Interactive Media Use and Youth:

Learning, Knowledge Exchange and Behavior

Elza Dunkels
Umeå University, Sweden

Gun-Marie Frånberg
Umeå University, Sweden

Camilla Hällgren
Umeå University, Sweden

INFORMATION SCIENCE REFERENCE

Hershey · New York

Senior Editorial Director:	Kristin Klinger
Director of Book Publications:	Julia Mosemann
Editorial Director:	Lindsay Johnston
Acquisitions Editor:	Erika Carter
Typesetters:	Michael Brehm, Milan Vracarich, Jr., and Julia Mosemann
Production Coordinator:	Jamie Snavely
Cover Design:	Nick Newcomer

Published in the United States of America by
Information Science Reference (an imprint of IGI Global)
701 E. Chocolate Avenue
Hershey PA 17033
Tel: 717-533-8845
Fax: 717-533-8661
E-mail: cust@igi-global.com
Web site: http://www.igi-global.com/reference

Library of Congress Cataloging-in-Publication Data

Interactive media use and youth: learning, knowledge exchange and behavior / Elza Dunkels, Gun-Marie Frånberg, and Camilla Hällgren, editors.
       p. cm.
   Includes bibliographical references and index.
   Summary: "This book provides a comprehensive collection of knowledge on interactive media based on different perspectives on quantitative and descriptive studies, what goes on in the contemporary media landscape, and pedagogical research on formal and non-formal learning strategies"--Provided by publisher.
   ISBN 978-1-60960-206-2 (hardcover) -- ISBN 978-1-60960-208-6 (ebook) 1. Interactive multimedia. 2. Mass media and youth. 3. Cognition in adolescence. I. Dunkels, Elza, 1960- II. Frånberg, Gun-Marie. III. Hällgren, Camilla, 1973-
   QA76.76.I59I573 2011
   302.23'1083--dc22
                                  2010050365

British Cataloguing in Publication Data
A Cataloguing in Publication record for this book is available from the British Library.

All work contributed to this book is new, previously-unpublished material. The views expressed in this book are those of the authors, but not necessarily of the publisher.

Editorial Advisory Board

Table of Contents

Section 1
The Context of Interactive Media

Section 2
Contemporary Learning

Section 3
Learning Environments

Section 4
Contemporary Challenges

Detailed Table of Contents

Section 1
The Context of Interactive Media

Chapter 1
Youth and Contemporary Learning 1
    Gun-Marie Frånberg, Umeå University, Sweden
    Elza Dunkels, Umeå University, Sweden
    Camilla Hällgren, Umeå University, Sweden

This chapter deals with contemporary and future challenges of education. The aim is to problematize the concept of learning and common views on transformed conditions for learning; have contemporary digital media reformed the processes of learning? What is seen as meaningful learning, and why?

Chapter 2
Educational Technologies for the Neomillenial Generation 12
    Regina Kaplan-Rakowski, Southern Illinois University, USA
    David Rakowski, Southern Illinois University, USA

The purpose of this chapter is to provide educators, researchers, and policy-makers with an overview on how modern technology has been influencing the learning styles of the "neomillennial" generation. The authors conclude by summarizing the characteristics of the neomillennial generation. They also discuss why technological changes are likely to influence educational practices for them, as well as how these changes fit in the broader context of educational theory.

Chapter 3

Birgitte Holm Sørensen, Aarhus University, Denmark
Karin Levinsen. Aarhus University, Denmark

The knowledge society's demands to its citizens profoundly affect the educational system and this chapter presents and discusses how the implementation of it in schools gradually moves from an industrial paradigm towards an emerging knowledge society paradigm. The knowledge society school is exemplified through a Danish primary school and finally extrapolated into the vision of the future local global school of the knowledge society.

Section 2
Contemporary Learning

Chapter 4

Simon Lindgren, Umeå University, Sweden

The overarching question in this chapter has to do with cooperation dynamics in social networks on YouTube. The chapter will focus on community aspects of vlogging (video blogging) and it is suggested that networked publics and participatory cultures offer valuable opportunities to the educational system.

Chapter 5

Christina Olin-Scheller, Karlstad University, Sweden
Patrik Wikström, Jönköping International Business School, Sweden

In this chapter the authors problematize fan fiction sites as informal learning settings. These settings and their relations to teaching and learning within formal learning settings are explored. The system of on-line co-production of literary texts on fan fiction sites enables young people to develop literacies in a safe environment in a way which previously have been almost impossible.

Chapter 6

Natalie Wakefield, McGill University, Canada

The importance for educators to implement a media literacy approach in their classrooms and school environments is emphasized in this chapter. It is suggested that there is an urgent need to recognize the impact that new technologies have on the lives of their students, as well as how they are used to building relationships between people.

Chapter 7

Kathy Sanford, University of Victoria, Canada
Liz Merkel, University of Victoria, Canada

This chapter will demonstrate how students were engaged in a powerful, emergent learning experience, one that is very different to the traditional Eurocentric schooling approach, one often not recognized or understood as credible learning. The authors introduce emergence theory to illuminate how students' understandings and skills can be used to provide more meaningful learning experiences in formal learning/school experiences.

Section 3
Learning Environments

Chapter 8

María Luisa Zorrilla Abascal, University of East Anglia, UK & Universidad Autónoma del Estado de Morelos, Mexico

The history of educational media has been a succession of technologies, where film and radio gave their place to television and now CD-ROMS and educational software have been displaced by the Web and videogames. This chapter focuses on media convergence of educational content particularly intended for television and the internet at the phase of its use in the classroom.

Chapter 9

Neriko Doerr, Ramapo College, USA
Shinji Sato, Columbia University, USA

The incorporation of blog activities in language education classes as an equalizing practice is discussed by the authors of this chapter. It is seen as important to acknowledge the existence of relations of dominance. The authors show that a teacher-student hierarchy still seeps into the blog space and that learners can be involved by educators in the understanding and transformation of such relations of dominance.

Chapter 10

Wu Liwei, Xiamen University, China
Fan Yihong, Umeå University, Sweden & Xiamen University, China
Yang Sujuan, South China Normal University, China

It is suggested that good teaching includes teaching the student how to learn, to memorize, to think and to motivate oneself. This chapter reports on a study of how the learning competence of young people may be improved. The authors report on the design and development of a learning strategy guidance system based on learning styles and how this system can provide young learners with support in their learning process.

Section 4
Contemporary Challenges

Daunting obstacles remain to the internet's becoming a source of political information for a segment of the population as wide as there was for newspapers and television during their heydays. The chapter focuses on the increasing dependence on digital information and tools to make informed judgments and that the skills involved in those judgments are very unequally distributed.

The approach in this chapter is to recognize what is said to be important regarding the feeling of being a part of the information society. The chapter is an exploration into the amount that social factors, digital skills, self-efficacy and a relationship with technology are able to explain the variance in perceived feelings regarding participation.

Focusing on the social and cultural aspects of digital learning, the concept hybrid media engagement is introduced in this chapter to capture the creative ways in which African art students overcome limitations in infrastructure, while exploring new forms of cultural production.

In the twenty first century new expectations and demands on education are mounting rapidly, as social and economic development becomes geared around the concept of constructing a Society of Knowledge. Challenges and opportunities of learning in arapidly changing digital age will be identified in this chapter. The authors also propose a theoretical framework for classifying potentially useful learning competences for youths.

Foreword

I began writing this Foreword on my way back from an international lecture. I was surrounded by people talking on their cell phones, listening to music, doing email, texting, playing games, surfing the Web, typing on their computers and net books, and the list goes on. The age levels of the people varied, but one thing was clear. "Reality" was being highly mediated. New technologies were everywhere. This is occurring in homes, places of paid and unpaid labor, schools, the sites of popular culture, and nearly every public and private space—at least for those who can afford or have access to these technologies. Indeed, what now counts as public and private is often being redefined, a fact brought home to me when in the airport and then in the plane people seemed to think nothing of having phone conversations about their most private thoughts and actions that were overheard by anyone who was sitting within hearing distance.

Often subtly but sometimes radically, these technologies are changing our workplaces, our schools, our actions, our time commitments, and often our very identities since such technologies can also create new forms of sociality and collectivity (Apple 2006). All of this raises crucial issues about educational priorities, about the connections between education and a changing economy, and about the connections between educational policies and practices and the daily lives of teachers and students. This book demonstrates that new media can challenge our accepted understandings of teaching, learning, literacies, what counts as "legitimate knowledge" and who has it, and so much more.

Interactive Media Use and Youth also documents that context counts and it counts in important ways. Context counts in terms of the socio-economic distribution of skills and knowledge. It also is important in terms of what structures and resources are available and how these resources will be used, and by whom. All of these elements are important for our understanding of the place of new media in institutions and in people's lives.

There can be no doubt that new technologies and new media offer new possibilities. But let us be honest. They also can be the site for the reproduction of relations of dominance and subordination and for the production of new hierarchies and inequalities. Just as importantly, they can also provide crucial spaces for actions and meanings that contest dominant forms and hierarchies. These contradictory tendencies can occur at one and the same time. Thus, our focus needs to be unromantic. There are positives and negatives, possibilities and limits. And all of this is occurring in educational and other institutions that are already structured in particular ways.

Even given the possible contradictory processes, uses, and outcomes of these new media, they do offer exceptional ways of rethinking our actions as educators. Let me give an example. In *Official Knowledge* (Apple, 2000), I describe some of my experiences as a film-maker working with a group of young women. This was no "ordinary" group of youth. They were incarcerated in a juvenile detention center, placed there for such things as drug use and small scale drug selling, prostitution, violence in schools, and similar kinds of things. These were 13-17 year old "girls" who were tough, hardened by abuse, by alienating educational experiences, and by impoverishment. And yet they were fragile on the inside. They were in essence part of society's throwaway populations.

Working with them on a joint film-making project had powerful effects on me and on the young women involved. Their emerging sense of competence, their ability to see themselves collectively as meaning makers and as creative, when they had constantly been told that they were basically unworthy and that they had little or no future, provided a space for alternate understandings of who they were and who they could be. This convinced me that media—when connected to the lives and creative capacities of youth--has the capacity to illuminate the ways in which popular cultural forms and content connect one with processes of cultural production that are powerful meaning-making acts. And it also provided ways in which these young women could create new forms of expression and new identities that were radically different than those that society had made available to them.

There is a powerful tradition within cultural studies that seeks to make us aware of these possibilities. For example, Paul Willis (Willis, 1990) has argued that popular cultural forms and technologies—even those that are simply mass produced as commodities for a lucrative youth market—are often taken up in what can best be described as aesthetic and self-making forms. Thus, the aesthetics, politics, and realities of consumption cannot be reduced to the economics of production without doing damage to the creative possibilities inherent on new technologies and cultural forms. A similar case has been made by DuGay and his colleagues in their discussion of the genesis, sale, and multiple uses of such things as the SONY Walkman (DuGay, et al. (1997). Each of these analyses in grounded in the insights of figures such as Richard Johnson (1986) who argues that any cultural commodity, technology, and cultural form needs to consider what he calls the *circuit of cultural production*, a circuit that has 3 moments: production, circulation, and reception. All three need to be taken up seriously, especially when we are interested as the book you are reading is, in the intricate connections between new media and the ways they can provide insights into the world of education, new knowledge, youth culture, and altered social relations (see also Dyson 1996; 2007).

Readers of *Interactive Media Use and Youth* would do well to pay close attention to what this fine book tells us about this circuit and about the ways in which new media operate on and in the lives of youth. The chapters in this book provide important insights into the complicated realties and possibilities of media and their connections with and uses by youth inside and outside the sphere of formal education.

Michael W. Apple
John Bascom Professor of Curriculum and Instruction and Educational Policy Studies
University of Wisconsin - Madison, USA

REFERENCES

Apple, M. W. (2000). *Official Knowledge: Democratic Education in a Conservative Age* (2nd ed.). New York: Routledge.

Apple, M. W. (2006). *Educating the "Right" Way: Markets, Standards, God, and Inequality.* New York: Routledge.

DuGay, P. (1997). *Doing Cultural Studies: The Story of the SONY Walkman*. Buckingham: The Open University Press.

Dyson, M. E. (1996). *Between God and Gangsta Rap: Bearing Witness to Black Culture*. New York: Oxford University Press.

Dyson, M. E. (2007). *Know what I mean? Reflections on hip-hop*. New York: Basic Civitas Books.

Johnson, R. (1986). What is Cultural Studies Anyway? *Social Text, 16*, 38–80. doi:10.2307/466285

Willis, P. (1990). *Common Culture: Symbolic Work at Play in the Everyday Cultures of the Young*. Boulder, CO: Westview Press.

Preface

The subject area of youth and online social practices deals with research that concerns children and youth and their use of interactive media. This research consists of a broad range of different perspectives such as quantitative and descriptive studies of what goes on in the contemporary media landscape, psychological and sociological research on online social practices, pedagogical research on formal and non-formal learning strategies, to mention a few. The aim of this book is to outline this emerging research area, evolving around young people and contemporary digital arenas. The field is growing in size, shape and complexity and the need for study is urgent. The book is a valuable contribution by providing critical perspectives and a broad overview.

The book, *Interactive Media Use* and *Youth: Learning, Knowledge Exchange and Behavior,* cover current areas of research on young people's use of interactive media. The chapters represent cutting edge research with a critical perspective as a common denominator. As editors we were pleased that our call for chapters had such good results. All authors were interested in the critical perspective that we emphasized in our call. So you will find chapters presenting novel ideas, different aspects of young people's net cultures and ground-breaking research that will be of great value to the academic society as well as to policy makers. The book aims at providing relevant theoretical frameworks and the latest empirical research findings in the area.

The target audience of the book will be composed of students, professionals and researchers working in the field of young people and the internet in various disciplines (e.g., education, library and information science, psychology, sociology, computer science, linguistics, informatics, media and communication science). The book may serve as literature at an undergraduate level and provide an overview of the area for researchers, teachers, students and policy makers. It is written for professionals as well as students who want to improve their understanding of online social practices from a young people's perspective. *Interactive Media Use and Youth: Learning, Knowledge Exchange and Behavior* focuses on young people's use of interactive media in general and learning, knowledge exchange and behavior in particular.

During our planning process we tried to find a way to involve young people in the making of the book. The aim was to make young people not only the objects of studies but also subjects. The idea was to find students who were willing to give their side of the story. This is not as easy as it may seem; we needed to find students who were sufficiently good at English, who were interested in reading a substantial amount of academic text and who had the time to go through a writing process together with us. And since the chapters from the adult authors were to be submitted in spring 2010, we had to ask the students to do this work during the busiest period of school. Luckily enough, there is an International Baccalaureate Diploma Programme in Umeå, Sweden, quite close to the university. Their English teacher Neil Duncan presented our idea to one of his classes and some of the students wanted to participate.

The contributors are students in the IB1 class of the International Baccalaureate Diploma Programme at Östra Gymnasiet in Umeå. All IB students have CAS – Creativity, Action, Service as part of their diploma, and these students volunteered their contributions here as Service – helping other people who need or ask for help – in this case by giving their time and sharing their ideas, opinions and experiences in print with us when editing this book. The students were first presented with the abstracts of every adult chapter. After reading through the abstracts some of the students wanted to read entire chapters, which at this stage were in the form of drafts. Our instructions for the writing were deliberately vague, because we wanted to avoid steering these young authors into writing in a traditional academic style. Even though there may be educational winnings from training young people in academic writing, we wanted their tone to be authentic since they were to write about their own thoughts and feelings. After the first reading of the adult chapters, we presented the students with questions like "What are your thoughts about this? Did anything particular catch your attention, either in a positive or a negative way? Do you have any ideas what to write about this?" We also pointed out that the students did not have to comment on the adults' chapters, their chapters could just as well be separate texts. Today, we are very proud to present this way of getting young people's views on research concerning the internet and we hope that the readers will appreciate this vantage point. We also encourage other editors and publishers to follow our example, since it has been a valuable experience for us and these students and hopefully beneficial to the book.

The theme of *Interactive Media Use and Youth: Learning, Knowledge Exchange and Behavior* is the different learning aspects of the contemporary media landscape. As researchers having young people and the internet as our focus we have slowly come to understand that learning is one of the burning issues of today. The educational system was slow in discovering that there was very much learning going on in front of the computers, be it learning not being steered by curricula. This learning, often labeled informal learning, is a recurring theme in the chapters of this book. Furthermore, even though schools discovered the potential of interactive media they often had problems incorporating these new, powerful processes into the pedagogical practice. In fact, today we can no longer call them new processes. Instead, we have to admit that it is not the technology that is new but the teachers and the educational system that have become older.

To counteract this dichotomy between old and new, the first section of this book consists of the young authors' chapters. The students from a Swedish upper secondary school have focused mainly on three different aspects of learning: media literacy, learning styles and informal learning.

In the second section of this book the chapters focus on the context of interactive media; what does the setting for learning, knowledge exchange and behavior look like? What approaches can we take on to manage learning today? The opening chapter in this section is the editors' own, *Youth and Contemporary Learning*. The chapter problematizes the concept of learning and asks if and in what ways contemporary media have influenced the processes and outcomes of learning. We also pose the question of how the educational system may exploit and benefit from this. In the next chapter Regina Kaplan-Rakowski and David Rakowski give us an overview on how modern technology has been influencing the learning styles of the young of today. Their chapter *Educational Technologies for the Neomillennial Generation* gives a description of the neomillenial learner and outline why technological changes are likely to influence educational practices for them, as well as how these changes fit in the broader context of educational theory. This particular chapter has deeply inspired our student authors as the reader will see in the first section. To conclude this opening section, *School in the Knowledge Society – a Local Global School* by Birgitte Holm Sørensen and Karin Levinsen report findings from a study of schools that proactively meet the challenges for teaching and learning. The findings are then extrapolated into a vision of the future local global school in the knowledge society.

The third section in this volume zooms in on the perspective of learning in the individual's perspective. This does not in any way mean that the individual learners are on their own, which the reader will become very aware of. In fact, the opening chapter of this section focuses on collaborative learning among young people. In his chapter *Collective Problem-Solving and Informal Learning in Networked Publics. Reading Vlogging Networks on YouTube as Knowledge Communities*, Simon Lindgren focuses on community aspects of video blogging on YouTube. Lindgren stresses the learning aspects of this activity, an aspect that may be hidden to many outside observers. Along the same lines, collaborative processes, Christina Olin-Scheller and Patrik Wikström write about informal learning settings such as fan fiction sites, and their relations to teaching and learning within formal learning settings. In their chapter *Literacies on the Web. Co-production of Literary Texts on Fan Fiction Sites* the authors discuss learning processes connected to the development of literacies. Following this, Natalie Wakefield's chapter discusses the related issue of *Media Literacy Education*. The author points out that although curricula predominantly focus on reading and writing, educators need to reach beyond basic learning skills and include the development of the complete individual. Serving as a bridge to the next section, the last chapter on this theme is Kathy Sanford's and Liz Merkel's chapter *Emergent/See: Viewing Adolescents' Video Game Creation Through an Emergent Framework*. The authors studied a class where students created their own video games as a way to learn programming. To understand the processes, an emergence theory is introduced. The theory outlines how students' understandings and skills can be used to provide more meaningful learning experiences in a school setting.

Zooming in further on the learning and teaching practice, the fourth section focuses on what once was called the classroom. This is perhaps not always a suitable a term today when learning environments in most cases reach far beyond the walls of the school building. Opening this section, María Luisa Zorrilla Abascal writes about media convergence of educational content. Her chapter *BBC Schools Beyond the TV Set: Educational Media Convergence in the Classroom* presents an enquiry into how educational television and related websites converge in an era in which the boundaries between different media are disappearing. In their chapter on how blogs may be used in language studies, Neriko Doerr and Shinji Sato stress the importance of recognizing the existence of relations of dominance in online settings. Their chapter *The Modes of Governmentality in Language Education: Blog Activities in a Japanese-as-a-Foreign-Language Classroom* examines language studies. This examination is carried out with a power relations' perspective and the authors discuss the validity of incorporating blog activities in language education classes as an equalizing practice. Closing this section, Wu Liwei, Fan Yihong and Yang Sujuan investigate learning styles and learning strategies in their chapter *Designing Web-Facilitated Learning Strategy Guidance System: Based on Young Learners' Learning Styles*. The authors' research aims at improving young learners' learning competence and effectiveness. In this process, the authors developed a Web-Facilitated Learning Strategy Guidance System (WFLSGS).

The final section focuses on society in a very general sense; what challenges do we face because of the fact that interactive media use is changing the conditions for learning, knowledge exchange and behavior? Opening this section, Henry Milner discusses obstacles that remain to be dealt with before the internet could become a source of political information for everyone. In his chapter *Political Dropouts and the Internet Generation* Milner stresses that even though citizens are expected to exercise independent, informed judgments in order to make use of the internet as a source of political information, the skills needed to do this are very unequally distributed. Touching on the same subject, Sheila Zimic points out that the ability to participate in, and thus feel like a part of, the information society is related to digital skills, self-efficacy and relations to technology. In her chapter *Predicting the Participation in Information Society*, Zimic gives a report of a study on Swedish young people's perceived feeling of participation. In the next chapter, *African Art Students and Digital Learning*, Paula Uimonen investigates the development of digital media skills. Focusing on social and cultural aspects of digital learning, the concept hybrid media engagements is introduced to capture the creative ways in which African art students overcome limitations in infrastructure, while exploring new forms of cultural production. The closing chapter of this section and in fact the entire book is Yang Sujuan's and Fan Yihong's *Learning Competence for Youth in Digital Lifelong Learning Society*. This chapter aims at identifying challenges and opportunities of learning in a rapidly changing media landscape, and at proposing a theoretical framework of classifying potentially useful learning competences for young people in a contemporary learning setting.

Altogether, the different chapters represent many of the joys and troubles that are part and parcel of contemporary learning and we hope that you will have much use of, and much pleasure from reading them.

Elza Dunkels
Umeå University, Sweden

Gun-Marie Frånberg
Umeå University, Sweden

Camilla Hällgren
Umeå University, Sweden

Acknowledgment

During the editing of this book there have of course been a number of obstacles to overcome and we would like to thank those people who have helped us with this. First of all, we would like to thank the authors who heeded our call for chapters. They represent the finest, most important research at this turbulent period of time and we are happy that they chose to come together in our book. Among the authors we would like to extend a special thank you to the student authors. They showed such commitment to their task and also proved to have the courage to write about their own thoughts in an academic, perhaps sometimes intimidating, context. Furthermore, they had to finalize their chapters at the end of the semester when all the tests and assignments were due as well. If it had not been for their teacher Neil Duncan, who freely gave us and the students of his time, this task would have been so much harder if not impossible. We would also like to extend our gratitude to the Editorial Advisory Board who patiently and diligently assisted us with the delicate questions of publishing. A problem when recruiting a board is that we are not the only ones who appreciate the work of these professors and consequently they have been very busy. Nevertheless they have helped us selflessly and we are deeply grateful for this. Professor Michael Apple, John Bascom Professor of Curriculum and Instruction and Educational Policy Studies, University of Wisconsin-Madison, USA, also a busy and sought-after scholar, has contributed greatly to this book with his insightful foreword.

As in any book project there are also a number of people who may think that they have done nothing to help but they have; by providing time, by excusing us from meetings, by cooking and cleaning at home, by encouraging. So we want to thank our colleagues at the Department of Applied Educational Science, Umeå University, Sweden and, not least, our husbands and children who patiently wait for us to send this manuscript.

Elza Dunkels
Umeå University, Sweden

Gun-Marie Frånberg
Umeå University, Sweden

Camilla Hällgren
Umeå University, Sweden

Young Authors' Thoughts on Contemporary Learning

THREE STUDENTS' RESPONSES TO MEDIA LITERACY EDUCATION

Åsa Johansson, Franziska Messinger, and Josefin Lindgren

In 2008 the public upper secondary schools in Umeå started a campaign to give all the first year students a free laptop to use for work related to school. Our class has been a part of this, and now two years later, we have gained experience of how computers have both advantages and disadvantages for schoolwork. We intend in this text to give examples of this and provide suggestions on how to improve those causes that we have discovered to be a problem.

First, computers sometimes malfunction in the form of crashing, viruses or other errors. This can destroy some of the data on the computer, for example an essay you have worked on for several days. This happens when you least expect it, even though the reason for the crashing can be questioned. This problem can however be solved quite easily as it is possible to copy and save an essay on a different space rather than the laptop, such as internet, USB or in this case, the school server. The students I have asked do not know that we have a server, however, and some do not own a USB. By supplying students with USBs or information about local storage, the problems with computer crashing will be history.

In addition, teachers find that multitasking is a problem. The internet distracts the students from their writing, with games, music, and blogs. I myself know about this problem really well as I am at this very moment both writing this and on Facebook, chatting via msn and reading my friends' blogs. I know very well that I have better things to do and still I take some of my time to enjoy some of the things on internet. Though I do get my work done, it takes more time; if I had lacked more discipline, then this might not have been written at all. However as I am sitting here studying with my friends outside of class, I see a web-based game to my left and the site flashback on my right. This is a regular thing that happens but we are all silent and minding our own business. In this kind of self-study situation I feel that multi-tasking is okay, as it only depends on you yourself. Without the computers at hand I feel that we would probably start to have a conversation instead and lose track of time.

In a classroom, on the other hand, I find it hard to concentrate when using the computer. It is really effective for taking notes but if I am lacking in energy I tend to take a break and read other things. During these breaks I do not listen at all and when I start to concentrate once again, I have missed valuable information. This is a problem for many students, and it might be hard to find an easy solution. If the teacher were able to turn the internet off it would improve a bit but when the internet connection is connected to all the computers around the school this is not an option. Other solutions would be to use the computer more efficiently by integrating it into the lecture or when the computer is not needed the teacher should tell the students to put it away. **ÅJ**

Today's society has become more and more based on the use of computers. Therefore it is reasonable that computers also become more and more integrated into the school system.

Nevertheless I do not think that we should move completely away from using pen and paper at school, for various reasons. Personally, I remember things much better if I write them by hand than if I type them into the computer. When I study for exams, for example, I usually take notes by hand, writing on the computer does not have the same effect. Everybody learns differently, of course, but I think that there are many people that learn better by writing by hand. In many lessons essays and notes are almost exclusively written on the computer and have to be handed in via internet, so that we do not even get a choice whether we would like to use the computer or not. Then I sometimes miss "good old pen and paper".

Another disadvantage with writing texts on word processors can be that word processors often correct slight mistakes automatically, so that you do not notice if you make a mistake. Other errors are underlined in red by the program and you can simply correct it by clicking on the right alternative without really thinking about it. Sometimes this might be good because your mistakes are shown to you immediately, but I think that for long-term learning it would be better to write a text by hand and let a teacher correct it. If the teacher corrects the mistakes and perhaps even discusses major mistakes with the student, the student would probably learn better from the mistake. Also writing a correction could be sensible. In the German school system we were always forced to write corrections to the mistakes made in our exams, which I found rather annoying then, but now I think it actually helped me a lot.

In addition, I prefer looking at notes I made by hand as well. This might sound very old-fashioned, but I think that it can be quite tiring to look at a computer screen too long. And if you think about it, it cannot be too good for the eyes either if you spend a whole day in front of the computer screen doing schoolwork. It also takes rather long time to start the computer, so that I would not consider starting it if I only quickly want to check something in my notes, in that case it would also be easier with notes made on paper.

I do agree that writing texts on the computer can also have advantages and that it is an important skill we should also learn at school. But a good balance should be found between the use of computers and writing by hand. And it should be kept in mind that technology is not necessarily always better than the "old school methods". **FM**

Many of the things that have been brought up are issues involving the use of computers. The problems with word processors correcting the writer's mistakes, or the student's work disappearing because of a computer crash were both mentioned before, but a solution to these two problems is easily obtained. The correction-function in some writing programs is actually possible to turn off, if you know how to do it. The same with a computer crash: the crash itself is probably hard to prevent from happening, but you should always be prepared for it and know how to save the files separately from the computer hard drive – some people even know how to recover the files from the computer after it has been reinstalled! But all these things require knowledge. So the solution to the problem would be some sort of computer course.

A computer course is something that already exists for students that start at upper secondary school in Sweden, and I personally have not taken the course, but I asked a friend about it that has. His opinion was that the course was unnecessary to some extent since he already knew many of the things the course took up (he has been a regular computer user his whole life, and is therefore accustomed to them). But he still thought that the course in total was not unimportant to him, since he learned new things about word- and calculation processors, and those types of programs that he would not have learned by himself, simply because it was not in his interest to do so. But he also thought that there were many students that did not know any of these things, and it was therefore very important for them. One thing that limited the course in terms of knowledge about computers and obtaining knowledge with them was the teachers' view of the Internet. They seemed to have the attitude that Internet was a dangerous device that should be avoided as much as possible, and they got instructions about how to use the Firewall to protect them from it. So the students never learned, for example, how to search on the internet or to be critical of the sources used when obtaining information on the web.

I was in Korea a couple of weeks ago and I got to meet a politician and doctor named Daein Kang who told me a very interesting story about a project he had been a part of to develop their young people's use of computers[1]. He had been the advisor to South Korea's president Kim Dae-jung, and they had started out by giving out free computers to all children/teenagers in Korea, including the children living out in the countryside, to see if they could find a specific pattern for who learned best. The results from the experiment were quite surprising: children with mothers that were engaged in their children's use of computers developed a bigger understanding and knowledge about computers as well. So the government's next program was to give free courses in computers to one million mothers in Korea. Two million applied, which encouraged the president to extend the program to two million mothers. This was around ten years ago, and now, when their children have grown up, Korea is known worldwide for having the best game-players in the world[2], and is very powerful on the internet because of their great knowledge about everything that has to do with computers. If this is a coincidence I do not know, but it shows that if other governments took risks like this, they might be able to compete with the Korean professionals, and certainly be better at using the computers to obtain knowledge in school work. It is very often the knowledge about how computers work that is lacking, and I think that is where we have to start to develop the knowledge acquired through computers. But giving out computers in school is a good start towards a more proficient society. **JL**

In conclusion, computers in education are shown to be both effective and troublesome. The computers themselves are not the problem, but the way we use them can still be developed considerably. So these issues are something that the government should take into account when offering computers to the students in the schools – there is still lots to work on to make it as efficient as possible!

THE NEOMILLENNIAL LEARNING STYLE

Ida Wånge

The neomillennial generation is what we can sometimes call the internet generation. We grew up with the internet, so it has always been a part of our life, both during our free time and for schoolwork. This chapter will focus on our learning style; what role the internet plays in it, and how we incorporate it to improve our learning style.

In comparison to the previous generation, the neomillennials are often described as being faster paced and having a better aptitude for multi-tasking. But to what degree do we agree with this image of our generation and what role has internet played in this? Internet has changed our way of retrieving information, which has contributed to the fact that we are fast paced. Instead of searching for certain information in a book, or multiple books, we can find it right away by putting it into Google. Books now take too much, unnecessary time, we even find quotes from books on the internet instead of looking in the book. This has resulted in us most often just collecting information, without being critical of its source or analysing different information. Many students in the neomillennial generation have most likely, at one time or another used the copy-and-paste technique for homework. However, for the ones that possess the skill of being critical to sources, and who analyse the information, the internet offers endless opportunities. We have easy access to information from all around the world, all in the same place, in comparison to books, where even university libraries might not possess the material that we need for a work.

When we sit in front of the computer, we don't usually do just one thing. We're on Facebook, we listen to music, chat and do our homework, all in the same time. This can of course be very distracting sometimes, and popular groups on Facebook deal with procrastination from schoolwork, such as "How did our parents ever procrastinate without Facebook, MSN or YouTube?"[3] and "I won't procrastinate any longer... LOL jk, back to facebook."[4]. However, even if we do get distracted from our learning sometimes, it has also gotten us used to multi-tasking. Multi-tasking allows us to be more effective, and we can thus get things done more quickly. It also prevents us from getting bored a lot of the time, as we always have something on our mind, or something to do.

The computer is usually with us all day every day. A normal weekday, we bring the computer to school, and some of us even check out Facebook, for example, before going to school (and it was also the last thing we did before going to bed). In school, we use the computer in most classes, and the teachers expect us to. If we do not bring the computer with us, we won't be able to do some of the tasks that we are assigned during the day. During the breaks, most of us sit in front of the computer as well, we even communicate more and more with each other through the computer. An example of this was one Tuesday afternoon, when our teacher came in to the classroom, and all the students were sitting in the back-row with their computers. Everyone was looking at their screens, not talking to or looking at each other. It might have looked like we were deeply concentrating on our task, but in fact we were all communicating through msn, even though we were sitting right next to each other. When we then get home from school, the first thing we do is to open the computer, either to do schoolwork or for personal use. Hence, the computer plays a major role in our daily life, and even a day without it can lead to symptoms of abstinence.

The public upper secondary schools in Umeå each have a website with a learning platform. Here the teachers put up all necessary information that we need to know, and if you do not have a computer, you are not be able to access this. This learning platform, as the teachers call it, is where we hand in most of our assignments. As we are given a laptop when we start school, this is very practical. For us, it is easier to write on the computer than with pen and paper, and with the learning platform, we can easily submit our work, without going through the hassle of printing it out.

Thus, I believe that the internet has improved our learning style, although it could be better if the learning style of the previous generation was incorporated as well. We would then receive the best parts of two worlds; endless and easy accessible material from the internet, as well as the teacher's knowledge and the skill to collect and then analyse the information from the traditional learning style.

GAMES AND SUBCONSCIOUS LEARNING

Andrea Kallin

One way of learning for the Neomillennial generation is the learning through games, electronic games that we play on the computer and on other gaming consoles

Through games we can learn a lot and about an extensive range of things. There are a lot of different genres of games and this text is going to focus on offline RPG and strategy-games since this is what I, Andrea Kallin, play for the most part.

Firstly, perhaps I should explain and elaborate what RPG and strategy games are. RPG is an abbreviation for Role-Playing-Games, these type of games which let you become a character you can customize and change in certain ways e.g. their looks, skills, moral standing, clothing, and so on. The main ingredient in RPG is that the player can decide for her/himself *how* s/he wants to play – if the character should be good or evil, what specialization the character focuses on (e.g. magic, archery or melee/swordsmanship). The story in RPG often changes according with what decisions the player makes during the play-through. Strategy games, on the other hand, are not based on a single character. Instead they let the player control a nation. A nation that the player is supposed to make strong, influential and powerful. This can be done in a number of ways, e.g. by building massive armies, strong fortifications and by investing in advanced technology, infrastructure and trade. Most often the goal in strategy games is to become the dominant power in the game. By becoming the dominant power and by showing that the title can be sustained, the game is won.

Most of my friends and I have played a lot of games since our early childhood – most of the games being in English without any Swedish manuals or interfaces. This has without a doubt made English easier for us. One example of this is the game "Age Of Empires 1" by Microsoft. I got it from a friend when I was 8 years old and it is a strategy game where you are building your own nation and developing it from the stone age up to the iron age. During this time, you build up its army, infrastructure, agriculture and you increase its population to try to overthrow the other nations which also occupy your continent. You can overthrow the other countries by either crushing them with your colossal army or by your advanced superior technology.

As an 8 year-old, I could not speak any English except the ordinary phrases of "Hello" and "How are you" and, as my dad often reminds me, I really detested having to do my English vocabulary homework. The first time I had to do it, I threw an angry fit and sulked for hours because whoever or whatever created us did not make just one language too!

However, I happily drank in and memorized every new word I encountered in "Age Of Empires 1". Without any difficulty I learned, e.g., what a "shepherd", "ruin", "horse", "town square" and what a "villager" were. I also learned to spell words like "pepperoni pizza", "flying Dutchman" and "black rider". In themselves, these phrases might not be so impressive for an 8 year-old to be able to spell and understand, however, by playing "Age Of Empires 1" my English vocabulary, and my understanding of it, greatly increased in a short span of time.

Games always include some form of problem-solving, whether it is to make a household go around as in "The Sims" or to find the best way past a way too vigilant guard in the "Thief"-series – it is all the same: problem-solving.

Problem-solving in games can involve many things. However, my friends and I can agree for the most part that while games do not always give us explicit knowledge or tools we can use in the real world, they always improve or make use of our logic, our ability to plan in advance (strategize) and our multi-tasking skills. Even when playing a first-person shooter or a splatter game (games where you kill basically everything you can see with random weapons) we strategize and multi-task.

In "Call of Duty", for example, (a first person shooter where you play as an Allied soldier in a number of famous battles from WWII) multi-tasking and strategizing takes place while you shoot, move, look for cover and equip your character which you do under enemy fire and while advancing! It is a hectic game where you have to keep track of at least 5 different things on screen while planning your next couple of moves.

Many adults do not see the value of electronic games and have a tendency to only see the increasing inactivity and obesity in the youth of today. However, electronic games, both offline and online, are a great medium that can be used for educational purposes - they already contribute on a subconscious level. The principal advice I can give someone going to make a game for educational purposes is to do it thoroughly. *Put your energy and focus on the layout, story and graphics!* Educational games are often unappealing because they do not even try to appeal to the players! For a product to succeed it needs to attract its possible consumers – this is where educational games fail. Of course we all know that the big games have big budgets, which put educational games at a disadvantage simply because they have smaller financial resources. However, money is not everything: by using funny, cute or cool graphics and interesting and smart dialogue the amount of money put into a game does not matter.

THE NEOMILLENIALS' LEARNING STYLE IN THE CLASSROOM

Sharon Mateke

The learning style in the classroom has changed since the last generation, our parents, grew up. We, the neomillenials, imagine the last generations' classroom as a strict environment where you had to sit still, be extremely quiet and do nothing but eagerly listen to the teachers' lectures and follow their writings on the board. There were strict rules, you had to have respect and be disciplined. In some countries (e.g. Germany) you even got a grade on how nice and clear you were writing in your notebooks. Today it looks a lot different; we mostly take responsibility for our learning and often work in groups and share our own knowledge instead of sitting straight up in our chairs and listening to the teacher all day long.

The teachers often let us work in groups: for almost every assignment we get they want us to work in groups. They say that it is good to work together both when it comes to helping each other out and in achieving the best possible result on a task. They want us to be able to co-operate with any person. Not only because they want us to learn to respect each other no matter whom it is but also because they think that the learning process is enhanced.

However, students sometimes feel that this has gone too far; teachers sometimes give us an assignment without any guidance and put us together in groups and let us do the working or the thinking ourselves for a large number of lessons. This can create an uncertainty among the students. We can feel that the teachers trust too much in our own shared knowledge and that we are expected to rely on our own competence. Sometimes we feel that there is a great lack of guidance from the teacher and there are large numbers of students that would feel more comfortable with actually following the teacher on the board a bit more often, to get guidance for what we need to know, learn or look for. Sometimes we wish for and would like to be provided with more authoritative knowledge from the teachers in order to feel secure in our learning.

Another noticeable difference in the learning style (when comparing with) the last generation is of course that today we have computers in the classroom. This also contributes to the feeling of uncertainty when it comes to learning in the everyday school-day. We get a task, type it into a search machine on the web, click, read it, click, write it and then forget it. We look for immediate information which we then immediately also tend to forget. The last generation had to rely on books when they had to research for an essay or other assignments. By doing that, the thinking process is a lot more encouraged in comparison to ours when typing a word or phrase into Google and directly getting what we are looking for. As mentioned before we are or we tend to be fast paced and always look for shortcuts. We have almost totally lost the ability to use books for research. We do not even know how to find a book in the library; instead of trying to learn the system (which everyone should be familiar with) we go straight to the librarian to directly ask for what we want: shortcut. By having the computers in the classroom the teachers naturally expect us to use them for learning.

They give us tasks that allow us to use the computer almost every day, which also can contribute to the feeling that we have to rely on self study because we are doing the work on our own and we are looking for knowledge ourselves, often without being critical of sources. Sometimes the teachers should insist that we use books for our research so that we do not lose that ability and so that we enhance our thinking/learning process when looking for information and also in order to use reliable sources.

Even though teachers think that it is a very good opportunity for students to share their knowledge, most of us do not want to work that way for the majority of the lessons, not because we cannot, but because we would like to be provided with more authoritative knowledge in order to feel secure in our studies. Furthermore, it is almost the same when it comes to computers. People think that by providing students with computers they ease both studying and teaching and that this creates great opportunities for learning as well. That however does not mean that we students always like to work with computers as our learning process is not really enhanced by them. Because to ease is the thing that computers do, they do not challenge us, they only supply us with shortcuts.

CONCLUSION

We wrote this section because we wanted to share our opinions and feelings about the neomillennial learning style, because we are the ones that it affects. By writing this we hope to give an insight into our perspectives so that improvements can be made, so that we will be able to get the best out of our learning.

The internet provides us with endless opportunities in our learning style. However, we need to consider other ways of learning as well, such as the traditional learning style, to get the best out of it. Technology is an opportunity to neomillennial kids, who grow up with it, but parents should be more updated to be able to help neomillenial kids with school work that is done on a computer, for example, or that needs to be done with some other technology, otherwise it could lead to an imbalance or disequilibrium. Games are a great medium to reach neomillenial learners. However, games that are made for educational purposes must be well made and enticing to the neomillenials. We are hard to please when it comes to technology and the games that do not meet our standards will have the opposite effect of what they were trying to do. Furthermore, computers and group assignments are appreciated in the classroom but students still want to be learning from the teacher and want to follow written material on the whiteboard/Smartboard.

The focus of the learning styles should not be put on these two methods in order to make the students feel secure and comfortable in their studies.

ENDNOTES

[1] http://ir.lib.sfu.ca/bitstream/1892/9940/1/b37359885.pdf, pp 38-39, 25/5-10

[2] http://www.wcg.com/6th/history/ranking/ranking_wcgrank.asp#01, 25/5-10

[3] http://www.facebook.com/pages/How-did-our-parents-ever-procrastinate-without-Facebook-MSN-or-Youtube/115633695142505?ref=search&sid=584789642.3335359385..18/05/10

[4] http://www.facebook.com/pages/I-wont-procrastinate-any-longer-LOL-jk-back-to-facebook/120738361287199?ref=search&sid=584789642.3335359385..18/05/10

Section 1
The Context of Interactive Media

Chapter 1
Youth and Contemporary Learning

Gun-Marie Frånberg
Umeå University, Sweden

Elza Dunkels
Umeå University, Sweden

Camilla Hällgren
Umeå University, Sweden

ABSTRACT

This chapter deals with contemporary and future challenges of education. The text falls into two interconnected parts. One part relates to societal changes that have relevance to education issues worldwide. The other explores the challenges inherent in the context of information technology and knowledge society.

The aim of the chapter is to problematize the concept of learning and common views on transformed conditions for learning; have contemporary digital media reformed the processes of learning and if so, how can the educational system benefit from and exploit this? The chapter highlights changes and reflects on contemporary and future aspects of learning. What is seen as meaningful learning? Is learning more demanding today or does the open and abundant access to information simplify it?

INTRODUCTION

In a broad sense, education is a universal human activity with a long history and a future directed ambition. It is culturally situated and allocated at global, international and local levels. Thus, as an essential human activity the educational phenomenon is interlaced with societal structures and human interactivities, governed by political ideologies, expressed as different values in the laws, curricula, course handbooks, examinations and teaching practices. At the same time, it is also true that values, practices and artefacts of formal education evolve in different ways in different parts of the world.

Furthermore, education has endured two powerful historical shifts; The Industrial Revolution and The Information Revolution. In relation to

DOI: 10.4018/978-1-60960-206-2.ch001

educational impact there is at least one major difference between these two historical changes: "While the industrial revolution gave rise to a universal schooling system where none had previously existed, the information technology revolution presses a very real, active system to reconsider its fundamental practices." (Collins & Halverson, 2009). Learning became associated with schooling at the time as public schools arised. Before that, learning was incorporated in an era of apprenticeship (Collins & Halverson, 2009).

During the last few years educational institutions have also gone through many reforms that have had an impact on how we arrange learning situations on the one hand and also how we understand learning as a concept, on the other. Today we understand learning as a lifelong process and not only as an activity taking place in school. This particular notion of learning has, however, little correspondence with steering documents aimed at formal educational settings. Another feature of today's approach to education is that the emphasis has shifted from teaching to learning. But since learning has been understood as an essentially individual process, and education as an institutional one, we now see a clear separation between formal, non-formal and informal learning environments (Jarvis, et al 2003).

SOCIETAL CHANGES AND LEARNING

Not only is the approach to education transforming but also the conditions of human society have changed profoundly. E.g. English sociologist Zygmunt Baumann (2003) explores the conditions and claims that we have moved from the solid stage of modernity to the liquid stage of modernity in the recent decades. The metaphor of liquidity is a demanding view and a challenging condition for contemporary society. For the first time in history, fluidity is a major logic for structuring

human life, since ideas of instability and change are more prevalent than ever.

To picture living in a society under thorough transformation there might be a need for an extension of the classic change-analogy; that we are not able to step into the same river twice. Perhaps the continuously shifting structures of our everyday life are better compared to an online game, that deals with adaptation and power? Given the proposed fluid logic of societal structures, players and rules are shifting continuously and randomly. Even the scripts of the everyday game are under constant change. Synchronicity is irrelevant at times. The ability to identify important information, learning new rules and being flexible becomes key competences. Thus, in the end, the winner is not necessarily the player with the most points, or the one who played by the rules. The winner is most likely the one who could create and recreate truth, meaning and reality; the one who had the power and ability to adapt to change and generate the best storyline.

Following the ideas from the Game Analogy it becomes essential to develop ways of acting, and ways of interacting, which are fit for living in a state of constant change and uncertainty. This demands a different approach to learning; our culture today has become as much a culture of learning as it is a culture of forgetting in order to clear the ground for new things to replace the old ones. Learning is now more or less understood as a life-long process. And above all, today learning consists of the ability to change what is considered true, appropriate, usable, and effective knowledge.

The internet provides us with information, tools and resources. The combination extends memory and improves the quality of retrieving. In other words, internet extends accessible facts and concepts. But what is seen as important information seems to change from one day to another and the learners have to be ready to review their prior knowledge.

Psychologist Herman Ebbinghaus, as early as in the late 1800's, had a keen interest in memory and other higher cognitive processes. He was the first to describe the "learning curve" and to characterize memory. What he found through his experiments was e.g. that things that are connected to one another are more easily remembered together. He also found that we remember best what we first and last come across and tend to forget inbetween items. But he also discovered that most humans are likely to forget 50% of newly learned knowledge in a few days or weeks. Remembering and forgetting are important issues in human learning, in general, and has been a burning issue for psychologists and educationalists for a long time.

The realm of post modernity also includes what Ziehe describes as cultural redundancy (Ziehe, 2000). Cultural redundancy takes into consideration that humans today to a greater extent than did previous generations, independently, on their own, construct their identity. Ziehe argues that existence and identity are created by a reflexive project where individuals using media experience are constructing and reconstructing their identities. This is why present-day individuals to a greater extent than previous generations renounce traditions and mandatory procedures. It is also common to refuse to accept social rituals that might create restricted social structures. Following these ideas we can assert that the influence of factors such as gender, class and ethnicity is falling. But have we achieved equality in these matters? And if so, what implications does this have on identity construction in general?

What are the challenges of education in a current liquid modernity then? In the first chapter of Democracy and Education (1916) Dewey asserts that as societies become "more complex in structure and resources, the need of formal or intentional teaching and learning increases (p 9)." This was true for the beginning of the 20th century, but what about today? Is formal education a keyword in contemporary and future society?

Is progressivism still a useful concept when we talk about the purpose of education and learning?

The development of modern society is according to German sociologist Ulrich Beck (2000) based on exceptional progress in many areas. Technical, social and cultural development has paved the way for the beginning and development of modernity. In the wake of this development, expert systems have been developed, and constantly more areas of the world have come to be characterized and monitored by experts.

British sociologist Anthony Giddens (1990, 1991) stresses concepts such as relativism of space and time in his description of post modern society. Modernity, Giddens points out, is largely a matter of the extent of social relations in time and place. But social relationships on the other hand do not require shared geographic locality and concurrency any longer. It is in light of this fact that many modern period features can be understood. Now the whole world is covered by this degree of social relations, which has far-reaching consequences for all social dimensions of life.

Concepts that are important to take into consideration in contemporary society are thus relativism of space and time, reflexivity, the media and the increasing importance of individualization. But what are the consequences in relation to education, knowledge and learning? If you on the one hand understand knowing as basically a social act, it has significant implications for the way we think of and try to support learning. If you on the other hand understand learning as an essentially individual activity it will have other consequences for how learning is facilitated.

A SHIFT FROM TEACHING TO LEARNING

What is learning then? In a historical perspective several views on learning have existed. One long-lived issue is if learning is to be looked upon as a product or a process. Different learning theories such as cognitivism or behaviorism have focused on internal mental processes or changes in behavior as an effect of learning. The socio-cultural perspective emphasizes that learning is about how knowledge and skills circulate and are re-created in a society, i.e. how previous knowledge lives on in new contexts and how new knowledge comes about (Säljö, 2002). How learning takes place is dependent on prevailing social circumstances and cultural patterns, particularly the ways in which the communicative transfer of skills takes place. Access to technical equipment also plays a big role. The socio-cultural perspective emphasizes the relationships between collectives and individuals. In today's society, it is not only school that teaches: individuals take part in a variety of public contexts, where learning is an explicit or implicit part of the social relation.

Considering learning and teaching, scholars claim that we are facing a paradigm shift. The paradigm that has been at stake for a long time is often called the Instruction Paradigm. In the educational atomism of the Instruction Paradigm, the parts of the teaching and learning process are seen as discrete entities. The parts exist prior to, and independent of, any whole; the whole is no more than the sum of the parts. Today, focus has moved to the Learning Paradigm where student learning and success set the boundaries (Barr & Tagg, 1995).

The contemporary Paradigm of Learning does not prescribe one answer to the question of how to organize learning environments and experiences. It supports any learning method and structure that work. The Learning Paradigm requires a constant search for new structures and methods that work better for student learning.

The fact that focus has shifted from teaching to learning can thus be described as a paradigm shift, which can also be related to the change in the perception of knowledge in relation to IT. But the abundant availability of information existing on the internet needs to be transformed into knowledge in order to promote learning in school context.

What we are facing today is an increasing complexity of knowledge mediation (NSF 2008). New technological tools for learning, communicating, collaborating, information gathering and production are introduced to us nearly every day. Our lives are seen as becoming increasingly easier to lead as we are becoming more and more connected through an ever-growing dependence on cell phones, e-mail, blogs, video conferencing, and other technological applications. From this strongly interconnected world and the potential immediate access to information emerges a new approach to learning (Brown, 2006).

FUTURE VIEWS OF LEARNING

Views on education and learning might also be mirrored in research about the future of learning. Future directions for education and technology that are currently visible in the research field were mapped and analyzed in a recent, 2-year study by Facer & Sandford (2010). Insights from over 100 researchers, from four disciplines, and 130 organizations and individuals from various societal groups contributed to a set of future scenarios which formed three future worlds. The future scenarios can most likely be described along three lines. Firstly, the changing demography with global migration that has an effect on the labor market and thus contributes to explaining international differences in age and gender, and employment and unemployment rates. Secondly, new human-machine relations are evolving as the internet trickles down to even the smallest devices and into every-day use (Vasseur & Dunkels, 2010). Thirdly, we see a weakening of institutional boundaries as the affordances of technology and access to e.g. online databases support student learners (Czerniewicz & Brown, 2010). Students are able to disregard content selected by others and take control of content choice. It is suggested that the next 25 years will challenge our contemporary organization of education around the unit of the individual child, the school and the discourses of the knowledge economy.

Researchers thus paint new scenes that give us indications about what will characterize future learning environments. Globalization seems to be a key concept that most futurists mention when talking about changing conditions related to education. Furthermore, advancements in technology will afford new opportunities to enhance learning experiences (Flynn & Vredevoogd, 2010). Students are supposed to take greater control of their own learning and they might therefore ask for more assorted and holistic approaches to e.g. inclusive learning. Inclusive learning can be understood as a process of increasing the attendance, participation and accomplishment of all learners in educational settings in their local community. In this sense inclusive learning can be seen as a form of personalizing learning, and IT can play a key role in supporting this process. The average age of students will according to Flynn & Vredevoogd (2010) rise and the mix of cultures, ages and learning styles will become gradually more varied.

In post-modern societies undergoing social and economic changes, high-quality education has become more important than ever before due to a larger and more demanding and specialized labor market. Global policy has led to a growing convergence of values, interdependence and global awareness. Also concepts such as inclusion, multiculturalism, pluralism and post-modernity are frequently used when describing the present-day society when education issues are being discussed.

On the other hand, Bauman (2003), addresses the challenges of education in modern society by asserting that the fundamental values underpinning the concept of knowledge has not changed in 2 500 years. The world is still perceived as stable, unchangeable, and the individual is seen as someone who must adapt to the existing structures rather than the other way around.

As little as forty years ago learners would complete the required schooling and enter a career that would often last a lifetime. Information development was slow and the time of knowledge was measured in decades. Today, these foundational principles have been altered and knowledge can be said to be growing exponentially. In fact, in many fields the life span of knowledge is now measured in months and years.

YOUTH AND LEARNING

Young people have a central position in the digital revolution. Their lives are intimately interlaced with the move towards a globally connected society and the growing complexity of relations and learning. Only a few years after the initiation of the world wide web, Katz (1997:173-174) suggested that "Children are at the epicenter of the information revolution, and ground zero of the digital world. Children can for the first time reach past the suffocating boundaries of social convention, past their elders' rigid notions of what is good for them". Yet, thirteen years later into the digital revolution, the metaphor of epicenter is still applicable. Discourses of fear are also present in the prevailing picture of young people and emerging technologies (Sandoval & Latorre, 2008). Parents fear the dangers online and want to protect their children from unwelcome contacts of potential perpetrators. They also feel that children should be protected from bullying and similar harassing acts on the internet (Frånberg, 2009).

But when we discuss risks on the internet, we also have to reflect on how the construction of childhood is made (James & Prout, 1997). To look at childhood as a separate part of life means that we at the same time contribute to the reinforcement of the concept of generational differences.

Prensky (2001) introduced the expressions digital natives and digital immigrants to catch the different attitudes towards the internet. This difference may also occur in many other attempts to label the young in relation to technology.

In the discourse of youth, learning and digital media the young generation have been given labels such as net-generation, digital generation, millennial learners and the YouTube generation (Cf. i.e. Tapscott, 1998; Oblinger & Oblinger, 2005). These are all labels constructed by an adult generation. As Herring (2008) points out, adults' power to interpret and construct contemporary technologies and practices are often normative and built on stereotyped assumptions. This may create a process of othering, defining youth as "The Other" as well as it may contribute to exoticizing the digital context and its associated activities. But, as Herring (2008) continues, this divide may also be seen as a rich site for cross-generational conversation.

Several researchers, such as Tingstad (2003), Veen & Vrakking (2006), Dunkels (2007) and Moinian (2007) have accentuated the importance of trying to view contemporary phenomena from the points of view of the young users. Herring (2008) even calls for a paradigm shift in this kind of research, emphasizing the need for both a change in methodology and for contextualized interpretations.

As mentioned above the new experiences of educational institutions can be understood as a paradigm shift where new roles and practices have emerged (Barr & Tagg, 1995; Brown, 2006). Son & O'Neill (2006) assert that in the space of approximately one hundred and thirty years, we have moved from the industrial age through the scientific age to the technological information age and the knowledge economy. With regards to pedagogy, this dramatic shift has placed traditional approaches to teaching and learning directly in the darkest shadow compared to a new, possible vision about the learner, in a more and more globalised world. Yet the relationships between technology, teaching, learning and pedagogy have not been fully explored (Paulsson, 2008). Watson (2001) asserts that despite the ubiquity of technology, no clear role has emerged in education. After many years of national policies and investment in IT in most countries, technology is still an imposed and novel outsider in the pedagogy of schools. Understanding the problematic of using IT demands a consideration of some more fundamental educational issues. IT is often perceived as a means for change; change in teaching style, change in learning approaches, and change in access to information. Yet research indicates that teachers are both threatened by change, and conversely not impressed by change that appears to focus on what the technology can do rather than on learning. Notably, teachers are seen to be 'immigrants' with regard to the new digital practices, appearing to lack knowledge about how children and young people engage with the net in informal, out-of-school contexts (Dunkels, 2007). While at school, teachers are challenged by young digital natives of the net who are members of an established digital culture from which teachers are generally, and for different reasons, excluded. Thus there is a risk that the young digital culture is ignored within schooling and that student experiences are not respected or considered in school.

As a result, this impacts on the relationship between students and teachers in the classroom and places constraints on the learning process and interaction (van't Hooft 2007; Prensky 2001, 2006). This is particularly influential on teachers' possibilities to act, respond to and prevent the abuse as well as the possibilities of the digital culture.

EMERGING LEARNING THEORIES

The advent of contemporary digital learning arenas, the shifting conditions for human society and the transformed approach to education demand extended ways of understanding knowledge and learning. Existing pedagogical theories build on ideas deriving from behaviorism, cognitivism and constructivism. They use language and logic as major components to describe knowledge. These traditional theories were also developed to understand learning situated in a pre-digital age society. Thus, how may learning situated in today´s society be understood? What theories might be helpful to understand online social learning today?

As a complement to cognitivist views on knowledge, connectivism (Siemens, 2005) may be of interest to further the understanding of the non-linear, formal and informal learning on the net (Dunkels, et al, 2008). Connectivism explains knowledge as 'the set of connections formed by actions and experience' (Downes, 2007:1b). Siemens (2005) suggests a learning theory that acknowledges technological shifts in a society where learning is no longer an internal, individualistic activity. It integrates principles of 'chaos, network, complexity and self-organization theories' (Siemens, 2006:30). Other central principles of connectivism are that learning and knowing are seen as continuous, on-going processes as opposed to end states or products and that this process is collective. Furthermore, decision-making is equal to learning in the sense that choosing what to learn and the meaning of incoming information is seen through the lens of a shifting reality. While there is a right answer now, it may be wrong tomorrow due to alterations in the information environment affecting the decision (Siemens, 2006). According to Siemens the abilities to see connections and recognize patterns constitute core skills today; "Learning and knowledge require diversity of opinions to present the whole and to permit selection of best approach" (Siemens, 2006:31).

There are some significant trends in contemporary ways of learning, according to Siemens (2005), which are mirroring the challenges of educational systems worldwide. He asserts that many learners will move into a variety of different, possibly unrelated fields over the course of their lifetime. He also states that informal learning is a significant aspect of our learning experience. Formal education no longer comprises the majority of our learning. He further states that learning is a continual process, lasting for a lifetime and that technology is changing our brains; the tools we use define and shape our thinking. Many of the processes previously handled by learning theories, especially in cognitive information processing, can now be supported by technology (Siemens, 2005).

If we understand learning as an individual process, in which previous conceptions about human and society are being challenged and changed we have to consider: What particular change and development are we talking about? Whose are the choices of the selection of learning content and who have the power to decide what is important to learn? Again, if we understand learning as a collective and social process where communication and dialogue in general are central, we have to ask: In what particular situations will learning as such take place? What kind of communication and interaction do we have in mind?

Another burning issue deals with the risk of fragmentation and a development towards an even more disrupted worldview and identity. Do really millennium learners think differently? Do their cognitive skills and competences develop in a different way? Do we in fact have to deal with Papert's (1994) "grasshopper minds" meaning that learners quickly jump from one topic to another without lingering over a subject? And if so what are the implications for the learning environments in the future?

Further on, is there a risk that independent thinking will be lost if we get caught in the compulsion to continually consume information just because it is available? Or if we no longer can sort and evaluate the flow, to distinguish the important from the unimportant?

The fact that we are familiar with assumptions underlying cognitive or constructivistic theories might help us understand how connectivism could contribute to the understanding of learning today. But on the other hand, learning is something much more complicated than connecting different pieces of information to each other. To have access to different sources of information and also to get this information through different media might have a positive impact on the interest and motivation of students in learning situations. It is rather a choice among the large quantity of information that is the crucial decision and to be able to critically examine the sources used.

CONCLUSION

Several parallel conditions have been highlighted in this chapter. For example, the theory about a fluid regime for structuring human life and technological meta trends, suggesting an overall increased complexity of knowledge mediation. Further key conditions are young people's continual central position on digital arenas and how this is influencing learning contexts. Emerging technologies, social, cultural and learning issues are interlaced with school practice and youth everyday life.

Contemporary technology is clearly changing the way people behave, talk, react, think, remember and learn. Similar to other human social activities such as identity work and socialization, learning is intangible and difficult to grasp. We suggest however, that in the same way as emergent technologies have yielded new ways of socialization and identity work, new learning experiences are a possibility. Consequently, opportunities to enhance and broaden our learning process have increased. But has learning in itself changed?

This may also be true for contemporary learning generated by the liquid state of modern society; a constant repetition of construction and deconstruction. However, equating learning with knowledge acquisition and reducing the learning process to the omnipresent access of information in the form of text, images, video, and audio is overly one-dimensional and lacks an understanding of the development of higher order thinking skills. Rather than simply register information, learning has more to do with making links between people, ideas and concepts in a particular context. Technology can surely be used to identify potential connections in these matters, but it also takes reflective thought and dialogue to make meaning of these relations. There is obviously a need for critical school-based research on the relationship between contemporary digital arenas, young people, and learning.

Overarching research questions are for example: What are the possibilities of and dilemmas associated with contemporary digital channels? How do they interact with and influence learning possibilities for young people? How can this together be analyzed and understood from an intersectional perspective? Have contemporary media influenced the processes and outcomes of learning and if so, how can the educational system exploit and benefit from this? The contemporary technology transformation has impacted on how we value, think, and talk about learning. But how the core essences in learning processes are affected needs to be further explored.

Further, we suggest there is a need of developing a critical framework to be able to conduct and analyze the outcomes of research findings in the area of young people, learning, and contemporary digital arenas. It is thus necessary to develop both theoretical and analytical concepts to make it possible to critically examine learning in today's society. Connectivism, as referred to in this chapter would be a fruitful starting point and a way forward for such a development. In addition, there is a need to include a critical perspective. This, together with a constructivistic approach, in relation to research questions, design and analysis will contribute to develop a more comprehensive and elaborative perspective on learning in the Google Era.

FUTURE RESEARCH AND DEVELOPMENT

In our opinion there is a need of developing a post connectivistic theory construction together with intersectional perspectives on identity that would be fruitful (Dunkels et al, 2008). Critical constructivistic connectivism is an approach we have begun to develop in relation to this research field. The theoretical framework will consider a critical perspective, a constructivistic approach as well as a modified theoretical approach on learning. This will hopefully give us opportunities to develop comprehensive analytical concepts in this research field. Further research aims are to embrace social and cultural perspectives on contemporary technology by focusing on social values and net cultures at the intersection of age, class, gender and ethnicity (Hällgren, 2006). Overall, such perspectives are important since they encourage adopting a critical approach towards education and technology use.

REFERENCES

Barr, R., & Tagg, J. (1995). *From Teaching to Learning – A New Paradigm for Undergraduate Education*. Philadelphia, PA: Change Magazine.

Bauman, Z. (2003). *Diogenes, 50*. Educational Challenges of the Liquid-Modern Era.

Beck, U. (2000). *The Risk Society and Beyond: Critical Issues for Social Theory*. London: Sage.

Bloom, D. E., & Canning, D. (2005). *Global Demographic Change: Dimensions and Economic Significance*. Boston: Harvard Initiative for Global Health.

Brown, T. H. (2006). *Beyond constructivism: navigationism in the knowledge era*. In On the Horizon, 3.

Collins, A., & Halverson, R. (2009). *Rethinking Education in the Age of Technology: The Digital Revolution and Schooling in America*. New York: Teachers College.

Czerniewicz, L., & Brown, C. (2010). Strengthening and weakening boundaries. Students negotiating technology mediated learning. In Sharpe, (Eds.), *Rethinking Learning for a Digital Age. How Learners are shaping their own Experiences*. Amsterdam: Routledge.

Dewey, J. (1916). *Democracy and Education: an introduction to the philosophy of education*. New York: The Macmillan Company.

Downes, S. (2007a). *What Connectivism Is*. 20081020Retrieved from http://www.webcitation. org/5bCyoI12E

Dunkels, E. (2007). *Bridging the Distance - Children's Strategies on the Internet*. Sweden:Umeå, Umeå universitet.

Dunkels, E., Frånberg, G.-M., & Hällgren, C. (2008). Young People and Contemporary Digital Arenas - Identity, Learning and Abusive Practices. In *Journal of Research in Teacher Education*.

Facer, K., & Sandford, R. (2010). The Next 25 Years?: Future Scenarios and Future Directions for Education and Technology. *Journal of Computer Assisted Learning, 26*(1), 74–93. doi:10.1111/j.1365-2729.2009.00337.x

Flynn, W., & Vredevoogd, J. (2010). The Future of Learning: 12 Views of Emerging Trends in Higher Education. *Planning for Higher Education, 38*(2), 5–10.

Frånberg, G.-M., & Gill, P. (2009). *Vad är mobbning? I På tal om mobbning och vad som görs*. Stockholm: Skolverket.

Giddens, A. (1990). *The Consequences of Modernity.* Cambridge, UK: Polity Press.

Giddens, A. (1991). *Modernity and Self-Identity. Self and Society in the Late Modern Age.* Cambridge, UK: Polity Press.

Hällgren, C. (2006). *Researching and Developing Swedkid: A Swedish Case Study at the Intersection of the Web, Racism and Education.* Doktorsavhandlingar i Pedagogiskt arbete. Nr. 5. Fakultetsnämnden för lärarutbildning. Umeå universitet.

Herring, S. (2008). Questioning the Generational Divide: Technological Exoticism and Adult Construction of Youth Identity. In D. Buckingham (Ed.) *Youth, Identity and Digital Media*, Pp. 71-92. John D. and Catherine T. MacArthur Foundation Series on Digital Media and Learning. Cambridge, MA: MIT Press.

James, A., & Prout, A. (Eds.). (1997). *Constructing and Reconstructing Childhood: Contemporary Issues in the Sociological Study of Childhood.* London: Falmer Press.

Jarvis, P. (2003). *The Theory and Practice of Learning.* London: Kogan.

Jenkins, H. (2006). *Confronting the challenges of participatory culture: media education for the 21st century.* Chicago: The MacArthur Foundation.

Katz, J. (1997). *Virtuous reality: How America Surrendered Discussion of Moral Values to Opportunists, Nitwits and Blockheads like William Bennett.* New York: Random House.

Moinian, F. (2007). *Negotiating Identities: Exploring children's perspectives on themselves and their lives.* Dissertation, SU - Stockholms universitet.

NSF [National Science Foundation] (2008). *Fostering Learning in the Networked World the Cyber Learning Opportunity.* Retrieved from 20080827: http://www.nsf.gov/pubs/2008/nsf08204/nsf08204.pdf

Oblinger, D., & Oblinger, J. (2005). *Educating the Net Generation.* Boulder, CO: Educause.

Papert, S. (1993). *The children's machine: rethinking school in the age of the computer.* New York: Basic Books.

Paulsson, F. (2008). *Modularization of the learning architecture: supporting learning theories by learning technologies.* Stockholm: KTH.

Prensky, M. (2001) Digital Natives, Digital Immigrants. *On the Horizon, 9*(5). NBC University Press. 20070402: http://www.marcprensky.com/

Prensky, M. (2006). *Don't Bother Me Mom - I'm Learning!* St. Paul, MN: Paragon House.

Säljö, R. (2005). *Lärande i praktiken: ett sociokulturellt perspektiv.* Stockholm: Nordstedts akademiska förlag.

Sandoval, C., & Latorre, G. (2008). Chicana/o Artivism: Judy Baca's Digital Work with Youth of Color. In A. Everett (Ed.) *Learning Race and Ethnicity: Youth and Digital Media.*, pp. 81-108. John D. and Catherine T. MacArthur Foundation Series on Digital Media and Learning. Cambridge, MA: MIT Press.

Siemens, G. (2005). Connectivism: A learning Theory for the Digital Age. In Donald G. Perrin (Ed International Journal of Instructional Technology and Distance Learning. 2(1) Article 1. 20081020: http://www.itdl.org/Journal/Jan_05/index.htm

Siemens, G. (2006). *Knowing Knowledge.* 20081020: http://www.knowingknowledge.com/book.php

Son, J.-B., & O'Neill, S. (2006). *Enhancing Learning and Teaching: Pedagogy, Technology and Language*. Queensland, Australia: eContent Management.

Tapscott, D. (1998). *Growing Up Digital: The Rise of the Net Generation*. New York: McGraw-Hill.

Tingstad, V. (2003*). Children's chat on the net: A study of social encounters in two Norwegian chat rooms*. Norsk Center for barneforskning.

van 't Hooft, M. (2007). Schools, Children and Digital Technology: Building Better Relationships for a Better Tomorrow. *Journal of Online Education 3,* (4). 20070410: http://www.innovateonline.info

Vasseur, J.-P., & Dunkels, A. (2010). *Interconnecting Smart Objects with IP - The Next Internet*. Reading, MA: Morgan Kaufmann.

Veen, V., & Vrakking, B. (2006). *Homo zappiens: growing up in a digital age*. London: Network Continuum Education.

Watson, D. (2001). IT and pedagogy - teachers - change - information – knowledge. Pedagogy before Technology: Re-thinking the Relationship between IT and Teaching. *Education and Information Technologies, 6*(4), 251–266. doi:10.1023/A:1012976702296

Ziehe, T. (2000) *Modernisierungsprozesse und Jugendkultur*. InPlebuch-Tiefenbacher, L. u.a. (Hg.), Geschlechterfrage in der Schule, Weinheim.

Chapter 2
Educational Technologies for the Neomillennial Generation

Regina Kaplan-Rakowski
Southern Illinois University, USA

David Rakowski
Southern Illinois University, USA

ABSTRACT

The purpose of this chapter is to provide educators, researchers, and policy-makers with an overview on how modern technology has been influencing the learning styles of the "neomillennial" generation. The authors begin by describing the demographic and cultural characteristics of the neomillennial genera-tion and how they differ from preceding generations. They follow with a discussion of how neomillen-nial learning styles have changed as a result of new technology. The authors then take a detailed look at two examples of how modern technology can be used to design novel learning approaches: digital game-based learning and learning in virtual worlds. Disadvantages, difficulties, and barriers to accep-tance of these approaches are then examined. They conclude by summarizing the characteristics of the neomillennial generation and why technological changes are likely to influence educational practices for them, as well as how these changes fit in the broader context of educational theory.

INTRODUCTION

Today's youth represent a diverse group of indi-viduals with profound differences in background, race, ethnicity, social status, and access to tech-nology. Nevertheless, there exist common trends among this group that distinguish them from

prior generations. The very recognition of such diversity, as well as unprecedented acceptance of it, is one of the most widespread characteristics of this group (Kohut, Parker, Keeter, Doherty, and Dimock, 2007). While within-group differ-ences abound, and perhaps are even stronger for many variables for this group than for previous generations, the synthesis of modern technology with popular culture provides a degree of novel

DOI: 10.4018/978-1-60960-206-2.ch002

social transformation which very few members of this generation are untouched by. We provide a generalized description of several of these current socio-technological influences on youth behavior and how these factors have the potential to transform selected educational practices.

Any study which endeavors to describe "young people" or "youth culture" suffers from the problems inherent with generalizations, and this chapter is no exception. However, in order to provide our readers with information relevant to understanding a wide pool of students, we have attempted to present an analysis of broad trends that have relevance across individuals, with the caveat that individuals will always exhibit their own idiosyncratic departures from broad generalizations. We do not provide a strict definition of who is included in our description of the "neomillennial generation" because some aspects of our discussion are more generalizable than others, and therefore encompass different groupings of individuals. Therefore, the analysis of educational practices discussed in our chapter potentially applies for any students whose lives and experiences are shaped by the socio-technological trends discussed below. These trends are most widespread for members of the neomillennial generation and we therefore frame our analysis in that context.

The most important feature of modern youth culture for our purposes is the extended exposure to multimedia interactive technology. American teens display this characteristic, with the majority of them (age 12-17) using the Internet on a daily basis (Lenhart, Madden, and Hitlin, 2005). While this feature is most common for students born roughly between the 1980's and the early years of the 21st century, other researchers have used a variety of slightly different age-based definitions for this group, depending on their resources and goals. The generation of students we consider has also been tagged with many different names. Labels focusing on the cultural aspects of this group include "millennials" (Wilson and Gerber, 2008),

"neomillennials" (Oblinger, 2003), "Generation Y" (Strauss and Howe, 2000), "Generation Next" (Lenhart, Kahne, Middaugh, Macgill, Evans, and Vitak, 2008), "the Net Generation" (Tapscott, 1998), and "Generation M" (Cvetkovic and Lackie, 2009). These cultural labels generally stress the importance of interactive technology, such as the Internet, on these individuals. Demographers and marketers often use terms such as "Echo Boomers" (Zolli, 2007) to highlight that this generation is large compared to the "Generation X" that precedes it. We follow Oblinger (2003) and refer to our subjects of interest as the "neomillennial" generation. We use the term "neomillennial" in order to draw attention to our focus on the younger members of this generation who are still in school, as the leading members of this group have already reached graduate school and are themselves entering society as educators.

This chapter is primarily written from the perspective of classroom-based educators in the United States. This is especially true with regard to the discussion of demographic trends and their potential impact on educational practices. However, the spread of interactive multimedia technology is a phenomenon common to all economically-developed countries, often to a greater degree than in the USA. Our examination of interactive multimedia technologies on youth learning is therefore extended to consider the experiences of other countries where this technology is available on a suitable scale. We have also noted, where appropriate, how these technological advances can potentially be used by students in developing countries to increase access to educational materials and practices that may otherwise not be available. The ability of developing countries to modify and apply modern technology in their own unique settings represents one of the most important potential future benefits offered by the combination of technology and education.

Across all countries with sufficient access to modern technology, numerous studies maintain that current youth cultural and technological development can be considered more sophisticated than for generations preceding them (Prensky, 2001a, 2001b; Gee, 2003, 2004; Johnson, 2005). However, others have argued for shortcomings of neomillennial learning styles and claim that modern educational habits "demean complex thinking, technical language, and sophisticated problem solving" (Shaffer and Gee, 2005, p. 9). Although there seem to be many potential strengths to the learning styles of the new generation, their shortcomings become apparent when these individuals are forced to conform to educational practices developed for a very different pool of students. We therefore examine common learning styles of this generation and provide examples of how educational practices can be modified to build on the new ways of thinking displayed by many members of this generation.

THE NEOMILLENNIALS VS. PREVIOUS GENERATIONS

There are specific differences that distinguish past generations of schoolchildren from the generation that is at school now. Eighty-seven percent of American teens (age 12-17) regularly use the Internet (Lenhart et al., 2005), which is the same proportion of this population (aged 14-17) who attend high school (US Census, 2008). Despite the pervasive reach of both the Internet and the school system, an important minority of potential students is not currently being reached through either of these channels, and these children rightfully deserve attention and research targeted to their unique situation. However, because the vast majority of the high-school-age population does have access to both the school system and Internet-based interactive technology, we focus on this potential inter-relationship. Furthermore, the use of the Internet by these potential students has increased from 73% in 2000 (Lenhart et

al., 2005) while school enrollment has dropped slightly (by 1%) over the same period (US Census, 2000, 2005). Therefore, access to interactive multimedia technology delivered through the Internet is growing while the percentage of students reached through the traditional school system is not. Furthermore, Internet use is more common among some minority groups, such as Hispanics (Lenhart et al., 2005) who are less represented in the traditional educational system than other groups (US Census, 2008). The widespread and growing access to multimedia interactive technology, represented by Internet access, is one of the most important transformative characteristics of the neomillennial generation.

The importance of cyclically recurring generational characteristics is studied in detail by Strauss and Howe (2000) who have produced several best-selling books, as well as a popular consultancy business, on the art of identifying and responding to shifts in generational characteristics. The intrinsic relationship between interactive technology and the neomillennial generation fits prominently in virtually all analyses of this group. The access of the neomillennials to technology is due to several interconnected factors which must be considered in order to understand the complex influence of media technology on youth culture. The rapid development of interactive technology during this generation's developmental years as a result of political and economic factors has been vital. However, technological change itself is not unique to this time period.

Widespread access to innovative technology has been just as important for neomillennials as the development of the technology itself. Access is unprecedented for this group (Wilson and Gerber, 2008; Strauss and Howe, 2000) because of the economic and demographic cycle in which this group has come of age. These economic characteristics include one of the longest periods of consumption growth in developed countries ever recorded, even after considering the economic setbacks of

2008-2010. For better or worse, this period has seen the dominance of a capitalistic-consumerist society that has encouraged the consumption of technology items that may have been considered frivolous luxuries by previous generations.

An additional demographic factor is that the neomillennials are the product of a parenting revolution, or reaction, in response to the distinctly anti-parenting attitudes prevalent during the 1960's and 1970's (Strauss and Howe, 2000). The parents of the neomillennials, born during the 1980's and 1990's, were not only more prosperous economically, but also more concerned with spending on children than the parents of Generation X, born in the 1960's and 1970's. A further influence is that the parents of the neomillennials are on average significantly older than parents of preceding generations (Strauss and Howe, 2000). This increased age further adds to the affluence and interest in education of the typical parent of a neomillennial child. The combined result of these factors is that the neomillennials' parents have more money to spend, more motivation to spend it on their children, and more technology to purchase, during the years when the neomillennials have been growing up (Lenhart et al., 2005). Although these factors have led to increased access to technology and education, they are also reflected in the narcissistic attitudes shown by this generation in their social relationships and self image (Twenge, 2006).

The differences between generations are stark enough that some researchers have concluded the wiring of a typical neomillennial brain has been physiologically altered according to the input it has received. The neuroscientist Paula Talla asserts that "you create your brain from the input you get" (Kurzweil, 2005, p.175), implying that the nature of media technology is a relevant influence on physical brain structure and cognitive processes. While past generations may have also had important differences from each other due to their modes of sensory input (recalled in the ancient shift from spoken to written communication), the current pace of technological advancement may have led to an accelerated change for the current generation. These technological factors embrace the duration and the style of media, which differ from the past. Examples of these include the way current television programs are now made, with short clips and dynamic shots (Prensky, 2007). It has been argued that the differences in cognitive processes between people who are immersed in digital culture from those who are not are comparable to the differences between literate and illiterate individuals with regard to traditional reading skills (Prensky, 2001a). The implication is that teaching or learning methods developed for people with one cognitive structure (i.e., those who are unable to read or not experienced with digital technology) may actually be counterproductive when applied to students whose thought processes have been molded by very different stimuli.

Many studies and analyses which compare learners based on their exposure to modern technology classify subjects as "Digital Natives" or "Digital Immigrants", after Prensky (2001a). Prensky provides us with an observation of how the cognitive styles of Digital Immigrants and Digital Natives may differ. His list contains contrasting features of the two groups with regard to their thought processes (the Digital Natives' and the Digital Immigrants' respectively): "twitch speed vs. conventional speed, parallel processing vs. linear processing, graphics first vs. text first, random access vs. step-by-step, connected vs. standalone, active vs. passive, play vs. work, payoff vs. patience, fantasy vs. reality, technology-as-friend vs. technology-as-foe" (p. 52).

Whenever Digital Immigrants deal with technology, they are said to have "an accent" (Prensky, 2001a), in that they are more comfortable with traditional media formats, even when they have learned to be proficient with technological innovations. This classification is highly correlated with the generational status of a student, with the neomillennials being far more likely to display the characteristics of Digital Natives (Jones and Fox, 2009; Lenhart et al., 2005). In contrast, the parents and educators of the neomillennial generation often display the characteristics of Digital Immigrants. The different levels of comfort with these technologies are reflected in the goals of use reported by neomillennials and previous generations. Older generations report using the Internet as a tool for research and shopping while neomillennials are significantly more likely to describe it as their primary method of communication and entertainment (Jones and Fox, 2009).

The Neomillennials' Learning Styles

The tendencies displayed by the neomillennial generation when learning have been labeled as "neomillennial learning styles" (Dede, 2005). These learning styles reflect many of the distinct characteristics that distinguish this generation from those preceding it. First, as mentioned above, this neomillennial generation is special, in that it has received increased attention from parents compared to previous generations. This increased attention is reflected both in increased spending and consumption by these children and increased legislation devoted to their needs (Wilson and Gerber, 2008; Strauss and Howe, 2000). For our purpose, this is reflected in their expectation of personalized attention while learning, which must be balanced with the contradictory fact that the number of people of teaching age is set to decline relative to the number of students.

The second relevant characteristic of the neomillennials is their team-orientation. This generation is used to group projects, collaborative effort, and cooperation. The interactive nature of modern technology may then be a result of these characteristics rather than a cause of them. Social networks, virtual worlds and online games allow for group socializing, play, and entertainment. Media are increasingly developed spontaneously and collaboratively through Internet sites such as *Facebook*, *YouTube*, *Flickr*, and *MySpace*. For our purposes, it is suggested that a successful educational strategy could benefit from incorporating the team-oriented technologies which are an integral part of the generation's persona.

A distinctly negative aspect of the neomillennials is that they have been documented to have higher stress and anxiety than the generations before them, especially with regard to academic performance (Wilson and Gerber, 2008). This is apparently the result of the increased attention from parents, as well as the increasingly competitive economic and professional environment which this generation faces. Educational strategies could therefore benefit from recognition that the anxiety levels of these students may necessitate alternative approaches to learning. The increased use of digital games for education is one way to address this factor.

The new generation's learning process does not commonly follow the traditional paradigm of beginning with a clear starting point and then proceeding in sequential steps to the conclusion. Instead, they follow a non-linear path of exploration by taking several paths in different directions as they search, filter, and synthesize different multimedia sources of information. Some search paths are abandoned and some are combined to lead to the task's completion (similar to browsing a website). This illustrates the nature of the nonlinear learning style popular with the new generation.

Multitasking is usual not only for daily activities but also within media. One fourth of the time that the young spend with one media, they also do something that relates to another media form (Roberts, Foehr, and Rideout, 2005). Moreover, the prevalence of multitasking is increasing over time. Wallis (2006) reports on a study by the director of UCLA's Center on Everyday Lives of Families, Elinor Ochs, who found "it [the impact of multitasking gadgets] to be one of the most dramatic areas of change". It is unsurprising these days to see the young talking and/or texting on a phone, listening to music, having a TV on, browsing the Internet on multiple monitors, and playing a video game at the same time. This multitasking tendency highly resembles situations when, on our computer, multiple windows are open for easy access and manipulation between and among them. This invention makes it possible to multitask easily. As a consequence, it provides methods to work in a faster and more efficient way, once one is comfortable with the nonlinear patterns of thought stimulated by such a process. For young students, such thinking is second-nature, while for older people it can seem to be only an unproductive distraction.

Tapscott (1998) and Howe and Strauss (2000), among others, describe the way the characteristics discussed above come into play when neomillennials use modern digital media. To take the World Wide Web as an example, one can see that the multiplicity of sources of information obliges one to search, filter and synthesize. This process highly contrasts with the traditional reception of information, which comes from a single authoritative source, such as the teacher's lectures or books. Therefore, the new generation uses a very different process (search, filter and synthesize) than the previous generations (memorize the master source that was given to them). Furthermore, the neomillennials' styles also encourage experiential activities, entertainment while learning, and the integration of technology. These characteristics lead to improvement in goal orientation, positive attitude, and technical savvy (Raines, 2003) and should be considered alongside the personalized attention, group-orientation, high-stress levels, non-linear cognitive processes, and multi-tasking features that define this generation. Such influences on styles of learning are difficult to incorporate when relying on traditional media formats such as printed texts and spoken lectures. However, environments such as digital games or virtual worlds offer an ideal setting to build on the

opportunities offered by neomillennials' distinct styles of processing information and organizing the tasks they face.

EXAMPLES OF NEW TECHNOLOGIES FOR LEARNING

The neomillennial generation is especially well-prepared to adopt innovative technological gadgets, as well as Internet-based learning environments (Lenhart et al., 2005). Internet users are increasingly able not only to retrieve information from the web but also to customize it to their specific tastes, as well as to participate actively in its creation. This possibility gives more confidence to the users of such applications. The emergence of "Web 2.0" with its focus on user-generated multimedia interactivity, is both a result of, and a further stimulus to, the collaborative and contributory nature of modern information technology. The interactive nature of these platforms leads to a generation of students who are uncomfortable with passively absorbing information. Instead, they expect to actively take part in the creation, modification, and customization of that material. In this sense, the neomillennial generation is the exact opposite of the "couch potato" generation that preceded it.

A full examination of the impact of the Internet on neomillennials' education is too broad a topic to be adequately addressed in a concise book chapter. Numerous sources attest to the growing usefulness of, as well as concerns with, innovations such as blogs (Ferdig and Trammell, 2004; Williams and Jacobs, 2004; Duffy and Bruns, 2006), social networking (Baird and Fisher, 2005-2006), file-sharing (Godwin-Jones, 2005), wikis (Notari, 2006; Lamb, 2004; Duffy and Burns, 2006), etc. We therefore focus on two specific examples of innovative and interactive technologies and how they can be integrated into the learning experience for students. The two platforms we examine are instructional digital games and online virtual worlds.

Digital Games for Instruction

It is estimated that 97% of teenagers in the USA play video or computer games (Rainie, 2009). This might make us wonder what makes digital games so popular. Is it their accessibility, their multimedia attractiveness, their storyline, or their engagement? The answers to those questions are hard to find, especially considering that each gamer might be attracted by a different feature that games have. However, what is difficult to dispute is that such a high rate of gaming should not be overlooked by educators. Wouldn't teachers (and learners) one day be glad to see statistics reporting: "it is estimated that 97% of teenagers in the USA do their homework voluntarily and with pleasure?" This question should be very easy to answer.

Simply said, the possibility of delivering learning content through games is like killing two birds with one stone – that is, providing students with entertainment and motivation, as well as with an educational experience. The use of digital games is gaining ground, with 34% of American teens reporting to have played a digital game as part of a school assignment (Lenhart et al., 2008). Therefore, the field of digital game-based learning needs to be further explored, as game-based learning fits many psychologically-based theories of how effective learning occurs but empirical evidence of the effectiveness of these games is lacking.

Vygotsky (1978) states that engaging and motivating play is necessary to enhance learning. However, besides motivation and educational factors, there is much more to games. It comes by no surprise then that the field of serious gaming (educational / instructional gaming) has been growing, with digital games increasingly advocated for learning. As a basis for the rationale of why games could work as an effective instructional tool,

Becker (2007) illustrates how effective games correspond with established instructional approaches, such as Gagné's Nine Events (Gagné, Briggs, and Wager, 1992), Reigeluth's Elaboration Theory (Reigeluth, Merrill, Wilson, and Spiller, 1980), Bruner's Socio-Cultural Approach to Education (Bruner, 1996), and Merrill's First Principles of Instruction (Merrill, 2001). These approaches have been used extensively in educational, military and corporate training for several decades and they have often been reported to be effective. As we pinpointed in a previous section of this chapter, the neomillennials display certain characteristics, such as experience with collaborative effort, multi-tasking, and high-anxiety, which suggest that a game-based learning environment may be more appropriate for them than for previous generations.

While using games for education is not a new idea, the flexibility offered by using computer-based digital games allows for an immense expansion of the educational possibilities available in terms of content, interactivity, assessment, and structure. There are times when teachers would want to go on a field trip with their students for better immersion in a topic. However, sometimes it may be too dangerous (e.g. a nuclear reactor), too expensive (e.g. going abroad), or simply impossible (e.g. ancient Greece) (Kluge and Riley, 2008). That is when modifiable role-playing games come in handy. These games, that are daily part of the neomillennials' life, provide opportunities for teachers to create immersive and educational scenarios for students where the danger, complexity, and expense can be appropriately adjusted or diminished (Kaplan-Rakowski and Loh, 2010).

Shaffer and Gee (2005) criticize schools that do not prepare students for high-quality future jobs and life experiences. They claim that traditional educational methods are increasingly shunting students into commodity jobs[1], while those students would benefit more from preparation for innovative work. This rationale leads Shaffer and Gee to suggest that young students would benefit from education by means of epistemic games. Those games are ones that will foster innovation and creativity in the young generation. They state:

"in epistemic games students learn facts and content in the context of innovative ways of thinking and working. They learn in a way that sticks, because they learn in the process of doing things that matter" (p. 24).

In a similar manner, Weigel (2005) suggests that "a 21ˢᵗ-century education should prepare students to be knowledge creators – not simply receptacles of existing knowledge." They further propose that "discovery and discernment" should play an important role in modern education while "absorption and recall" should not. Because the traditional curriculum focused on the effective transfer of an accepted body of knowledge to students, it was well-suited to the mass production of workers for standardized factory jobs. However, because the most productive jobs of the future will require initiative, innovation, and creativity, the traditional methods may no longer be effective. The use of instructional games is one method to encourage initiative, innovation, and creativity in the current and future generations of students.

Research on the potential aspects of using digital games for instruction has been growing as educators increasingly recognize the effectiveness of this mode for encouraging the development of the characteristics needed by future members of society. However, this research has yet to provide consistent empirical evidence for if these games actually improve learning by students. For a more-in-depth analysis, one could consult, for example, Gee (2003, 2008); Johnson (2005); Becker (2007); Wong (2007); Young, Schrader, and Zheng (2006); Annetta, Murray, Laird, Bohr, and Park (2006); Squire and Jenkins (2003); Squire (2002); Van Eck, (2006); Bellotti, Berta, De Gloria, and Primavera (2009); Moreno-Ger, Burgos, and Torrente (2009); Michael, and Chen

(2006), and Kaplan-Rakowski and Loh (2010). Much of this research finds that as the technology for digital games has matured, these games have become more effective in stimulating interest by students, fulfilling a variety of psychologically-based theories of cognition. Simultaneously, the unique characteristics of the neomillennials and the changing requirements of economics and society have elevated the particular skills fostered by games relative to traditional educational practices.

Virtual Worlds

In addition to instructional games, the use of virtual worlds (VWs) and related environments such as multi-user virtual environments (MUVEs) have been attracting the interest of educators. While many of the features of virtual worlds that are important for learning overlap with the characteristics of digital games, there are some important aspects of VWs that can be distinguished from digital games. Although gaming may be either a solitary or cooperative activity, VWs are by nature collaborative social experiences. Therefore, while games possess strengths in the experiential side of learning, VWs have a relative advantage in facilitating the social interaction and exchange of information that accompanies learning.

Using VWs (or online games) gives educators a method with which they may transition from teacher-centered instruction to student-centered instruction (Kluge and Riley, 2008), which is a fundamentally important step (Polka, 2001). However, because educators may possess a more flexible environment for interaction with students in a VW, they may present a more effective platform for integrating the actual classroom with interactive technology than games alone can. Active engagement and practical experience by students in the VW are effective means to foster more meaningful learning (Kaplan-Rakowski, 2010). In this type of environment, the instructor's role is one of a facilitator, as opposed to one of a lecturer (Hargis, 2005).

The potential of VWs is not limited only to hierarchical instruction; it can also provide an opportunity for a combined implementation of "peer-teaching, autonomous learning principles, intellectually rich content-based instruction, individualized learning, and play" (Von der Emde, Schneider, and Kotter, 2000, p. 210). VW's generative nature lets students build environments through which they create their unique learning experiences. Since the nature of VWs is highly social, they also provide opportunities for collaborative work. As Calongne (2008, p. 48) adequately put it:

"The use of virtual worlds expands on the campus-based and online classrooms, enhancing learning experiences. Some people learn best by listening to the course content, others by seeing and visualizing the content in context, and the rest by using a hands-on approach to demonstrate course competencies. In virtual worlds, we can leverage a mix of content and activity to support all learners: auditory, visual and kinesthetic. Virtual worlds support these different learning styles and give students opportunities to explore, discover, and express their understanding of the subject".

While in the past it was difficult to create environments for many teaching activities, VWs (as well as games and simulations) now provide us with more feasible opportunities. VWs encompass a wide range of complexity, with the simplest uses serving only as a receptacle for course material online. However, the full advantage of the environments is often gained when educators use the possibility of placing educational material in context by manipulating the virtual environment.

An example of using a VW to place educational experiences in context is a foreign language class set in a virtual location corresponding to the native environment where that language is spoken (Kaplan-Rakowski, 2010). The audio-visual flexibility of the virtual world allows for a simulation of the setting in a way that would be infeasible in a traditional classroom. The technological tools offered by VWs to facilitate social interaction also provide useful tools for both the transmission of material and assessment by the educator. These tools include voice and text chat, allowing for private or group conversations; logging of conversations, useful for recall of material at a later time for review by the student or assessment by the instructor; instant messaging as a "virtual clicker" for speed drills and timed assessment; and virtual gestures, as a non-verbal communication option. One may refer to Kaplan-Rakowski (2010) for several examples of educational activities set in a virtual world which are specifically tailored to the neomillennial learning styles.

CRITIQUES OF THE USE OF NOVEL TECHNOLOGY FOR LEARNING

What has prevented digital games and virtual worlds from being properly and widely implemented for education so far, given that they appear to be well-suited to the neomillennial learning styles? In addition to the upfront technology cost, one problem concerns mistakes in identifying and generalizing the relevant characteristics of any group of individuals, such as the neomillennial generation. However, the issues of access, represented by funding and generalizability concerns, are not confined to digital games or virtual words, but are common to any revisions to educational practices. Further criticism, directed specifically against the technologies described above, is the lack of empirical evidence on their efficacy. These criticisms generally fall into three related categories. First, the use of digital games and virtual worlds have not fully proven their effectiveness over alternative formats for instruction due to the poor design of many initial games used for instruction, and the relatively recent emergence of virtual worlds for instruction. Second, research on games has suffered from inadequately designed methodology, leading to a lack of consistent evidence on the value of instructional games (Clark, 2007). Related to this, the lack of available data from virtual worlds presents difficulties for the identification and assessment of learners. Third, the valuable characteristics of both environments can have side-effects, such as over-use, unintended behavioral influences (Anderson and Bushman, 2001; Anderson et al., 2008) and exposure to inappropriate content.

Access

Despite the apparent potential for the use of digital games and virtual environments in education, they have not been quickly or enthusiastically adopted by the majority of mainstream educators. Part of this lies in the resistance to the upfront cost in time and financial resources required for any transformation of educational practices. One of the apparent advantages of traditional instruction is that it requires little hardware other than a blackboard or some other simple means to display information. However, the use of digital games and VWs require substantial initial hardware and infrastructure spending. The budgetary advantage of technology in education is achieved only when it can be scaled up to provide instruction to additional students for little marginal cost. Therefore, while these costs are true impediments in the short term, they are less relevant over the medium and long term. However, when the budgetary outlook of an educational institution is more uncertain, then the present value of long-term capital investments in technological infrastructure is diminished. Therefore, the value of technological improvements is dependent on society's willingness to provide stable sources of support for educational institutions.

Further concerns arise because students with sufficient access to the required technologies are unlikely to be fairly distributed across social, economic, ethnic, and national lines. The unequal distribution of access can be both a blessing and a curse for new technologies in education. Lower-income groups are less likely to use the Internet, with 73% of families earning less than $30,000 using the Internet, compared to over 90% Internet use for families earning more than $50,000 (Lenhart et al., 2005). However, evidence on the relative impact of equity in access is mixed. On one hand, students from more privileged backgrounds are more likely to have experience and access to multimedia technology than students from minority or lower-income backgrounds. However, students who have less access to multimedia technology are often from the same groups that are already being under-served by the existing school system. For example, although Hispanic teens display higher rates of Internet use than the general population (89% versus 87%), African-American teens display lower rates (77%) (Lenhart et al., 2005). However, this rate is not very different than the 79.5% of African-Americans (US Department of Education, 2008) who are already not provided with a high-school degree by the existing educational system.

Variation in the initial access to technological infrastructure is a legitimate concern for educators, as it implies the possibility of greater benefits for students who are already from privileged backgrounds. However, the scalable nature of educational practices over the Internet allows content to be delivered to students who would not otherwise have access. Furthermore, the use of modern technology represents the possibility of designing education methods that are relatively more beneficial for students who are not currently being well served by the existing educational system. Educators should therefore take care to consider the balance between these factors when designing educational content to be delivered through either games or virtual worlds. More evidence is needed in order to distinguish between innovations that simply reinforce the advantage already held by dominant groups, from those practices that allow for the advancement of students for which traditional educational methods are ineffective.

Effectiveness

Extrapolating from the disappointing results of earlier technologies and attempts at "edutainment", such as with TV, it was first concluded by many educators that the new technologies discussed here would remain ineffective as well (Oppenheimer, 1997; Postman, 1985; Tyack and Cuban, 1995). Moreover, the classic discussion in the field of instructional technology, the debates of Clark (1983, 2001) vs. Kozma (1991, 1994) reveal a history of discord on the two sides of the educational establishment as to whether technology is considered to have a positive impact on learning or not. Kozma (1991, 1994) provided support for advocates of the positive side of technology, while Clark (1983) summarized the arguments that "media are mere vehicles that deliver instruction but do not influence student achievement" (p. 455) and concluded that they are not better than traditional instruction through lecturing. These debates and criticism began back when interactive technology was at its embryonic stage. The criticisms still linger now, even though interactive multimedia technology has progressed and penetrated society.

Researchers such as Gredler (1996) and Hayes (2005) concluded that students do not learn better from games than from other approaches, with Hayes adding that the studies that show serious game instruction as favorable are the ones that are deficiently designed. Chen and O'Neil (2005) and O'Neil, Wainess, and Baker (2005) report that only 19 papers (out of 4,000 published in peer-reviewed journals up to that point) analyzing "data

about learning or motivation" used quantitative or mixed-research methods. Because the qualitative methods dominating the literature were often restatements of the existing arguments for why technology may or may not be effective, little actual evidence on effectiveness was produced.

We believe that many of these criticisms aimed at new technologies stemmed from the fact that these technologies faced several decades when they had to mature before effective uses could be evaluated. In considering the research on the effectiveness of instructional games, one must be careful to distinguish between early studies conducted when educational games where largely in a pilot stage, with many bugs yet to be resolved, and later studies when game development was considerably refined. We may not yet have reached the stage when games are truly perfected and accurate assessment of their value is possible, but we do appear to be moving closer. The personal side of this is that users of interactive multimedia technologies also faced a generation of sometimes difficult transition. Generation X, on which early research about these technologies and education was based, represented a phase in education and culture when these technologies were just being developed and therefore could not be expected to be comfortable with these new practices and immature technologies. In contrast, one of the most defining characteristics of the neomillennial generation is that they have spent their entire lives with these technologies and face no transition in using them. Therefore, we currently face the need for a broad range of research on the effectiveness of innovative technologies for education. Past studies have failed to definitively provide evidence either for or against these technologies, and have also failed at documenting the variation in any benefits that may be achievable.

Teacher Training

Despite growing funds for technology, its integration into the curriculum has often proved challenging (Ficklen and Muscara, 2001). A part of the reason lies with teachers, who often have negative attitudes towards new technology. Therefore, increased funding alone will not necessarily lead to the success of innovative technologies in the classroom unless the perspectives of teachers are better incorporated into the implementation of technology.

The two most apparent obstructions to technology implementation on the part of educators are teachers' shortage of time and shortage of training (Beggs, 2000; Newhouse, 1999). Tolmie (2001) concludes that it is not enough to provide technology resources if the effective integration into instruction does not take place. Therefore, a critical shortcoming of early digital games and virtual worlds is that they were either designed by instructors with good pedagogical training, but poor technological skills, or by programmers with advanced technological skills, but poor pedagogical training. Either way, many applications ended up being ineffective for instructional purposes.

Anderson and Becker (2001) point out that whether educational technology works depends highly on the "human element". That means that it is essential for teachers to have both technical skills and pedagogical expertise so that they will be able to design computer-based activities that will enhance students' learning. While today's education programs provide thorough pedagogical training, they do not always provide the necessary technical knowledge. What is needed then is a way to provide the necessary technological abilities to educators who already have the required pedagogical training. As more members of the neomillennial generation become educators themselves, this problem will be partially addressed. Until then, educators should keep in mind that poorly designed digital and online environments will not necessarily provide benefits to students.

Side Effects: Inappropriate Content and Overuse

Several studies draw attention to certain side-effects of modern media. Educators, in particular, need to guard their (especially young) students from exposure to inappropriate content of some digital games and VWs, and the risk of overuse of modern technology and media.

As for content, there exist concerns about both violence and sexually-explicit material. Violence is mainly encountered in commercial video games, and with traditional media, such as TV. The young, in particular, are susceptible to the influence of violence. Anderson and Bushman (2001) and Anderson et al. (2008) account that media with violent content increase the degree of aggressive behavior, aggressive cognition, physiological arousal and aggressive affect, while decreasing their measures of helpful behavior. This finding needs to be kept in mind while designing activities using commercial games (COTS) or when designing games or VWs ourselves (Kaplan-Rakowski and Loh, 2010).

Sexually-explicit material is more prevalent in virtual worlds (Bugeja, 2007), although several games have also raised concern, with Senator Hillary Clinton famously calling for an investigation into both violent and sexually-explicit content in the game *Grand Theft Auto*. While exposure to material is one facet of using virtual worlds, possible contact with sexual predators by young students raises even stronger concerns. Educators may respond to these issues by restricting educational interactions to limited areas of virtual worlds, but at the cost of eliminating much of the unbounded social interaction that these worlds provide. If one of the motivations in using virtual worlds is to expose students to alternative ideas and cultures then restricting access will be counterproductive.

Another side-effect associated with modern media is game, or Internet, overuse, which in extreme cases has been interpreted as addiction (Young, 1996). Because the new technology is attractive and engaging, it naturally poses the danger of students becoming overly dependent on it. Games and the Internet, in particular, carry this danger, as well as related risks, such as obesity and social withdrawal. Young (1996) portrays this overuse as a clinical disorder. More recent studies confirm the likelihood of hazardous effects of overuse of the Internet (Chou, Condron, and Belland, 2005; Young, 2004; Young, 1996) and they caution users against media overuse, claiming it may negatively influence mental and physical states and behavior. On the other hand, the investigation by Campbell, Cumming, and Hughes (2006) finds that extensive Internet use does not correlate with anxiety, depression, or social fearfulness. Further, a study by Wood (2008) suggests that some gamers play excessively because of their ineffective time management skills or as a way to escape from problems. An alternative explanation of the overuse is provided by Smahel, Blinka, and Ledabyl (2008) who claim that players' addiction is due to their strong identification with the characters they play.

Looking from another perspective, the bad connotation of the word "addiction" in the case of educational games could turn into a benefit. Which educator would not want her students to be "addicted" to learning? Prensky (2006) advocates this beneficial "addiction" (that is "learning") in his book on digital game-based learning entitled *"Don't bother me Mom - I'm learning"*.

CONCLUSION

This chapter has described the social, cultural, and technological characteristics of the neomillennial generation. These characteristics provide tempting support for the hypothesis that these current and future students could benefit from the integration of modern interactive multimedia technology into their education. We have provided concrete examples of two such technologies, digital games and virtual worlds, as well as the problems associated with implementing these technologies for education. However, it is unclear whether these potential tools will be used for the benefit of students or if they will present an additional impediment to the progress of students, as conclusive evidence is lacking for either position.

As technology advances, the nature of its influence will evolve as well. Educators commonly misunderstand the fact that although teens today read far fewer books than earlier generations (Wilson and Gerber, 2008), they actually read more material than previous generations (Rainie, 2009). Therefore, while it first appears that students are underperforming their predecessors on a variety of traditional reading-and-writing-based measures, it is unclear if this represents a technology-induced stunting of intellectual achievement, or if these students are simply learning skills and material in a format that is poorly suited to traditional methods of evaluation.

The incorporation of technologies such as digital games and virtual worlds offers a potential means to combine the media culture of the neomillennial generation with their learning environment. This chapter provides educators and administrators with the demographic background which drives this opportunity and specific examples of the potential technological tools that may result from it. The shift of social engagement online, represented by the explosive growth of interactive applications such as social networks, is likely to increasingly dominate the interaction between members of society as the neomillennial generation moves out of school and takes its place at the center of our cultural and business world. Traditional communication skills may rapidly decline, as styles better suited to the available technologies come to dominate.

Part of the transformative, yet troubling, nature of information exchange for neomillennials arises because youth today are used to absorbing information from a variety of multimedia interactive formats rather than through linearly-delivered media, such as books, lectures, or television. The production of this content goes hand-in-hand with the reception of it for neomillennials using Web 2.0 and related media. Recognition that the creation of this information has changed, as well as its delivery, is essential to understand the future progression of technology, as well as the social and cognitive development of future students and members of society. The two-way flow of information will likely lead to predictable developments, as well as the disruptive and unforecastable innovations that spur future progress.

In many cases the transition to new technologies for education is unnecessarily disruptive because teachers do not always have enough skills to use technology in the appropriate way. Such difficulties are probably as old as institutionalized education itself, with surprisingly similar difficulties being described by Plato when encountering the shift from oral to written transmission of educational content in ancient Greece (Gibson, 2009). A common mistake is to view new technologies as mere delivery devices for traditional content, rather than focusing on their implications for the creation of new content. This is well shown by the disappointing early results from incorporating television into educational instruction (Postman, 1985; Boyse, 2009; American Decades, 2001), before its value as a supplement was painstakingly demonstrated much later (Prensky, 2005). Therefore, it seems that it would be more logical to first make sure that equipment, such as computers, and Internet resources will have an effective use before the actual investment is made. This could be done by organizing workshops that would prepare teachers for the challenge. Even more, if the necessary changes to the curriculum are thought out and teachers' input is incorporated

before hardware is purchased, then it is more likely that teachers will make effective use of new technology.

The second common problem is the issue of generality – that is, falsely considering all students to be the same. The neomillennial generation is unique in being one of the most diverse groups in recent history (Kohut et al., 2007). Some experts, such as Prensky (2001), argue for the alteration of all instruction into games. Some schools have even gone so far as to attempt performing all instruction via digital games, although it will take some time to evaluate their progress (Davidson, 2009). Even though for some it may seem an exciting learning method, as educators, we have to remember that not all the students in our class are the same. Some students might dislike technology or feel uncomfortable around it. Therefore, forcing such students to base their education on games or virtual worlds is not necessarily effective for all students – not to mention the fact that right now there are very few good educational games available and by the time there will be more, the newer generation will likely have progressed to even newer technologies.

One must also consider the access of students to new technologies. Some forms of modern technology, such as basic Internet access and cell phones, are available to a wider range of social and economic groups than earlier forms of new technology (Lenhart et al., 2005). However, more advanced and expensive innovations may be available only to those students of privileged backgrounds. Educators must strive to balance the opportunities for advancement offered by modern technology against the difficulties of access experienced by some students.

Third, increased use of technology for education inevitably leads to the issue of losing the "human factor". In virtual worlds, human representation is in the form of an avatar[2]. It is not yet clear what the consequences will be for society of this loss of face-to-face physical interaction.

Again, similarities exist with the shift from face-to-face dialogues for education to the reading of impersonal written texts in ancient Greece (Gibson, 2009). This focus on the efficient transfer of information via technology, if accompanied by the abandonment of face-to-face interaction, raises important questions of what exactly schools are meant to teach children. Should the focus be the transmission of knowledge or the molding of social practices? These questions go to the heart of alternative theories of the purpose of education (Schiro, 2008).

For those that are unsatisfied with educational practices that promote total digital classrooms and those that are unsatisfied with traditional instruction, hybrid learning has been suggested (Young, 2002) as a useful transitional mode of instruction. This method blends conventional face-to-face instruction with interactive multimedia technology, as well as additional e-learning facilities (Koohang and Durante, 2003). Seimens (n.d.) claims that the hybrid learning "takes the best of both worlds", and therefore enhances the learning experience. However, as evidence of the effectiveness of these methods is either not yet available, or is inconclusive, this remains a potentially beneficial area for further study.

REFERENCES

American Decades. (2001). *Television's effect on education*. Retrieved April 5, 2010, from http://www.encyclopedia.com/doc/1G2-3468301851.html

Anderson, C. A., & Bushman, B. J. (2001). Effects of violent video games on aggressive behavior, aggressive affect, physiological arousal, and prosocial behavior: A meta-analytic review of the scientific literature. *Psychological Science, 12*(5). doi:10.1111/1467-9280.00366

Anderson, C. A., Sakamoto, A., Gentile, D. A., Ihori, N., Shibuyya, A., & Yukawa, S. (2008). Longitudinal effects of violent video games on aggression in Japan and the United States. *Pediatrics, 122*(5), 1067–1072. doi:10.1542/peds.2008-1425

Anderson, R. E., & Becker, H. J. (2001). School investments in instructional technology. *Teaching, Learning, and Computing, 8*. Retrieved March 15, 2010, from http://www.crito.uci.edu/tlc/findings/report_8/startpage.htm

Annetta, L. A., Murray, M. R., Laird, S. G., Bohr, S. C., & Park, J. C. (2006). Serious games: Incorporating video games in the classroom. *EDUCAUSE Quarterly, 29*(3), 16–22.

Baird, D. E., & Fisher, M. (2005-2006). Neomillennial user experience design strategies: Utilizing social networking media to support "Always on" learning styles. *Journal of Educational Technology Systems, 34*(1), 5–32. doi:10.2190/6WMW-47L0-M81Q-12G1

Becker, K. (2007). Pedagogy in commercial video games. In Gibson, D., Aldrich, C., & Prensky, M. (Eds.), *Games and simulations in online learning. Research and development frameworks* (pp. 26–34). Hershey, PA: Information Science Publishing.

Beggs, T. A. (2000). *Influences and barriers to the adoption of instructional technology*. In Proceedings of the Mid-South Instructional Technology Conference. Retrieved November 25, 2008, from http://frank.mtsu.edu/~itconf/proceed00/beggs/beggs.htm

Bellotti, F., Berta, R., De Gloria, A., & Primavera, L. (2009). Enhancing the educational value of video games. *Computers in Entertainment (CIE), 7*(2).

Boyse, K. (2009). Television and Children. *YourChild Development & Behavior Resources*. Retrieved April 1, 2010, from http://www.med.umich.edu/yourchild/topics/TV.htm

Bruner, J. S. (1996). *The culture of education*. Cambridge, MA: Harvard University Harper Perennial.

Bugeja, M. J. (2007). Second thoughts about *Second Life*. *The Chronicle of Higher Education*, C1.

Calongne, C. M. (2008, September/October). Educational frontiers: Learning in a virtual world. *Educause Review, 43*(5), 36-48. Retrieved April 3, 2010, from http://www.educause.edu/EDUCAUSE+Review/EDUCAUSEReviewMagazineVolume43/EducationalFrontiersLearningin/163163

Campbell, A. J., Cumming, S. R., & Hughes, I. (2006). Internet use by the socially fearful: addiction or therapy? *Cyberpsychology & Behavior, 9*(1), 69–81. doi:10.1089/cpb.2006.9.69

Chen, H. -H., & O'Neil, H. F. (April, 2005). *Training effectiveness of a computer game*. Paper presented in a symposium titled "Research Issues in Learning Environments" at the annual meeting of the American Educational Research Association, Montreal, Canada.

Chou, C., Condron, L., & Belland, J. C. (2005). A review of the research on Internet addiction. *Educational Psychology Review, 17*(4), 363–388. doi:10.1007/s10648-005-8138-1

Clark, R. E. (1983). Reconsidering research on learning from media. *Review of Educational Research, 53*(4), 445–459.

Clark, R. E. (Ed.). (2001). *Learning from media: arguments, analysis, and evidence*. Greenwich, CT: Information Age Publishing.

Clark, R. E. (2007). Learning from serious games? Arguments, evidence and research suggestions. *Educational Technology, 47*(3), 56–59.

Cvetkovic, V. B., & Lackie, R. (Eds.). (2009). *Teaching generation M: A Handbook for Librarians and Educators*. New York: Neal-Schuman Publishers, Inc.

Davidson, C. (2009). *Game school opens in New York: Quest to learn. HASTAC*. Retrieved April 4, 2010, from http://www.hastac.org/node/1959

Dede, C. (2005). Planning for neomillennial learning styles: Shifts in students' learning style will prompt a shift to active construction of knowledge through mediated immersion. *Educause Quarterly, 28*(1). Retrieved March 20, 2005, from http://www.educause.edu/apps/eq/eqm05/eqm0511.asp?bhcp=1

Duffy, P. D., & Bruns, A. (2006, September 26). *The use of blogs, wikis and RSS in education: A conversation of possibilities*. Paper presented at Online Learning and Teaching Conference 2006, Brisbane, Australia.

Ferdig, R. E., & Trammell, K. D. (2004). *Content delivery in the 'Blogosphere'*. Technological Horizons in Education Journal, 31.

Ficklen, E., & Muscara, C. (2001). Harnessing technology in the classroom. *American Education, 25*(3), 22–29.

Gagné, R. M., Briggs, L. J., & Wager, W. W. (1992). *Principles of instructional design* (4th ed.). Fort Worth, TX: Harcourt Brace Jovanovich College Publishers.

Gee, J. P. (2003). *What video games have to teach us about learning and literacy* (2nd ed.). New York: Palgrave Macmillan.

Gee, J. P. (2004). *Situated language and learning: A critique of traditional schooling*. London: Routledge.

Gee, J. P. (2008). Learning and games. In Salen, K. (Ed.), *The ecology of games: Connecting youth, games, and learning* (pp. 21–40). Cambridge, MA: The MIT Press.

Gibson, T. G. (2009). *Plato on the Break Boundary: Implications for the Digital Revolution.* Paper presented at the meeting of the International Communication Association, Montreal, Quebec, Canada. Retrieved May 23, 2009, from http://www.allacademic.com/meta/p234593_index.html

Godwin-Jones, R. (2005). Emerging technologies: Messaging, gaming, peer-to-peer sharing language learning strategies & tools for the Millennial Generation. *Language Learning & Technology, 9.*

Gredler, M. E. (1996). Educational games and simulations: A technology in search of a research paradigm. In Jonassen, D. H. (Ed.), *Handbook of research for educational communications and technology* (pp. 521–540). New York: Simon & Schuster Macmillan.

Hargis, J. (2005). Collaboration, community and project-based learning? Does it still work online? *International Journal of Instructional Media, 32*(2), 157–161.

Hayes, R. T. (2005, November). Effectiveness of instructional games: A literature review and discussion. *Technical Report 2005–004.* Retrieved April 3, 2010, from http://www.dtic.mil/cgi-bin/GetTRDoc?AD=ADA441935&Location=U2&doc=GetTRDoc.pdf

Johnson, S. (2005). *Everything bad is good for you: How today's popular culture is actually making us smarter.* New York: Riverhead Books.

Jones, S., & Fox, S. (2009). Pew Internet Project data memo. *Pew Internet and American Life Project.* Retrieved March 22, 2010, from http://www.pewinternet.org/~/media/Files/Reports/2009/PIP_Generations_2009.pdf

Kaplan-Rakowski, R. (2010). Foreign language instruction in a virtual environment: An examination of potential activities. In Giovanni, V., & Braman, J. (Eds.), *Teaching through multi-user virtual environments: Applying dynamic elements to the modern classroom.* Hershey, PA: Information Science Reference.

Kaplan-Rakowski, R., & Loh, C. S. (2010). Modding and rezzing in games and virtual environments for education. In Baek, Y. K. (Ed.), *Gaming for classroom-based learning: Digital role playing as a motivator of study.* Hershey, PA: Information Science Reference. doi:10.4018/978-1-61520-713-8.ch012

Kluge, S., & Riley, L. (2008). Teaching in virtual worlds: Opportunities and challenges. *Issues in Informing Science and Information Technology, 5.*

Kohut, A., Parker, K., Keeter, S., Doherty, C., & Dimock, M. (2007). How young people view their lives, futures and politics: A portrait of "Generation Next". *The Pew Research Center for the people and the press.* Retrieved March 28, 2010, from www.people-press.org

Koohang, A., & Durante, A. (2003). Learners' perceptions toward the web-based distance learning activities/assignments portion of an undergraduate hybrid instructional model. *Journal of Information Technology Education, 2,* 105–113.

Kozma, R. B. (1991). Learning with media. *Review of Educational Research, 61*(2), 179–211.

Kozma, R. B. (1994). Will media influence learning? Reframing the debate. *Educational Technology Research and Development, 42*(2). doi:10.1007/BF02299087

Kurzweil, R. (2005). *The singularity is near. When humans transcend biology.* New York: Penguin.

Lamb, B. (2004). Wide open spaces: Wikis, ready or not. *EDUCAUSE Review, 39*(5).

Lenhart, A., Kahne, J., Middaugh, E., Macgill, A. R., Evans, C., & Vitak, J. (2008). Teens, video games, and civics: Teens' gaming experiences are diverse and include significant social interaction and civic engagement. *Pew Internet and American Life Project*. Retrieved January 1, 2010, from http://www.pewinternet.org/Reports/2008/Teens-Video-Games-and-Civics.aspx

Lenhart, A., Madden, M., & Hitlin, P. (2005). *Teens and technology: Youth are leading the transition to a fully wired and mobile nation*. Washington, D.C.: Pew Internet & American Life Project.

Merrill, M. D. (2001). First principles of instruction. *Journal of Structural Learning and Intelligent Systems, 14*(4), 459–466.

Michael, D., & Chen, S. (2006). *Serious games: Games that educate, train, and inform*. Boston: Thomson Course Technology.

Moreno-Ger, P., Burgos, D., & Torrente, J. (2009). Digital games in eLearning environments. *Simulation & Gaming, 40*(5), 669–687. doi:10.1177/1046878109340294

Newhouse, P. (1999). Examining how teachers adjust to the availability of portable computers. *Australian Journal of Educational Technology, 14*(2), 148–166.

Notari, M. (2006). How to use a Wiki in education: Wiki based effective constructive learning. *Proceedings of the 2006 international symposium on Wikis*, 131-132.

O'Neil, H. F., Wainess, R., & Baker, E. (2005). Classification of learning outcomes: Evidence from the games literature. *Curriculum Journal, 16*(4), 455–474. doi:10.1080/09585170500384529

Oblinger, D. (2003). Boomers & Gen-Xers Millennials: Understanding the "new students". *EDUCAUSE Review, 38*(4).

Oppenheimer, T. (1997, July). The computer delusion. *Atlantic Monthly, 280*(1), 45–62.

Polka, W. (2001). Facilitating the transition from teacher centered to student centered instruction at the university level via constructivist principles and customized learning plans. *Educational Planning, 13*(3), 55–61.

Postman, N. (1985). *Amusing ourselves to death: Public discourse in the age of show business*. New York: Penguin.

Prensky, M. (2001a). Digital Natives, Digital Immigrants. *Horizon, 9*(5), 1–6. doi:10.1108/10748120110424816

Prensky, M. (2001b). Digital Natives, Digital Immigrants, part II: Do they really think differently? *Horizon, 9*(6), 1–6. doi:10.1108/10748120110424843

Prensky, M. (2006). *Don't bother me mom – I'm learning!* St. Paul, MN: Paragon House Publishers.

Prensky, M. (2007). *Digital game-based learning*. St. Paul, MN: Paragon House.

Raines, C. (2003). *Connecting generations: The Sourcebook*. Berkley, CA: Crisp Publications, Inc.

Rainie, L. (2009). Networked Learners. *Pew Internet & American Life Project*. Retrieved January 1, 2010, from http://www.authoring.pewinternet.org/Presentations/2009/52-Networked-Learners.aspx

Reigeluth, C. M., Merrill, M. D., Wilson, B. G., & Spiller, R. T. (1980). The elaboration theory of instruction: A model for sequencing and synthesizing instruction. *Instructional Science, 9*(3), 195–219. doi:10.1007/BF00177327

Roberts, D. F., Foehr, U. G., & Rideout, V. (2005). *Generation M: Media in the lives of 8-18 year-olds*. Washington, DC: Henry J. Kaiser Family Foundation.

Schiro, M. S. (2008). *Curriculum theory. Conflicting visions and enduring concerns*. Los Angeles, CA: Sage Publications.

Seimens, G. (n.d.). Blended. *elearnspace*. Retrieved April 3, 2010, from http://www.elearnspace.org/doing/blended.htm

Shaffer, D. W., & Gee, J. P. (2005). *Before every child is left behind: How epistemic games can solve the coming crisis in education.* Manuscript submitted for publication.

Smahel, D., Blinka, L., & Ledabyl, O. (2008). Playing MMORPGs: Connections between addiction and identifying with a character. *Cyberpsychology & Behavior, 11*(6), 715–718. doi:10.1089/cpb.2007.0210

Squire, K. (2002). Cultural framing of computer/video games. *The International Journal of Computer Game Research, 2*(1).

Squire, K., & Jenkins, H. (2003). Harnessing the power of games in education. *Insight (American Society of Ophthalmic Registered Nurses), 3*(1), 5–33.

Strauss, W., & Howe, N. (2000). *Millennials rising: The next great generation.* New York: Vintage.

Tapscott, D. (1998). *Growing up digital: The rise of the Net Generation.* New York: McGraw-Hill.

Tolmie, A. (2001). Examining learning in relation to the contexts of use of ICT. *Journal of Computer Assisted Learning, 17*(3), 235–241. doi:10.1046/j.0266-4909.2001.00178.x

Twenge, J. M. (2006). *Generation Me: Why today's young Americans are more confident, assertive, entitled—and more miserable than ever before.* New York: Free Press.

Tyack, D., & Cuban, L. (1995). *Tinkering toward utopia: A century of public school reform.* Cambridge, MA: Harvard University Press.

US Census Bureau. (2000). *School enrollment--Social and economic characteristics of students: October 2000* [Data file]. Available from http://www.census.gov/population/www/socdemo/school/ppl-148.html US Census Bureau. (2005). *School enrollment--social and economic characteristics of students: October 2005* [Data file]. Available from http://www.census.gov/population/www/socdemo/school/cps2005.html

US Census Bureau. (2008). *School enrollment--Social and economic characteristics of students: October 2008* [Data file]. Available from http://www.census.gov/population/www/socdemo/school/cps2008.html

US Department of Education. (2008). *Digest of education statistics.* Retrieved March 27, 2010, from http://nces.ed.gov/programs/digest/d08/tables/dt08_012.asp

Van Eck, R. (2006). Digital game-based learning: It's not just the digital natives who are restless. *EDUCAUSE Review, 2*(14), 16–30.

Von der Emde, S., Schneider, J., & Kotter, M. (2000). Technically speaking: Transforming language learning through virtual learning environments (MOOs). *Modern Language Journal, 85*(2).

Vygotsky, L. (1978). *Minds in society: The development of higher psychological processes.* Cambridge, MA: Harvard University Press.

Wallis, C. (2006, March 19). The Multitasking generation. *Time.* Retrieved from December 23, 2009, from http://www.time.com/time/magazine/article/0,9171,1174696,00.html

Weigel, V. (2005). From course management to curricular capabilities: A capabilities approach for the next-generation course management system. In McGee, P., Jafari, A., & Carmean, C. (Eds.), *Course management systems for learning: Beyond accidental pedagogy* (pp. 190–205). Hershey, PA: Information Science Publishing.

Williams, J. B., & Jacobs, J. (2004). Exploring the use of blogs as learning spaces in the higher education sector. *Australasian Journal of Educational Technology, 20*(2), 232-247. http://www.ascilite.org.au/ajet/ajet20/williams.html

Wilson, M., & Gerber, L. E. (2008). How generational theory can improve teaching: strategies for working with the "Millennials". *Currents in Teaching and Learning, 1*(1).

Wong, W. (2007, May/June). Gaming In Education. *Ed Tech Magazine*. Retrieved April 10, 2008, from http://www.edtechmag.com/higher/may-june-2007/gaming-in-education.html

Wood, R. T. A. (2008). Problems with the concept of video game "addiction": Some case study examples. *International Journal of Mental Health and Addiction, 6*(2).

Young, J. R. (2002). "Hybrid" teaching seeks to end the divide between traditional and online instruction. *The Chronicle of Higher Education, 48*(28), A33–A34.

Young, K. S. (1996). Internet addiction: The emergency of a new clinical disorder. *Cyberpsychology & Behavior, 1*(3), 237–244. doi:10.1089/cpb.1998.1.237

Young, K. S. (2004). Internet addiction. *The American Behavioral Scientist, 48*(4), 214–246. doi:10.1177/0002764204270278

Young, M., Schrader, P. G., & Zheng, D. P. (2006). MMOGs as learning environments: An ecological journey into Quest Atlantis and The Sims Online. *Innovate: Journal of Online Education, 2*(4).

Zolli, A. (2007, December 19). *Demographics: The Population Hourglass*. Retrieved December 15, 2009, from http://www.fastcompany.com/magazine/103/open_essay-demographics.html

ENDNOTES

[1]   Commodity jobs are those that can increasingly be done at any location by low-trained workers for low pay. For example, transferring the commodity task of technical support to lower-paid workers in developing countries while keeping the highly trained and highly paid "innovative" work of R&D in Western Europe or the United States.

[2]   A representation of a user in a game/simulation/VW

Chapter 3
School in the Knowledge Society:
A Local Global School

Birgitte Holm Sørensen
Aarhus University, Denmark

Karin Levinsen
Aarhus University, Denmark

ABSTRACT

Implementation of ICT in Danish and Nordic schools is gradually changing from an industrial to a. At the same time ICT, digital literacy and the school's physical and social organization are constantly negotiated. In schools that proactively meet the challenges, new designs for teaching and learning emerge while teacher-student relations transform and the children and young people's competencies are resources in the processes of learning. This chapter presents research based on the proactive schools and exemplifies possible outlines of the school, in the knowledge society. Finally, the findings are extrapolated into a vision of a future local global school in the knowledge society.

INTRODUCTION

In recent years, the school as institution has been challenged at all levels, from political decisions, school management, and teacher education to the everyday school practice. These challenges are rooted in society's structural transformation from industrial- to knowledge society, i.e. digitaliza-

tion and ubiquitous ICT, Internet and mobility are core drivers of globalization and affects all levels of society. The knowledge society's demands to its citizens differ radically from those of the industrial society and have a profound impact on the present and future educational system. At the present stage of transformation, ICT and the key competencies of the knowledge society have become interdependent and inseparable.

DOI: 10.4018/978-1-60960-206-2.ch003

The school is not only challenged by the present and future society's and business' need for new competencies due to the knowledge society's increasing demand for production and processing of knowledge and innovation. The children and youth in schools belong to a generation for whom mobiles, wireless Internet, Web 2.0 and social software are everyday phenomena and they frequently use these digital resources outside school (Stald 2009). School and the teachers are still reluctant to integrate ICT and digital media in the everyday school practice. To a large extent, children and youth are self-taught bricoleurs through the learning communities that exist or emerge in the respective children and youth cultures. Accordingly, children and young people can in an ICT perspective be regarded as a potential resource for the school.

That students are often more competent than the teachers when it comes to the use of the dominant infrastructure of society has already led to new relations between the school's actors. It means that the contact between teachers and students and between students no longer is restricted to a physical room; it may also take place in a virtual room. The school's physical classroom as the local setting for learning activities has expanded with the advent of Web 2.0, mobility and wireless Internet from being merely an interactive communication process on a local level between the school's actors to comprise increasingly globally oriented teaching and learning activities.

This paper will take its departure in the relationship between the school and society's transformation. Since one of the basic factors of change at present is the digitalization of the media and Internet, we will focus on the corresponding changes in school in relation to teaching and learning processes, ICT-based designs for learning and teaching, teacher and student relations and positions, including the school's relations to the local and global world.

We will apply an ICT perspective to the social changes that occurred in the transition from the industrial society and its school to the knowledge society and its school. Next, we will describe the recent decades' use of ICT in schools and provide examples from Denmark and the Nordic countries. In the following section, the ICT perspective will be applied to web 2.0 and the opportunities offered by the new technology for design for classroom teaching and learning. The technology aspect is continued in the section on teachers and students – relations and positions, focusing on the actors' positions in relation to the technology, and how the technology may create new relations between teachers and students. Before we place the school in a local and global perspective in a concluding section, we will provide a concrete example from a school that may be seen as a blueprint for a knowledge society school.

CHANGES IN SCHOOL CAUSED BY THE TRANSITION FROM THE SCHOOL OF THE INDUSTRIAL SOCIETY TO THE SCHOOL OF THE KNOWLEDGE SOCIETY

Industrial societies gradually shift away from industrial production methods and a growing number of countries can now be called as knowledge societies (Qvortrup 1998, 2002; Beck 1998; Giddens 2007). Due to architectural theory the succeeding periods of school's organisation and physical appearances mirror the corresponding social formation and the changed demands from society (Sørensen, Audon & Levinsen 2010). Accordingly, present schools that strive to cope proactively with the challenges in terms of management, everyday organisation and practice as well as the design of the physical environment also bears similarities to the emerging knowledge society.

The industrial society's signature mode of production is the assembly line, where primary products are transformed into manufactured goods through mechanical production systems. At present, the societal changes appear in the companies that have a large impact on the economy. These companies can be characterized as knowledge- or service companies, and their new products are the result of knowledge production and innovation. These companies' primary mode of production is project-oriented development processes in open, transparent organizations. In such organizations, knowledge-sharing and cooperation are central issues for the staff (Castells 2000; Qvordrup 2000). Knowledge-based organizations gradually replace traditional companies and institutions so that the constant production of new knowledge becomes an integrated part of, and condition for, the function of society, which is a key characteristic of a knowledge society (Fink, Harder, Holm, Jakobsen & Stjernfelt 2004:6). Likewise, the tendencies that point towards a school of the knowledge society exist alongside the industrial society school paradigm. Sometimes this co-existence is even evident in a specific school (Sørensen, Danielsen & Nielsen 2007; Sørensen, Audon & Levinsen 2010: 27-40).

As a social category, the concept 'knowledge society' indicates that all parts of society's organizational, institutional and professional activities have become knowledge-based. In this way, knowledge becomes an open concept that is not exclusively tied to the sciences, but which constitutes an essential condition for society's production and service companies (Fink, Harder, Holm, Jakobsen & Stjernfelt 2004:21). A concept such as knowledge society may cause some confusion, because 'information society' and 'network society' are often used synonymously with knowledge society. The concept information society has been discussed since the 1950s and concerns technology and the fact that data has become a primary product and information

processing is the most important production form (Masuda 1980). The concept knowledge society (Stehr 1994) indicates that knowledge constitutes the dominating component in all human activities, and that knowledge processing is the most important production form. The concept network society (Castells 1996 & 2000) has a broader social scope, and denotes a society in which the principal organization and the economy is global, ad hoc networks made possible by digitalization.

As mentioned above, certain features of the school of the industrial society resemble the industrial society's organizational form such as strong routines in everyday life. The industrial society's school was clearly divided into age groups, classes and courses, the school day was according to a fixed timetable, and teachers were in charge of the teaching. Thus, the school shared a number of features with a 'machine' that rarely deviates from the structure (Scott: 2003). In the school that emerged from the industrial society, the teacher organized the classroom teaching according to the curriculum. The traditional teaching approach was based on knowledge imparted by teachers and compulsory assignments of a factual nature given by teachers. The objectives were determined according to the cultural practice and defined by legislation. The students were isolated within the defined school context and rarely experienced that the world outside had any consequence in the daily teaching. In the classroom, it was mainly a matter of doing one's homework and solving given assignments in time, controlled and affected by an explicit power hierarchy between teachers and students. The books contained the essential knowledge, and books were the central medium for teaching and learning processes (Sørensen, Danielsen & Nielsen 2007).

In the last decades of the twentieth century, the situation changed. The traditional school day divided by groups, classes, courses and the familiar timetable, was maintained, but now group work such as subject assignments and project weeks were added. Double modules were introduced, more emphasis was placed on the students' own productions, and the teacher – student relations became a more equal relationship. A number of approaches to teaching and work processes were developed. In the last decades, the digital media have slowly been integrated into schools, which is another important similarity with companies in the transition from the industrial society to the knowledge society's school. In general, ICT integration has been much faster in the business sector (Ibid.).

In the transformation from industrial society to knowledge society, the schools' belated adjustment to the surrounding society becomes quite apparent (Sørensen, Audon & Levinsen 2010). As such, the school is an interesting example of an institution that was once the most important source of inspiration and progress in society, but now in many cases finds itself in a position where it must find its place in a globalized and e-permeated world. This leads to a unstable situation for the school, and in Denmark we currently witness a fierce public debate about the school while several actors propose different solutions to the current fluid situation. The Danish government wants "The world's best public school" and has launched a *360 degrees check* conducted by a governmental task force. The task force has recently publish their findings and points to inclusion and teacher education as major challenges. The *Digital council* who represent the digital industry have suggested comprehensive digitalization in order to save teacher resources, while the *Local government Denmark* has suggested that the grade, time- and space organization of the everyday school practice is made more flexible.

First and foremost, school in a knowledge society needs to take a new approach to meet and incorporate knowledge society's demands and possibilities. Studies of the, still rare, examples from schools, and the loosely connected network that organization characterize the knowledge society

indicates school in the knowledge society: The teacher - student relations will reflect a decrease in hierarchy; contact between teachers and students will increasingly be by electronic means, e.g. when teachers comments on work processes and students have to hand in their written work. ICT has changed from being concrete well-defined tools to an all-pervading social infrastructure. In the industrial society, ICT, learning processes, academic traditions and teaching forms were gradually assimilated. In a knowledge society, ICT, learning processes, academic traditions and teaching forms increasingly affect each other in a radically changing and accommodating process. Owing to Web 2.0, students' informal and recreational approach to information and communication technology will play a part in the organization of classroom teaching. In addition, the distinctive features of globalization have started to emerge in some learning processes, as students collaborate across national borders[1]. Thus, the digital media transcend the school life of former times and place the school in the physical and virtual field between the local and global world.

RECENT DECADES' USE OF ICT IN SCHOOLS

The school has been criticized for acting insufficiently and too slowly to changes in society (Erstad 1997; Selfton-Green 1998). Due to social changes, a number of political initiatives to force ICT into schools were introduced throughout Europe. In several countries, including the Nordic, this was very much a top-down process; recent educational policies have launched initiatives such as subsidizing the schools' purchase of computers and providing ICT courses for teachers. In addition, grants were given to development projects to further ICT integration in the classroom.

The ICT development in schools has gone through several phases. The first phase focused on providing schools with computers. The Danish government argued that, once the computers were installed, they would be used. In some countries, the first phase also included the introduction of electronic data processing as a special course. However, in Denmark, electronic data processing did not last long as an independent course. The second phase was characterized by educational ICT integration in the classroom. In this period, schools in Denmark and several other countries would employ educational ICT instructors to support teachers in their use of ICT. As a follow-up, a number of comprehensive government supported development projects with corresponding research on the use of ICT in classroom teaching were initiated in several countries in the beginning of the 2000's, e.g. *Project PILOT* in Norway, *ICT in School* in Sweden and *ICT, Media and Primary and Lower Secondary School* in Denmark. In the UK, similar projects have been carried out under BECTA.

In an OECD report from 2004 (OECD 2004) the Nordic countries rank among the best in terms of number of computers in schools. But it is one thing to have many computers, another thing to use them. In continuation of these projects, a study was made on a Nordic level about application of ICT and the effect of the application of ICT on the primary and secondary school level (E-learning Nordic 2006). In the study, teachers and students were asked about how many hours they had used ICT in a teaching and learning context in the week prior to completing the questionnaire. The study showed that a third of the teachers had not used ICT, and about half the teachers had used ICT 1-5 hours per week. Between 5% and 17% (difference in the four countries: Denmark, Finland, Norway and Sweden) had used ICT for six hours or more per week (Ibid p. 40) In addition, the study showed that teachers focus more on using ICT when it supports the academic content in their teaching than if ICT supports their educational methods (Ibid p. 48). These studies have recently been followed by similar findings in several Danish studies (Levinsen & Sørensen 2008; Pedersen & Hornskov 2009; Sørensen, Audon & Levinsen 2010; Gynther 2010).

The entire period was characterized by the concept 'educational ICT integration'. However, it is problematic to talk about educational ICT integration at a general level if we look at the practice in school, because ICT integration differs from discipline to discipline. In terms of content, the disciplines differ; different designs for learning and teaching are connected to different disciplines, learning strategies differ, and the technology applicable in individual disciplines is not the same, or it is applied in different ways. ICT integration in schools concern ICT in relation to discipline related learning. Studies in Denmark indicate that teachers need to develop ICT in a discipline design for learning and teaching perspective (Pedersen & Hornskov 2009; Sørensen, Audon & Levinsen 2010).

Today, the ICT architecture has more or less been implemented in most schools in Denmark, which is also the case in several Nordic countries. The schools have computers, access to the Internet and interactive whiteboards in many classrooms. Experiences have been gained from using ICT in classroom teaching and learning processes, a number of teachers have acquired basic ICT literacy and many students are very computer literate, that is they possess the functional and basic skills required to perform particular operations (Oblinger 2003; Malyn-Smith 2004; Sørensen et al. 2004; Dede 2005; Oblinger & Oblinger 2005; Levinsen 2006; Ryberg 2007). The major challenge for the next phase in the school's ICT development is to combine ICT, discipline and designs for learning and teaching in such a way that it will improve discipline related learning results and make it easier for students to learn. Another challenge is to apply the digital media in inter-disciplinary projects.

Seen in a historical and educational perspective, changes and developments in schools in Denmark and other Nordic counties are often part of a bottom-up process: They often occur in the daily practice through teachers' initiatives to experiment and do developmental work, and when such practices have become sufficiently widespread, they eventually result in legislation pertaining to the field. Apart from a small group of ICT-interested teachers, it has turned out that digital media is not a field that teachers include of their own accord in their teaching practice. Development as a bottom-up movement has not worked for the ICT field in school. On the contrary, many teachers have found the education policy initiatives as something that have been 'pulled down' over their usual way of teaching, and therefore they have held back, hesitated and in some cases acted reluctantly (Sørensen et al. 2004; Petersen & Hornskov 2009; Sørensen, Audon & Levinsen 2010; Gynther 2010). Later in the chapter we present research findings from the schools that take a proactive approach to the challenges.

WEB 2.0 – NEW DESIGNS FOR LEARNING AND TEACHING

Web 2.0 is characterized by *social networking* and cooperation between users and with the users' new status as active participants and producers, the concept *user-generated content* has appeared. The concept user-generated content is tied directly to Web 2.0 and should be understood as the accumulation of users' own productions, which are either uploaded to the net or produced directly in Web 2.0 services on the net. Such productions can be processed further together with others in the same services. The concept covers several phenomena such as user-generated content on different websites, *peer-to-peer file sharing* and *social networking* (Ryberg 2007).

For decades, the printed book has been the central learning artefact, but in the last decade it has met a growing competition from digitalized teaching and learning artefacts. In recent years, we have seen the development of a large supply of digitally based teaching and learning instruments derived from different designs for learning and teaching. As a parallel to this development, more and more Web 2.0 resources become available. In this connection, affordance is a central concept, which originally comes from Gibson (1979), who uses the concept about the options of artefacts and actions available in a given environment. Due to the schools' access to the Internet and thus Web 2.0 resources, the scope of both artefacts and actions are increased in the school's learning space. Many of these resources present and allow new approaches to and forms of

- Participation
- Sociality
- Cooperation
- Production
- Publication
- Creativity

These approaches and forms of action are not new in the school, but digitalization, online technology and new forms of multimodality present new opportunities for developing designs for new and alternative ways of teaching and learning within the school context.

In a Web 2.0 perspective and to comply with the students' interests, it is relevant to use several approaches to design for teaching and learning processes. In the knowledge society's school, design for learning and teaching is performed in a fluid context, where the technology allows us to differentiate and design with the individual student in mind. The technological development is a constant challenge for the school, which means that learning and teaching design is constantly developing and changing. Apart from theories on learning and different educational approaches, theories on multimodality, communication, play and games become relevant. Multimodality has a clear potential and allows for both different learning approaches and ways of expression. Communication in a teaching perspective does not only involve face to face communication, it is mediated in a profusion of ways according to whether the communication takes place via Messenger, blogs, Twitter or Facebook. Thus, the classroom repertoire is constantly expanding allowing students in different ways to take an active part in their learning processes related to the academic and interdisciplinary disciplines. For several years, play has been included in the design for teaching and learning. In recent years 'playware', which comprises digitally based play and learning objects, has introduced new opportunities for a number of courses in school, e.g. sports, music and science. Games have also been digitalized and developed in many forms, such as entertainment games where e.g. SimCity has a learning potential and learning games with a learning- and teaching perspective on various disciplines.

STUDENTS AND TEACHERS – POSITIONS AND RELATIONS

Teaching and learning practices rooted in the school of the industrial society represent decades of traditions both for teachers as well as parents and even students. This affects the level of expectations and contributes to preserve the status quo. When digital media are introduced in school, they often become an object of learning themselves as it is vital to understand how to use the technology before including the media as options in learning and teaching practices. Thus, replacing handwritten assignments by assignments written on a computer represents an instance in a gradual assimilation of digital media into existing practice,

provided that the activity is kept within the school's curriculum and teaching. Another instance of this gradual assimilation applies to developing digital learning tools, which often falls into the category of switching on 'the power to books'. Only rarely do we see radically changing and accommodating processes, i.e. where the media's potential is seen as an inspiration to a new way of thinking and a change of practice, that most students welcome because it corresponds to how they use the digital media outside school (Sørensen, Audon & Levinsen 2010; Gynther 2010).

A number of studies show that students' use of New Digital media is far more sophisticated and differentiated outside school than in school (Drotner 2001; Livingstone & Bowill 2001; Sørensen, Jessen & Olesen, 2002; SAFT 2003; Stald 2009). The introduction of digital media in the classroom is defined by the traditional way of teaching and thinking about the use of physical space.

Children's and youth's competencies in relation to digital media differ greatly, but in general they acquire their competencies by using and experimenting with the media. To a large extent, children and youth are self-taught bricoleurs in learning-communities that exist or emerge. Children and young people can be regarded as a potential for the school. They have an open informal learning approach to ICT, and they share knowledge about ICT and they have the necessary competencies.

Then we have a large 'course-teacher group', with an entirely different approach to the media. *How can I use that machine in my teaching when I haven't been to a course yet?* is a frequent remark from teachers (Sørensen, Audon & Levinsen 2010). Children never talk about whether they have attended a course or not or consider it important whether they have had any training. They just immerse themselves as they do any other thing they want to learn.

People are constantly exposed to changes and new interpretations to which they must create and reproduce themselves continuously (Hastrup

2003). Digital media present a new element in culture and society to which the school's actors must relate. Many children do not even think about it as they have grown up with the digital media, which are now an integrated part of their play culture and everyday life. But for some teachers, digital media present a new learning medium that provides new means of expression and content, which they must learn to deal with as a fact.

The encounter between technology and teachers is rarely uncomplicated. A study made in a Danish municipality demonstrates teachers' range of attitudes and approaches to their respective use of digital media (Sørensen et al. 2004). The study concludes that a number of teachers has a *deprecating approach* and feel that the digital media take time away from *real* teaching, i.e. actual 'academic' teaching. When a class attempts to use a new computer program, it takes time to introduce it and learn how to use it, and this will often be at the expense of the 'academic' teaching. For some teachers, time used on computers is time taken away from academic issues, a finding that is also present in a Norwegian study (Lund & Almås 2003:33) and in recent Danish studies (Pedersen & Hornskov 2009; Sørensen, Audon & Levinsen 2010). These teachers do not see the media as an integrated part that may be productive and strengthen academic teaching and students' learning; they view it as a top-down decree or as something secondary in relation to 'real teaching'. But in contrast to these teachers there is another group of teachers with a different attitude. We call them promoters. Sometimes these teachers are single frontrunners, but by now many promoters have gathered in communities of practice initiated by the ICT-supervisor network or in *msPilotschools* initiated by Microsoft Denmark. A few municipalities also engage and initiate local financed development and research projects such as use of multitouch tables (Georgsen & Konnerup 2009), ICT supported inclusion of young children with reading-writing difficulties (Levinsen 2010)

and recently initiated project where all children in first to third grade (introductory period) in two primary schools are equipped with notebook computers (Sørensen & Levinsen – in print).

These frontrunner teachers can be subdivided into two groups:

A. These teachers have not attended courses, nor do they have any special competencies, but they can see it will be both beneficial and necessary that students as well as teachers learn how to use the media. They remain *open* and have the same approach as children who typically start working with the media without any special qualifications. Similarly, this group of teachers just start work with the media, relying on students' competencies. They acknowledge and admit to the students that they are no wizards in computers, but hope that they all can solve the problems together. They accept the challenge both in relation to the media and their function and position as a teacher. Together with the students, the teachers develop projects, in which the use of the digital media is optimized, and as such the teachers are part of the learning process. Often, an open attitude might be a better approach for integrating digital media into teaching than attending compulsory courses, in which you have no particular interest.

B. These teachers have an *innovative* approach and the competencies to use digital media, and they apply them deliberately and competently as an integrated part of academic teaching. This category of teachers is also full of ideas about how to combine the media with specific disciplines or use it as mediator in an interdisciplinary perspective resulting in productive, academic benefits for students. Such approaches to the media's potential may often act as a source of inspiration activating the connection between students' competencies and ideas. This group of teachers have an innovative and investigative approach to the potential of digital media. They examine available digital learning resources and think creatively about the possibilities of the Internet. They let themselves be inspired and challenged to include digital facilities in their teaching, as e.g. a teacher who read a novel with his Danish class and arranged with the author that the students, via an e-platform, could ask him/her questions and go into dialogue with him/her about his/her novel (Sørensen et al. 2004). This group of innovative teachers are experimenting and testing the options of digital media and learning tools, including programs, the Internet and Web 2.0 to evaluate the educational and academic value.

The digital encounter between students and teachers differs in nature depending on their respective background and attitudes, which affects how the scope of action is experienced in the social field within the different learning cultures. The Norwegian PILOT project reflects the same relational characteristics as described above. In some cases, the students' competencies become a 'natural' and often crucial part of the work expanding the scope of action for both students and teachers. Conversely, teachers' opposition or resistance to the use of digital media may cause students to feel that their scope of action in school has been limited. Especially, some children will find that they are cut off from using options that they know will facilitate their learning processes (Lund and Almås 2003).

By acquiring their competencies outside school, children have gained a new position in school. Now, some children have more sophisticated digital competencies than many adults, and this in a field of great social importance. Within a relatively short timeframe, children have gained skills and become important actors in the family's everyday life as indispensable helpers in practice. The nature of digital practice learning first and foremost takes place within the children's own ranks, either in a specific children and youth culture or between children. Thus, their learning is detached from their family, but on the other hand it is applied at home, where their parents are not particularly familiar with the media. In this way, children play a completely new role in many homes. Children's handling of the new media provides them with another status in school, a status that leads to re-structuring of relations and authorizations between teacher and student as well as to a new perspective on the concept 'student qualifications'.

Recent studies find that teachers who belong to the group with a *deprecating approach* and who rely on the students' digital literacy risk that integration of web 2.0 resources may produce what may be called Web 2.0 trivia (Levinsen & Sørensen 2008, Gynther 2010), In order to use digital media and Web 2.0 in a competent way as an integrated part of academic and interdisciplinary teaching, teachers must gain certain qualifications and adopt an investigative, open and innovative approach to the potential of digital media. In terms of working with different designs for learning and teaching, teachers must examine the digital learning resources available, as well as facilities provided by the Internet and how the Internet is used. In their training, teachers must therefore acquire competencies that allow them to be self-programming in relation to new knowledge and new technologies (Castells 2000).

Based on their informal and bricoleur approach to technology, some students already possess self-programming competencies, because they master new technologies on their own or together with friends. Often, this takes place through knowledge-sharing and network learning outside school or in school, where knowledge-sharing and -distribution is central. Some teachers also adopt a network- and self-programming approach.

Self-programming is a central element in the knowledge society's change and development measures. As such, it is important that all teachers and students acquire this competency. Therefore, teachers must work on developing self-programming while simultaneously supporting students in developing the approach. To further these processes in students, teachers must see themselves as educational knowledge leaders and apply different knowledge leadership designs. Of course, these new demands to the actors must be seen in relation to a changed understanding of practice among teachers, leaders and decision makers.

THE SCHOOL OF THE KNOWLEDGE SOCIETY: AN EXAMPLE

In the following, we will present an example of a school that proactively met the challenges of the knowledge society. It is a school that has been rebuilt to accommodate the educational principles in a knowledge society, where project work and knowledge sharing plays a major part in teaching, and where ICT is included in the physical design. The following is based on our research projects at Maglegårdsskolen in the period 2002-2008 (Levinsen & Sørensen 2008; Sørensen, Audon & Levinsen 2010).

The school is situated in a district north of Copenhagen. The school has been reconstructed, and its physical structure complies with the open and changing fluid educational approach. The overall organization of the school is based on a principle that includes an introductory period, an intermediate period and a final period. Each section consists of three 'home areas' with three grades and comprises 70-80 students from 1th to 3rd grade (introductory period), 4th to 6th grade (intermediate period) and 7th to 9th grade (final period) respectively. In this way, the mix of grades increases the actors' social radius of action

enabling knowledge-sharing between students across classes.

Normally, a home area will consist of five rooms, where the three classes each have their own room, home space, and the fourth room functions as a 'quiet room'. The space between these rooms is open and without any walls, but is furnished with chairs and tables, sofas and sofa corners, and also a kitchen and room for desktop computers. It is in this space, which rightly may be called 'the in-between space' that students' social learning processes thrive. The open space and the organizational form with a division into different school periods enable information to circulate in networks between children across classes. In this way, information is not isolated in a certain class. It is normally around the digital media that children like to expound on their experience and share their knowledge, which is why the space around the computers is social and open in nature. The computers create, so to speak, a space in the space by placing themselves with the mobile, digital media in a corner or a strategic place, where they become a central focus for other students' interests and distributed inspiration.

Kurokawa's architectural metabolism' concept covers a number of aspects connected to the knowledge society's open and changeable school. The concept describes space as metabolic systems, i.e. an open, flexible and changeable room with a focus on creating spatially flexible conditions that essentially reinforce change on different levels and allow certain structures to remain unchanged (Kurokawa 1977). The open room and open school increase the individual student's radius of movement and allow a form of openness that is essential for a learning environment. But this openness also presents an agenda for the school's educational development that focus on creating dynamic space in accordance with the unavoidable need for change in a society that is changing continually (Sharp 2001:9). By allowing open structures without identifiable centres, the space is formed by the people who use it.

The important incentive in educational learning principles is the organization of home areas across age groups, which leads to cooperation across classes, a fact that is underlined by the physical environment's organization. In the large common space, students can work together on projects and assignments across classes. Throughout the day, many different activities based on different individual and collective learning strategies take place in the 'home area'. We saw for instance how an entire class can be part of a learning- and teaching community in one part of the home area, while other students worked together in groups on a project in the large common space. The large space in the middle is furnished with tables, chairs and sofas in different forms and sizes. There are books alone with other learning objects, just as decorative objects and articles for everyday use are placed on tables and windowsills. This type of arrangement focuses on the 'home' metaphor, which is further underlined by comfortable furniture, candles and flowers. Another important feature in this setup is the different media on display such as TV, video viewers, desktop computers with Internet access, laptops, digital video recorders, digital cameras, projectors, scanners and printers. They are all clearly on display, indicating that they can be used freely.

The open and fluid school space functions as connecting hub between the classroom, *home space*, and the network possible routes that connect the home space with the rest of the *home area*. But it is often in the spaces between the firmly established and functional rooms that a 'transformation of energy' takes place in the form of knowledge-sharing. This 'in-between space' is used spontaneously and situational; and as such, it presents an unpredictable, flowing and ad hoc use of possibilities. It is a matter of 'time communities', where individuals are not tied by tradition to certain places and localities, but on the contrary to different activities carried out over time, and depending on the situation, they may include or exclude the surroundings (Kurokawa 1977:17 and 36).

The digital media play a major role in creating and mediating the physical space and the space that emerges socially around the media. Because pupils can move the digital media about, activities are moved out of the class and into the surrounding space, which attracts social attention. In other words, when the media are used as completely natural and ordinary tools, they expand the available space. Thus, the 'in-between space' is not in opposition to the classroom's closed space. It creates a meaningful sphere around children, and it is often in the 'in-between space', the physical interspace, that digital media are used. The technology is available and as such involved in a constant, dynamic exchange in different rooms and between teachers and students individually and collectively.

Based on our impressions and findings from Maglegårdskolen, we will present a vision of what may be the next step in the formation of the school in the knowledge society.

A LOCAL GLOBAL SCHOOL

The economic aspect is a central issue in globalization. But globalization also includes social and cultural processes that in recent years have grown in importance. In these processes, technology is a constant and all-pervading dominating drive (Castells 2000). In other words, globalization has an impact on many levels of our everyday life.

If we look at children today and their use of digital media outside school, the global aspect has already become part of their growing up. English has, for many of the oldest children, due to their online activities become a familiar language (Sørensen, Audon & Levinsen 2010; Stald 2009).

The electronic media play an important role in cultural globalization processes. The time-space dimension is reduced through the proximity that children and young people feel when they communicate online with children and young people in other countries and continents when they exchange knowledge in online communities. Proximity is the feeling that you are connected to the rest of the world and the emotional (Bruun 2002:53).

Children and young people's physical, everyday lives with other children in the same age group comprise their cultural context. When children have learned how to communicate in English, a significant part of their online everyday life takes place in global, virtual rooms, where they meet children and young people from other countries with other cultural backgrounds. Thus, globalization in terms of cultural processes across time and space is a recurring item on children's agenda. Online, they search for information and experience, or they produce for a global audience in form of pictures in Flickr or profiles in English for various social communities as e.g. MySpace and Facebook. Around the world, children and young people communicate and establish relations and web-friendships with other children and young people in other countries and cultures (Sørensen, Jessen & Olesen 2002; Stald 2009).

Globalization is closely connected with students' everyday lives. To improve learning processes, school should therefore be discussed in a global perspective to profit from the potential in the virtual and communicative globalization. Thus, the present schools answer to the knowledge society's school would call for strengthening and developing competencies within communication, innovation and creativity through learning processes. A self-programming person's main competencies are innovation and creativity (Castells 2000). As such, innovation and creativity are key concepts in the work processes that have replaced the industrial sector's mechanical work functions. If the school adopts a global perspective, Web 2.0 and mobile solutions may be used actively in a change-oriented teaching focusing on students' informal learning potential. The many different Web 2.0 and mobile resources enable us to generate globally oriented teaching and learning that correspond to the challenge of the knowledge society.

Communication is a central issue in learning processes, and technological development has now allowed us to expand communicative processes to include different geographic destinations. Today, Web 2.0 resources are available for communication, social network and knowledge-sharing between different continents. The challenge is to teach students to handle the encounter with the unfamiliar, to change their perspective and to see how their own narratives are created in the meeting with another culture. As such, we might say that globalization is part of a normal school day. Many academic topics can be discussed and transformed into shared online learning processes between students in different countries.

It stands to reason that it is a good idea for the school to benefit from ICT-experienced pupils' competencies. It will be possible to develop teaching with a global dimension if teachers and students cooperate to create ideas to develop productive learning processes in different academic fields. On this basis, we may develop concepts for global projects that focus on using websites that allow us to draw on information about academic issues relevant to different actors' global network and the potential embedded in the new Web 2.0 services.

To understand why the school had to undergo a change alongside the industrial society's transformation into a knowledge society, we must realize how competencies required to act as a citizen and employee in an ICT-permeated and globalized society differ radically from the industrial society's requirements. Buckingham argues that an ICT-user in a digitalized world needs to understand him/herself and the other actors on the net in an interaction with the intentions, styles and actions that create the present ICT world (Buckingham 2003).

At the same time, the most important social trend at present indicates that we not only choose to participate as actors in an ICT-context, which we may opt out of again (e.g. Second Life, Arto), but our world has basically been permeated by digital media and ICT, which we can neither opt for or out of. This means that ICT now plays an active part in constituting our world, and as citizens we no longer have a choice regarding ICT. Thus, a thoroughly digitalized society is characterized by an economy exercised as information and knowledge that are transported in data systems in a globalized world, where all important relations are network relations. Castells (2000) explains the difference between general shared view on ICT and technology before the wireless and mobile solutions became a prevalent phenomena and now. In the industrial society, ICT was seen in relation to production. According to Castells, this view no longer makes sense as technology and ICT in a knowledge society are just as important for production as they are for performance of politics, military and financial power, and for that matter in our personal relations. In a knowledge society, we must accept that ICT is an integrated part of the overall social package (Ibid.: 9). In Castells' view, ICT has become a fundamental factor in human beings' lives and actions. ICT has been woven into everything, and as such it has an effect on creating and changing the way we relate to each other, the world and our social structures.

On this background, Castells describes a person's future prospects in view of the future's labour requirements, which basically may be divided into self-programming and generic employees (Ibid.: 12). A self-programming employee may respond to new challenges in informal ways, train him/herself and adjust to new tasks, processes and types of information to comply with the constant increase in society and technology's rate of change. In contrast, the generic employee is only capable of changing through formal training, and therefore he/she can easily be replaced or dismissed. Castells sees a danger in this development and argues that people incapable of being self-programming will end up as local and global casualties. These observations have had a great influence on international and national bodies' definition of future competencies, their connection with the civic concept and the formulation of a framework for a far-sighted educational policy (G8 2006; OECD 2001; the Danish Ministry of Education 2005). In this society, ICT and ICT related competencies will have a great impact on how an individual person will perform in society. Therefore, it is imperative that the educational systems respond to the future challenge, as persons who understand and are able to use e-facilities have significant advantages in terms of educational success, occupational opportunities and other vital aspects in life (Elearning Europa 2005).

SOLUTIONS AND RECOMMENDATIONS

In terms of ICT in school, it is relevant to start development and research projects on the link between ICT, academic disciplines and designs for learning and teaching. To improve development, teachers in different disciplines must be able to investigate technology's learning potential and evaluate whether an ICT resource will facilitate learning processes and/or improve learning results. In addition, they must be able to indicate how teaching and learning processes with ICT should be designed to achieve the results requested. In other words, it is necessary to design models for an innovative ICT teaching development. Important elements in such models should be user based innovation and cooperation.

In terms of training teachers, we recommend that they learn to act self-programming and able to meet new challenges in an informal way by participating in knowledge sharing processes, training themselves and adjusting to new tasks, processes and types of information to comply with the constant increase in society and technology's rate of change.

FUTURE RESEARCH

To pursue research on ICT in relation to professional standards, future research projects should be tied to ICT application in academic contexts. We need research in how ICT may facilitate academic learning processes and improve learning results. In addition, we need research to clarify the potential of ICT in relation to students with specific needs. It applies to students that are up against difficult challenges and therefore may benefit from ICT as a compensating measure and to students whose specific needs may be met through substituting ICT facilities enabling them to participate in normal classroom teaching. In a global perspective, we need research in global teaching projects.

CONCLUSION

In the industrial society, the code word in the educational system was adjustment. Today, the ability to manage unpredictable and unfamiliar issues is a requirement, i.e. to choose, interpret and act in different situations where you do not know the answer and have no previous experience. Compared to what used to be practice in the educational system, the knowledge society opens up for countless new possibilities, but also demands completely new future oriented competencies and a reduction of complexity.

Adjusting to a given issue or adopting a future oriented approach to solve unpredictable and unfamiliar situations may be related to the generic employee and the self-programming employee, respectively. In line with Castells' explanation

of his concepts, a central element in the knowledge society's educational system is support and training of self-programming individuals. In this connection, it is necessary to rethink ICT as a concept in relation to design for teaching and learning. ICT has changed from being a tool that can be used by means of acquired skills to being an all-pervading basic framework for the function of society. Introduction of new wireless and mobile technologies, Web 2.0 services and the change in users' role from merely using tools to participating in producing content and meaning construction are vital elements in the dynamics that permit incorporating the technologies in school and launching a future oriented education of citizens in an ICT permeated society. Research made in schools that have worked actively with organization of space, cooperation forms and ICT integration shows that changed student-teacher relations and roles together with a flexible organization support a positive development in both academic learning and self-programming competencies. Last but not least, social development points to an active incorporation of the global perspective in school. In this respect, Web 2.0 services provide new opportunities for intercultural cooperation and knowledge sharing as well as research into other societies and cultures.

REFERENCES

G8. (2006). *G8 Wold Summit in St.Petersburg.* July 16, 2006. Retrieved April 01,2008 http://en.g8russia.ru/docs/12.html, Georgsen, M. & Konnerup, U. (2009). Mobil læring på Søndervangskolen, *Rapport nr. 1 fra følgeforskningen til projektet "Bæredygtighed i elevernes nærmiljø* Aalborg: Center for User-Driven Innovation, Learning & Design, 54 s.(eLearning Lab Publication Series; 18).

Beck, U. (1998). *Democracy without enemies.* Cambridge, UK: Polity Press.

Bruun, H. (2002). Global Tv-genre og komplekse nærhedsoplevelser. *Dansk Sociologi,*2/13.

Buckingham, D. (2003). *Media Education: Literacy, Learning and Contemporary Culture.* Cambridge, UK: Polity Press.

Castells, M. (1996). *The rise of the network society*, Oxford, UK: Blackwell (2nd edition, 2000).

Castells, M. (2000). Materials for an exploratory theory of the network society. *The British Journal of Sociology, 51*(1), 5–24. doi:10.1080/000713100358408

Dede, C. (2005). Planning for Neo-Millennial Learning Styles. *EDUCAUSE Quarterly,* (1): 7–12.

Drotner, K. (2001). *Medier for fremtiden: børn, unge og det nye medielandskab.* København: Høst.

E-learning Nordic. (2006). *Effekten af it i uddannelsessektoren.* Retrieved January 22,2010, from http://www.elearningeuropa.info/files/media/media10112.pdf

Erstad, O. (1997). *Mediebruk og medieundervisning. En evaluering av medieundervisningen i norsk skole:intensjoner... elever på ungdomsskolen og videregående skol.* Oslo: NOVA Rapport 8/04.

Europa, E. (2005). *A European Framework for Digital Literacy.* Retrieved January 15,2010, from http://www.elearningeuropa.info/directory/index.php?page=doc&doc_id=6007&doclng=6).

Fink, H., Harder, P., Holm, P., Sonne Jacobsen, K., Stjernfelt, F., & Pahuus, A. M. (Red.). (2004). *Humanistisk viden i et vidensamfund.* Temarapporter fra Forskningsrådet for kultur og kummunikation. København: Statens Humanistiske Forskningsråd

Gibson, J. J. (1979). *The Ecological Approach to Visual Perception.* Boston: Houghton Mifflin.

Giddens, A. (2006). *Sociology.* Cambridge, UK: Polity Press.

Giddens, A. (2007). Living in a Post-Traditional Society. In U. Beck, A. Giddens & S. Lash, *Reflexive Modernization.* Cambridge, UK: Polity Press.

Gynther, K. (2010). *Didaktik 2.0.* København: Akademisk Forlag.

Hastrup, K. (Ed.). (2003). *Ind i verden. En grundbog i Antropologisk metode.* København: Hans Reitzels Forlag.

Kurokawa, K. (1977). *Metabolism in Architecture. London: StudioVista. Catalogue to an exhibition at Cube Gallery London.* London: BookArt.

Levinsen, K. (2010). Effective use of ICT for Inclusive Learning of Young Children with reading and writing Difficulties. In Mukerji & Tripathi (Eds.) *Cases on Interactive Technology Environments and Transnational Collaboration: Concerns and Perspectives,*pp.56-73. Hershey, PA: IGI-Global.

Levinsen, K. & Sørensen, B.H. (2008). *It, faglig læring og pædagogisk videnledelse: rapport vedr. Projekt It læring.* Gentofte Kommune /DPU, AU.

Livingstone, S., & Bowill, M. (Eds.). (2001). *Children and their Changing Media Environment: A European Comparative Study.* New York: Erlbaum.

Lund, T. & Almås, A.G. (2003). *På vei mot god praksis? En beskrivelse og analyse på tvers av ni skoler i PILOT.* Tromsø: Universitetet i Tromsø.

Malyn-Smith, J. (2004). Power Users of Technology - Who are they? Where are they going? Why does it matter? *UN Chronicle Online Edition,* (2), pp 58 [online], http://www.un.org/ Pubs/chronicle/2004/issue2/0204p58.asp

Masuda, Y. (1980). *The Information Society.* Tokyo: Institute for the Information Society.

Oblinger, D. (2003). Boomers, Gen-Exers and Millennials: Understanding the New Students. *EDUCAUSE, 38,* 36–43.

Oblinger, D., & Oblinger, J. (Eds.). (2005). *Educating the Net Generation*. EDUCAUSE, [online], e-book, www.educause.edu/educatingthenetgen/

OECD. (2001). *Meeting of the OECD education ministers*, Paris, 3-4 April 2001. Retrieved April 01, 2008 http://www.oecd.org/dataoecd/40/8/1924078.pdf.

OECD. (2004). *OECD-rapport om grundskolen i Danmark – 2004*. http://pub.uvm.dk/2004/oecd/oecd.pdf

Pedersen, S.G. & Hornskov, M.B. (2009). *It I skolen – erfaringer og perspektiver*. Købenahvn: EVA (English summary)

Qvortrup, L. (1998). *Det hyperkomplekse samfund. 14 fortællinger om informationssamfundet*. København: Gyldendal.

Qvortrup. L. (2002). *Samfundets uddannelsessystem*. Arbejdspapir, Kolding: Institut for Pædagogisk Forskning og Udvikling, Syddansk Universitet.

Ryberg, T. (2007). *Patchworking as a Metaphor for Learning: Understanding youth, learning and technology*. Aalborg University: e-Learning Lab Publication Series; 10.

SAFT. (2004). Retrieved July 07, 2004, http://www.medieraadet.dk/html/saft

Scott, W. R. (2003). *Organizations: rational, natural and open systems*.(5 ed) Upper Saddle River, NJ: Prentice Hall.

Selfton-Green, J. (1998). Introduction: Being Young in the Digital Age. In Selfton-Green, J. (Ed.), *Digital Diversions: Youth Culture in the Age of Multimedia* (pp. 1–20). London: UCL Press.

Sharp, D. (2001). *Kisho Kurokawa. Metabolism + Recent Work. Catalogue to an exhibition at Cube Gallery London*. London: BookArt.

Sørensen, B. H., Audon, L., & Levinsen, K. (2010). *Skole 2.0*. Aarhus: Klim.

Sørensen, B. H., Danielsen, O. & Nielsen, J. (2007). Children's informal learning in the context of school of knowledge society. *Education and Information Technologies*. Official Journal of the IFIP technical committee on Education, 12, 1

Sørensen, B. H., Hubert, B., Risgaard, J., & Kirkeby, G. (2004). *Virtuel skole. ITMF Forskningsrapport*. København: Danmarks Pædagogiske Universitet.

Sørensen, B. H., Jessen, C., & Olesen, B. R. (Eds.). (2002). *Børn på nettet. Kommunikation og læring*. København: Gads Forlag.

Stald, G. (2009). *Globale medier – lokal unge. Institut for Medier, erkendelse, formidling*. København: Københavns Universitet.

Stehr, N. (1994). *Knowledge Societies*. London: Sage.

Undervisningsministeriet (2005). *Det nationale kompetenceregnskab – hovedrapport*. Retrieved from http://pub.uvm.dk/2005/NKRrapport/

ADDITIONAL READING

Andreasen, L. B., Meyer, B., & Rattleff, P. (Red.). (2008). *Digitale medier og didaktisk design: Brug, erfaringer og forskning*. København: Danmarks Pædagogiske Universitetsforlag.

Benjaminsen, N. (2009). *Authorisations - A STS approach to computer based teaching*. Aarhus, Denmark: The Danish School of Education, Aarhus University.

Brown, J. S., & Duguid, P. (1998). Organizing Knowledge. *California Management Review, 40*(3).

Dillenbourg, P. (1999). Introduction: What Do You Mean By "Collaborative Learning". In Dillenbourg, P. (Ed.), *Collaborative Learning: Cognitive and Computational Approaches*. Oxford, UK: Elsevier Science.

Dunkels, E. (2009). *Vad gör unga på nätet.* Malmö: Gleerup Utbildning AB.

Erstad, O. (2005). *Digital kompetanse i skolen – en innføring.* Oslo: Universitetsforlaget.

Jewitt, C., & Kress, G. (2003). *Multimodal Literacy.* New York: Peter Lang.

Katz, I. R. 2007: Beyond Technical Competence: Literacy in Information and Communication Technology. *An Issue Paper from ETS,* www.ets.org/Media/Tests/ICT_Literacy/pdf/ICT_Beyond_Technical_Competence.pdf (16/11 2007) (13/10/ 2007)

Kreiner, K. (1995). In search of relevance: Project management in drifting environments. *Scandinavian Journal of Management, 11*(4), 335–346. doi:10.1016/0956-5221(95)00029-U

Kress, G. (1993). *Communication and Culture.* Australia: New South Wales University Press.

Kress, G. (2003). *Literacy in the New Media Age.* London: Routledge. doi:10.4324/9780203164754

Levinsen, K. (2008a). Reinventing Papert's Constructionism - Boosting Young Children's Writing Skills with e-Learning Designed for Dyslexics. *EJEL, 6,* 3.

Littleton, K., & Häkkinen, P. (1999). Learning together: Understanding the Processes of Computer-Based Collaborative Learning. In Dillenbourg, P. (Ed.), *Collaborative Learning: Cognitive and Computational Approaches.* Oxford, UK: Elsevier Science.

Littleton, K., Mercer, N., Dawes, L., Wegerif, R., Rowe, D., & Sams, C. (2005). *Talking an Thinking Together at Key Stage 1.* http://anubis.open.ac.uk/thinking/downloads/publications/Early%20years%20paper%20D2%20HO%20April%20 20041.pdf (10.2.2005)

Livingstone, s. & Haddon, L. (2009). Lids online. Opportunities and risk for children. Bristol, UK: The policy Press, Bristol University.

Rostwall, A.-L., & Selander, S. (2008). *Design för lärande.* Stockholm: Norstedts akademiska förlag.

Selander, S. & Svärdemo-Åberg, E. (red. 2009). *Didaktisk design i digital miljö. Nya möjligheter för lärande.* Stockholm: Liber.

Sørensen, B. H. (2004). *ICT and the Gab Between School Pedagogy and Children's Culture.* Journal Pedagogy. Culture and Society.

Sørensen, B. H., & Olesen, B. R. (Red.). (2000). *Børn i en digital kultur.* Forskningsperspektiver. København: Gads Forlag.

Tingstad, V. (2003). *Children's chat on the net: A study of social encounters in two Norwegian chat rooms.* Trondheim: Norges teknisk-naturvitenskabelige universitet.

Wenger, E. (1998). *Communities of Practice. Learning, Meaning, and Identity.* Cambridge, UK: Cambridge University Press.

Wenger, E., McDermott, R., & Snyder, W. M. (2002). *Cultivating Communities of Practice: A guide to Managing Knowledge.* Boston: Harvard Business School Publishing.

Williams, P. (1999). The net generation: the experiences, attitudes and behaviour of children using the Internet for their own purposes. *Aslib Proceedings, 51*(9). doi:10.1108/EUM0000000006991

ENDNOTE

[1]   e.g., Friends and Flags http://www.friendsandflags.org and Kidlink http://www.kidlink.org/kidspace/index.php

Section 2
Contemporary Learning

Chapter 4

Collective Problem-Solving and Informal Learning in Networked Publics:
Reading Vlogging Networks on YouTube as Knowledge Communities

Simon Lindgren
Umeå University, Sweden

THE RISE OF SMART MOBS

This chapter will focus on community aspects of *vlogging* (video blogging) on *YouTube* (Figure 1). This site, familiar to most, is a popular video sharing platform with built-in social networking functions such as tagging, commenting, favoriting and the possibility to leave video replies. The typical vlog entry consists of a clip that is a few minutes long and features the vlogger looking straight into the camera, addressing the viewers.

Vlog entries are generally based on oral narratives that sometimes build on previous entries by the same person, and sometimes serve as video replies to entries posted by other vloggers.

The chapter is based on a qualitative case analysis focusing on vlogging as *participatory culture* (Jenkins, 2006, 1992). While *YouTube* started out as a straightforward video sharing platform, it has increasingly come to offer a number of social networking site (SNS) features (Lange, 2008). The meanings of SNS practices vary across sites and individuals (boyd, 2006). This case study will explore how the affordances of the site may be

DOI: 10.4018/978-1-60960-206-2.ch004

Figure 1.

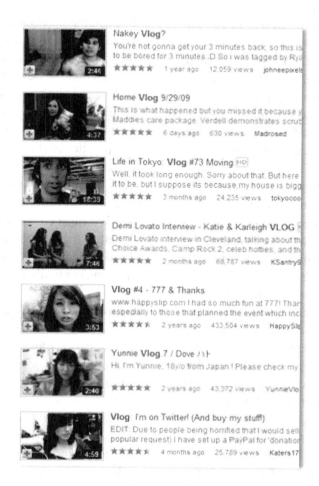

employed by vloggers in order to establish and maintain social networks. My analyses serve to illuminate, from various perspectives, community and social network aspects of *YouTube*. The overarching question has to do with finding basic dynamics of this cooperation system.

American technology writer Howard Rheingold (2002) predicts that one result of the ongoing development of digital media will be the rise of ever more so called *smart mobs*. These are communities – much like the vlogger community – which "consist of people who are able to act in concert even if they don't know each other. The people who make up smart mobs cooperate in ways never before possible because they carry devices that possess both communication and computing capabilities. Their mobile devices connect them with other information devices in the environment as well as with other people's telephones" (Rheingold, 2002, p. xii). But similar to what Henry Jenkins writes about convergence culture – we are still "testing the waters and mapping directions" (Jenkins, 2006, p. 246) – there is a need for more practical knowledge of the dynamics of these cooperation systems (Rheingold, 2002, p. 202).

In the early forms of virtual communities (Rheingold, 1994), participation was limited to being present in physical spaces where internet connections were available. Those types of virtual communities transcended space in the sense that the participants were not physically co-present, but they frequently found themselves in similar types of environments (offices, teenage bedrooms, home offices, living rooms, etc.). In the virtual communities of today – where phones, palms, netbooks, laptops, and similar portable devices are increasingly used to access the internet – participation is hardly limited by space and time at all. Today's mobile phones, smart phones, and digital cameras are pervasive tools. They have become such an important part of the daily life that they are no longer mere technological objects but rather key social objects.

Young people in particular are embracing the emerging participatory cultures. According to American data (Lenhardt & Madden, 2005), 57 percent of teen internet users can be considered media creators. They have created blogs or web-pages, posted original content online, or have remixed online content to create new expressions. Swedish data (Findahl & Zimic 2008) show that around 20 percent of 15 to 20-year olds have their own blogs, 60 percent upload photos, and 10 percent post their own videos.

Though some research has been made on *You-Tube* since its launch in 2005, not very much of it has focused on vlogging (see for example the work of Burgess & Green 2009b or Lange 2007 for a couple of examples). Even less has been done on *YouTube* as a platform for informal learning. Still, several aspects of its participatory potential have been dealt with in books such as *The YouTube Reader* (Snickars & Vonderau 2009), *Video Vortex* (Lovink & Niederer 2008) and *YouTube* (Burgess & Green 2009a).

VLOGGING, PARTICIPATORY CULTURE AND INFORMAL LEARNING

Concerns are sometimes raised that the internet might be alienating people and fragmenting social

relations (Fuchs, 2008, pp. 328-330; Kraut et al, 1998). On the other hand, it has been argued that new media attract "colonies of enthusiasts" because the technology "enables people to do things with each other in new ways" (Rheingold, 1994, p. xxi). According to Yochai Benkler (2006, p. 357), digital media provides "an information environment that both technically and as a matter of social practice enables user-centric, group-based active cooperation platforms". According to Fuchs (2008), there is an antagonism in cyberculture between cooperation and competition. This opposition is most clearly expressed in the question of whether it generates socialized (communicating and cooperating) or alienated (atomized and competing) individuals.

Colonies of Enthusiasts

Social network sites like *Facebook* or *MySpace*, allow their users to create a public (or semi-public) profile and to articulate their relations to other users in a way that is visible to anyone accessing their profile (Ellison & boyd, 2007). As these sites have become increasingly popular, many other sites – like *YouTube* – have started to adopt SNS features. According to Cheng et al (2008, p. 235), *YouTube* is indeed a social media application. This can be illustrated of how social networks are established on the vlogging arena on *YouTube*. To be able to assess this issue in a smaller scale, vloggers with a specific interest – in this case the urban art form of free running, so called *parkour* – were selected.[1]

As Figure 2 illustrates, the commentaries exchanged in between the parkour vloggers give the image of a tight social network existing within the much larger and presumably much looser *YouTube* network as a whole. The vertices represent the individual vloggers, and the arrows – which are sometimes unidirectional and sometimes bidirectional – show the flow of communication in the form of commentaries. So, even though *YouTube*

Figure 2. Sociogram of a 21-person vlogger subcommunity

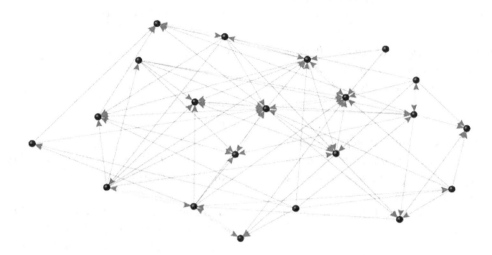

is a technological environment at its basis, a lot of human social interaction is obviously taking place here.

In directed graphs, such as the one above, the share of edges (relations) that are mutual is interpreted as a measure of reciprocity or symmetry. In previous research (Mislove et al 2008), a high level of reciprocity has been found in the directed networks on social networking sites such as *Orkut* and *flickr*. With a reservation for the fact that the *YouTube* dataset presented above is much, much smaller than those analyzed by these researchers, it seems as if the reciprocity principle is quite strong here too. To be more precise, 28 percent of the relations are mutual, and this must be seen as a relatively high number considering the character of *YouTube* as a whole. The site audience is global and much of the communication is random and occasional. Still, the fact that interactive networks as tightly knit as the example above are formed bear witness to the large community building potential of this arena.

The Exchange of Knowledge

Looking closer at the content of the interaction taking place among the individuals under study,

the image of a knowledge community emerges. The two dominant categories of commentaries flowing throughout this network are encouraging comments about the parkour activity as such, and technical tips relating to vlogging in general. The following excerpts are examples of this.

[Parkour Vlog clip #1, including footage of actual parkour]

commentator 1: awesome 5/5

commentator 2: very nice video

commentator 3: this is really nice:) i like it:)

vlogger: cheers, glad you like it, coming to [city] tomorrow if you up for it

[Parkour Vlog clip #2, parkour enthusiast at home talking about future plans]

commentator 1: if u have MSN can u write it down pls.

commentator 2: come to [city] and trane with me and lots and lots of other teams

[Parkour Vlog clip #3, including footage of actual parkour]

commentator 1: Man that HD camera is nice, I think I've seen your youtube name on the [geographic area] Parkour forums also, what a weird coincidence.

vlogger: The camera is pretty cheep 150 on sale for 130 and this wasn't even filmed in the highest quality. I have the same [user name] on every thing I sign up for but I don't think I have made a profile on [...] parkour since I live in [city]. But I could be wrong.

[Parkour Vlog clip #4, including instructional footage of parkour]

commentator 1: WHAT R THE SHOES??? I NEED THE NAME

vlogger: the shoes are called ariakes

commentator 2: u dont need those fuckin shoes...i wear adios

commentator 3: me too i wear aididas bounce 2008+ lol

commentator 4: just don't get not good absorbing impact shoes or u will break your bones.. in an few years, and you will regret it. always tuck when jumping and taking high impact!

commentator 5: you shouldn't rely on your shoes, if you have to you have pretty much failed as a traceur. Why not tape blocks of foam to your shoes if you want impact absorbtion.

commentator 6: dnt listen to a word dey r sayin dey are all shit search pk generations dey r professional teachers and btw dnt use ariakes dey r

shit aswel dey dnt have gd grip its bullshit buy a pair of glenjies or nike darts

commentator 7: I agree completely, I had a pair of ariakes, they suck DICK, I reccomend a good pair of asics, because they are lightweight, they have great shock absorbtion, also asics are pretty cheap.

commentator 8: I Have Ariakes, I Slipped On A Gap And Almost Diiiied, XD

I'd Recommened Kalenji Success's, A Lot Of Professional Traceurs Use Them, Or Asics and New Balance are Also Good Makes. Peace, Much Love

commentator 9: I recommend you practice more. Shoes will not make you a good athlete. I wear beat up skate shoes and can do 3 step wallflips on flat walls with ease.

As all of these excerpts illustrate, vloggers utilize this forum to form ties that may lead to meetings and collaboration in virtual ("MSN"; "Parkour forums") as well as physical ("come to [city]") places. The fourth and final excerpt which pictures a discussion about which shoes to use for parkour, and whether the choice of shoes plays any part in parkour success, is a telling example of how "appropriate" and "right" ways of thinking and speaking are negotiated. In other words, of how a specific form of knowledge relating to parkour is produced.

In sum, this is an example of how a social community based on certain forms of knowledge is emerging within the confines of the infinitely larger and much more complex *YouTube* community as a whole. In a large quantitative analysis of clicking, commenting, favoriting, and subscription patterns on *YouTube*, Santos et al (2007, p. 8) came to the very general conclusion that the site is "a technological network whose topology and connections are heavily influenced by human social behavior". This leads to the conclusion that it is important to study *YouTube* in terms of those micro communities of young people – "colonies of enthusiasts" – that constitute the building blocks which make up the site and its sociality as a whole.

Cheng et al have also examined the social network of *videos* on *YouTube*. Their conclusion was that networks of videos on the site have so called small-world characteristics, with short chains of acquaintances linking any two videos. Patricia Lange (2008) has studied social networking among *people* on *YouTube* and concludes that adding other users as "friends" is neither the only nor the most prominent way of building social networks on the site. Rather, as illustrated above, the sharing and commenting of video clips often function as a basis for negotiating membership to certain networks and to maintain these relations. The commentary to a clip can lead to further social connections, if the initial uploader sustains communication and interaction with the commentator. Lange writes that the character of this process varies in relation to what information the participants display about themselves and how, and in relation to what content they produce. She also suggests that "(f)uture studies could examine different types of media exchange to see what they reveal about underlying social relationships" (Lange, 2008, p. 14).

Producer-Consumers

Using a clustering methodology, Maia et al (2008, pp. 4-5) have identified five typical user behaviors on *YouTube*. The first one of these is the "Small Community Member", which is a user who is part of small by tightly knit communities (families, colleagues, class mates). These users are not highly active. They simply create accounts and subscribe to videos from their peers. The second is the "Content Producer". This type of user visits many channels, and also watches and uploads many videos. These users get subscribed by a varied audience,

and also subscribe a lot themselves to be in contact with other producers. The material produced can be professional as well as homemade. The third is the "Content Consumer" – a typical user with a focus on clicking around and watching various clips. The fourth is the "Producer & Consumer" – a mixture of the second and third categories. This is the largest group (48 percent), and it consists of users with a moderate amount of subscribers, and uploads (like producers). They also browse around and watch and subscribe to videos (like consumers). Because of the social character of vlogging, most vloggers would probably be found in this category. Like ordinary blogging, vlogging is as much about producing texts of your own as it is about consuming and interpreting the texts of others in order to create community (Efimova, Hendrick, & Anjewierden, 2005). Finally, Maia et al identify a fifth group of "Other" users with low values on every feature (watching, subscribing, being subscribed to, uploading, etc.).

Let us now focus on qualitatively analyzing the inner workings of the "Producer & Consumer" category. By making a reading of the *YouTube* profile of successful video blogger Blade376, I will explore how affordances of the site can potentially be used in order to make and support social networks.

British 22-year old Myles Dyer is a vlogger who regularly posts to *YouTube* under the nickname of Blade376 since May 2006. His channel is the 76th most subscribed in the UK (23,679 subscriptions), he has had around 600,000 channel views, and all of his clips have been viewed thousands of times ranging from around 5,000 to 450,000 (for his 2007 clip "How to make your 1st Vlog!." See Figure 3).

Entering <http://www.youtube.com/user/Blade376> one is met by the profile area where Blade376 lays down his *YouTube* manifesto: "Hello to everone out there from all over the world, from all walks of life! I just make videos because I truly believe together with the internet,

Figure 3.

we can change the world for the better! And as long as I have people like you, we will succeed, one step at a time!".

Under the heading "My world has many portals…", Blade376 lists all entrances to his internet presence. Except from vlogging on *YouTube,* he blogs in text format on *livejournal.com,* socializes on *Myspace* (2694 friends), posts vlogs and personal info at SNS *stickam.com,* does podcasts, and shares his own music (also on *Myspace*) (see Figure 4).

Under the "Playlists" heading, he has posted his current vlogging project "Sixty Second September" which entails "Posting a new 1 minute vlog everyday for the whole of September 2009!", ending the information with asking "Who's with me!?". Blade376's list of channel comments include 12,877 posts, many of them relating to the social activity of vlogging and to technical aspects.

*hey, I made my own Vlog, BECAUSE OF YOU. yes you enspiard me, so it would mea alot to me if you cheked it out some time^^*

hey blade i just whanted to say i posted my second vid and i finaly wasable to edit it!

Any chance you could sub me please man? Been a subscriber of yours for a long time, really enjoy your videos. Thanks x

please could you check out my channel, not for your subscription or anything just for some feedback on how to improve my videos maybe?

hey Myles do u know any good progams that i can use for an hp to edit videos?

As is common among vloggers, Blade376 gets video replies to his entries by other vloggers.

Figure 4.

Most conspicuously his previously mentioned post "How to make your 1st Vlog!" has yielded 490 video clips showing beginner vloggers following his recommendations. Dyer himself claims to have been inspired to start vlogging after watching the, now classic, *YouTube* clip "First try" posted in 2006 by then 79-year old Peter Oakley (aka Geriatric1927), and being impressed by the amount of response to that vlog entry. The early posts by Blade376 revolved around getting advice for film scripts that he was working on, but as he states in the clip "My YouTube Story", he soon realized that this technology allowed him to explore other passions – in his case mainly socializing with and inspiring, as well as being inspired by, other people. Dyer soon became a *YouTube* celebrity (Levy, 2008). He was recognized in the street in the UK as well as in the US, and was often interviewed by various media as a spokesperson for vloggers and for *YouTube* users in general. In the summer of 2007 he met up with Geriatric1927 and they co-produced the clip "Closing The Generation Gap".

Dyer has co-hosted a number of real life gatherings of vloggers in the UK, the US and Canada. In June of 2008 he was instrumental to the creation of the largest collaborative video ever on *YouTube* ("What is Online Community to you?"), including 300 people explaining what this technology and the social network meant to them. Dyer was also invited to give lectures at universities and learning conferences, before taking a break from *YouTube* due to personal issues in late 2008 to early 2009. Since February 2009 he is actively vlogging again, his first entry after the hiatus ("You are not alone") aiming to give words of advice and hope to anyone struggling with "self-acceptance after tough circumstances".

Even though the case of Blade376 is extreme – he has been a highly active, recognized and successful vlogger – it can still be used to discern a set of core processes in the vlogging community. As classic sociologist Émile Durkheim wrote, the study of distilled and dense social forms – the analysis of examples that may seem too perfect – have a scientific value. By looking at these cases, one can potentially "isolate the constituent elements" of a phenomenon. This "aids in its explanation [...] (b)ecause the facts are simpler, the relations between them are more apparent" (Durkheim, 1912, p. 6).

In interviews and in his own vlog entries, Myles Dyer talks of something that he calls "the *YouTube* experience". This is his name for what is "in between" the videos on the site – the social exchange. One way of understanding many of the characteristics of Dyer's *YouTube* story, as well as what is going on in between the videos is supplied by Jenkins and his co-authors of the report *Confronting the Challenges of Participatory Culture: Media Education for the 21st Century*

(Jenkins et al, 2009). According to them, forms of participatory culture include:

Affiliations — memberships, formal and informal, in online communities centered around various forms of media, (such as Friendster, Facebook, message boards, metagaming, game clans, or MySpace).

Expressions — producing new creative forms, (such as digital sampling, skinning and modding, fan videomaking, fan fiction writing, zines, mash-ups).

Collaborative Problem-solving — working together in teams, formal and informal, to complete tasks and develop new knowledge (such as through Wikipedia, alternative reality gaming, spoiling).

Circulations — Shaping the flow of media (such as podcasting, blogging) (Jenkins et al, 2009, p. 3).

As the analyses throughout this chapter have shown, vlogger community on *YouTube* is at its core about *affiliations*. About formal membership to the site, and about informal relations through tagging, subscribing, commenting, and by posting video replies. Vlogging is also, very obviously, about what Jenkins et al label *expressions* and *circulations*. It is about users producing their own material, and distributing it to others. It has also been shown that *YouTube* vloggers constitute a knowledge community based on *collaborative problem-solving* relating particularly to vlogging techniques and strategies. As Jenkins et al (2009, p. 4) state, "(p)articipatory culture shifts the focus of literacy from one of individual expression to community involvement".

The case of Blade376 illustrates how a number of participatory literacies – all of them involving social skills that are developed through networking and collaboration – come into expression in the participatory culture of vlogging. Myles Dyer channels several of the new and important skills

listed and detailed by Jenkins et al (2009, p. 4). His inspirational approach to vlogging is an example of the *performance* skill, which is about staging one's identity for purposes of discovery. The movie editing skills, as well as the more general ability to interact with the tools needed to produce content in a meaningful way illustrates the skills of *appropriation* and *distributed cognition*. The ways in which Blade376 operates with "many portals" (many simultaneous web technologies and platforms) are expressions of *multitasking, negotiation* and *transmedia navigation*. He possesses the ability to move across various communities and modalities, and to shift focus as needed. Furthermore, his use of the medium to exchange experiences and pool knowledge with others relating to anything from personal crises to 'how to vlog'-issues are illustrative of the process of *collective intelligence* (Lévy 1999).

CONCLUSION

The aim of this chapter has been to give a picture of the basic dynamics of *YouTube* vlogging as a cooperation system. Prominent patterns have been discussed from the perspective of previous writings on semiotic dynamics (Cattuto et al, 2007), "colonies of enthusiasts" online (Rheingold, 1994), and participatory culture (Jenkins et al, 2009).

Overall, I have shown that there is definitely something "in between" the videos on *YouTube*. When trying to discern what this "YouTube experience" is, one finds a culture of participation characterized by social exchange and informal learning processes fostering a set of new literacies relating to collective-problem solving, community involvement and transmedia navigation. The patterns described in this chapter can be conceived of in terms of "networked publics". Mizuko Ito (2008, pp. 2-3, my underscoring) defines this:

*The term networked publics references a linked set of social, cultural, and technological developments that have accompanied the growing engagement with digitally networked media. The Internet has not completely changed the media's role in society: mass media, or one-to-many communications, continue to cater to a wide arena of cultural life. What has changed are the ways in which people are networked and mobilized with and through media. The term networked publics is an alternative to terms such as audience or consumer. Rather than assume that everyday media engagement is passive or consumptive, the term publics foregrounds a more engaged stance. Networked publics takes this further; now publics are communicating more and more through complex networks that are bottom-up, top-down, as well as side-to-side. Publics can be reactors, (re)makers and (re)distributors, **engaging in shared culture and knowledge through discourse and social exchange** as well as through acts of media reception.*

Young people acting as parts of these networked publics are, as Ito puts it, "mobilized through media". This relates to what Jenkins writes of in *Convergence Culture*: At this moment, large numbers of young people are hard at work learning how to participate in "knowledge cultures outside of any formal educational setting" (Jenkins, 2006, p. 259).

No Major Investment Necessary

At present, many of these activities are largely taking place in the – to employ James Gee's (2004) term – "affinity spaces" that relate to popular culture. Young pirates are writing network protocols and softwares, young movie enthusiasts are translating subtitle files, fan fiction is written and commercial content is remixed and subverted. Benkler, relating to the file sharing example, writes:

[A] few teenagers and twenty-something-year-olds were able to write software and protocols that allowed tens of millions of computer users around the world to cooperate in producing the most efficient and robust file storage and retrieval system in the world. No major investment was necessary (Benkler, 2006, p. 85).

It is therefore important to stress that instead of focusing one-sidedly on the risks and dangers of digital media and the internet, media education must aim to foster these opportunities for informal learning as well as to educate teachers and other adults in how these platforms work.

Both Gee (2004) and Jenkins et al (2009) argue that the emerging affinity spaces – of which vlogging networks are an example – and the participatory cultures inhabiting them constitute important environments for learning. It seems, they contend, as if young people participate more actively, learn much more and engage more deeply in activities such as these than they do in traditional schooling. This, of course, is a challenge as well as an opportunity for teachers and educators. Jenkins et al (2009) claim that while traditional, formal, education is often conservative, the collective problem-solving and peer-to-peer learning processes within the domains of popular culture are more experimental, innovative, and stimulating. Furthermore, the participator in a networked public can stay on the move, opting in and out of communities should they fail to meet their needs. This is a big difference compared with formal schooling and education.

Livingstone (2003) writes that the fact that many young people are already producers of media content is often neglected, except when discussed in terms of risks. The ways in which online cultures enable young people to become proficient at maneuvering, judgment, and expression must be included in discussions of media literacy.

Distinction and Various Modes of Acquisition

Bourdieu (1984, pp. 65-74) has shown how various modes of acquiring compentencies in the form of cultural capital lead to insurmountable distinctions between classes of individuals.

[...] for some [cultural competence] is neither taught nor learnt [...]; for others, a field of pedagogy like any other (Bourdieu 1984, p. 74).

Young people with parents who introduce them to certain books, movies, works of art, or classical recordings, and who take them to museums, on trips and who engage in dinner conversations, almost automatically develop skills which enable them to get good results in school. Similary, Lyman et al (2004) have shown that the skills acquired by young people online are largely shaped by a number of social and cultural factors such as gender, race, class, nationality, age and point of access. Those who can rely on technology and peer assistance in their homes become more autonomous in school where they seem superior to others, which further boosts their confidence and their will to develop further. As Livingstone & Bober (2005, p. 12) put it, young people will be increasingly divided into:

those for whom the Internet is an increasingly rich, diverse, engaging and stimulating resource of growing importance in their lives and those for whom it remains a narrow, unengaging, if occasionally useful, resource of rather less significance.

Sometimes when digital cultures and youth are discussed it seems to be assumed that digital literacies are acquired automatically, without support or supervision. But adults, teachers and educators must in fact engage actively in these processes in order to ensure that distinctions and divides are diminished and minimized. There are deep-seated differences in young people's access to digital technologies as well as to the opportunities they offer. Aside from this participation gap (Jenkins et al 2009) or digital divide, young people will indeed need support in reflecting actively on their experiences with digital technology, and sometimes also with navigating the complexities of the new media landscape.

When I conducted field studies in 2008 following the effort of the municipality of my home town to provide its high school students with "digital competence", the main conclusion was that the simple passing out of technology does not do the trick. All highschool students were given a laptop of their own, as part of the strategy for achieving this goal, but in most cases there was a marked absence of any form pedagogical strategy for incorporating this equipment in school work. This is similar to Wartella et al's (2000, p. 8) conclusion that "[c]losing the digital divide will depend less on technology and more on providing the skills and content that is most beneficial". The following are excerpts from student's blogs reflecting on this:

Among the bad things are that I would like things on paper as well. The computer distracts you and makes it hard to concentrate during lessons. It's better for gaming than for working.

You stay up much longer at nights, even though my parents have blocked the internet from 10.30 every night:S. How do they think that should work!? When I need to send in assignments, the deadline is 11.59. Oh well, still, the computer makes everyone less social, and it gets messier in class.

The computer is both good and bad. I like games, but I get tired when I stay up for too long. What I really want to say is this: "Procrastination is like Masturbation; In the end you're just screwing yourself."

If the goal of education is to ensure that students are enabled to participate in society, the skills developed through digital particiapatory activities such as vlogging must be fostered by those responsible for curriculums and in classrooms. Jenkins et al (2009, p. 7) write that:

In such a world, many will only dabble, some will dig deeper, and still others will master the skills that are most valued within the community. The community itself, however, provides strong incentives for creative expression and active participation. Historically, we have valued creative writing or art classes because they help to identify and train future writers and artists, but also because the creative process is valuable on its own; every child deserves the chance to express him- or herself through words, sounds, and images, even if most will never write, perform, or draw professionally. Having these experiences, we believe, changes the way youth think about themselves and alters the way they look at work created by others.

Vlogging may seem to some as simply play, as self-occupied identity work, or as an expression of youthful narcissism. However, it is also an activity which points to the fact that networked publics and participatory cultures offer opportunities to the educational system. Schools and universities have generally been quite slow in responding to these emerging phenomena. Now, politicians, teachers and educators must start working to ensure that all young people get access to the new skills and literacies discussed in this chapter, and that those who have acquired them get to develop them. Digital literacies represent a new form of "cultural competencies and social skills" (Jenkins et al 2009, p. 18) that are needed in the future.

REFERENCES

Benkler, Y. (2006). *The Wealth of Networks: How social production transforms markets and freedom.* New Haven, CT: Yale University Press.

Bourdieu, P. (1984). *Distinction: A Social Critique of the Judgement of Taste.* London: Routledge.

boyd, d. (2006). Friends, Friendsters, and MySpace Top 8: Writing Community Into Being on Social Network Sites. *First Monday, 2006*(11:12).

Burgess, J., & Green, J. (2009a). *YouTube: online video and participatory culture.* Cambridge, UK: Polity.

Burgess, J., & Green, J. (2009b). The Entrepreneurial Vlogger: Participatory Culture Beyond the Professional–Amateur Divide. In Snickars, P., & Vonderau, P. (Eds.), *The YouTube Reader* (pp. 89–107). Stockholm: National Library of Sweden.

Cattuto, C., Loreto, V., & Pietronero, L. (2007). Semiotic dynamics and collaborative tagging. *Proceedings of the National Academy of Sciences of the United States of America, 104*(5), 1461–1464. doi:10.1073/pnas.0610487104

Cheng, X., Dale, C., & Liu, J. (2008). Statistics and social network of YouTube videos. In *Proceedings of the 16th International Workshop on Quality of Service* (pp. 229–238). Enschede: IWQoS.

Durkheim, É. (1912). *The Elementary Forms of Religious Life.* New York: Free Press.

Efimova, L., Hendrick, S., & Anjewierden, A. (2005). *Finding 'the life between buildings': An approach for defining a weblog community.* Presented at the Internet Research 6.0: Internet Generations, Chicago. Retrieved from https://doc.telin.nl/dscgi/ds.py/Get/File-55092/AOIR_blog_communities.pdf.

Ellison, N. B., & Boyd, D. (2007). Social Network Sites: Definition, History, and Scholarship. *Journal of Computer-Mediated Communication, 13*(1), 210–230.

Findahl, O. & Zimic, S. (2008): *Unga svenskar och Internet 2008*. Gävle: WII.

Fuchs, C. (2008). *Internet and society: Social theory in the information age*. New York: Routledge.

Gee, J. P. (2004). *Situated language and learning: a critique of traditional schooling. Literacies, 99-3117527-3*. New York: Routledge.

Ito, M. (2008). Introduction. In Varnelis, K. (Ed.), *Networked publics* (pp. 1–14). Cambridge, MA: MIT Press.

Jenkins, H. (1992). *Textual poachers: Television fans & participatory culture*. New York: Routledge.

Jenkins, H. (2006). *Convergence culture: Where old and new media collide*. New York: New York University Press.

Jenkins, H., Purushotma, R., Clinton, K., Weigel, M., & Robinson, A. (2009). *Confronting the Challenges of Participatory Culture: Media Education for the 21st Century*. Cambridge, MA: MIT Press.

Kraut, R., Patterson, M., Lundmark, V., Kiesler, S., Mukopadhyay, T., & Scherlis, W. (1998). Internet paradox: A social technology that reduces social involvement and psychological well-being? *The American Psychologist, 53*, 1017–1031. doi:10.1037/0003-066X.53.9.1017

Lange, P. G. (2007). "The Vulnerable Video Blogger: Promoting Social Change Through Intimacy". *The Scholar & Feminist Online, 5*(2).

Lange, P. G. (2008). Publicly private and privately public: Social networking on YouTube. *Journal of Computer-Mediated Communication, 13*(1), 361–380. doi:10.1111/j.1083-6101.2007.00400.x

Lenhardt, A., & Madden, M. (2005). *Teen Content Creators and Consumers*. Washington, DC: PewInternet. Retrieved from http://www.pewInternet.org/PPF/r/166/report_display.asp

Levy, F. (2008). *15 Minutes of Fame: Becoming a Star in the YouTube Revolution*. New York: Alpha.

Lévy, P. (1999). *Collective intelligence: Mankind's emerging world in cyberspace*. Cambridge, MA: Perseus Books.

Livingstone, S. (2003). *The Changing Nature and Uses of Media Literacy*. Working paper. London: London School of Economics. http://www.lse.ac.uk/collections/media@lse/mediaWorkingPapers/ewpNumber4.htm

Livingstone, S., & Bober, M. (2005). *UK Children Go Online*. London: Economic and Social Research Council. Retrieved from http://personal.lse.ac.uk/bober/UKCGOfinalReport.pdf

Lovink, G., & Niederer, S. (2008). *Video vortex reader: responses to YouTube*. Amsterdam: Institute of Network Cultures.

Lyman, P. with Billings, A., Ellinger, S., Finn, M., & Perkel, D. (2004). *Literature Review: Digital-Mediated Experiences and Kids' Informal Learning*. San Francisco: Exploratorium. Retrieved from http://www.exploratorium.edu/research/digitalkids/Lyman_DigitalKids.pdf

Maia, M., Almeida, J., & Almeida, V. (2008). Identifying user behavior in online social networks. In *Proceedings of the 1st workshop on Social network systems* (pp. 1–6). New York: ACM.

Mislove, A., Koppula, H. S., Gummadi, K. P., Druschel, P., & Bhattacharjee, B. (2008). Growth of the flickr social network. In *Proceedings of the first workshop on Online social networks* (pp. 25–30). New York: ACM.

Rheingold, H. (1994). *The virtual community: finding connection in a computerized world*. London: Secker & Warburg.

Rheingold, H. (2002). *Smart Mobs: The Next Social Revolution*. Cambridge, MA: Perseus.

Santos, R. L., Rocha, B. P., Rezende, C. G., & Loureiro, A. A. (2007). *Characterizing the YouTube video-sharing community, (Technical report)*. Retrieved from http://security1.win.tue.nl/~bpontes/pdf/yt.pdf.

Snickars, P., & Vonderau, P. (Eds.). (2009). *The YouTube Reader*. Stockholm: National Library of Sweden.

Wartella, E., O'Keefe, B., & Scantlin, R. (2000). *Children and Interactive Media: A Compendium of Current Research and Directions for the Future*. New York: MarkleFoundation. http://www.markle.org/downloadable_assets/cimcompendium.pdf

ADDITIONAL READING

boyd, d. (2006). *Identity Production in a Networked Culture: Why Youth Heart MySpace*. Presented at the American Association for the Advancement of Science.

Castells, M. (1997). The Information Age: Economy, society and culture.: *Vol. 2. The Power of Identity*. Oxford, UK: Blackwell.

Ellison, N. B., & Boyd, D. (2007). Social Network Sites: Definition, History, and Scholarship. *Journal of Computer-Mediated Communication, 13*(1), 210–230.

Fattah, H. M. (2002). *How peer-to-peer technology is revolutionizing the way we do business* (p. 2P). Chicago: Dearborn Trade Pub.

Felix, L., & Stolarz, D. (2006). *Hands-on guide to video blogging and podcasting: emerging media tools for business communication*. Amsterdam: Elsevier.

Jenkins, H. (2006). *Fans, bloggers, and gamers: exploring participatory culture*. New York: New York University Press.

Levy, F. (2008). *15 Minutes of Fame: Becoming a Star in the YouTube Revolution*. New York: Alpha.

Lindgren, S. (2007). From Flâneur to Web Surfer: Videoblogging, Photo Sharing and Walter Benjamin @ the Web 2.0. *Transformations*, 2007(15), http://www.transformationsjournal.org/journal/issue_15/article_10.shtml.

Saco, D. (2002). *Cybering democracy: Public space and the Internet*. Minneapolis, MN: University of Minnesota Press.

Sveningsson, M. (2001). *Creating a sense of community: experiences from a Swedish web chat*. Linköping studies in arts and science, 233 (1st ed.). Linköping: Linköping University.

Tapscott, D. (1999). *Growing up digital: the rise of the Net generation*. London: McGraw-Hill.

Varnelis, K. (Ed.). (2008). *Networked publics*. Cambridge, MA: MIT Press.

KEY TERMS AND DEFINITIONS

Networked Publics: A gathering term for a number of socio-cultural and technological developments in the field of digitally networked media that have altered the ways in which people are engaged, networked and mobilized.

Participatory Culture: The concept "participatory culture" refers to the lowered barriers to civic engagement and artistic expression in the new media arena. Instead of strictly divided categories of producers and consumers, we now see a number of "participants" interacting trough media according to new rules.

Reciprocity: In network and graph theory, the level of reciprocity – or symmetry – represents the share of edges (relations) that are mutual.

Smart Mobs: A smart mob is a technology-mediated form of spontaneous social organization. The concept was coined by Howard Rheingold and refers to how peer-to-peer networks and pervasive computing empowers people.

Vlogging: A short form for "video blogging", which refers to blogging using the video medium to create posts.

ENDNOTE

[1] This example is part of a larger project wherein studies of parkour groups on *You-Tube* play a more important role. For the purpose of this chapter, however, this is an example as good as any other. The point here is simply to map and evaluate the patterns of communication among people with specific interests using *YouTube*, in order to see whether the idea of alienation or the one of 'colonies of enthusiasts' is the more valid one.

Chapter 5
Literacies on the Web:
Co-Production of Literary Texts on Fan Fiction Sites

Christina Olin-Scheller
Karlstad University, Sweden

Patrik Wikström
Jönköping International Business School, Sweden

ABSTRACT

In this chapter the authors discuss and informal learning settings such as fan fiction sites and their relations to teaching and learning within formal learning settings. Young people today spend a lot of time with social media built on user generated content. These media are often characterized by participatory culture which offers a good environment for developing skills and identity work. In this chapter the authors problematize fan fiction sites as informal learning settings where the possibilities to learn are powerful and significant. They also discuss the learning processes connected to the development of literacies. Here the rhetoric principle of "imitatio" plays a vital part as well as the co-production of texts on the sites, strongly supported by the beta reader and the power of positive feedback. They also display that some fans, through the online publication of fan fiction, are able to develop their craft in a way which previously have been impossible.

INTRODUCTION

Young people today spend a lot of time communicating and socializing via digital media. The so called social medias have become a big and important part of many children's and teen-agers' lives. Through a number of communities on the Internet, they find new and old friends all over the world with whom they share the same interest, values and attitudes (f.e. Medierådet 2008; Livingstone & Bober 2005; Sjöberg 2002). In this chapter we explore some learning processes related to being

10.4018/978-1-60960-206-2.ch005

a contributor to these web communities, often known as informal learning settings. We have a specific focus on competences involving reading and writing skills, so called literacies.

Grownups sometimes wonder, not only *what* children or students are doing on the computer, but also *why* they spend so much time there. The answer is simple: Internet and web communities offer things that young people desire and find meaningful to be a part of. First of all, not every child and teenager is an expert and a virtuoso on the computer. Not everyone even has one! In Sweden today however, the spread and access to computers and the Internet is very high among young people (Findahl & Zimic 2008; Findahl 2009a and 2009b). Some young people are more active than others, and for the individual the time spent on the computer and the Internet can change over time. At times school, sports or other interests take up most of their spare time. However, for a lot of Swedish kids Internet is a vital part and there are no signs that the impact that the Web has on young people's everyday life is declining. On the contrary the trend is quite the opposite. *What* you do on digital media might differ but time spent on the same media is increasing (Medierådet 2008; Findahl 2009a and 2009b).

Digital Natives, Digital Immigrants

One way of understanding young people's engagement at different web communities is the difference between the so called messenger generation and the (often) older "mail generation" (Selg & Findahl 2008). Here we would like to emphasize that difference in using the Web doesn't have to be connected with age at all – primarily it has to do with using habits and attitudes to the Internet.

However, a lot of young people can be described as what sometimes is called "digital natives", having the language of the computer and of Internet as a mother tongue (Prensky 2001). The digital natives have developed Internet based skills

and competences without taking a detour around older analogue technologies. Their competences differ radically from the so called digital immigrants who were not born into the digital world but gained their digital media skills later in life.

It is not necessary though, that the digital natives have more knowledge than the digital immigrants. But the two groups and various generations certainly have different skills and act differently on the Web (Prensky 2001; Selg & Findahl 2008). For example, the digital immigrants have difficulties in fully accomplishing the digital language and don't use the Internet as a first hand source for information etc. In comparison to the messenger generation who practically always is on-line and therefore often use this way of communicating, the mail generation prefer e-mail and telephone when contacting others (Selg & Findahl 2008). Using the computer as a main tool when reading and writing, the digital natives might change, not only their way of dealing with literacies, but also notions about the traditional way of regarding printed texts and books as something representing a high cultural value.

Fan Fiction as an Informal Learning Setting

Then, what is different from before? And what impact does the new media landscape have on learning processes related to reading and writing on the Web? First of all, digital media technique has radically changed the possibilities for people to find, create, process and distribute cultural products. Today, instead of a few strong actors, a lot of people can be active in producing culture and spreading information at a number of levels. The changing role of the consumer is obvious in practically all digitalized forms of culture – music, film, computer games, news and books (Brynjolfsson, Hu & Smith 2003; Jenkins 1992 & 2008; Tapscott 1996).

Secondly cultural production is today a matter of "user generated content" where the borders between producers and consumers are loosened. The concept "prosumer" – a person that not only want to listen to, watch or read different text, but also is eager to be an active participant of the content – is widely spread (Jenkins 1992; Tapscott 1996; Herman et al. 2006). As fans the prosumers are busy creating fan works, i.e. texts, pictures, films based on already published material (Buckingham 2005; Jenkins 1992 & 2008).

Thirdly, web communities and social media are often characterized by participatory culture (Jenkins 1992 & 2008). Here there is a strong support for creating and sharing products with one another. Gee (2004) describes these communities as informal learning settings or "affinity spaces" where the possibilities to learn are powerful and significant. With affinity spaces Gee develops the wide spread notion of "communities of practice" (Wenger 1999) where novices learn through scaffolding and apprenticeship. In affinity spaces people create communities of practice, but also interact and communicate with each other around a common interest, passion or endeavor. Apart from formal learning settings such as school, an informal learning setting is not adapted to formal syllabuses etc. It has no specific curriculum or timetable and is not organized professionally. Nor is it planned consciously and systematically in relation to school subjects, tests or examinations. Contributors to web communities can participate in the way they want according to ability and interest, and the sites are also characterized by an informal mentorship. As informal learning settings, these media offer a good environment for identity work as well as developing skills connected to reading and writing (Björneloo & Sträng, 2006; Gee 2004; Olsson 2005).

Fan fiction sites are good examples of vital informal learning settings where knowledge about reading and writing is developed (Black 2009; Thomas 2006: Olin-Scheller & Wikström

2010a). Fan fiction is stories based on already published works.[1] The genre is strongly linked to fan culture and is often produced by the fans themselves, without any commercial purpose. In fan fiction the original settings and characters are moved into other contexts in which new stories are created. It's also common that the fans develop relationships between characters from different works and usually the stories are based on romantic *pairings* between two persons. These pairings are often presented with a slash between the first names, such as Harry/Hermoine, Aragorn/ Bilbo or Bella/Edward.

In fan fiction it is important to stick to the *canon*, i.e. the textual universe that the original author has created and which the fans are seeking to replicate using the source text's language and style. Stories that diverge from this idea have to declare that the text differentiate by marking it "OOC" (Out of Character) or "AU" (Alternate Universe). OOC denotes stories that develop the characters away from the original and AU is moving stories to places, times, and settings that do not match the original work (e.g. Pugh 2005).

The writers of fan fiction make their texts available on various web communities where readers across the world in interaction with the authors can comment on and influence the stories (cf. www.fanfiction.net). The stories can also be linked to other fanworks like images (fanart, cf.www.deviantart.com) and films (fanfilm, cf. www.youtube.com).

People who want to identify as fans as well as readers and writers produce fan fiction. Thus, to take an active part in an informal learning setting such as a fan fiction community involves using *literacy* ability (Black 2009; Leppänen 2007; Thomas 2006). Traditionally literacy has been connected with the ability young students have to deal with when reading and writing printed texts. Today literacy often is used to describe the complicated relationship between reading skills and different genres and media (Lankshear &

Knobel 2006). Obviously this can't be covered by one single competence, and we therefore prefer to talk about literac*ies* rather than literacy.

Moreover, a widespread view is that literacies can't be considered as a basic skill once acquired which remains constant. Instead the socio-cultural dimension of the concept is stressed (e.g. Barton 2007, Street 2001, Säljö 2005). Literacies can therefore be understood as a practice based on socio-cultural aspects. The digital technique, the virtuality and participatory culture create new ways of apprehending and constructing literacies. For example, on fan fiction sites the readers play vital and important parts for how the writers develop their stories. The participatory culture also strengthens the view of literacies as competences created collectively.

On fan fiction sites an ongoing process is always present where frames for reading and writing are communicated and negotiated (Olin-Scheller 2008). By interacting the fans create *interpretive* and *discursive* communities with specific norms concerning text and narrative (Fish 1993; Bizell 1992). These communities are arranged round common conceptions about language discourses and how texts ought to be written and constructed for different purposes.

In this chapter we explore these learning aspects from several perspectives. One is the perspective of the fan writer – how do fans look upon their own learning processes as contributors to fan fiction sites? Another is the perspective of relation between the source text and the fan text. What skills must fan writers comprise in order to stay trustworthy within the textual universe? A third perspective is fan fiction in a Swedish context, a field scarcely examined.

Method and Empirical Material

In this chapter we explore results based on empirical material from a study where the primary purpose is to learn more about Swedish fan fiction writers' production and consumption of web-based fiction. Here we have combined quantitative and qualitative methods, mainly because the knowledge on the topic is scarce. With the purpose of mapping the field we first conducted a small survey study (1000 respondents) followed by an interview study. The informants for the interview study were selected based on the findings from the survey. All in all 31 fans were interviewed during fall 2008, 9 interviews were answered via email, 20 were conducted via telephone, and 2 at real-life meetings. The interviews, which in average lasted for 30 minutes, were recorded and transcribed independently by the two authors. The data was then merged and both authors analyzed the entire material in parallel. The authors' findings were then discussed and any dissonances between the two analyses were sorted out. This process ensured that the data that was created is of high quality and reliability. In addition to the interviews with fan fiction writers we also base our findings to this chapter on text analyses of texts written and published by some of the fans interviewed.

We immediately found how difficult it was to find male fan fiction writers and among the 31 fans interviewed, there are no boys. The female domination of the fan fiction scene has been previously noticed (e.g. Gray 2008). There are some different plausible explanations to the situation which lie outside the scope of this chapter but which are discussed in Olin-Scheller & Wikström (2010b).

TO DEVELOP LITERACIES – AND ONESELF

The informants who participated in our interview study gave three different explanations why they are interested in fan fiction.[2] Beside pure entertainment the fans are eager to describe their *development* as readers and writers and how fan fiction have helped them growing as individuals. By comparing their first contributions to the sites to their present texts, they point out that they have learned language skills such as spelling as well as dealing with grammatical and genre issues. One of the respondents Jennie, aged 21, explains her development:

My writing has changed and developed enormously. When I started as a 13-year-old, I was really only good at writing dialogues. It's very embarrassing to read the first fanfic I wrote, it is so full of clichés and a really bad fanfic. But it was my first try, the first time I wrote something like that. Now I'm better at describing characters, feelings, settings, thoughts etc. I've also improved my English and I've learned many more words and expressions. But by reading and writing fan fiction I have also learned things about other cultures, philosophies etc. Moreover, I have started to reflect upon Swedish norms and codes compared to other countries. Fan fiction also is a good way for me to remember what I've learned in history, since I always mix real happenings with fiction in my stories.[3]

Just like Jennie many other of our respondents are able to distinguish different learning processes. Some of these processes, to learn how to avoid clichés, to learn "many more words and expressions" and to be better at "describing characters, feelings, settings, thoughts etc", are directly related to the development of literacies. But in a socio-cultural context also learning "things about other cultures, philosophies etc" and starting to "reflect upon Swedish norms and codes compared to other countries", have a relation to developing literacies.

Another of the respondents, Maria, aged 22, describes a development involving different genres and media. She says:

I have developed much as a writer during the years I've been active. My first ff was really lousy. I wrote it by hand before I wrote it on the computer. Now I write more descriptions and can

be more implicit and don't have to say everything explicitly. I've also tried to paint fan art, and have just started with fan film. I've put together cuts from one of the films about Harry Potter, added music and published it on YouTube.

The third explanation the fans gave why they are interested in fan fiction is connected to a community aspect where a strong general feeling of solidarity among the contributors is created. The fans in our study all describe that their knowledge and literacies are products of a collective creating process within the fan fiction communities. In this collective process there are several factors that, based on participatory culture, together have a great impact on the development of literacies and form the fans' co-production of cultural products. Here we will explore and discuss three of them – the creation of stories based on active replication, the power of positive feedback and the function of the beta reader.

Learning by Co-Production

One aspect of co-producing fan fiction texts is that the fans write together, literally speaking. "We sit beside each other at the computer and when we write dialogues we take one character each – very dynamic", one of the fans explains in an interview. But mostly the co-production is more implicit, based on specific structures that many fan fiction communities rely on. Sara, aged 15, describes how she does when writing and publishing stories:

My first story about Naruto [from the fandom of Manga] was a hit! More than 600 reviews up till today and only 3 of them said something bad! I tried to stick close to the canon and first wrote in Swedish. But after 10 chapters I said to myself, why not write in English so more people can read it? When I published a chapter in English some persons gave med feed-back on grammar. Then there was this girl who offered to be my beta, and has been so ever since. She is awesome! I get constructive feed back from most of my readers and it helps a lot to know what they like about the story and the language. Then I can write more of that.

This quote shows how Sara, together with other prosumers, uses the participatory culture in creating user generated content on fan fiction sites. She mentions how she in her writing sticks to "canon", a learning process that in this chapter will be and further explored as a process based on active replication. Sara also illuminates the importance of the reviewing function at fan fiction sites. This aspect is discussed below under the heading "The power of positive feedback". Finally Sara also speaks about how she gets help from "her beta". We develop this aspect below under the headline "The beta-reader".

The affinity spaces and communities for discourse and interpretation that are negotiated among the fans on fan fiction sites, implies an active participation from the contributors. This is also a presumption for participatory culture and for the role of the prosumer as well as an important aspect of the learning processes that take place at the sites. In aesthetical learning processes, Holgersen (2002: 159ff) have found four strategies of participation – reception, imitation, identification and elaboration. These strategies form different phases of the learning process and describe how new knowledge and skills are captured.

The first strategy, reception, is connected to a role where the main activity is watching and listening. Here you can engage yourself emotionally and cognitively without having to contribute actively. In the following step, imitation, actions are replicated and the participants are focused on (parts) of the activity rather than the expressions and impressions as a whole. You simply imitate the parts you find interesting. The third strategy, identification, prerequisites a holistic understanding of the meaningful aspects in the creation process. This strategy is also an expression of a deeper understanding where you use the other participants as role models. The last strategy, elaboration, is characterized by the searching for something new, something unknown. Here you want to be independent and free from your role models. As we discuss below, the fans use at least three of the strategies in their process of developing literacies.

To Expand a Textual Universe by Active Replication

The fans creations of new texts within textual universes very closely follow the strategies of active replication based on the rhetoric principle of imitatio (Olin-Scheller & Wikström 2010a). Imitatio includes an ambition to collect an arsenal of different methods, which is done after a pattern that reminds about the four strategies of participation. The knowledge about the different methods can be found in our *copia*, i.e. our register or repertoire of possible choices of language (Sigrell 2008).

According to the principle of imitatio, the teacher in formal learning settings has an important role giving positive feedback (Sigrell 2008). This is central for the processes of learning and also in the development of the repertoire of the student's copia. Since the participatory culture at fan fiction sites strongly is characterized by positive and supporting feedback to the writers of the stories, the given conditions for developing repertoires there are very good (Parrish 2007). "We basically want good things in our copia", Sigrell (2008:144) says. And to be able to discover and appreciate good examples we have to practice as well as being inspired by things that are good. This is just what the fans do when they contribute to fan fiction sites. To be active on a fan fiction site therefore means expanding a textual universe by replicating an original work and other fan fics, but also different genres, literary language, style and form.

By using the source text as a point of departure and through a number of strategies, the fans develop characters, settings, stories and relations. Already in 1992 Jenkins found in his mapping of the fan fiction genre, 10 different strategies that the fans use and combine when constructing new stories (Jenkins 1992: 162ff). Here we concentrate mainly on three of these strategies, refocalisation, to develop a story and to combine different genres.

The fans' ambition of expanding a textual universe has partly its origin in a basic human need to continue telling stories. In the academic field of literature, this is known as intertextuality, a principle on which all stories are created (Allen 2000). One of the fans interviewed, Lina, aged 21, describes:

It's like… instead of free-drawing you use a co-louring book and kind of fill in the contours… so you learn the skills even if you don't make up the world yourself…

But the will of expanding a textual universe it is also dependent of the fans curiosity to know more about the characters, their actions and relations. In doing so, they stick to canon and strive to replicate the language and style of the source text.

Mixing Old and New Stuff

Taking a specific text as a point of departure, how can active replication and the participation strategies be described? Some of the fans are fascinated by the character Lord Voldemort and the fact that Rowling describes him as a person born evil. One of the respondents, 14-year-old Kate, explains that she wants to develop the character of the evil magician because she finds it inadequate. She says:

I don't want to criticize Rowling, I never would do that, but I thought an explanation to why he never

has been able to feel love was missing. I refuse to believe that Voldemort never has felt love or warm happiness not caused by another person's pain. I wanted an explanation to why he became the person he did and to find some goodness in him. It's so unfair that he never should have been able to love at least one person, and that everyone just takes it for granted that he was born as a killing machine.

In her story Kate unfolds a period of Lord Voldemort's life as a young student at Hogwarts, then named Tom Riddle. In her participation strategy Kate uses both imitation and identification and by changing the telling perspective (refocalisation), she switches the protagonist from Harry to Tom Riddle. In doing so, completely different perspectives of the story can be revealed and insufficient descriptions of the characters can be explored.[4]

In her story Kate is replicating J.K Rowling in many aspects. She is faithful to the canon and uses the source text's settings, characters, themes and frames. Even if she has changed the focalisator, the story resembles Rowling's when it comes to how dialogues and descriptions alternate. However, in Kate's story another character, Sarah, is introduced. She is not to be found in the source text and Kate uses the pairing Tom/Sarah in her narrative and put their romantic relation is in focus.

In order to be loyal to Rowling's version, Kate is letting Tom speak "parseltounge", a sort of snake language that just Harry Potter, Dumbledore and Tom master. As in the source text, Kate is occupied with the struggle between good and evil. In her story, Kate also develops the magical track to embrace the magic of love, and she makes connections between violence, power and mutual addiction. By Kate Tom Riddle is a young man who has difficulties with close relations. He is so fascinated by Sarah that his love to her prevents him from becoming what he wants – the ruler of the world.

In Kate's story Tom finally decides to end up the relation with Sarah by sacrificing her. In this part Kate actively uses the readers' knowledge of details of the textual universe and by giving hints only known to someone familiar with the canon, she reveals that Sarah is dead. Just like J. K. Rowling she uses "horcruxes" and a "testral" – both symbols of death in Harry Potter. By interpreting these symbols the readers, who are expected to be well-oriented within the textual universe, understand that Tom has killed his girlfriend.

Thus, to make her story stand out as reliable, Kate expands the original textual universe by balancing on the line of OOC, which is a process of challenging as well as developing literacies. By doing so she partly uses the strategy of elaboration. At the same time she takes some old stuff – what is already known as typical for the Harry Potter-world and mixes it with new stuff when introducing new themes and deepen the characterization.

Recontextualisation

Besides refocalisation, and expanding the texts timelines, Kate also uses recontexualisation, i. e. to fill in gaps of the original story. Many fans mean that this complementary addition is needed in order to entirely explain the course of events in the story or different actions made by the characters.

In her recontexualisation Kate takes a very short passage from the sixth book in the series, *Harry Potter and the Half-Blood Prince* (2005) and develops it into a longer chapter. By using the strategies identification and elaboration she fills in the gaps Rowling is leaving around Tom Riddle's experiences at the orphanage where he grew up. In this chapter Tom remembers the solitude, the degradation and the isolation he felt during his early years at the orphanage. He also recalls how he tormented the other children for his own pleasure. This content is collected from the original work, but Kate takes the story one step further.

Fan fiction often focuses on emotionally strong events and relations, and usually psychological dilemmas are explored. The episode Kate chooses to develop is an emotionally strong part of the story where Tom, during a summer excursion, lured a girl and a boy from the orphanage, Dennis Bishop and Amy Benson, to an inaccessible cave by the sea. Kate's reason for further exploration, she says in an interview, is that since Rowling almost totally neglects this episode, she was "curious of what really happened in the cave".

When writing her story, Kate reuses and replicates not only Rowling's style, form and narratological structures, but also typical words from the original text. She weaves the small and scattered pieces of information that Rowling gives in her book, together with her own picture of the episode. By choosing typical words full of meaning such as "the yearly summer excursion", "the orphanage", "the coast", and "a little village", she reconstructs the atmosphere of the original text. She also continues Rowling's descriptions of the wild coastal setting with wordings such as "the endless sea which waves beat hard against the hard cliffs". Here she functionalizes the principle of imitatio actively and constructively.

The Power of Positive Feedback

However, without the readers to Kate's narrative and their feedback to what and how she writes, no story would be written. In many aspects the system of feedback that characterizes fan fiction sites, can be considered as a basic and important factor of the co-production. Many fan fiction writers receive a great deal of feedback from the readers of their stories – Kate above has hundreds of comments on her story. The fans point out that their readers give feedback on grammar, but also on content and how the story develops.

According to Parrish (2007) approximately 95% of the feedback is positive, and, as discussed above, due to the active replicating process and participation strategies, this has a great impact on the learning processes and development of literacies on fan fiction sites. One of the fans interviewed explains the importance of the feedback:

At first I wasn't sure I would dare to publish on ff.net. I was ever so scared to get bad feedback, but in spite of this I published my first chapter. I told myself that it could remain there until I got a comment. If the critique would be poor, I would throw it away and never ever publish anything again. But the nest day it had become a hit! Since then I have been writing on different stories and shared them all with others. The feedback helps me go on writing, everyone says what they think, what they like and dislike. I can laugh when I read them, this gives me self-confidence, I feel I do a good thing and that I'm appreciated.

The feedback supports the fans and gives them enough courage and self-confidence both to continue writing and to make their texts public by publishing them on the site. You can easily understand the importance and the power of positive feedback, when you take a look at what usually is said to the writers of fan fiction. Here Lizzie gives her view of a story she has read:

Oh, I really love you (well not in THAT way, but you get it)... Everyone from the book that died, I cried over them and I love the way you got your text together even though it was so short. Incredible! (And I would never be able to do the same, no way ;D). I hope you have motivation enough to go on writing on a new fic, so we can "meet" again:). Good Luck with your future fics!!! I'm glad there are persons like you!!!

The quotes from the fans are examples of that fan fiction is not written in solitude but is aimed for an audience consisting of peers in the fan fiction community. The peers fulfill a very important role by giving comments and feedback on the texts the

writer has published and encouraging the writer to continue the story, to help the writer by pointing to issues related to language, narratological structure, or how the story relates to the norms and rules of the original story.

Also, the fan Sara's choice to write in English, as described above, has to do with the importance of feedback and maximizing audience. Among the fans interviewed, many argued that by writing in English – even many of them struggled – enabled them to get far more feedback than if they had written in Swedish only.

But the feedback also is important for how the stories unfold. One of the fans interviewed explains:

The feedback means ever so much. If I didn't get any feed-back, there would be no point in publishing. I write for myself, but also for other people to appreciate what I do. I bring the readers views and ideas with me when writing the following chapters, and if someone suggests something I often try it.

The conception that knowledge is built up gradually and together with others, is widely spread among our respondents. Obviously the positive feedback has a great impact both in the process of creating new stories and how the co-production helps the fans to learn and develop.

The Beta Reader

At school the frames for reading and writing are often a product of the teacher's norms and attitudes. In informal learning settings there are no teachers who can serve as role models. Instead the participatory culture with its informal mentorship functions as support and a guide for those with less experience. One of our respondents, Frida, aged 26, has been interested in fan fiction for a long time. She is among the oldest and most experienced on the site where she is active and says that being experienced gives here a certain responsibility. "I feel I have to give constructive feedback with concrete suggestions how to improve the story", she says.

Overall the feedback practice and the learning that this generates on the sites are fundamental to the fan fiction phenomenon. In fact it has even become institutionalized into a role which is referred to as a "beta reader", or "beta", a role which anyone within the community can take on.[5] The function of the beta reader is a sort of peer-review activity which is an important part of the informal learning setting. As a beta you play an even more active part in helping less experienced fan fiction writers in their development. A beta reader reads a fan fiction text sometimes before it is published online in order to improve the quality of the text before it reaches the larger community.

In addition to the feedback, the function of the beta reader is a part of the co-production of literary texts on fan fiction sites. It helps the fans developing literacies in a number of aspects, such as language, form, style and composition. Through the beta reader the fans are also guided in how to give and receive feedback and how to encourage other fans by giving them constructive advice about how to improve a story. Together the participants create what Jenkins describes as a collective intelligence where everyone gives contributions to the final product (Jenkins 2008).

Writing Something of One's Own

The fans are fully aware of the importance and power of positive feedback for getting enough courage to develop as a writer. One important part for some of the informants in their development as fan writers, is to become independent towards the source text and to reach the participant strategy of elaboration. When she was younger, Ellie, 19 years states, she would be happy for feedback that said that she wrote like J.K Rowling. "Now my ambition is to develop my own style and that everyone shall be sure of that it isn't Rowling",

she continues. Ellie, as well as a number of other fans interviewed, carry a strong dream of one day becoming "successful" professional writers. They have a very clear opinion of the hierarchy they have to climb in order to succeed and are very reflective on their own development within this hierarchy.

The right to publish fiction was once a career defining event – those whose work got published were referred to as "writers" or "authors" while everybody else were "readers". Fan fiction, and other similar phenomena change this structure by introducing the far more flexible concept of the "contributor". "Writers", "authors" and "readers" all contribute in different ways to the collaborative production of fiction where authorship becomes fuzzier concept than in the old days. It is possible to place these different roles on a spectrum of "contribution to a textual universe" where the traditional fiction readers, who contribute very little, or not at all, to the textual universe, are placed at one end of the spectrum and the professional authors who has writing as their primary source of income are placed at the other end (Figure 1).

Inspired by Bakhtin we choose to think of the contribution to the textual universe of a fandom as a matter of *utterances*. For Bakhtin (1986) "language is realized in the form of individual concrete utterances (oral or written) by participants in the various areas of human activity" (p. 70). When you make an utterance you appropriate the words of others and transform and develop them with your own intention. Thus, with help of words, sentences, messages, novels etc, we form genres where every utterance is linked in a chain of other utterances. According to Bakhtin (1986), each separate utterance is of course individual and specific, "but each sphere in which language is used develops its own *relatively stable types* of these utterances" (p. 70).

In this sense fandoms are created by a large amount of different utterances made by the fans. Through these utterances conventions and at-

Figure 1.

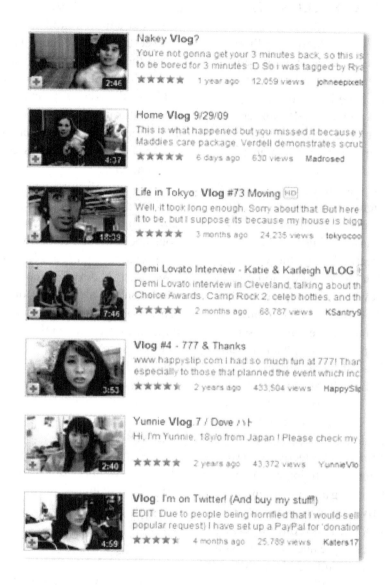

titudes are formed within the fandom, factors which have impact on learning and development of literacies among the contributors. The development of the fan fiction movement in concert with the establishment of services such as *Lulu.com*, *Vulkan.se*, *WeBook.com*, and many other similar brands, indicate a fundamental transformation of how one develops into a "writer". Through the online publication of fan fiction, young people are able to develop their craft in a safe environment in a way which previously have been impossible for most aspiring writers.

Among our informants we have found that the higher involvement in contribution to the fandom, the more development as readers, writers and critics. Therefore our figure can serve as a model for how fans as prosumers move and develop within a textual universe.

DISCUSSION AND CONCLUSION

The system of on-line co-production of literary texts on fan fiction sites enables young people to develop literacies in a safe environment in a way which previously have been almost impossible. By interacting as prosumers the fans create interpretive and discursive communities with specific norms concerning text and narrative. In the interaction and the construction of these communities between readers and writers on a fan fiction site, the fictive text is used as a tool by the fans to understand themselves as well as other people and the surrounding society.

Thus, the digital technologies, the virtuality and participatory culture as they function on fan fiction sites, create new ways of apprehend and construct literacies. Feedback is fundamental in any learning process and, as we have presented above, the power of positive feedback is fundamental in the collaborative production of fan fiction stories. Also, the role of the beta reader is an important aspect of the co-production. For developing literacies, active replication in the way we have given examples of above, offers big opportunities. When the fans collectively as well as individually use different participant strategies, they understand that learning and development of literacies is about active replication and sharing knowledge with others. The fans replicate genres, narratological structures, style and language and successively become more independent towards the source text. All this together give the fans tools to be powerful actors within formal as well as informal learning settings.

The learning processes described in this chapter can also be related to what is known as the zone of proximal development (Vygotskij 1978). To education and learning this conception is central and he maintained the child follows the adult's example. Vygotskij (1978) writes: "While imitating the elders in culturally patterned activities, children generate opportunities for intellectual development" (p. 129). Like us, Vygotskij advocates that children gradually develop the ability to do certain tasks without help or assistance. He called the difference between what a child can do with help and what he or she can do without guidance the zone of proximal development. On fan fiction sites the contributors are supported in their zone of proximal development by a number of factors. We have discussed some of them in this chapter.

There are, of course a number of opportunities for future research into the fan fiction phenomenon. For instance, fan fiction raises several questions about the fan fiction writers' development. How do their writing skills develop over time and how can this development be linked to formal education? It also raises questions concerning professional production of fiction. What are the implications for the authors' creative processes? Further more, an important research topic could concern the gender differences we have discovered during the study.

REFERENCES

Allen, G. (2000). *Intertextuality*. London, New York: Routledge.

Bakhtin, M. M. (1986). *Speech Genres and Other Late Essays* (5th ed.). Austin, TX: University of Texas Press.

Barton, D. (2007). *Literacy: an introduction to the ecology of written language* (2. ed.). Malden, MA: Blackwell.

Black, R. (2006). Digital Design: English Language Learners and Reder Reviews in Online Fiction. In M. Knobel & C. Lankshear (Eds.), *A New Literacies Sampler*. (pp115-136). Peter Lang. Retrieved December 18, 2009, from http://www.soe.jcu.edu.au/sampler/.

Black, R. (2008). *Adolescents and Online Fan Fiction. New Literacies and Digital Epistemologies*. New York: Peter Lang Publishing Group.

Brynjolfsson, E., Hu, Y., & Smith, M. D. (2003). Consumer Surplus in the Digital Economy: Estimating the Value of Increased Product Variety at Online Booksellers. *Management Science, 49*(11), 1580–1596. doi:10.1287/mnsc.49.11.1580.20580

Buckingham, D. (2005). The Media Literacy of Children and Young People. A Review of the Literature. *Centre for the Study of Children Youth and Media Institute of Education*, London. Retrieved November 11, 2009, from http://www.ofcom.org.uk/advice/media_literacy/medlitpub/medlitpubrss/ml_children.pdf.

Findahl, O. (2009a). *Svenskarna och Internet 2009*. Hudiksvall: World Internet Institute. Retrieved January 25, 2010, from http://www.wii.se.

Findahl, O. (2009b). *Internet 15 år. Visionerna möter vardagsverkligheten – om hur svenskarna blev Internetanvändare*. Stockholm. SE (Stiftelsen för Internetinfrastruktur).

Findahl, O., & Zimic, S. (2008). *Unga svenskar och Internet 2008 – en rapport som baseras på en pilotstudie av barn och ungdomars internetanvändning*. Hudiksvall: World Internet Institute. Retrieved February 20, 2010, from http://www.wii.se.

Fish, S. E. (1993). Att tolka Variorumupplagan. In Entzenberg, C., & Hansson, C. (Eds.), *Modern litteraturteori* (pp. 164–190). Lund: Studentlitteratur.

Gee, J. P. (2004). *Situated Language and Learning: a Critique of Traditional Schooling*. New York: Routledge.

Gray, L. (2008). A Fangirl's Crush. *Houston Chronicle*. Retrieved November 29, 2009, from http://www.chron.com/disp/story.mpl/moms/5611220.html.]

Hellekson, K., & Busse, K. (Eds.). (2006). *Fan Fiction and Fan Communities in the Age of the Internet: New Essays*. Jefferson: McFarland & Co.

Herman, A., Coombe, R. J., & Kaye, L. (2006, March/May). YOUR SECOND LIFE? Goodwill and the performativity of intellectual property in online digital gaming. *Cultural Studies, 20*(2-3), 184–210. doi:10.1080/09502380500495684

Holgersen, S. (2002). *Mening og deltagelse: iagttagelse af 1-5 årige børns deltagelse i musikundervisning. Diss*. Diss. København: Danmarks Paedagogiske Universitet.

Jenkins, H. (1992). *Textual Poachers: Television Fans & Participatory Culture*. New York: Routledge.

Jenkins, H. (2008). *Convergence Culture: Where Old and New Media Collide*. (New ed.). New York: New York University Press.

Kress, G. R. (2003). *Literacy in the New Media Age*. London: Routledge. doi:10.4324/9780203164754

Lankshear, C., & Knobel, M. (2006). *New Literacies: Everyday Practices and Classroom Learning*. London: Open University Press.

Leppänen, S. (2007). Youth Language in Media Contexts: insights into the functions of English in Finland. In *Word Englishes, 26* (2), 149-169.

Livingstone, S., & Bober, M. (2005). *UK Children Go Online. Final Report of Key Project Findings*. London: LSE Research Online. Retrieved February 10 2010 from http://eprints.lse.ac.uk/archive/00000399.

Medierådet. (2008). *Ungar och medier 2008: fakta om barns och ungas användning och upplevelser av medier*. Retrieved January 15, 2010, from http://www.medieradet.se/upload/Rapporter_pdf/Ungar_&_Medier_2008.pdf.

Olin-Scheller, C. (2008). Trollkarl eller mugglare? Tolkningsgemenskaper i ett nytt medielandskap. In *Didaktikens forum*, 3, pp. 44-58. Stockholm: Stockholms universitet.

Olin-Scheller, C. (fourthcoming). Förvärva, förvalta och förädla. Ungas läsande och skrivande av fanfiction. In Anne Banér (ed.), *Kulturarvingarna, typ. Vad ska barnen ärva – och varför?* Stockholm: Centrum för barnkulturforskning.

Olin-Scheller, C., & Wikström, P. (2010a). Young People's Reading and Writing in a New Media Landscape. In *Education Inquiry 1(1)*. Literary Prosumers.

Olin-Scheller, C., & Wikström, P. (2010b). *Författande fans*. Lund: Studentlitteratur.

Olsson, T. (2005). *Alternativa resurser: om medier, IKT och lärande bland ungdomar i alternativa rörelser*. Rapport. Lund: Lunds universitet.

Parrish, J. J. (2007). *Inventing a Universe: Reading and Writing Internet Fan Fiction*. Pittsburgh, PA: University of Pittsburgh. Retrieved November 14, 2009, from http://etd.library.pitt.edu/ETD/available/etd-08072007 170133/unrestricted/Parrish2007.pdf

Prensky, M. (2001). Digital Natives, Digital Immigrants. In *On the Horizon, 9 (5)*. NCB University Press. Retrieved November 2, 2009, from http://www.marcprensky.som/writing/default.asp.

Pugh, S. (2005). *The Democratic Genre: Fan Fiction in a Literary Context*. Glasgow, UK: Seren.

Rowling, J. K. (2005). *Harry Potter and the Half-Blood Prince*. London: Bloomsbury.

Säljö, R. (2005). *Lärande i praktiken: ett sociokulturellt perspektiv*. (1. uppl. uppl.). Stockholm, Sweden: Norstedts akademiska förlag.

Selg, H., & Findahl, O. (2008). *InternetExplorers – Delrapport 6, Nya användarmönster. Jämförande analys av två användarstudier*. Uppsala, Sweden: Uppsala universitet. Retrieved January 25, 2010, from http://www.foruminternet.se/downloads/20081105-Forum-Internet-Internet-Explorers-Delrapport-6-Nya-anvandarmonster.pdf.

Sigrell, A. (2008). Lärarens förebildlighet och elevens förmåga att efterbilda. In A. Palmér et al (Eds.), *Sjätte konferensen i svenska med didaktisk inriktning. Muntlighetens möjligheter - retorik, berättande, samtal*. Uppsala, Sweden: Uppsala universitet.

Sjöberg, U. (2002). *Screen Rites: A Study of Swedish Young People's Use and Meaning-making of Screen-based Media in Everyday Life*. Lund, Sweden: Lunds universitet.

Street, B. V. (2001). *Literacy and Development: ethnographic perspectives*. London: Routledge. doi:10.4324/9780203468418

Tapscott, D. (1996). *The Digital Economy: Promise and Peril in the Age of Networked Intelligence*. London: McGraw-Hill.

Thomas, A. (2006). Blurring and Breaking through the Boundaries of Narrative, Literacy and Identity in Adolescent Fan Fiction. In M. Knobel & C. Lankshear (Eds.), *A New Literacies Sampler*. Peter Lang. Retrieved December 3, 2009, from http://www.soe.jcu.edu.au/sampler/.

Vygotskij, L. S. (1978). *Mind in society: the Development of Higher Psychological Processes*. Cambridge, Mass.: Harvard University Press.

Wenger, E. (1999). *Communities of Practice: Learning; Meaning and Identity*. Cambridge, UK: Cambridge University Press.

ENDNOTES

[1]   For a description of the fan fiction genre see for example Jenkins (1992); Pugh (2005); Helleksen & Busse (2006); Olin-Scheller & Wikström (2010b)

[2]   In order to protect the respondents' net-identities and to ensure confidentiality we've changed their nick-names. The ones used in this chapter are therefore made up by us.

[3]   This, and the following quotations by the fans are originally in Swedish and translated by us.

[4]   See also Olin-Scheller (fourthcoming).

[5]   The term "beta" comes from the computer business where the concept of alpha and beta is used for products and services that isn't yet developed since they need to be tested internally and in a smaller scale before they are released on the market. (Black 2006; 2008).

Chapter 6
Media Literacy Education

Natalie Wakefield
McGill University, Canada

ABSTRACT

In order to prepare students for the information age, educational leaders have a responsibility to establish and maintain school environments where media literacy is valued, encouraged and understood. The implementation of media literacy should be an integrated approach and involve all stakeholders in the school community.

Although curricula predominantly focus on reading and writing, educators should have a responsibility to reach beyond basic learning skills and should include the development of the complete individual. This requires an understanding of how children grow, develop and interact, and how their social, cultural and educational environment influences them.

Media literacy education offers educators a vehicle by which they can promote and foster social responsibility. It prepares students for the technological world in which they are required to be active participants and contributing producers of knowledge. Technology allows students to explore the various methods of communicating their ideas, expertise and opinions with others in a participatory culture; it is therefore important for student to develop analytical skills that will help them create, interact and engage effectively in a socialized network. The challenge for educators is to understand the cultural needs of students in today's technologically advanced society and to incorporate media literacy programs as an integral part of education. In order to achieve these goals, teachers should be encouraged to attend seminars and hands-on workshops and more importantly, practical resources should be developed and made available for their use in the classroom.

DOI: 10.4018/978-1-60960-206-2.ch006

INTRODUCTION

Media, in its various forms, has evolved rapidly in the last few decades and is playing an increasingly prominent role in all aspects of our lives – social, cultural, industrial and political. These advancements in technology, and especially the strides made by Internet communication, have also played a major role in the lives of students and youth, and have both increased and altered their perceptions of society (Kaiser Family Foundation, 2005). Unlike the written venues of newspapers, the audio venues of radio, and even the audio and visual influences of television, the Internet has greatly increased the volume of accessible information and the speed at which it can be accessed. Its influence has altered and shaped our perception of information and events, and its authoritarian presence has replaced individual interpretation and use of imagination with visual reality. This 'reality' is deeply embedded in the social lives of children and youth, as teenagers and children spend an average of 6 ½ hours a day consuming electronic media (Kaiser Family Foundation, 2005). Hence, the problem lies in the fact that the information available can be overwhelming, and young people lack the knowledge and experience to sift through and analyze what is relevant. The Internet is a wonderful source of information, but young people need the tools and guidelines to effectively organize and analyze various sources of information in order to differentiate between what is worth analyzing and internalizing, and what should be discarded. Furthermore, they need guidance with the various ways of communicating responsibly with others on-line.

The need for media literacy education can easily be justified by analyzing the life style of many young people today. With easy access to the Internet, email and text messaging, as well as popular web sites such as Facebook and MySpace, it is generally believe that a great number of young people function in isolation, and have become disengaged and disconnected from their school, families, peer groups and communities. Encouraging young minds to participate actively and responsibly in their society should include incorporating their talents and personal interests into positive learning experiences and opportunities. It is therefore important to initiate programs and initiatives that will motivate and encourage students to actively participate outside of their 'nests' or comfort zones and expose them to real life situations.

In this chapter, I will discuss and define the various concepts of media literacy education and their implications. Secondly, I will explain the reasons for the need of media literacy education and the benefits it provides for a positive and participatory learning environment. Finally, I will explore the various critiques of media literacy education and offer some insight into possible solutions over this debate.

THE EVOLUTION OF TECHNOLOGY AND CONCEPTS OF MEDIA LITERACY EDUCATION

Media literacy is not a new concept but it has been redefined and altered over time. Seymour Papert, a mathematician and educator, first introduced the concept of using computers to teach children in classrooms in the 1960's. He believed that computers would offer many opportunities for children and could revolutionize the way they learn (Armstrong & Casement, 1998). Over the following few decades, as schools witnessed a decline in student achievement, a new approach of 'back to the basics' reemerged, and the computer and its software programs were implemented as a convenient tool to improve student test scores through drill and practice (ibid). In the 1980's, when the CD-ROM emerged, the computer was recognized as a valuable tool for research and information, and many schools incorporated programs in their curriculum that necessitated the integration of computers into the classroom instead of confining them to the school computer rooms. During the late 1990's, a new advancement of technology emerged in the form of the Internet, which brought with it a great opportunity for global communication. With this revolutionary tool, schools could no longer teach in the traditional way, as a new form of literacy emerged, and with it the need for a new approach to teaching this technological phenomenon.

Just as the use of computers in schools has evolved to suit the learning needs of students, so too has the definition of concepts such as literacy, media literacy, media education and digital literacy. In general, literacy is viewed as the ability to read and write, which are important skills that schools have been required to teach their students in order to prepare them for a future in a working society. It is argued, however, that this traditional definition of literacy does not encompass the literacy practices of the ways in which we communicate with each other through technology in our every day lives (Hoechsmann & Low, 2008). With the continuous technological advancements in society, the definition of literacy has been reformulated as a 'new literacy' that represents the new digital age (Withrow, 2004). This new approach, also known as 'technoliteracy', shapes the way we presently define literacy in schools, homes and the workplace and has a direct impact on the ways in which we view and teach language in a new literacy world (Leu, Kinzer, Coiro, & Cammack, 2008).

Media literacy is defined as "the ability to decode, evaluate, analyze, and produce both print and electronic media" (Aufderheide, as cited in Kubey, 1997, p. 79). Just as literacy requires a student to read and write, media literacy incorporates the ability to read or analyze media texts through critical analysis and evaluation, as well as the ability to create media texts by producing messages based on personal experiences and points of view (Frechette, 2002). However, the goal of media literacy is not only to enable students to read and write media texts, but its purpose should be to prepare students to make sense and reflect on the complex system of visual codes and conventions that are represented to them, and through this process, to understand their own experiences as discerning readers and writers of various media texts (Buckingham, 2003). Johnson (2001) further ascertains that these codes and conventions define the language of a text, and the way in which we read and interpret the language involves active and meaningful participation. Thus, an in-depth analysis of media texts requires interpretation, metacognition and decoding. Based on these principles, important questions arise: "How does the text come to have meaning? How is it that I came to think of that?" (p. 34).

Buckingham (2007) outlines a number of core skills that define media literacy, which include access, understanding, interpretation, and creation of media. Students need to understand not only how to access information, but also how to develop a set of skills that will help them process, analyze and extract relevant information. Students need to have a sense of self-regulation, where they can independently select appropriate and relevant sources of information. Secondly, learners have to develop an understanding of the information that is available to them. Their ability to sort through and synthesize the vast amounts of information is a crucial component of media literacy education. Finally, students should have the opportunity to create and share their own interpretations and messages through the production of media. In this way, students internalize and identify with the information, become producers of knowledge, and are empowered to share their ideas and creations with others in what Jenkins (2007) calls a participatory culture. Moreover, media literacy should empower students with the "ability to choose and select, the ability to challenge and question, the ability to be <u>conscious</u>

about what's going on around them – and not be passive and vulnerable" (Thoman, as cited in Schwarz, 2001, p. 112). Therefore, according to Potter (2004), media literacy is multidimensional and requires a plethora of knowledge and skills, which include media studies, human thinking and pedagogy. Students must have an awareness of where the sources of information come from, how their understanding and interpretation (as well as others) are constructed through media texts, and then develop the required skills to become educated about what information is delivered.

If media literacy centres on the knowledge and skills that students need to acquire, media education is defined as "the process of teaching and learning about media" (Buckingham, 2003, p. 4). Media can include both written and visual texts, and media education recognizes the importance for learners to understand and deconstruct not only written information, but the visual images, sounds, text features and the use of language that are used to convey a message. It enables students to reflect on the processes of reading and writing and make connections to what their interpretations might be as they come to understand their own experiences as both readers and writers (Buckingham, 2003).

The central focus of media education is to empower students' understanding and participation in the culture of media that surrounds them and is regarded as an extension of democratic citizenship (Buckingham, 2007). Democratic citizenship incorporates a teaching method that encourages the growth of competence, character, communication, team building and leadership in students. The classroom, the school, and its surrounding environments play a vital and intertwined role in promoting and fostering socially responsible citizens.

Another important definition specifically related to the skills students need in relation to the Internet is digital literacy. This is defined as "the ability to understand and use information in multiple formats from a wide range of sources when it is presented via computers" (Gilster, 2000, p. 215). At the core of digital literacy is learning the skills needed to search for and critically evaluate the vast amounts of information on-line. Potter (2004) explains two types of information that is available to us in the form of messages. The first, referred to as factual information, is information that is raw, unprocessed, context free and can be verified by reliable sources. The second type of information, known as social information, is a product of cultural, philosophical and political influences. It is comprised of accepted beliefs that cannot be objectively verified. It is the latter type of information that requires a form of conscious processing from readers.

Nicolas Burbules and Thomas Callister extend the notion that sophisticated web users who evaluate and question sources and information found on-line are known as 'hyper readers'. They have the knowledge and skills to compare different information sources and question the basis and motivation of the information in order to understand who produces the information, what is relevant and irrelevant, and what might be missing in the way it represents various ideologies (as cited in Buckingham, 2007). This is extremely important when sorting through vast amounts of information when authorship is often open, anonymous, and unedited. With these skills, learners are able to not only critically evaluate the information, but most importantly, to use the acceptable information and transform it into knowledge (Buckingham, 2007).

CRITICAL MEDIA LITERACY AND THE CONCEPT OF MEDIA MINDFULNESS

There are many definitions that incorporate the required skills to read, write and produce media texts in the new digital age, but perhaps the most significant definition that covers the broad range of this new literacy is referred to as critical media literacy. This stems from the original definition of media literacy, but the critical factor extends to include a "heightened sense of awareness regarding the content and context" (Serafin, 2007, p. 178) of media texts. Critical media literacy demands a conscious and active participation from its members and includes what is referred to as a 'mindful' approach to media. "A mindful approach has three characteristics: the continuous creation of new categories; openness to new information; and an implicit awareness of more than one perspective" (Langer, as cited in Serafin, 2007, p. 179). This approach focuses on the process of learning from the abundance of material available from media texts, visuals and sounds, and challenges the sense of automaticity—the passive or 'mindless' consumption of information, from what Potter (2004) terms 'information fatigue'.

Media mindfulness is a key factor in critical media literacy education because it incorporates awareness, active participation and responsibility for learners to navigate consciously and discriminatingly through the digital world of the Internet and its sources. This skill should be internalized, and this requires continuous awareness, discussion, reflection and practice. When students are given opportunities to engage in discussions and debates about what messages are reflected back at them, they will gain a better sense of how ideologies and constructions of knowledge are formulated, and have the ability to synthesize the plethora of information that is available to them. They learn how information can be interpreted in multiple ways and that interpretations vary among individuals and are based on one's personal beliefs, experiences, opinions, values, etc. (Frechette, 2002). Being mindful requires us to acknowledge that all messages are constructions and that they are carefully created to reflect an individual's or group's personal agenda or viewpoint (Serafin, 2007). This is particularly important for media educators to incorporate in their teaching, as learners require guidance and support to avoid

believing everything at face value; in other words, mindfulness should replace automaticity (Potter, 2004). The critical media literate individual neither accepts all information at face value nor the commonsense assumption of a media's message, as s/he is aware that the source of information may be tainted by cultural, ideological or political experiences. S/he is sensitive to the multidimensional influences and is capable of deconstructing and reconstructing these multiple layers of meaning, as well as considering alternative viewpoints and interpretations (Potter, 2004). In other words, the viewer or the reader of media texts is astute, knowledgeable and possesses a heightened sense of control over the process of influence and has an increased awareness of the content and context of the information being presented. "Media-literate people make their own choices and interpretations. They know how to recognize a wide range of choices; then, they use their personal elaborated knowledge structures for context to make decisions among the options and select the option that best meets their goals" (Potter, 2004, p. 57). The end result will be that the information they retain and work with will have a personal stamp. No knowledge exists in isolation. All knowledge is interpreted in the context of one's experiences, cultural influences and presence of mind. The more exposure and training that is available to young people and adults, the more objective and analytical their interpretation of information becomes, and the more empathetic and relevant will be their approach and involvement in the community in which they live and work.

THE NEED FOR MEDIA LITERACY EDUCATION THROUGH A CONSTRUCTIVIST APPROACH

"Education in a democratic society is charged with preparing children for the workplace, for citizenship, and for daily human interaction...

the skills needed for success in each of these areas changes radically in the information age" (Kuhlthau, as cited in Kubey, 2001)

Over recent decades, we have seen a shift in the methods of teaching. Educators can no longer prepare students for simply an industrial or manufacturing society; they must provide the skills students will need for a more intellectual and knowledge oriented society that focuses on collaboration, communication and networking. "Educating students has shifted from providing information to students to opening doors for them to explore topics and create meaningful learning experiences for themselves" (Smaldino, Lowther, & Russell, 2008, p. 126). When students are encouraged to have an active role in the learning process, they feel confident and more secure. Lickona, a developmental psychologist and professor of education (2004), states that when students have opportunities to be active participants in their school and community, they display a greater liking for school, a greater empathy towards others' feelings, a stronger motivation to be kind and helpful, a higher academic self-esteem, and stronger feelings of social competence. In addition, they are more willing to make an effort to connect and contribute to the learning environment, which can help expand and reinforce their knowledge, attitudes and appreciation for learning. This pedagogy, known as 'constructivist education', promotes the idea that students become the authors of their own understanding when they feel comfortable and confident to engage in meaningful and relevant learning experiences through interactive, effective, experiential and hands-on learning (Owings & Kaplan, 2003). In such an environment, students are much more integrated in the learning process because they have access to authentic learning experiences where they can participate, collaborate, communicate and teach others about their experiences, knowledge and expertise.

CONSTRUCTIVIST THEORY FOR EDUCATION

Constructivist theory is based on the idea that learning takes place when the learner is actively participating and constructing his/her knowledge—it is a social practice that incorporates experience and interaction between people in their environment (Jones & Bronack, 2008). It promotes the idea that students assemble the pieces to form their own understanding when they feel comfortable and confident to engage in meaningful and relevant learning experiences through discussions and debates (Carlsson-Paige & Lantieri, 2005).

A conceptual framework of social constructivist learning was developed at the Reich College of Education at Appalachian State University. It outlines five basic assumptions of this theory (Jones & Bronack, 2008).

1. Knowledge is created and maintained through social interactions. In classrooms and schools, learning experiences need to be collaborative, where students and teachers both share their knowledge and learn from one another in formal and informal ways.
2. Learning is participatory. Teachers are facilitators in the learning process and students are actively engaged in the learning process. In this type of environment, learning is social and students are encouraged to discuss and reflect on alternative viewpoints, share their ideas and opinions and engage in problem solving.
3. Learning leads to development of knowledge. This is a gradual process that has learners moving through different stages; from novice to expert. Learning is continuous and is shared among participants.
4. Knowledge emerges from meaningful activity with others. Shared values and goals develop and shape the way the group develops and works towards a common goal.

5. Learners develop dispositions relative to the community of practice. The more opportunities students have to interact with one another, the more they show willingness to engage in more productive and meaningful ways.

These five assumptions that comprise the social constructivist theory can play a significant role in media literacy education. Learning is and should be a social process, where learners collaborate and experiment together. Educators encourage and promote this type of learning environment and serve as facilitators for student learning. This helps not only in the retention of the information that the student acquires, but can significantly increase student awareness and practice with media and technology and can help break down some of the barriers of the digital divide within the classroom. With this theory, learning is promoted as a lifelong process where students continue to share and learn from one another. An essential element of learning through digital media requires a process of trial and error through which students explore, experiment and play in social environments, both in the classroom and in the virtual world (Buckingham, 2003).

Some argue that since children and youth are already immersed in media and technology outside the educational system, they can simply acquire media literacy skills on their own. However, Jenkins (2007) argues that this laissez-faire approach disregards three core problems: the participation gap, the transparency problem, and the ethics challenge. These problems can and should serve as a framework for the support and implementation of media literacy education in schools. In such a setting, educators can ensure every student has access to the skills and tools needed to participate and collaborate responsibly within a larger community.

THE PARTICIPATION GAP

The participation gap does not recognize the inequalities that exist among learners' access to and participation in technology. There is in fact a great divide between the digital haves and have-nots; those that have exposure and unlimited access to technology and those who do not. This digital divide contributes to further inequalities for students and can jeopardize the learning environment. Schools must encourage and provide access to technology for all students in the classrooms, libraries and computer labs. They must also encourage collaboration, peer teaching and leadership among their students so that all learners have equal opportunities to share what they know and learn what they don't know. Furthermore, schools must invest in useful and engaging resources that allow for open-minded and creative learning with various forms of media (Buckingham, 2007). To be effective, learning must be meaningful and continuous and provide all learners with equal access to the skills and tools needed to function in the digital age. Every student has the right to an education that will help him/her succeed in the future, and schools have the responsibility to foster and provide the means for equal opportunity.

It is important for these learning experiences to be implemented in schools and classrooms, as they are the place of instruction for the majority of young people between the ages of six and seventeen, and a place where they spend most of their weekdays. There is a responsibility for the school to reinforce the development of children's social skills and virtues by providing them with the tools to make critical decisions, judgments and choices. It is also a place where students can collaborate with one another and share or communicate their prior knowledge. Jenkins (2007) argues that schools' inability to close the participation gap has negative consequences for both the experienced and novice media literate learners.

He states that students who are comfortable and knowledgeable with a variety of media skills are often denied the opportunity to share what they know, while students who do not have equal access find it difficult to keep up with their peers. For this reason, it is clear that bridging the digital divide and the participation gap need to occur in schools, as this may be the only setting where these two groups can engage with and learn from one another.

A crucial step in incorporating meaningful digital inclusion in schools is directly related to the methods of access students receive when engaging with media and technology. It is not enough for students to learn basic skills of computer processing and drill and practice exercises; they must engage in discussions and build their technological skills through critical thinking, production, experiential learning, creativity and expression (Cuban & Cuban, 2007). Schools must invest in the methods and conditions they use to implement and integrate technology for effective learning and teaching, and not just in the number of computers on hand (Kleiman, 2000). Therefore, the essential question for educators to help close the participation gap becomes: "How do we ensure that every child has access to the skills and experiences needed to become a full participant in the social, cultural, economic, and political future of our society?" (Jenkins, 2007, p. 56). The implementation of media literacy education in schools can simultaneously engage students from a multitude of backgrounds and can provide them with more opportunities to integrate into and contribute to a larger participatory community. It is difficult to control and supervise digital access in the home, and therefore, educational institutions are the ideal settings for providing quality education in media literacy skills. These will not only include building familiarity by exposing students to computers and technology, but also the set of tools needed to manage the abundance of information provided to them through these mediums (McAdoo, 2003).

THE TRANSPARENCY PROBLEM

The second argument for teaching media literacy in schools is the transparency problem, which assumes that children are actively reflecting on their media experiences and are independently capable of analyzing and expressing their thoughts, feelings and ideas about these experiences. Buckingham (2003) explains that there is a naiveté in regards to young people's capabilities of processing computer information, and children are often referred to as 'cyberkids' who somehow "possess a natural affinity with technology, and are automatically confident and autonomous in their dealings with digital media" (p. 174). This is not to say that cyberkids do not exist, however, they most probably make up a minority, and do not represent young people as a whole (Buckingham, 2007).

Media and technology play an influential role in our lives and "significantly help to frame how we think about ourselves, our culture, and our perceptions of reality; however, most of us simply take the impact for granted" (Johnson, 2001, p. 42). Students must learn how to develop a critical approach to the information available on the Internet and increase their ability to evaluate the reliability and validity of the variety of sources they are exposed to. In order for students to effectively maximize the benefits from the information available, it is important that they have access to a set of tools; these can only be acquired through education, reflection and discussion. It is the responsibility of educators to give students the necessary information and support to empower and enable them to make informative decisions independently. Students need to be equipped with meaningful experiences that contribute to their understanding and participation with the new technoliteracies, which are complex and multidimensional. Education, and more specifically, media education should "help learners understand how one moves from information to knowledge, and how to make selective, critical judgments about the quality of information" (Lankshear, Snyder, & Green, 2000, p.xvi). Part of decoding information, involves dissecting the various layers of meaning in the information that is presented on-line. Analysis is a key ingredient for sorting through the chaos of information and there are two components that comprise this skill. First, students need to know how to navigate and locate relevant information. Secondly, and perhaps more importantly, they need to develop an analytic filter system that allows them to evaluate information and pose specific questions as to where the information comes from and what purpose it serves (Tally & Burns, 2000). Students must have fundamental knowledge in how to make sense of disconnected facts and get to the root of the essential information (Burniske & Monke, 2001). Careful assessment of information must be explicitly taught to students so they become critically autonomous in finding accurate information, synthesizing that information into their own ideas, and communicating those ideas coherently to others. Once they possess the ability to recognize what information is valuable to their goal of research, it is important for students to know that they are not required to become "experts" in their research but that they have the right to tap into the expertise of others, and learn from the distributive knowledge that exists in the virtual world of on-line research (Dede, 2000).

Surfing the web can seem to be an overwhelming and confusing exercise with no apparent end. It is here that the educator's role can significantly increase the learner's confidence and independence. Navigating on-line requires a sophisticated level of decision-making and students need continuous assistance and training in order to do this effectively; otherwise they may be "unable to distinguish among the important, the trivial, the inadequate, and the simply erroneous" (Armstrong & Casement, 1998, p. 125). The Internet's main appeal to most young people is primarily focused on the social and entertainment sites. It is therefore important that their experiences be broadened in scope, and that they are exposed to the many opportunities the Internet has to offer as a tool for research, education and information. This is an area into which they may not venture on their own, whereas educators can direct and encourage them to broaden their horizons and interact with technology in meaningful ways that add value to their learning.

In summary, media literacy education, or information literacy, as it is sometimes referred to, fosters critical independent thinking, and encourages learners to make informed choices about what information they select on-line. It also enables them to consciously analyze, evaluate, synthesize and extract the appropriate information and decide if sources are unbiased, accurate and reliable (Heil, 2005). Although these skills will take time to develop, once students have the educational training and opportunities to practice and experiment with them, their decisions will be based on a set of "personal and elaborate knowledge structures for context to make decisions among the options and select the option that best meets their own goals" (Potter, 2004, p. 57). To summarize, becoming media literate means taking control of one's own learning by constructing meaning from the messages and information that we are consistently bombarded with and learning how to discriminately assemble the information we need. It involves dissemination and interaction with the information rather than simple absorption and transmission of it. When students have the ability to do this, they are informed and capable of setting their own expectations for what information is relevant, can go beyond surface meanings to construct their own interpretations, and can gain control over the process of influence (Potter, 2008).

Media and technology can offer a wide variety of entertainment, information and interaction for students, however, it is important to acknowledge that in order for students to maximize the benefits of learning and comprehension through these mediums, intervention from educators is necessary as they need assistance and guidance to search for truth, meaning, judgment, comprehension and critical thinking. There is a human component to engaging with media and technology as we seek to help students reach their highest human potential, while developing their sense of reflection and expression, and "nurture exploratory discourse rather than the recitation of homogenized thought" (Burniske & Monke, 2001, p. 57). The transparency initiative seeks to help students engage in their learning process and help improve their contextual understandings of media texts. This notion investigates the essential question of: "How do we ensure that every child has the ability to articulate his or her understanding of the way that media shapes our perceptions of the world?" (Jenkins, 2007, p. 56). We cannot continuously think for our students, therefore, we must provide them with the appropriate skills so that they have the ability to think for themselves.

THE ETHICS CHALLENGE

Finally, there is the ethics challenge; the notion that children develop an independent awareness of what is considered appropriate when contributing and participating in a social on-line environment. This environment, referred to as a participatory culture, is described as "a culture with relatively low barriers to artistic expression and civic engagement, strong support for creating and sharing one's creations, and some type of informed mentorship whereby what is known by the most experienced is passed along to novices" (Jenkins, 2007, p. 3). However, in such an environment, ethical norms and expectations are not clearly defined and students should be prepared to accept or reject concepts and not be unduly exposed to or influenced by situations beyond their understanding. Media literacy strives to educate students to reflect on how their choices affect others and the importance and value of respecting alternative viewpoints. Jenkins (2007) explains that participatory cultures take many forms and can include *affiliations*, such as Facebook and MySpace; *expressions*, such as video making and fan fiction; *collaborative problem solving*, where members can contribute information in teams, such as *Wikipedia*; or *circulations*, such as podcasting—audio or video files that are shared among users.

Social networking sites such as Facebook, You Tube, MySpace and others, offer participants opportunities to engage and connect with others and to establish a sense of community (Hoechsmann & Low, 2008). The social connections that make up participatory cultures are important for students to engage in, but they also need practical strategies in order to participate effectively, responsibly and respectfully. It is important for learners to recognize their own points of view, but it is also important for them to validate and respect other viewpoints and interpretations in order to make informed decisions about how they interact with others in an on-line community. Although self-expression is important, participants on-line need to be able to listen to each other and exchange ideas in thoughtful and meaningful ways without resorting to inappropriate or disrespectful banter (Wilhelm, 2004). Buckingham (2003) further states that learners require a specific set of skills in language when engaging in conversations on-line. They need to 'read' the nuances and learn the rules of online social etiquette (known as 'netiquette'). This is reflective of an approach to citizenship education, where students will learn how to engage in different, and sometimes in difficult conversations with others, but can acquire the necessary skills to participate effectively in a democratic society.

Media literacy prepares students for the technological world in which they are required to be active and reflective participants, as well as contributing producers of knowledge. Through the use of various technological mediums, such as the Internet, students develop critical skills that help them create, interact and engage in a socialized networking system. Thomas (2007) argues that, "as children become well versed in the literacies of technology, they are in fact educating themselves into becoming active and participatory citizens, complete with access to the language of power. For educators not to recognize this and act upon it would be a travesty indeed" (p. 196). The learning process is more meaningful and rewarding when students learn by participation and interaction rather than by more passive methods.

The ethics challenge strives to answer the question: "How do we ensure that every child has been socialized into the emerging ethical standards that will shape their practices as media makers and as participants within online communities?" (Jenkins, 2007, p. 56). Schools and classrooms must establish learning environments that foster student growth both intellectually and socially in order to empower students to be contributive and thoughtful members of society.

Media literacy education can help assist in overcoming the participatory gap, the transparency problem and the ethics challenge. Providing meaningful learning opportunities and access to media and technology, fostering critical student reflection, and promoting socially responsible on-line participation, are key components of teaching media literacy in schools. The process involves learning by doing, experimentation, discussion and collaboration, rather than direct instruction (Buckingham, 2003). Most importantly, it is a social process that "arises through immersion in a 'community of practice' " (Lave & Wenger, as cited in Buckingham, 2003, p. 176). Preparing

students for the future involves equipping them with the skills needed to function in a complex and ever-changing information age, where social skills and collaboration are essential to exchanging ideas across a multitude of different learning forums and communities, both locally and internationally.

CHALLENGES TO MEDIA LITERACY IMPLEMENTATION AND POSSIBLE SOLUTIONS

Although media literacy education promotes both the intellectual and social development of students, the concept itself is relatively new, and therefore, those who wish to incorporate, promote and execute the program in schools face numerous challenges. Multiple criticisms have emerged, including the lack of teacher training to successfully implement critical media literacy education in classrooms and schools; the generation gap that is redefining the concepts and roles of child and adult; and the threats that exist with on-line participation, such as inappropriate content and cyber bullying. However, these challenges should not serve as the basis for excluding a media literacy approach to education, and there are numerous solutions and alternatives that can be introduced in order to ensure that students gain a critical understanding of how they should behave on-line. In addition, it is only through education and guidance that students will be equipped to handle the many negative aspects and threats they may encounter.

THE LACK OF TEACHER TRAINING IN MEDIA LITERACY EDUCATION

The first challenge for media literacy education is the limited amount of training and preparation that is available to teachers in both acquiring technical knowledge and the know-how to pass this information on to their students. Although teacher education programs may introduce technology, much of it is related to disconnected skills training, such as the operation of the technology itself, rather than on the pedagogy of how it could be used in the classroom to complement the curriculum (Lawson & Comer, as cited in Buckingham, 2007). In most programs, teachers are given the basics about the automation of technology, but not the opportunities to explore, evaluate and practice with technology and media. When teachers' media literacy is limited to technical knowledge, the information that is transferred to their students will be limited to the same kind of computer-mediated learning (Goodson, Knobel, Lankshear, & Mangan, 2002). This restricted knowledge results in a lack of confidence and a reluctance to venture into the world of digital technologies, thus creating an educational void and a further disadvantage to the development of a relevant program for students. Teachers who are better versed in the methodology and practices of integrating media and technology into the curriculum, are more likely to assign work to students that incorporates the use of computers (Franklin, 2008).

Media and technology advocates tend to criticize teachers and regard them as unwilling participants in the technological revolution (Buckingham, 2007). Adapting to change takes time, training and confidence, in addition to other factors that contribute to why and how teachers implement media literacy into their current practices. It is also important to recognize that computers and technology do not in themselves shape students' ability to learn; rather it is the influence of teachers that promote and foster positive learning experiences with these mediums. The benefits of media literacy education can only come to fruition when the very people that are responsible for it feel empowered and supported to teach it (Buckingham, 2003). Teacher critics need to pay close attention to the concerns and conditions that can affect the implementations of

new programs, such as media literacy education (Wiske, 2000). It is only when these concerns are heard and understood that possible solutions can emerge.

Educators are accountable to their students and the quality of education that teachers receive will reflect on what they can accomplish in the classroom. Therefore, school leaders and teachers should demand that media literacy education courses be integrated into teacher training programs. Furthermore, professional development opportunities should be readily available to practicing teachers so that they can easily upgrade their knowledge and skills, as "it takes an average of five to six years for teachers to change their method of teaching so that they are using computers in a way that benefits students" (Armstrong & Casement, 1998, p. 35). Once teachers' confidence improves, they become open to experimenting with new methods of teaching, become creative, and are more likely to engage in experiential learning with students in what is referred to as the *invention stage* of technology integration (Kleiman, 2000). Media literacy training is a process that is continuous, and teachers need time to explore and interact with various forms of media and technology in order to provide the same opportunities to their students. When teachers gain the skills and knowledge in media literacy, they will have a greater impact on students' ability to learn and collaborate with one another.

In the meantime, school leaders should help shape positive attitudes and perceptions with regards to media and technology by providing adequate resources and training for their staff members. If teachers have a supportive and collaborative atmosphere within the school, they will be encouraged to participate in a better understanding of the technology available to them, and will be more confident in their expertise (Franklin, 2008). They will also be more likely to exchange ideas and information with their peers and feel less intimidated in accepting help or suggestions from their own students. Schools need to establish safe learning environments where lifelong learning is promoted for both students and teachers.

Media literacy education deserves integration in teacher education programs because it encourages critical thinking for both teachers and students. Teachers have the right to experience the type of learning their students are provided with, and this includes the right to develop their own relationship with technologies through meaningful practice (Jacobsen & Goldman, 2001). Furthermore, these experiences will "offer new ways of engaging students in learning; and making connections—among students, between school and life, as well as between educators and students" (Schwarz, 2001, p. 112). When teachers have the capability and the training to think critically, communicate effectively, and possess the technical skills and creative innovations for implementing media literacy, they will be better prepared and empowered to help their students achieve the same goals (Schwarz, 2001). Effective media literacy education requires enthusiastic, trained teachers who can act as role models for their students, who are attuned and willing to listen to the needs of learners, and more importantly, who are not afraid to get their feet wet when facing new challenges with media and technology. These goals can only be achieved if teacher training and professional development programs are well thought out and carefully developed and implemented.

THE GENERATION GAP AND THE PROTECTIONIST APPROACH

A second challenge for media literacy education is the growing sense of panic about the quality and quantity of accessible information through the use of media and technology in the classroom (and at home). Since young people have embraced the new forms of media communication and unhesitatingly incorporated them into their daily lives, they are assumed to have a better grasp and a higher level of knowledge and confidence in the new technologies. As a result, there has been a significant shift in the relationship between expert and beginner users. The ensuing power struggle for recognition of authority has led to concerns and paranoia both over the younger generation's access to and participation in the digital environment, as well as the loss of adult control over this sphere of influence (Jacobsen & Goldman, 2001). Buckingham (2007) argues that adults may sense a loss of control or feel threatened when children and youth are given too much freedom and are capable of accessing things that might have otherwise been hidden or denied to them. Adults have always been the primary gatekeepers of children's rights and actions, and when the boundaries between adult and child are threatened or altered, or when adults feel a sense of exclusion, the need for rules and control are strongly reinforced, particularly in the domain of media technologies (Buckingham, 2000). This causes great hesitation on the part of teachers to introduce or even implement media literacy education. Moreover, the notion of what students experience or practice with media texts outside of the classroom may be regarded as leisurely and irrelevant to the educational curriculum, thus stripping the value of student culture and identity (Leu et al., 2008). It is important for teachers, as well as adults in general, to acknowledge that media technologies are embedded in the very fabric of the social and cultural lives of students, and excluding them from issues concerning access and participation is to minimize the values that are important to them. "Children will only be able to *become* competent if they are treated as though they *are* competent" (Buckingham, 2000, p. 197). Respect for their knowledge tempered with discretionary guidance will enhance their ability to make critical decisions regarding their actions with media technologies.

There is no watchdog on the Internet, and children can fall prey to pornography, hate literature, cyber bullying, violence, and adult chat sites, often without adult knowledge, mediation or supervision. It is the apprehension of these negative influences that has resulted in many schools blocking certain websites through V-chips or other filtering software, thus imposing parameters on accessibility. Although it might be necessary for certain types of appropriate measures to be in place for students, fear or panic cannot serve as an excuse to refrain from teaching students the skills and tools needed to synthesize the saturated world of media and technology. Censorship and the denial of freedom to on-line access by students are subjective methods of control and undermine the responsibility of educational institutions to teach students about the safety and ethics of on-line digital use (Murphy & Laferrière, 2001). Furthermore, students see these impediments as challenges and in many cases have the knowledge, determination and expertise to maneuver around the filters and access these sites, which become even more intriguing by the censorship that is put in place. As Goodson et al. (2002) argue, "the more elaborate the filter, the more elaborate the search to find ways around it, and the more powerful these resistances become" (p. 61). Clearly, a fine balance needs to be maintained in regulating what students have access to on the Internet, while providing and preparing them with the skills to discern the various types of information that they will need to sort through in their daily lives.

Since students cannot be continuously supervised, they must be given the tools and skills that will enhance their learning and contribute to their growth as individual, independent and thoughtful learners. Students should be aware of the dangers inherent in the use of media, and teachers have a responsibility to intervene and discuss problems as they arise. The learning environment can be significantly enhanced if students are given opportunities to engage in meaningful conversations about the content on-line. Interactive participation with their peers and teachers to understand and find solutions to problems will increase their enthusiasm and give them a sense of achievement that they might not otherwise attain if they were working in isolation (Burniske & Monke, 2001). A critical media literacy approach is needed to ensure that students are accountable for the choices they make on-line. Investing time and patience in media literacy is much more beneficial than quick fix solutions offered by the need to control.

Educational leaders must be proactive and prepared to overcome and deal with obstacles, but more importantly, they need to be aware of the range and diversity of the media experiences that their students possess (Buckingham, 2007), tap into their prior knowledge, and incorporate a program suitable to their needs. Media literacy education will require a shift in the traditional ways of teaching so that the roles of teachers and students can alternate and can complement one another through participation, problem solving and motivation. Teachers can no longer be compartmentalized as the providers of information, nor can students be the knowledge takers (Leu et al., 2008). Students should be provided with opportunities to act as mentors to their classmates and their teachers, which will help promote a collaborative learning environment. Teaching media literacy not only requires imparting knowledge to students, but it also demands that educators recognize that they cannot know everything, and they will need not only to be receptive to the knowledge their students possess, but recognize and respect the culture and interests of those students (Hoechsmann & Low, 2008).

It is insecurity and lack of knowledge that foster reluctance to learn from those that we should be teaching. Many students in our society, however, are better versed in digital technologies, and teachers can benefit from their knowledge. The technological experiences between teachers and students can vary drastically, and these differences must first be recognized, and then an effort should be made to integrate the various experiences and connect them to student learning. This bilateral exchange of ideas and information is not only beneficial for both sides, but would establish a bond of communication and cooperation in the classroom and provide educational potential for life long learning. Today's students are the new 'net generation', already having a significant amount of access to and knowledge of various forms of media, even sometimes without adult consent or knowledge (Tapscott, 1998). In contrast, "the use of information and communication technology in schools signally fails to engage with the ways in which young people are now relating information, and with the ways they choose to communicate" (Buckingham, 2007, p. 178). Students' experiences with media and technology need to be incorporated in schools and this will require consistent discussion and negotiation between what students already know and what new knowledge teachers can implement (Buckingham, 2003).

Media literacy education is a proactive approach that incorporates a philosophy of empowering students to be active members of their own learning. The protectionist approach does not prepare students to be critically autonomous members of society, rather it seeks to protect, and fails to give learners opportunities to engage in meaningful and purposeful dialogue regarding issues that may affect them in the future as adults. Understanding and recognizing what students already know in regards to media and technology is a good starting point for educators, and from there, they can discover what their students still need to learn. It is important to remember that educators need to provide students with meaningful learning opportunities in schools so that they have the skills to function independently, and the ability to discriminately process information. As Masterman eloquently states: "educators need to develop in pupils enough self-confidence and critical maturity to be able to apply critical judg-

ments to media texts *which they will encounter in their future*" (as cited in Frechette, 2002, p. 56).

CYBER BULLYING

The World Wide Web offers children and youth a wide range of opportunities to engage and participate in social networks and create online spaces where information is shared among different groups of people. It is a place where students have the freedom to create or hide their own identities and contribute or post information or comments that travel instantaneously to other virtual viewers. There is a legitimate concern that anonymity can be a dangerous tool for on-line users, as some students post harmful or derogatory comments about others without detection. Cyber bullying has become a challenge for educators in the digital environment as the on-line activities of students at home are often affecting the social, emotional and psychological well being of students at school.

Although there are various definitions of cyber bullying, there is a general consensus that it involves deliberate and hostile behaviour that is intended to harm others through the use of text, images, sounds and video (Bamford, 2004; Shariff, 2008). These messages can be communicated via a host of technological mediums, including cell phones, web sites, blogs, email, MSN chat, and social networking sites, such as Facebook, MySpace and You Tube. The on-line environment becomes increasingly difficult for adults and educators to patrol due to the ease with which students can create multiple identities or remain anonymous. The "cloak of invisibility" can influence some youth to become disinhibited; saying or doing things that they would not normally do if their identities were revealed (Kowalski, Limber, & Agatston, 2008 p. 65).

Schools play a leading role in building awareness and creating strategies and solutions to deal with cyber bullying. Blocking or denying access to digital technology in schools is not the appropriate solution. The lack of knowledge with media technologies creates a sense of panic and this leads to 'shutting down' the problem. It is more beneficial if educators focus on the message or the behaviour, rather than on the medium through which the message is sent. Students must therefore be given a venue where they are encouraged to openly vent their frustrations or discuss any concerns they may have encountered in their travel through cyber space. "Good teaching helps children and youth engage with, and understand difficult matters... helps students uncover things that have been hidden, and brings to life brand new questions, ideas and abilities" (Clifford & Friesen, 2001, p. 32). The virtual world has transformed into a socialized network and students must be provided with real life experiences and exposure to it in order to participate in it responsibly. Schools must pay closer attention to the ways in which they can integrate media technologies more effectively. This can include integrating popular culture or social networking sites where students are encouraged to create their own web sites or MySpace pages where they are promoting themselves in a positive manner, or participating in blogs, where they can share their opinions or knowledge in an ethical way (Kowalski et al., 2008). Engaging students in meaningful experiences with technology, while making them aware of the many pitfalls due to the anonymity of this form of communication, can create opportunities for them to use it wisely and responsibly. These attitudes need not only be implemented in classrooms, but should also serve as the framework for a school's culture.

Media literacy education can play a significant role in developing students' sense of responsibility and respectful behaviour in social situations both on-line and off. Since schools are a primary place for socialization for children and youth, they must share the responsibility for shaping student actions, choices and processes of thought. Educators must incorporate media technologies into their current

practices, as they are increasingly shaping the way students interact and communicate with each other, and the learning potential is far too great to be ignored (Shariff, 2008). This requires students to develop a strong sense of right and wrong and recognize that their actions have consequences (Bamford, 2004). Furthermore, part of this requires students to acknowledge, "facelessness of virtual communication does not mean it is victimless" (Bamford, 2004, p. 4).

Schools must also communicate and collaborate with parents on this issue and provide them with resources and support to enable parents to insert the appropriate and necessary measures that will maintain a sense of control at home.

"Cyber bullying is not a battle, but a plea for improved and increased attention to education, dialogue, bonding and engagement with our young people" (Shariff, 2008, p. 258). Media literacy education strives to help students develop a strong sense of social skills and responsibility that include critical decision-making, an appreciation for diversity, cooperation and collaboration. Students should be able to analyze their decisions and keep in mind how their actions can affect others through the use of media technologies, while at the same time become aware that they too could be the object of unscrupulous predators.

CONCLUSION

The technological revolution continues to have a significant impact on the way we communicate, share information and interact with others. Children and youth are engaging with new media technologies both inside and outside of school, and as a result, are creating their own identities through the use of language and communication (Hoechsmann & Low, 2008). There remains, however, a digital gap in what students are learning from educators and what they are learning on their own. Given the amount of time that young people are spending with these new technologies, it is imperative that educators implement a media literacy approach in their classrooms and school environments. They need to recognize the impact that these mediums have on the lives of their students, as well as how they are used to build relationships between people (Goodson et al., 2002).

We cannot assume that students can fully comprehend the complexities of media technologies independently, and with the implementation of media literacy, educators can serve as facilitators who guide and support them through this process. It is therefore important to initiate programs and learning opportunities that will motivate students to actively engage in the media literacy movement, where they become autonomous and lifelong learners who question and challenge what information and messages surround them in a discriminatory and orderly manner.

The challenge for educators, in this technologically advanced world, is to create synergy rather than friction with technological innovations. Re-educating and empowering educators with the skills to manage, monitor and understand the world in which today's students live, is crucial when implementing curriculum.

The implementation of programs to effectively teach media technologies in schools requires a shift in pedagogical practices. Integrating media technologies in schools "requires new questions, shifts power relations and roles, and demands that educators evaluate the needed changes that will enable students to take advantage of online resources, and to contribute to and extend those resources as they share their knowledge with the world" (Jacobsen & Goldman, 2001, p. 108). Media literacy education cannot wait for the future; it must be currently present in today's classrooms and school culture in order to prepare our students to feel confident, empowered and informed about the world.

REFERENCES

Armstrong, A., & Casement, C. (1998). *The child and the machine: Why computers may put our children's education at risk*. Toronto, Canada: Key Porter Books.

Aufderheide, P. (2001). Media literacy: From a report of the national leadership conference on media literacy. In Kubey, R. (Ed.), *Media literacy in the information age: Current perspectives* (pp. 79–88). Piscataway, NJ: Transaction Books.

Bamford, A. (2004, September). *Cyber-bullying*. Paper presented at the AHISA Pastoral Care National Conference, Melbourne, Australia.

Buckingham, D. (2000). *After the death of childhood: Growing up in the age of electronic media*. Cambridge, UK: Polity.

Buckingham, D. (2003). *Media education: Literacy, learning and contemporary culture*. Cambridge, UK: Polity.

Buckingham, D. (2007). *Beyond technology: Children's learning in the age of digital culture*. Cambridge, UK: Polity.

Burniske, R. W., & Monke, L. (2001). *Breaking down the digital walls: Learning to teach in a post-modern world*. New York: State University of New York Press.

Carlsson-Paige, N., & Lantieri, L. (2005). A changing vision of education. In Noddings, N. (Ed.), *Educating citizens for global awareness* (pp. 107–121). New York: Teachers College Press.

Clifford, P., & Friesen, S. (2001). The stewardship of the intellect: Classroom life, educational innovation and technology. In Barrell, B. (Ed.), *Technology, teaching and learning: Issues in the integration of technology* (pp. 31–42). Calgary, Alberta, Canada: Detselig.

Cuban, S., & Cuban, L. (2007). *Partners in literacy: Schools and libraries building communities through technology*. New York: Teachers College Press.

Dede, C. (2000). Rethinking how to invest in technology. In *The Jossey-Bass reader on technology and learning* (pp. 184–191). San Francisco: Jossey-Bass.

Franklin, C. A. (2008). Factors determining elementary teachers' use of computers. *Principal Magazine, 87*, 54–55.

Frechette, J. D. (2002). *Developing media literacy in cyberspace: Pedagogy and critical learning for the twenty-first century classroom*. Westport, CT: Praeger.

Gilster, P. (2000). Digital literacy. In *The Jossey-Bass reader on technology and learning* (pp. 215–228). San Francisco: Jossey-Bass.

Goodson, I. F., Knobel, M., Lankshear, C., & Mangan, J. M. (2002). *Cyber spaces/Social spaces: Culture clash in computerized classrooms*. New York: Palgrave Macmillan.

Heil, D. (2005). The Internet and student research: Teaching critical evaluation skills. *Teacher Librarian, 26*–29.

Hoechsmann, M., & Low, B. E. (2008). *Reading youth writing: Literacies, cultural studies and education*. New York: Peter Lang.

Jacobsen, M., & Goldman, R. (2001). The hand-made's tail: A novel approach to educational technology. In Barrell, B. (Ed.), *Technology, teaching and learning: Issues in the integration of technology* (pp. 83–111). Calgary, Alberta, Canada: Detselig.

Jenkins, H. (2007). Confronting the challenges of participatory culture: Media education for the 21st century. *MacArthur Foundation Website*. Retrieved October 27, 2009, from http://www.projectnml.org/files/working/NMLWhite Paper.html.

Johnson, L. L. (2001). *Media, education, and change*. New York: Peter Lang.

Jones, J. G., & Bronack, S. C. (2008). Rethinking cognition, representations, and processes in 3D online social learning environments. In Rivoltella, P. C. (Ed.), *Digital literacy: Tools and methodologies for information society* (pp. 176–206). Hershey, PA: Idea Group Inc.

Kaiser Family Foundation. (2005). *Generation M: Media in the lives of 8-18 year olds*. Retrieved October 30, 2009, from http://www.kff.org/entmedia/entmedia030905pkg.cfm

Kleiman, G. (2000). Myths and realities about technology in K-12 schools. In Gordon, D. T. (Ed.), *The digital classroom: How technology is changing the way we teach and learn* (pp. 7–15). Cambridge, MA: Harvard Education Letter.

Kowalski, R. M., Limber, S. P., & Agatston, P. W. (2008). *Cyberbullying*. Oxford, UK: Blackwell.

Kubey, R. (Ed.). (2001). *Media literacy in the information age: Current perspectives (Vol. 6)*. Piscataway, NJ: Transaction Books.

Lankshear, C., Snyder, I., & Green, B. (2000). *Teachers and techno-literacy: Managing literacy, technology and learning in schools*. St. Leonards, NSW, Australia: Allen & Unwin.

Leu, D. J., Kinzer, C. K., Coiro, J. L., & Cammack, D. W. (2008). Toward a theory of new literacies emerging from the Internet and other information and communication technologies. In Mackey, M. (Ed.), *Media literacies: Major themes in education (Vol. 2*, pp. 337–374). New York: Routledge.

Lickona, T. (2004). *Character matters*. New York: Touchstone.

McAdoo, M. (2003). The real digital divide: Quality not quantity. In Johnson, D. L., & Maddux, C. D. (Eds.), *Technology in education: A twenty-year retrospective* (pp. 35–48). New York: Haworth Press.

Murphy, E., & Laferrière, T. (2001). Classroom management in the networked classroom: New problems and possibilities. In Barrell, B. (Ed.), *Technology, teaching and learning: Issues in the integration of technology* (pp. 305–324). Calgary, Alberta, Canada: Detselig.

Owings, W. A., & Kaplan, L. S. (Eds.). (2003). *Best practices, best thinking, and emerging issues in school leadership*. Thousand Oaks, CA: Corwin Press.

Potter, W. J. (2004). *Theory of media literacy: A cognitive approach*. Thousand Oaks, CA: Sage Publications.

Potter, W. J. (2008). *Media literacy* (4th ed.). Thousand Oaks, CA: Sage Publications.

Schwarz, G. (2001). Literacy expanded: The role of media literacy in teacher education. *Teacher Education Quarterly*, *28*(2), 111–119.

Serafin, G. M. (2007). Media mindfulness. In Macedo, D., & Steinberg, S. R. (Eds.), *Media literacy: A reader* (pp. 178–186). New York: Peter Lang.

Shariff, S. (2008). *Cyber-bullying: Issues and solutions for the school, the classroom and the home*. New York: Routledge.

Smaldino, S. E., Lowther, D. L., & Russell, J. D. (2008). *Instructional technology and media for learning* (9th ed.). Upper Saddle River, NJ: Pearson Education.

Tally, B., & Burns, M. (2000). History: Mining for gold in a mountain of resources. In Gordon, D. T. (Ed.), *The digital classroom: How technology is changing the way we teach and learn* (pp. 111–116). Cambridge, MA: Harvard Education Letter.

Tapscott, D. (1998). *Growing up digital: The rise of the net generation*. New York: McGraw-Hill Inc.

Thomas, A. (2007). *Youth online: Identity and literacy in the digital age*. New York: Peter Lang.

Wilhelm, A. G. (2004). *Digital nation: Toward an inclusive information society*. Cambridge, MA: MIT Press.

Wiske, S. (2000). A new culture of teaching for the 21st century. In Gordon, D. T. (Ed.), *The digital classroom: How technology is changing the way we teach and learn* (pp. 69–77). Cambridge, MA: Harvard Education Letter.

Withrow, F. B. (2004). *Literacy in the digital age: Reading, writing, viewing, and computing*. Lanham, MD: Scarecrow Education.

ADDITIONAL READING

Bevort, E., & Bréda, I. (2008). Adolescents and the Internet: Media appropriation and perspectives on education. In Rivoltella, P. C. (Ed.), *Digital literacy: Tools and methodologies for information society* (pp. 140–165). New York: IGI Global Publishing.

Brown, J. A. (1998). Media literacy perspectives. *The Journal of Communication*, *48*, 44–57. doi:10.1111/j.1460-2466.1998.tb02736.x

Burniske, L. (2008). *Literacy in the digital age* (2nd ed.). Thousand Oaks, CA: Corwin Press.

Coppola, E. M. (2004). *Powering up: Learning to teach well with technology*. New York: Teachers College Press.

Covey, S. R. (2008). *The leader in me: How schools and parents around the world are inspiring greatness, one child at a time*. New York: Free Press.

Creighton, T. (2003). *The principal as technology leader*. Thousand Oaks, CA: Corwin Press.

Domine, V. E. (2009). *Rethinking technology in schools*. New York: Peter Lang.

Farmer, L. (2008). *Teen girls and technology: What's the problem, what's the solution?* New York: Teachers College Press.

Gardner, H. (2000). Can technology exploit our many ways of knowing? In Gordon, D. T. (Ed.), *The digital classroom: How technology is changing the way we teach and learn* (pp. 32–35). Cambridge, MA: Harvard Education Letter.

Green, H., & Hannon, C. (2007). *Their space: Education for a digital generation.* London: Demos Publications. Retrieved November 30, 2009, from http://www.demos.co.uk/publications/theirspace

Hillman, T. (2008, Summer). Canadian curriculum spaces for issues of online privacy. *Our Schools, Our Selves. The Canadian Centre for Policy Alternatives, 17*(4), 97–101.

Hird, A. (2000). *Learning from cyber-savvy students: How Internet-age kids impact classroom teaching.* Sterling, VA: Stylus Publishing.

Hobbs, R. (1998). The seven great debates in the media literacy movement. *The Journal of Communication, 48,* 16–32. doi:10.1111/j.1460-2466.1998. tb02734.x

Houston, P. D. (2003). Changes in the educational landscape. In Owings, W. A., & Kaplan, L. S. (Eds.), *Best practices, best thinking and emerging issues in school leadership* (pp. 255–260). Thousand Oaks, CA: Corwin Press.

Jacobi, E. F., Wittreich, Y., & Hogue, I. (2003). Parental involvement for a new century. *New England Reading Association Journal, 1-8.*

Jenkins, H. (2008). Media literacy-Who needs it? In Willoughby, T., & Wood, E. (Eds.), *Children's learning in a digital world* (pp. 15–39). Oxford, UK: Blackwell Publishing.

Jenson, J., Brushwood Rose, C., & Lewis, B. (2007). *Policy unplugged: Dis/connections between technology policy and practices in Canadian schools.* Montreal, Canada: McGill-Queen's University Press.

Kalmus, V. (2007). Socialization in the changing information environment: Implications for media literacy. In Macedo, D., & Steinberg, S. R. (Eds.), *Media literacy: A reader* (pp. 157–165). New York: Peter Lang.

Kellner, D., & Share, J. (2007). Critical media literacy, democracy, and the reconstruction of education. In Macedo, D., & Steinberg, S. R. (Eds.), *Media literacy: A reader* (pp. 3–23). New York: Peter Lang.

Kelly, F. S., McCain, T., & Jukes, I. (2009). *Teaching the digital generation.* Los Angeles, CA: Corwin Press.

Kist, W. (2005). *New literacies in action: Teaching and learning in multiple media.* New York: Teachers College Press.

Lenhart, A., & Madden, M. (2007). Teens, privacy and online social networks: How teens manage their online identities and personal information in the age of MySpace. *Pew Internet & American Life Project.* Retrieved November 29, 2009, from http://www.pewinternet.org/Reports/2007/Teens-Privacy-and-Online-Social-Networks.aspx

Livingston, S., & Bober, M. (2005, April). *UK children go online: Final report of key project findings.* Retrieved November 2, 2009, from http://www.comminit.com/en/node/217126

Livingstone, S., & Bober, M. (2006). Regulating the Internet at home: Contrasting the perspectives of children and parents. In Buckingham, D., & Willett, R. (Eds.), *Digital generations: Children, young people, and new media.* London: Lawrence Erlbaum.

Lotherington, H., Morbey, M. L., Granger, C., & Doan, L. (2001). Tearing down the walls: New literacies and new horizons in the elementary school. In Barrell, B. (Ed.), *Technology, teaching and learning: Issues in the integration of technology* (pp. 131–161). Calgary, Alberta, Canada: Detselig.

Media Awareness Network. (2005). *Young Canadians in a wired world: Trends and recommendations*. Retrieved December 2, 2009, from http://www.media-awareness.ca/english/research/YCWW/phaseII/trends_recommendations.cfm

Mueller, J., Wood, E., & Willoughby, T. (2008). The integration of computer technology in the classroom. In Willoughby, T., & Wood, E. (Eds.), *Children's learning in a digital world* (pp. 272–297). Oxford, UK: Blackwell Publishing.

Nanus, B. (1992). *Visionary leadership: Creating a compelling sense of direction for your organization*. San Francisco: Jossey-Bass.

Orr Vered, K. (2008). *Children and media outside the home: Playing and learning in after-school care*. New York: Palgrave Macmillan. doi:10.1057/9780230583979

Papert, S. (2000). Computers and computer cultures. In *The Jossey-Bass reader on technology and learning* (pp. 229–246). San Francisco: Jossey-Bass.

Partnership for 21st Century Skills. (2004). *Framework for 21st Century learning*. Retrieved November 28, 2009, from http://www.21stcenturyskills.org/index.php?option=com_content&task=view&id=254&Itemid=120

Partnership for 21st Century Skills. (2009). *21st Century learning environments*. Retrieved November 30, 2009, from http://www.21stcenturyskills.org/documents/le_white_paper-1.pdf

Patterson, W. (2003). Challenges to leading and sustaining school change. In Owings, W. A., & Kaplan, L. S. (Eds.), *Best practices, best thinking and emerging issues in school leadership* (pp. 37–43). Thousand Oaks, CA: Corwin Press.

Prensky, M. (2001). Digital natives, digital immigrants. *Horizon*, *9*(5), 1–15. doi:10.1108/10748120110424816

Quebec Ministry of Education. (2001). *Teacher training: Orientations and professional competencies*. Retrieved September 23, 2009 from www.mels.gouv.qc.ca/dftps/interieur/PDF/formation_ens_a.pdf

Rennie, F., & Mason, R. (2004). *The connecticon: Learning for the connected generation*. Greenwich, CT: Information Age Publishing.

Schlechty, P. (1997). *Inventing better schools: An action plan for educational reform*. San Francisco: Jossey-Bass.

Selwyn, N. (2007). Technology, schools and citizenship education: A fix too far? In Loader, B. D. (Ed.), *Young citizens in the digital age: Political engagement, young people and new media* (pp. 129–142). London: Routledge.

Shelly, G. B., Cashman, T. J., Gunter, R. E., & Gunter, G. A. (2008). *Integrating technology and digital media in the classroom* (5th ed.). Boston: Thomson Course Technology.

Sutherland, R., Robertson, S., & John, P. (2009). *Improving classroom learning with ICT*. London: Routledge.

Thornburgh, D., & Lin, H. S. (Eds.). (2002). *Youth, pornography, and the Internet*. Washington, D.C.: National Academy Press.

Wiburg, K. M. (2003). Technology and the new meaning of educational equity. In Johnson, D. L., & Maddux, C. D. (Eds.), *Technology in education: A twenty-year retrospective* (pp. 113–128). New York: Haworth Press.

Willard, N. (2004). I can't see you-You can't see me: How the use of information and communication technologies can impact responsible behavior. *Center for Safe and Responsible Internet use Website.* Retrieved on September 1, 2009 from www.cyberbully.org/cyberbully/docs/disinhibition.pdf

Willard, N. E. (2003). Safe and responsible use of the Internet: A guide for educators. *Center for Safe and Responsible Internet use Website.* Retrieved on October 3, 2009, from http://www.cyberbully.org/documents/

Zucker, A. A. (2008). *Transforming schools with technology: How smart use of digital tools helps achieve six key education goals.* Boston: Harvard Education Press.

Chapter 7
Emergent/See:
Viewing Adolescents' Video Game Creation through an Emergent Framework

Kathy Sanford
University of Victoria, Canada

Liz Merkel
University of Victoria, Canada

ABSTRACT

In the fall of 2006 the authors' ethnographic research study began in a response to increasing social concern regarding adolescent (dis)engagement in school literacy practices. The authors began data collection in a grade 9/10 Information Technology (IT) class wherein students were in the process of creating their own videogames as a way to learn programming. Through observations and interviews with students, teachers and parents, they have begun to consider how knowledge developed through creating video games informs the way young people see and engage in the world. They introduce emergence theory to illuminate how their understandings and skills can be used to provide more meaningful learning experiences in formal learning/school experiences. This chapter will demonstrate how these students were engaged in a powerful, emergent learning experience, and one that is very different to the traditional Eurocentric schooling approach, one often not recognized or understood as credible learning.

INTRODUCTION

Emerge: c. 1563, from Latin emergere, "rise out or up," from ex- "out" + mergere "to dip, sink". The notion is of rising from a liquid by virtue of

DOI: 10.4018/978-1-60960-206-2.ch007

buoyancy. *Emergency* "unforeseen occurrence". *Emergent* (adj.) was first recorded c.1450.[1]

It is the fall of 2006, and we are observing a grade nine Information Technology (IT) class in action. The students are in the process of creating their own videogames as a way to learn programming, and as we observe we begin to notice engagement and learning in this space that is very different from the conventional Eurocentric high school classroom we are used to as teachers and researchers. Imagine the following scenario if you will:

The lab is bustling. Students are seated--sort of--searching through a variety of windows open on their computers. Fingers click and clack keys, and there are murmurs of "Oh! I just died!" and calls from across the room: "Sam²! I just figured it out!" Some students get up and peer over the shoulder at a friend's computer. Where is the teacher? He is working one-on-one with a student and there is a list on the board where students may sign up if they would like some guidance from the teacher, but otherwise they are on their own. Alone, that is, with their friends, the internet, software tutorials and 'cheats', blog and wiki sites, game forums, YouTube and of course, their past experiences with technology and/or gaming. As written in a previous analysis, we found that this environment is a highly social and cooperative one wherein the "relationships develop to become more fluid, organic interconnections, where the students and teacher are both learning and guiding each other" (Sanford, Madill, Ticknor & Spencer; under review). The students approach problem solving in a multiplicity of ways (Squire, 2008) and realize that their expertise is developing in order to make them more capable. One student, Sam, is immersed, working through a problem and we are surprised that he has yet to ask for help from the teacher: "Ok, never during this time have you raised your hand for help," we say. Sam replies: "No, I don't know if the teacher could figure it out anyway. Might be able to, but I want to figure it out myself 'cause what am I going to learn if I just let him do it." The students are all working at different paces and timelines, on different steps and problems, and on different projects of their own choice but with the same software. They are engaged, immersed, and are both teachers

and learners in not only their individual learning process, but also the collective learning and knowledge acquisition of the class.

The engagement, social connectivity and motivation to learn in the above scenario does not represent the majority of high school classrooms in North America that still value and practice Eurocentric conventional schooling. Gee and Levine (2009) claim that schools are not meeting the learning needs of students who are deeply engaged in learning outside of school using technological advances like the ones the IT students were accessing in order to develop their games. Gee and Levine suggest that both teachers and students "witness a disconnect between the real world outside their classrooms and the contrived, dated world that exists within" (p. 51). Further, Shaffer, Halverson, Squire, and Gee (2005) remind us of this when they compare the internal motivation of students in the classroom and in the gaming world:

Whereas schools largely sequester students from one another and from the outside worlds, games bring players together, competitively and cooperatively, into the virtual world of the game and the social communities of game players. In schools, students largely work along with school-sanctioned materials; avid gamers seek out news sites, read and write FAQ's, participate in discussion forums, and most important, become critical consumers of information (p. 5).

This present research was developed through concern for, and in response to, this disconnect present in the lives of teachers and students in school life.

In developing our research questions we felt it integral that, as Gee and Levine (2009) suggest, "[a] crucial first step in promoting student engagement is to rethink literacy for the 21st century" (p. 49). This research sought to better understand the skills (particularly relating to literacy and learning through new/alternative texts and approaches) that youth are gaining through engagement with videogames. We consider how their knowledge informs the way they see and engage in the world, and how their understandings and skills can be used to provide more meaningful learning experiences in formal learning/school experiences. This paper will demonstrate how Sam and his classmates are engaged in a powerful, *emergent* learning experience, and one that is very different to the traditional schooling approach, often not recognized or understood as credible learning.

BACKGROUND

Context and Participants

In a high school with a population of approximately 1300 students, two technology teachers choose to use videogames as motivational entry points for students to learn the abstract concepts of computer programming. The Information Technology grade 9 and 10 classes used the open source software called *Game Maker* that has built-in programming language and students can create a variety of types of videogames. The students ranged in ability and experience with videogames and technology; some students rarely had played videogames, while others are considering careers in the videogame industry. The majority of students were male in both classes. This paper draws primarily on the transcript of one male student, Sam, who details his experience as he describes his process solving a challenging problem in creating his videogame, and also refers to the comments of some of his classmates in the IT course.

Methods of Data Collection

Beginning in the fall of 2006 our research team began to visit the IT classes, all the while taking extensive observational notes, photographs and video recordings of the students, formally interviewing the participating students twice, as well as collecting their videogame artifacts. The teachers were interviewed on two occasions, once individually and once together; additionally, they engaged in a follow up meeting to discuss the research findings. Demonstrations of participants creating videogames and describing the game creation process have been videotaped and screen captured using *Camtasia* (2008) in an attempt to more clearly understand the thinking behind the participants' actions as creators and in relation to their experiences as players.

Our analysis process included hand coding the transcripts of the interviews; each transcript was hand coded by two researchers. Then the transcripts were uploaded and coded using the NVivo software program where more specific coding was completed. The main themes from the hand coding are reported in a previous paper (Sanford, Madill, Ticknor & Spencer; under review), whilst this paper describes a further analysis using emergent theory to support our current thinking.

Below is an excerpt from Sam's first interview, wherein he explains to a researcher his problem solving process as he creates his videogame in class. We chose Sam's interview as he clearly articulates this process and by going into depth into one participant's experience, we can provide the reader with a rich analysis drawing on a framework based on emergence theory, as articulated primarily by Holland (1998). We feel this theory supports our developing understandings of learning through videogame development as described by Sam and his peers, and it also provides context and reference points for the study. Sam comments:

OK, so pretty much what I was doing was, there was a problem where my character wasn't stopping if the other character was moving. So, both of them had to stop or else the one character wouldn't stop. So I was trying to make it so they would stop by themselves. So basically what's happening right here is, I'm testing it for the first time just about to realize that what's going on right now is so bad... and there my friend there is trying to figure out what's going on and he can't figure it out so none of us can figure it out...so then I go back and... they stop when they hit a wall by themselves so I copied what was happening when he hit a wall to stop him then the problem was when you hit a wall you bounce off of it a little bit and so if you only tap the button you bounce off of yourself...off of nothing pretty much. So, that wasn't working. So, yeah here I'm copying and pasting everywhere back and forth changing numbers.

Theoretical Framework: Emergence and Complexity

Although this paper uses notions of emergence as the framework from which we analyze Sam's complex and sophisticated learning, this exploration must begin with a (too) brief discussion of the encompassing theories of complexity science under which emergence is a key element. A body of work is continuously developing that uses complexity science as a meaningful and transformative lens through which to see learning (Barab, et al. 1999; Collins & Clarke 2008; Davis & Simmt, 2003; Davis & Sumara 2006; Doll, 2008; Davis, Sumara & Luce-Kapler, 2008; Sanford & Hopper, 2009). As complexity theory is interdisciplinary, interconnected, intricate, complicated, and not matured in the field of education, researchers must develop markers with which to study complex phenomena. Sanford & Hopper (2009) present such markers for understanding videogame play using a complexity framework. Bringing a complexity sensibility to learning demands that we attend to both the diversity of the agents within a system, as well as a redundancy, or degree of commonality and recursion within a system. Complex systems exhibit decentralized control, wherein hierarchical positions are in flux and often negotiated for the needs of the whole. Davis' (2004) "guidelines and

limitations" are defined as liberating constraints, which allow agents to move freely within boundaries or rules that maintain the collective objective. Finally, the last marker Sanford and Hopper present is that learning is 'distributed'. This recognizes that "concepts like cognition or skill are not just confined to the brain, but are distributed over the body, other people and the tools at hand" (Putnam & Borko, 2000) and throughout the system. For a fuller discussion, refer to Sanford & Hopper, *Videogames and Complexity Theory: Learning through Game Play*, 2009].

Finally, complexity science, as defined by Davis & Simmt [2003] most simply, is the "the science of learning systems, where *learning* is understood in terms of the adaptive behaviours of phenomena that arise in the interactions of multiple agents" [p. 7, italics in original]. This implies that both adaption and emergence are integral to such learning. Adaption indicates a continuous assessment and response by an individual or individuals within a system to fit the needs of the whole, an adjusting that, by nature, transforms the system itself. Emergence, more difficult perhaps to define, is the interaction and dynamics between "players" or mechanisms in the system that allows a new and different system to arise: "much coming from little" (Holland, 1998, p. 1).

John Holland (1998), well-referenced author of the seminal work *Emergence: From chaos to order*, agrees that even he has difficulty in giving a definition of the complex and complicated science of emergence but that he can "provide some markers that stake out the territory" (p. 3). This paper uses Holland's markers as a backbone to *begin* to understand the complex learning demonstrated by these students, highlighting Sam as a case study, as they create videogames. Holland's emergence markers are as follows: Mechanisms and Perpetual Novelty; Dynamics and Regularities; Hierarchical Organizations. These markers and the science of emergence are underpinned by the use of models and modeling, which is (not coincidentally) also a property of game design and learning. The following serves as a reciprocal presentation of not only the emergent theoretical framework with which to view a young person's learning experience through videogame creation, but also, in the spirit of emergent theory, exemplifies videogame creation as a beginning model for emergent markers.

EMERGENT MARKERS IN VIDEO GAME CREATION

Mechanisms and Perpetual Novelty

SONIA

Descartes was the primary architect of the view that sees the world as a clock. A mechanistic view that still dominates most of the world today. And, it seems to me, especially you politicians.

JACK

"Mechanistic?" Is that a real word?

THOMAS

Mechanistic, mechanical, mechanics, yeah, it's a good word.

SONIA

Mechanistic, as if nature functioned like a clock. You take it apart, reduce it to a number of small simple pieces, easy to understand, analyze them, put them all back together again and then understand the whole.

(from the film Mindwalk, *1990, based on the book* The Turning Point, *by Fritjof Capra)*

The Cartesian view of the world is one challenged by theories of emergence and complexity science, though, sculpted through Newtonian science of mechanics, is a view often taken up to make meaning of a complex and unpredictable world. Wheatley (1999) states:

this reduction into parts and the proliferation of separations has characterized not just organizations, but everything in the world during the past three hundred years. Knowledge was broken into disciplines and subjects, engineering became a prized science, and people were fragmented - counseled to use different "parts" of themselves in different settings. (p. 27)

Reductionism seems the most straightforward way to understand life and how it works, but falls short in explaining phenomena such as the collective and unexpected behaviour of complex systems such as ant colonies (Johnson, 2001; Hofstadter, 1979; Holland, 1998). Reductionism would tell us that by examining an individual ant we would be able to predict and understand the behaviour of two ants, three ants or an entire colony: "Yet the colony exhibits a flexibility that goes far beyond the capabilities of its individual constituents" (Hofstadter, 1979). Hofstadter's metaphor of the ant colony is a seminal example of such systems and helps us to see how emergence theories provide a framework to better understand like phenomena, in this case, the phenomenon of creating a videogame. Emergent systems also reveal that Cartesian and Newtonian mechanistic theory has a place, but that those simple mechanisms are combined and in interaction with other mechanisms that create something novel.

Mechanistic theories alone neglect the world as an ever-changing, adapting and interacting environment. Emergence depends on the "ever-changing flux of patterns" (Holland, 1998, p. 4) in the interactions of simple mechanisms. Each change within a system creates a new whole; That is, something novel is perpetually emerging as the world and environment constantly shifts and changes at a mechanistic level: Hence, the term "perpetual novelty". Morowitz (2002) concurs that, in our understanding of emergence, "the real gain is that both reduction and novelty can exist together in the same framework" (p. 20). In fact, reduction and novelty can *and do* exist together, according to Holland. Thus, in regards to the writing and reading of this text, mechanisms and perpetual novelty must implicate and influence the other. The following continues Sam's problem solving exploration and highlights his recombining of mechanisms in order for a new whole entity to emerge:

I have changed something, but it's no good. If you hold down the keys it works fine, but if you just want to move a little bit it doesn't work at all... you just like bounce all over the place. So that was me typing in umm 32...so that was me trying to jump to position if I wasn't aligned with the grid. See I've got a grid....32 by 32 pixels that I keep aligning with so if I clicked one it would move me over so at a speed of four....so now I'm testing it here and it just doesn't work.

Sam continues to change one mechanism of the game, sometimes the speed, the grid or the commands to try and solve the problem of the avatars not stopping independently of the other. There is an aspect of unpredictability here, of how the avatars will respond to the change, to the other mechanisms and how the game itself will change. Sam is working under Johnson's (2001) assertion that mechanisms in the system "act locally, but their collective action produces global behaviour" (p. 74). Unfortunately, two minutes later in the transcript, Sam realizes that the change he has made causes his avatars to stop moving altogether and he must go back to those specific mechanisms again. Fortunately, however, a classmate asserts that this is a normal occurrence

and that game design *"teaches you that logic of how to jumble things around like that, and not be afraid to move it around, and then go back and redo it if you have to because that kind of thing happens a lot"* (James, participant). Those "things" that are jumbled around are individual mechanisms that, put in combination with other mechanisms, exhibit collective emergent properties. Said in another way, this jumbling allows for perpetual novelty.

As Holland describes, mechanisms can be thought of as building blocks, generators or agents within a system. Building blocks "range from mechanisms in physics to the way we parse the environment into familiar objects" (p. 224). Generators might be explained as the rules, principles or constraints playing within a system. Agents might be generalised as a mechanism "that processes input to become output" (pp. 123-124). These mechanisms are parts of systems that can be scrutinized individually by decomposing the system. However, changing/altering/replacing one of these mechanisms will combine in a different way with the other mechanisms, creating a different outcome: "the whole is greater than the sum of its parts in these generated systems. The interactions between the parts are nonlinear, so the overall behaviour *cannot* be obtained by summing the behaviours of isolated components" (Holland, 1998, p. 225). It is as Bateson (1972) asserts, "the pattern that connects" that makes the difference in such systems. It is the *interaction* between players and the combinations of building blocks/generators/agents that allow for a new behaviour or system to arise from simple mechanisms.

An aspect of emergence that Sam demonstrates in the excerpt and in his interaction with his game design is that of decentralized knowing and control (Johnson, 2001; Davis & Simmt, 2003; Salen, 2008). This happens in at least two levels from the researchers' perspective. What will happen is unknown and unpredictable as Sam plays with certain mechanisms in his game. Sam, in the first excerpt, says, *"I'm testing it for the first time, just, ahh, about to realize that what's going on right now is so bad....and there my friend is trying to figure out what's going on and he can't figure it out so none of us can figure it out"*. Later, when asked why he didn't refer to the teacher in the class, he thought that the teacher probably couldn't do it either, but that it was much better that he try so that he could learn which combination of mechanisms would work. Newtonian thinking has led western society to falsely rely on determinism and predictability (Wheatley, 1999), and that the teacher is expert, the student the apprentice. This is in contrast to emergent thinking that "the phenomenon at the cent[re] of each collective is not a teacher or a student, but the collective phenomena of shared insight" (Davis & Simmt, 2003, p. 153). What might emerge from different interactions isn't something the teacher could anticipate, nor could Sam without trying some different combinations of mechanisms. Within the class there seemed to be a collective approach to all the games being created wherein friends and teachers would add insight to game design in order to reach the best possible fit for solving problems.

The second layer wherein decentralized knowing/control appears is that each of the mechanisms is/could be as important as another. Sam isn't sure which mechanism needs to change, and thus each mechanism is as important as the other in these combinations. If one was missing or replaced, the system becomes something entirely different and adjusts accordingly. Therefore each mechanism is valued in the system, although the weighting of each mechanism shifts as Sam moves through the process, discerning which mechanism is important to the whole (or to his design).

Dynamics and Regularities

Holland offers that "[e]mergent phenomena in generated systems are, typically, persistent pat-terns with changing components" (p. 225). That is, there are both dynamics and regularities within emergent systems that interplay with one another, changing roles at times. There are patterns that are observed or generated by the combining of certain building blocks, which when they become recurring, are considered to be rules, or regularities within the system. As Sam works through his problem, he is looking for those patterns, those regularities, which might generate a configuration that works: *"So, I'm just looking at all the different possibilities"* (Sam). Sam comes closer to solving the problems as patterns emerge. He is engaged in very sophisticated learning wherein it is integral that he make critical choices and discard irrelevant detail as he comes closer to successfully creating a working videogame.

Sam is engaged in building and interacting with a dynamic model (modeling discussed below), and to do this he must be selective in his choices. As one of the researchers pondered, *"[these students must] look at all the different steps involved to see how each step affects the other step"* (Kathy). Holland calls this moving through the "tree of moves", or "tree of possibility." This metaphor of the tree is helpful in visualising the branching off in different directions when a new choice is made, or a new building block is added: "The root of the tree is the game's initial state, the first branches lead to the states that can be attained from the root, the branches on those branches lead to the states that can be attained by two moves…" (Holland, 1998, pp. 34-38) and so on. In short, the decisions made influence and manipulate the possibility, prediction, and situation of next decision, and perhaps create the grounds for innovation or, as Whitehead (1920/1971) writes, "the creative advance of novelty." The state of the situation/game changes through the succession of choices or new arrangements leading to new and newer states. This process is guided by a few simple rules, and in Sam's case, he was working with the software given and the discoveries/regularities found by trying out certain combinations. Through his testing and experience, Sam exhibits his skills in deciding what data is irrelevant to his problem and discards appropriately: "We learn what is irrelevant to 'handling' or understanding situations, and we refine our building blocks accordingly. We also learn to use rules [and regularities] to project the way in which the blocks will shift and recombine as the future unfolds" (Holland, p. 26). Choices are also made by the contextual significance of certain patterns: "context places boundary conditions on the particular meanings that occur" (Barab, et al., 1999; see also Holland, 1998, p. 226). The regularities are not always reliable, but they serve as tools to inform those choices or moves to future states. As Davis and Simmt (2003) concur, "decisions around planning are more about setting boundaries and conditions for activity than about predetermining outcomes and means—proscription rather than prescription" (p. 147). Feedback loops become important to agents within a system in setting those boundaries and conditions (Johnson, 2001; Bateson, 1979).

These 'enabling constraints' (Davis & Sumara, 2006) highlight the importance of creating and engaging in activities free enough to enable exploration but focused enough for specific outcomes to be generated by the rules of the system, in this case, game design. As Gee (2003) describes, games are designed to lead players to form good guesses about how to proceed when they face more challenging problems at later stages of the game. In this way, Sam was working not only to 'play' within the rules of game design and coding, but also he was anticipating how the game would be played and the enabling constraints he was setting up for consumers.

Hierarchical Organizations

The students who were involved in game design seemed genuinely engaged and immersed in the work they were doing. Sam was no different, and though he was struggling with this glitch in his game, he was determined to solve it out of class time: "*I've got my next class that I'm done all the assignments so I'm gonna work on it in that class too. I'm gonna work on it until this is done.*" As Sam continues to select and combine mechanisms, he will observe the way that they interact, and perhaps begin to recognize familiar patterns. Over time and with "enhanced persistence" (Holland, 1998), those patterns become generators themselves. In other words, Sam will not have to recombine certain mechanisms together to get the same result as he expects them to interact in similar fashion. He can now treat those patterns as a collective mechanism. This concept is referred to by Holland (1998) as "hierarchical organization."

As more and more patterns emerge, Sam has more possibilities of combinations to make. "Nonlinear interactions, and the context provided by other patterns…both increase the competence [of an emergent system]. In particular, the number of possible interactions, and hence, the possible sophistication of response, rises extremely rapidly (factorially) with the number of interactants" (Holland, 1998, p. 227). Consider the following example of the game *SimCity* given by Steven Johnson (2001):

Each block in SimCity obeys a set of rigid instructions governing its behaviour, just as our cells consult the cheat sheet of our genes. But those instructions are dependent on the signals received from other blocks in the neighbourhood, just as cells peer through gap junctions to gauge the state of their neighbours. With only a handful of city blocks, the game is deathly boring and unconvincingly robotic. But with thousands of blocks, each responding to dozens of variables, the simulated cityscape comes to life, sprouting upscale boroughs and slums, besieged by virtual recessions and lifted by sudden booms. As with ant colonies, more is different. (pp. 88-89)

A hallmark of emergent phenomena is that systems with very few, but firm, rules can produce a multiplicity of complex and unpredictable possibilities, "much coming from little". As more agents enter the system under the constraints of those firm rules, more unpredictability arises, with more possibility for innovation. Sam and his friends are bound by the rules of game design and the computer software used. As Sam adds more mechanisms to the game he discovers more possible situations and capabilities within his design; he learns what might be possible. As Sam's experience suggests, this is a messy, non-linear process and one that involves much play, tinkering and dreaming. As Wheatley and Kellner-Rogers (1996) assert: "All this messy playfulness creates relationships that make available more: more expressions, more variety, more stability, more support" (p. 18). To find the best-fit solution, Sam must proceed using this messy method, developing combinations of mechanisms that, together, exhibit new and collective properties.

More play with collective mechanisms results in more competencies within the system, which allows for more play with collective mechanisms, and so on in a recursive pattern. Sam's understanding of game design and working in this emergent fashion develops and grows deeper as his hierarchical organizations develop. Gee's (2003) principles of understanding articulate the competence and understanding Sam is developing:

1. system thinking – games encourage players to think about relationships, not isolated events, facts, and skills; players see each game and each genre of game as a distinctive semiotic system affording (or discouraging) certain sorts of actions and interactions
2. meaning as action image – players/game designers think through experiences they have had, and run possible scenarios of how to solve a problem in their imaginations

In this way, Sam's learning is not a short term, test-based event wherein he achieves an objective and then moves on to the next objective. Rather he is involved in deep, layered learning wherein mechanisms/parts become coupled or collective, building on past knowledge and experience.

Modeling

Underpinning John Holland's markers for emergent properties is the concept of modeling: "Models, especially computer-based models, provide accessible instances of emergence, greatly enhancing our chances in understanding the phenomenon. Moreover the model can be started, stopped, examined and restarted under new conditions, in ways impossible for most real dynamic systems" (p. 12). Human beings develop and look to models to make meaning of the world in a variety of disciplines. Holland's study on emergence is based on models like games (e.g., checkers), neural networks, weather patterns, and computer science. Further, in *Learning and Games*, Gee (2008) reminds us of model use in engineering (model planes), architecture (blueprints and model buildings/towns), and videogames (avatars and model environments/universes), for a few examples. Models give opportunity to imagine, to consider all possibilities, to experiment with design and play, and to acquire hypotheses about phenomena that may be too big, complex, expensive, dangerous to manipulate and/or understand. Models are often simplified and/or focused on specific properties of these phenomena, which allow more accessibility than the real phenomena/system itself.

Gee (2008) relates the importance of modeling in regards to learning: "models and modeling allow specific aspects of experience to be interrogated and used for problem solving in ways that lead from concreteness to abstraction" (p. 30). Further, in Sam's problem solving process he is relying heavily on model building and implementing. He has a model developed from prior knowledge about how avatars behave when they encounter obstacles in the game. He experiments with this model, inserting it into the situation at hand: "… *they stop when they hit a wall by themselves so I copied what was happening when he hit a wall to stop him then the problem was when you hit a wall you bounce off of it a little bit and so if you only tap the button you bounce off of yourself…*". Unfortunately this model did not fit the situation as he would have liked, but this strategy highlights that "copying" is intrinsic to the use of models.

Models and the thing being modeled by definition are self-similar, copies of one another at different scale. Although models may not work as predicted when reproduced in unknown situations, they allow the model-user to hypothesize, predict, test and adjust/adapt to the resulting action. Gee (2008) suggests, "in-game models are tools to facilitate, enrich, and deepen the problem solving the game designer is building" (p. 31). What is particularly noteworthy in Sam's case is that he is not only recognizing models by playing a game built by a commercial designer, but he is designing the game itself. He is using modeling to design a game in anticipation of the player's use of modeling to solve the problems he invents within his game, a complex layering of meta-modeling.

IMPLICATIONS

Sam's experience presents an in-depth and rich case study to demonstrate an emergent system. He learns in a way that is challenging, rewarding and engaging. He exhibits increasing confidence and competence not only with the software, but also with his storyline, how his avatar moves, how he best problem solves and what or who are his resources. The emergent understanding and competence developed could not have happened if the environment in which he was learning and exploring did not afford him the opportunity.

Consider some of the elements of the environment of the described IT class scenario:

1. Process based learning: Students in the IT class were working on long term projects wherein they worked through steps under their own timelines, contributing to their knowledge of videogame creation and appropriate software. Although they were working with an end goal in mind, they worked in a multiplicity of ways with a multiplicity of resources in order to solve problems throughout the process. These open ended goals present rules or constraints (using particular software and creating a videogame), but the product details are unknown as students value the learning along the way and use hierarchical organizations in further steps as novel situations emerge. The outcome of the project is not easily assessed with traditional methods as students adapt as new information arises through the interaction of mechanisms. Students, as the best assessors of their own learning and problem solving, should be consulted in the assessment of such long term projects in which they are invested and hold expertise.

2. Decentralized control: The students felt empowered to be working *with* teachers instead of *for* teachers. Emergent learning does not move in teleological paths wherein an end goal can be predicted and assessed. In this way, perpetual novelty is valued as an outcome of experimental systems. Students author their own knowledge in such systems and contribute to the collective. Teachers-as-facilitators allow students to be innovative, to take risks, and to feel confident in experimenting. In this way expertise is valued in every member of a class community and is used to generate collective knowledge.

3. Choice: Students were given choice in the theme of their project and how they ap-

proached problems. They developed great confidence by being able to choose the right path for the problem presented, looking for patterns which offered them both dynamics and regularities to manipulate. Students were involved in projects that were meaningful to their lives and their expertise. Meaningful learning was situated in their experiences outside of the classroom, then transferred inside the context of their own storyline and innovations in a classroom setting. In such classes, responsibility is on the student to make the choices that will best suit her or his project, and these choices are respected and supported by the teacher.

4. Teachers modeling and valuing new literacies: Finally, Gee and Levine (2009) support the notion that "[a] key challenge is to overcome traditional barriers to integrating the informal media that young people love into the more formal settings of schools" (p. 49). Teachers must become familiar with new literacies and be supportive in their uses. It is not good enough to rely on traditional teaching methods if the students recognize that they are not meaningful or engaging. Teachers must also honour that their students often (but not always) hold expertise in some or many new literacies. Instead of seeing this as unfavourable to a teacher/student relationship, teachers must perceive this as an opportunity for students to become engaged with schooling, to be innovative and to be part of a social community of learning.

FUTURE RESEARCH DIRECTIONS

The current research was designed in a response to increasing social concern regarding adolescent (dis)engagement in school literacy practices (Gee & Levine, 2009), and in particular those pertain-

ing to boys (Sanford & Madill, 2007; Sanford & Madill, 2007b; Sanford & Madill, 2006). As our relationships with our participants have grown over time, and we learn more about the complexities involved in playing video games (as illuminated in the above sections), we have recognized the importance of viewing this new literacy with a different lens. That is, we need to learn what is *actually going on* with/in these communities of players/creaters to be able to speak to the social concerns surrounding new media (e.g., concerns about violence, gender stereotyping and exclusion, perceived lack of literacy opportunities). Jenkins (2006) supports that he does not believe that "we can meaningfully critique convergence until it is more fully understood; yet if the public doesn't get some insights into the discussions that are taking place, they will have little to no input into decisions that will dramatically change their relationship to media" (p. 13). Through our work we have learned first hand from our participants who play with/in video games about *what* and *how* they are learning with/in the multiple forms of new media surrounding and including video games. Our research continues to move forward in this vein, coming to better understandings of emergent learning in video games through a complexity science lens, but also gaining more insight into what it means to assume a complexity science lens through a video game model.

The connection between video games and complexity is not a far stretch for the imagination: Complexity has often been articulated and modeled by computer science in seminal studies (Holland, 1998; Kauffman, 1992; Waldrop, 1992). Further, moving these understandings into a social constructivist realm, we see work generated to explain the creative, innovative potential of complex learning systems within communities of people (Johnson, 2001; Barab, et al., 1999; Hopper, in press). We propose that, with the aforementioned import and impact of modeling in mind, future research in the new literacies should aim to provide additional models of complex systems and emergent processes to the field. As the digital world(s) continue to provide new platforms for social/collective/individual learning at rapid pace, researchers must explore alternative lenses with which to see these phenomena in order to understand the potential and impact of new media.

The title of this book is *Media use and youth: Learning, knowledge exchange and behaviour,* calling to the active participation by individuals taking up new and multi-literacies and media. We feel that the ways in which we observe young people interact with/in digital worlds, both on and off-line, creates great possibility to view learning and knowing in other, more democratic ways: "the alchemy between youth and digital media has been distinctive; it disrupts the existing set of power relations between adult authority and youth voice" (Ito, et al., 2008, ix). Young video game players are often experts in this field and are more than capable of engaging in critical conversation about their practices with/in new media. The individuals we have observed in video game play are active participants in their learning, exploring and taking on multiple roles as fits the context. *Participatory culture* (Jenkins, 2006) represents the 'active and circular' shifting of roles individuals take in the consumption and creation of media content in this flow. The aforementioned notion of decentralized control that is often exercised within these realms allows for students to become teachers and vice versa (see Sanford & Madill, 2007). Decentralized control readily lends itself to disrupting conventional views of teaching and learning, offering a space in which young people, who are already exploring a multiplicity of roles within digital worlds, are empowered (Bennett, 2008). This shifting of power dynamics through new media challenges our taken-for-granted notions of schooling and teacher-as-expert, and presents new opportunities for educational researchers to adjust conventional thinking about schooling through their research

related to youth and media use. Our forthcoming research explores these shifting power dynamics in more detail and considers new media use as a disruptive, transformative space offering possibility for critical conversations with young people (Sanford and Merkel, forthcoming).

CLOSING (IN ON…)[3]

The participants from whom we learned exhibited high levels of sophisticated problem solving and understanding, and a competence in their work that could only be acquired from confident and layered exploration. That is, they are deeply *immersed* in this play. Immersion, as defined by Janet Murray (1997), is

a metaphorical term derived from the physical experience of being submerged in water. We seek the same feeling from a psychologically immersive experience that we do from a plunge in the ocean or swimming pool - the sensation of being surrounded by a completely other reality, as different as water is from air, that takes over all of our attention, our whole perceptual apparatus. (pp. 98-99)

This metaphor serves to begin to describe the deep engagement many students are finding in both playing and creating videogames. Most appropriately and coincidentally, the theoretical framework that makes the most sense in describing the innovative and complex learning involved, comes from another water metaphor: Emergence. The meaning of the word emergence is "to rise out or up", "[t]he notion is of rising from a liquid by virtue of buoyancy"(see etymological definition above). Together the words immersion and emergence produce a powerful metaphor for the study of learning in videogames. We see participants submerged into a different reality wherein they persist, play, work, spend time. When they reappear from this immersion, novel transformations have occurred and an unpredicted, complex, collective knowing is present. Researchers are seeking an understanding of the space between immersion and emergence. That is, what are the elements of emergence that young people are demonstrating that allow for such creative problem solving and layered, collective understanding? How do we explain, talk to/about, and begin to understand the learning that adolescents are taking up with this form of technology? We are observing the surface of this rapidly changing sea of knowing, but it is the complex world below that we need to dive into more deeply to see the rich, innovative possibilities within this development and understanding of emergent learning.

REFERENCES

Barab, S., Cherkes-Julkowski, M., Swenson, R., Garrett, S., Shaw, R., & Young, M. (1999). Principles of self-organization: Learning as participation in autocatakinetic systems. *Journal of the Learning Sciences*, *8*(3&4), 349–390. doi:10.1207/s15327809jls0803&4_2

Bateson, G. (1972). *Steps to an ecology of mind.* San Francisco: Chandler.

Bennett, W. L. (2008). Changing citizenship in the digital age. In W. L. Bennett (Ed.), Civic life online: Learning how digital media can engage youth *(The John D. and Catherine T. MacArthur Foundation Series on Digital Media and Learning)* (pp. 1–24). Cambridge, MA: The MIT Press.

Camtasia. (2008). Softwarecasa. Retrieved from http://www.softwarecasa.com/

Cohen, A. (Producer), & Capra, B. (Director). (1990). *Mindwalk* [motion picture]. America: Paramount.

Collins, S., & Clarke, A. (2008). Activity frames and complexity thinking: Honouring both the public and personal agendas in an emergent curriculum. *Teaching and Teacher Education, 24,* 1003–1014. doi:10.1016/j.tate.2007.11.002

Davis, B., & Simmt, E. (2003). Understanding learning systems: Mathematics education and complexity Science. *Journal for Research in Mathematics Education, 34*(2), 137–167. doi:10.2307/30034903

Davis, B., & Sumara, D. (2006). *Complexity and education.* Mahwah, NJ: Lawrence Erlbaum Associates, Inc.

Davis, B., Sumara, D., & Luce-Kapler, R. (2008). *Emerging minds: Changing teaching in complex times* (2nd ed.). New York: Routledge.

Doll, W. (2008). Complexity and the culture of curriculum. *Educational Philosophy and Theory, 40*(1), 191–212. doi:10.1111/j.1469-5812.2007.00404.x

Gamemaker 7.0. (2008). Yoyogames. Retrieved from http://glog.yoyogames.com/?p=535

Gee, J., & Levine, M. (2009). Welcome to our virtual worlds. *Educational Leadership,* 48–52.

Gee, J. (2003). *What videogames have to teach us about learning and literacy.* New York: Palgrave Macmillan.

Gee, J. (2008). Learning and games. In K. Salen (Ed.), The ecology of games: Connecting youth, games and learning *(The John D. and Catherine T. MacArthur Foundation Series on Digital Media and Learning)* (pp. 21–40). Cambridge, MA: MIT Press.

Holland, J. (1998). *Emergence: From chaos to order.* Reading, MA: Addison-Wesley.

Hopper, T. (In press). Complexity thinking and creative dance: Creating conditions for emergent learning in teacher education. *PHEnex, 1*(1).

Ito, M., Davidson, C., Jenkins, H., Lee, C., Eisenberg, M., & Weiss, J. (2008). Foreword. In W. L. Bennett (Ed.), Civic life online: Learning how digital media can engage youth *(The John D. and Catherine T. MacArthur Foundation Series on Digital Media and Learning)* (pp. vii–ix). Cambridge, MA: The MIT Press.

Johnson, S. (2001). *Emergence: The connected lives of ants, brains, cities and software.* New York: Simon & Schuster.

Morowitz, H. (2002). *The Emergence of everything: How the world became complex.* New York: Oxford.

Murray, J. (1997). *Hamlet on the holodeck: The future of narrative in cyberspace.* Cambridge, MA: The MIT Press.

Putman, R., & Borko, H. (2000). What do new views of knowledge and thinking have to say about research on teacher learning? *Educational Researcher, 29*(1), 4–15.

Salen, K. (2008). Toward an ecology of gaming. In K. Salen (Ed.), The ecology of games: Connecting youth, games and learning *(The John D. and Catherine T. MacArthur Foundation Series on Digital Media and Learning)* (pp. 1–17). Cambridge, MA: MIT Press.

Sanford, K., & Hopper, T. (2009). Videogames and complexity theory: Learning through game play. *Loading..., 3*(4). Retrieved October 31, 2009, from http://journals.sfu.ca/loading/index.php/loading/article/view/62.

Sanford, K., & Madill, L. (2007). Understanding the power of new literacies through videogame play and design. *Canadian Journal of Education, 30*(2), 421–455. doi:10.2307/20466645

Sanford, K., & Madill, L. (2007b). Critical literacy learning through video games: Adolescent boys' perspectives. *E-Learning and Digital Media, 4*(3), 285–296. doi:10.2304/elea.2007.4.3.285

Sanford, K., Madill, L., Ticknor, R. & Spencer, M. (under review). *Serious games: Meaningful learning through videogame creation.*

Shaffer, D., Squire, K., Halverson, R., & Gee, J. (2005). Video games and the future of learning. *Phi Delta Kappan, 87*(2), 104–111.

Squire, K. (2008). Open-ended video games: A model for developing learning for the interactive age. In K. Salen (Ed.), The ecology of games: Connecting youth, games and learning *(The John D. and Catherine T. MacArthur Foundation Series on Digital Media and Learning)* (pp. 167–198). Cambridge, MA: MIT Press.

Squire, K. (2008b). Video game literacy: A literacy of expertise. In J. Coiro, M. Knobel, C. Lankshear, & D. Leu (Eds.), *Handbook of research on new literacies* (pp. 635–669). Mahwah, NJ: Lawerence Erlbaum Associates.

Wheatley, M., & Kellner-Rogers, M. (1996). *A simpler way.* San Francisco: Berrett-Koehler.

Wheatley, M. (1999). *Leadership and the new science: Discovering order in a chaotic world* (2nd ed.). San Francisco: Berrett-Koehler.

Whitehead, A. (1971). *The Concept of Nature.* Cambridge, MA: Cambridge University Press. (Original work published 1920)

ADDITIONAL READING

Video Games and New Literacies:

Black, R., & Steinkuehler, C. (2009). Literacy in virtual worlds. In L. Christenbury, R. Bomer, & P. Smagorinsky (Eds.), *Handbook of adolescent literacy research* (pp. 271–286). New York: Guilford Press.

Buckingham, D. (Ed.). (2008). Youth, identity and digital media. *(The John D. and Catherine T. MacArthur Foundation Series on Digital Media and Learning)*. Cambridge, MA: The MIT Press.

Coiro, J., Knobel, M., Lankshear, C., & Leu, D. J. (Eds.). (2008). *Handbook of new literacies research*. Mahwah, NJ: Lawrence Erlbaum Associates.

de Castell, S., & Jenson, J. (2004). Paying attention to attention: New economies for learning. *Educational Theory, 54*(4), 381–397. doi:10.1111/j.0013-2004.2004.00026.x

Gee, J. (2005). Learning by design: Games as learning machines. *Telemedium: The Journal of Media Literacy, 52*(1&2), 24–28.

Gee, J. (2007). Are video games good for learning? In S. de Castell & J. Jenson (Eds.), *Worlds in play: International perspectives on digital games research* (pp. 323–335). New York: Peter Lang.

Gee, J. (2007). *Good video games and good Learning*. New York: Peter Lang.

Hopper, T. F., & Sanford, K. (In press). Occasioning moments in game-as-teacher: Complexity thinking applied to TGfU and videogaming. In J. Butler & L. Griffin (Eds.), *Second TGfU book: Theory, research and practice*. Windsor: Human Kinetics.

Hopper, T., Sanford, K., & Clarke, A. (2009). Game-as-teacher and game-play: Complex learning in TGfU and videogames. In T. Hopper, J. Butler & B. Storey (Eds.), *TGfU...Simply good pedagogy: Understanding a complex challenge* (pp. 246). Ottawa: Physical Health Education (Canada).

Jenkins, H. (2000). Art form for the digital age: Video games shape our culture. Its time we took them seriously. *Technology Review*, 117–120.

Kress, G. (2003). *Literacy in the new media age*. London, UK: Routledge. doi:10.4324/9780203164754

Lankshear, C., & Knobel, M. (2003). *New literacies: Changing knowledge and classroom learning*. Buckingham, UK: Open University Press.

McPherson, T. (Ed.). (2008). Digital youth, innovation, and the unexpected. *(The John D. and Catherine T. MacArthur Foundation Series on Digital Media and Learning)*. Cambridge, MA: The MIT Press.

Pearce, C. (2006). Productive play: Game culture from the bottom up. *Games and Culture, 1*(1), 17–24. doi:10.1177/1555412005281418

Capra, F. (1982). *The turning point: Science, society and the rising culture*. New York: Simon and Schuster.

Capra, F. (1996). *The web of life: A new scientific understanding of living systems*. New York: Anchor Books.

Cilliers, P. (1998). *Complexity and postmodernism: Understanding complex systems*. London: Routledge.

Cohen, J., & Stewart, I. (1994). *The collapse of chaos: Discovering simplicity in a complex world*. New York: Penguin.

Doll, W. (1986). Prigogine: A new sense of order, a new curriculum. *Theory into Practice, 25*(1), 10–16. doi:10.1080/00405848609543192

Doll, W. (1993). *Postmodern perspective on curriculum*. New York: Teachers College Press.

Doll, W., Fleener, J., Trueit, D., & St. Julien, J. (Eds.). (2005). *Chaos, complexity, curriculum, and culture: A conversation*. New York: Peter Lang.

Goodwin, B. (1994). *How the leopard changed its spots: The evolution of complexity*. New York: Scribner.

Hopper, T., Butler, J., & Storey, B. (2009). *TGfU... Simply good pedagogy: Understanding a complex challenge*. Ottawa, Canada: Physical Health Education Canada.

Jenkins, H. (2006). *Convergence culture*. New York: New York University Press.

Kauffman, S. (1992). *Origins of order: self-organization and selection in evolution*. Oxford, UK: Oxford University Press.

Lewin, R. (1992). *Complexity: Life at the edge of chaos*. New York: Macmillan.

Prigogine, I., & Allen, P. (1982). The challenge of complexity. In W. Schieve & P. Allen (Eds.), *Self-organization and dissipative structures: Applications in the physical and social Sciences* (pp. 3–39). Austin, TX: University of Texas Press.

Waldrop, M. (1992). *Complexity: The emerging science on the edge of order and chaos*. New York: Simon & Schuster.

KEY TERMS AND DEFINITIONS

Adaption: Individual agents or collectives of agents continually alter their work/role/play within a system in order to maintain the needs of the whole; thus transforming the system itself.

Complexity: An interdisciplinary lens through which to articulate the learning behaviours in/of systems wherein perpetual emergence and adaption occurs. Central to the understanding of complexity is the notion that individual agents within the system are involved in continuously negotiated and in-flux self-organization and de-centralized control.

Decentralized control: hierarchical positions and/or centres of expertise that are in constant flux and, through regular feedback loops, negotiated their actions base on the needs of the whole.

Emergence: The occurrence of new phenomena generated unpredictably by the interaction of simple rules and individual mechanisms that are in constant flux and interaction. Emergence suggests something novel is perpetually emerging at a systems/global level as the world and environment constantly shifts and changes at a mechanistic/local level.

Liberating constraints: rules or boundaries generated and acknowledged collectively that allow for individual agents to interact and innovate within a system whilst maintaining the context that the environment affords. This definition is extended from Davis' (2004) "guidelines and limitations" in complex systems.

Mechanisms: A broad title pertaining to the individual elements and/or simple structures within complex systems that can be identified by decomposing the system. The emerging system as a whole becomes unpredictable when mechanisms interact with and adapt to other mechanisms.

New literacies: A broad term developed to articulate literacy practices made available through the advent of new and multi-media, particularly (though not exclusively) pertaining to digital advances. Examples of such digital advances include: blogs, fan fiction, video games, websites, online social networking, etc. (For more see: Coiro, J., Knobel, M., Lankshear, C., & Leu, D. J. (Eds.) (2008). *Handbook of new literacies research*. New York: Lawrence Erlbaum Associates.)

ENDNOTES

[1] From online etymology dictionary, etymonline.com, retrieved October 15, 2009.

[2] All students' names are pseudonyms.

[3] Holland (1998) uses the word *closing* in two ways and both seem appropriate here: "The first meaning is 'ending' or 'finishing'; the second is 'coming closer'" (p. 221). As he asserts, emergence is too slippery and complicated a science to capture, but the best we can do is hope for a coming closer, or closing in on. This is yet another step in coming closer to understanding how emergent learning takes place in a variety of systems, this example being the creation of videogames.

Section 3
Learning Environments

Chapter 8
BBC Schools beyond the TV Set:
Educational Media Convergence in the Classroom

María Luisa Zorrilla Abascal
University of East Anglia, UK & Universidad Autónoma del Estado de Morelos, Mexico

ABSTRACT

The results here presented are part of a wider enquiry[1] into how educational television and related websites converge in an era in which the boundaries between different media are disappearing.

This chapter focuses on media convergence of educational content particularly intended for television and the internet at the phase of its use in the classroom. The case that best reflects the convergence of educational TV-Web contents is BBC Schools in the United Kingdom, which includes television series and corresponding websites.

INTRODUCTION

The history of educational media has been a succession of technologies, where film and radio gave their place to television and now CD-ROMS and educational software have been displaced by the Web and videogames. Probably the book has been the most resilient of all technologies, but that is also changing since the eruption of digital books. Each

new medium, at present the internet, is heralded as the one that will revolutionise education. Each new medium is seen as promising to extend the range and depth of access, while, simultaneously, shifting the emphasis from teaching to learning, claiming to give the learner direct access to content, without, presumably, the teacher's mediation.

Even the newest medium of all, the internet, has undergone its own path of evolution from *support material* (regarding educational TV) to

DOI: 10.4018/978-1-60960-206-2.ch008

a *stand alone* model and more recently to a *rich media* conception, where televisual, audio, internet and gaming resources are combined and delivered online (Zorrilla, 2008). This online media mix has received several names, *convergence* is one of them. For Jenkins (2006, p. 282) *media convergence* refers to a situation in which multiple media systems coexist and where media content flows fluidly across them.

Building around the concept of *convergence*, the aim of this work is to explore how educational media *converge* in the basic school classroom in the United Kingdom: the challenges and opportunities that the integrated use of media presents for educational purposes.

CONVERGENCE: A CULTURAL PERSPECTIVE

Convergence is an essential concept for this chapter. It is a term that has been widely used in referring to different ideas, although most of its applications within Cultural, Media and New Media Studies are related to the confluence of two or more media. There are two main understandings of media convergence: a) *platform integration* in the transmission-reception phases, which are possibilities based on technological development, such as online streaming video, webcasting, podcasting, PCTV, mobile television, interactive television, etc.; and b) *content integration* in the production and consumption phases, which refers to cultural practices and conceptions, such as simultaneous and collaborative TV-web production, transmedia storytelling and models for sharing and generating users' content.[2]

These two main understandings – technological and cultural convergence – might oversimplify the complex scenario of media convergence which is characterised by multiple levels and manifestations: media industries merge; media texts are marketed across several platforms; technological

devices, gadgets and services are brought together by an increasing connectivity and the magic of digitalization; viewers interact with content and choose to consume from a variety of delivery options; professional roles converge in merged media and non-merged media companies; and producers and consumers join in the creation of new forms of content.

Media convergence is also related to earlier concepts such as *multimedia* (McCormick, 1986; Schnotz 2005), *unimedia* (Lévy, 1997; Inglis et al., 1999) and *multimodal* (Lévy, 1997; Kress, 2003), which are later discussed at the light of some findings of this project.

However, as pointed out by Freedman (2006, p. 288) convergence "…is not the multimedia convergence long predicted by technologists and futurologists but media compatibility that points to the emergence of a new, varied and complex media environment co-habited by offline and online, mobile and fixed, visual and text-based technologies".

Henry Jenkins has a similar perception of the discourse around technological convergence, which he defines as the Black Box Fallacy:

Much contemporary discourse about convergence starts and ends with what I call the Black Box Fallacy. Sooner or later, the argument goes, all media content is going to flow through a single black box into our living rooms (or, in the mobile scenario, through black boxes we carry around with us everywhere we go) [...] Part of what makes the black box concept a fallacy is that it reduces media change to technological change and strips aside the cultural levels. (Jenkins, 2006, p. 14)

Jenkins focuses his analysis on the cultural dimension of convergence – the *convergence culture* – which "does not occur through media appliances, however sophisticated they may become" (2006, p. 3); from his point of view, convergence occurs within the brains of individual producers and consumers and through their social interactions (Ibid.).

One cultural competency related to convergence which is particularly relevant to this chapter is *transmedia navigation* (Jenkins et al., 2009) which is the ability to follow the flow of stories and information across multiple modalities. Kress (2003) defines this as *multimodality*, a characteristic of modern literacy which requires the ability to read and express ideas across a broad range of modes of representation and signification.

The concepts of *transmedia navigation* and *multimodality* are closely related to new media literacies:

[...which] involve the ability to think across media, whether understood at the level of simple recognition (identifying the same content as it is translated across different modes of representation), or at the level of narrative logic (understanding the connections between story communicated through different media), or at the level of rhetoric (learning to express an idea within a single medium or across the media spectrum). (Jenkins et al., 2009, p. 48)

Castells also refers to the concept of multimodality and multimodal processing:

Even if television is television and radio is radio, there is an increasing connection, a real-time interactivity, between different kinds of communications. We are now clearly moving towards an integration of all kinds of media and communications, which are deeply interconnected. Let's call it multimodal communication. (Castells interviewed by Rantanen, 2005, p. 139)

Kompare (2006, p. 336), from a more holistic point of view, argues that "the boundaries between previously discrete forms (text, film, broadcasting, video, and sound recordings) are increasingly blurred – aesthetically, technologically, industrially, and culturally –" and proposes a multiperspectival conception of convergence, where "technology, industry, and culture are not autonomous domains; each is shaped by the other in particular ways, helping construct particular media forms and practices in particular contexts" (Ibid.).

Building on previous ideas of convergence, within this chapter *media convergence* is understood as a cultural practice where contents from different media are integrated and combined at both ends of the media continuum: by producers and by users. Thus, when users (in this particular case: teachers and/or students) are able to follow, integrate and combine content across different media, we identify that practice as a manifestation of *convergence culture*.

Although media convergence usually starts at the production phase, or at least that has been happening with *BBC Schools* resources, it is the users' end the main focus of this chapter. From this cultural perspective of convergence, it is the user who flows from one content to other, from one medium to other, sometimes from one screen to other, stepping apart from the "mixed media" line of Multimedia Learning Studies (Mayer, 2005), in which most findings focus their analysis on one learning space (one screen) where different media mix.

Understanding media convergence as a cultural phenomenon more than a technological one, calls for a Cultural Studies theoretical perspective, which, as its name suggests, is about culture and its manifestations.

If educational television and related websites are considered cultural products, then Cultural Studies, and more specifically Media Studies and New Media Studies allow to explore these products from a variety of perspectives, including the industrial culture responsible for generating them, the cultural products themselves (educational TV programmes and websites) and the social practices of consumption, particularly the cultures of use of educational media in the classroom.

These perspectives are widely explored within this project (Zorrilla, 2008); however, for this chapter we focus on the practices in the classroom with the aim of understanding how teachers and students use educational convergent media.

It is important to point out that even though our main theoretical framework is Cultural Studies, we chose to define teachers and students as media "users", a term closer to New Media Studies, instead of "audience", which would be the current term within Cultural and Media Studies. For this chapter, audience is understood as users, as mediators, as people who do things with media and with each other.

The notion of *user*, although criticised by Lievrouw & Livingston (2006, p. 8) as too broad, too instrumental, too individualistic and too material, was ultimately accepted by New Media studiers as a working term, at least because it excludes the non-user, an indispensable distinction when studying the Information Society. Also from this perspective, mediation presented itself as a key concept for understanding a variety of media relations, like those between teachers and students around educational media, where, as I discuss later in this chapter, the figure of the teacher as mediator is essential.

According to New Media Studies, mediation is no longer perceived as necessarily distorting or corrupting; it's part of networked societies and the relations that thrive upon them, plural and engaging, where sharing and influencing are recursive practices (Silverstone, 2005, p. 30).

BACKGROUND: *BBC SCHOOLS'* RECENT EVOLUTION

Educational media in the United Kingdom, and more specifically resources generated by the BBC, known as *BBC Schools*, have been mainly characterised by a service named "school broadcasting". The history of distinctive educational resources aimed at British school children and teachers began in 1924 and its gradual evolution has brought together different media, including radio, television and the internet.

Along more than eight decades of history, the resources produced by the BBC for educational purposes have changed their role, nature, places and practices of consumption: a well documented history of school broadcasting can be found in Crook (2007). However, the focus of this project is to document the most recent phase of this evolution, particularly since the internet's irruption and how this is reflected in the classroom.

From the mid 90's to the present, the internet has been gaining terrain, and educational television and radio, at least as they traditionally used to be, have declined. There are several examples of this trend:

"[By 2000-2001] we stopped putting resources into the TV programmes [...] Now you can access *Bitesize* content, especially re-versioned online content, through mobile phone, there are interactive TV versions of *Bitesize* [and] audio downloads". (J. Millner, *BBC Schools* Online Editor, personal communication, June 8, 2007).

"Since 2003 all school radio programmes have been available as 'audio on demand' Internet services" (Crook, 2007, p. 224).

At the beginning of 2006, BBC launched its much anticipated 'digital curriculum', named *BBC Jam*, a rich educational media environment intended to gradually substitute *BBC Schools* Online, which was forced to close on March 2007 "following vehement complaint by commercial providers of educational software and online resources" (The Guardian, February 28, 2008); the closure of *BBC Jam* was shortly preceded by the closure of the BBC's commissioning arm for Children's Education, in charge of new radio and television educational products.

Another expression of the new pre-eminence of the internet was the announcement made by Channel 4 at the end of 2007 about spending their educational budget on multimedia online projects instead of traditional television programmes (The Guardian, December 3, 2007).

According to recent interviews with TV producers and web developers (Zorrilla, 2008), the concept of *BBC Schools* has evolved from a teacher centred model to a student-centred approach, where individual access to resources, available online, is supposed to transform the educational journey into a highly customized self-driven experience. But, is this really happening in the classroom?

METHODOLOGICAL APPROACH

This project followed the Cultural Studies tradition of applying ethnographic or "semi-ethnographic" methods to the study of media use and users; these terms refer to the use of qualitative methods of enquiry, including direct questioning and participant observation within the school environment.

The fieldwork was conducted in two schools in Norwich (Norfolk, U.K.), one First School[3] and one Middle School[4]. Seven teachers, two head teachers, one deputy head teacher and 128 children participated. A total of 27 media sessions were documented during the 2006-07 academic year.

For selecting participant schools it was first attempted to identify schools using *BBC Schools* resources in Norwich (the place where the research was going to take place) through the BBC Education Information Department. This attempt failed due to issues of privacy. Thus, an *opportunistic sampling* approach, as defined by Miles and Huberman (1994, p. 28), was undertaken. I contacted my son's school head teacher to ask for her advice, expecting her to know cases of schools in the area using *BBC Schools* resources. This attempt was more than successful: besides

putting me in contact with two other head teachers she volunteered her own school as a participant one. The three schools were using *BBC Schools* resources regularly.

Before starting the pilot study the work overload of one of the head teachers made it impossible to schedule the coordination meetings with the participant teachers, which were indispensable for starting the work. Consequently, at the end the study was only implemented in two of the three schools.

The methods for documenting media convergence in the classroom included: observation (video recording and field notes of media sessions), participant observation (given some of the teachers involved me in activities during media sessions), learning activities (designed by the teachers and which outcomes I analysed), interviews (with participant teachers) and questionnaires (for children).

The one-year fieldwork in schools produced an important volume of data integrated by field notes, audio recordings, video recordings and photocopies of children's work. All these bits of information put together outlined each session and reflected how media had (or had not) converged in the classroom. To recover that integrated view I designed a format which I named *Fieldwork data analysis matrix*. I used one matrix for each media session to concentrate in it all the data gathered from that particular occasion. After completing the fomats, I went through the data again to identify horizontal themes, common and particular issues. It was an exercise of categorising and coding, in order to make sense of this large amount of information and relate it to the wider field of enquiry around educational media and media convergence.

MEDIA CONVERGENCE CULTURE IN THE BRITISH CLASSROOM

During the first stages of this project it was wrongly assumed that combining the use of educational TV series and related websites was an established practice among British teachers, given the availability of the resources and the emerging convergence culture behind its production, according to the findings of the production phase of this project.

However, it was observed in the classrooms that media convergence culture, in Jenkins' sense, is just emerging. Instead of media convergence and transmedia navigation in the school, what was found in this study was a mosaic of coexisting and changing media cultures, some of them convergent, some of them not.

Since media convergence is understood within this study as a cultural practice, the findings of this work focus mainly on describing it through some of its different manifestations in the classroom: physical arrangements, practices, underlying concepts, opinions and perceptions expressed by teachers and children.

These findings are organised into three main areas: 1) Media settings and media practices in the school; 2) Underlying concepts: pedagogical model, roles assigned to teacher, pupils and media and types of users (active and passive); 3) Opinions and perceptions from teachers and children regarding the convergent use of educational media (TV and the Web).

Media Settings and Media Practices in the School

Media Settings in School

Even though the 21st century is a time of media convergence, the spaces for media use in the primary school, particularly in upper grades (Middle School), are less flexible than media contents themselves.

The TV Space in Middle School

The space for TV use has changed in schools following the technological evolution: during the 1960-70's there was usually a shared TV room used in turns by the whole school. Later, with the introduction of the video recorder during the 1980s this common space was mainly used for watching video recordings and the "TV trolley" was born as a result of portable technologies. During the 90s more equipment was bought and by the end of the 20th century each classroom had its own TV set and video player in most British schools. By 2004 the percentage of schools with electronic interactive whiteboards – and accompanying projectors – registered 63% (Department for Education and Skills, 2004) and, at the time of this research, the teacher's computer was one of the most common appliances for playing DVDs, CD ROMs and online videos. All the classrooms observed in this study had an interactive whiteboard, a projector, a teacher's computer and sound amplifiers. The means of video reproduction differed: some used desktop or laptop computers, one classroom had a DVD player (as the teacher's computer did not have DVD ROM) and VHS series were used in two different classrooms.

The use of different technologies, from broadcast TV to video on whiteboards (whatever the source), has had an impact on the spaces used for viewing, from common rooms for the whole school to the convenience and privacy of the classroom. However, the practices of viewing have not changed significantly, including the physical arrangements.

Classrooms still have a focal point, which is the "board space", now shared by the traditional board where the teacher writes and the more recent whiteboard or smartboard, an interactive screen which is mainly used as an amplification of the teacher's computer monitor and also as a big TV set in combination with technologies such as video and DVD players.

Even when the whiteboard is a much bigger screen than the old TV set's one, the observed teachers tended to gather the pupils at the front of the classroom, near the screen, either sitting on the carpet or using their chairs in tight rows or in semicircle. This is a practice inherited from the old TV set days, when the screen was smaller, but it is also a way of keeping children under control.

Watching the television programme is a silent process and the children are shushed if they giggle or talk during the video reproduction.

For viewing the video it is common practice to close the blinds (or curtains) and turn off the lights to have a semi-dark atmosphere very much like the theatre. In two sessions where children were instructed to take notes the teachers solved the writing in different ways: one teacher opted for leaving the curtains open but turning off the light; the other teacher paused the video at strategic points and turned on the lights for allowing them to write.

The notions of quietness and dark environment can be seen as a reflection of how teachers understand the traditional televisual experience: children must be viewing and listening, mentally active, but physically passive. When children need to be actively involved, as in note-taking, lighting conditions change.

The Internet Space in Middle School

Children in Middle school access the internet individually, either in the ICT suite or using the laptop trolley in their classroom. ICT rooms operate very much like the TV room in the old days: they are used in turn by different groups. However, computer portability is making it easier to move computers around the school rather than moving students to the ICT room.

When laptops are used, children remain in their places and the lights are kept on. The ICT room has large tables arranged perpendicularly to the focal point of the room, so that all the children can look at the whiteboard. Invariably lights are on when using this room.

Using the website, collectively or individually, is a relaxed experience in terms of communication dynamics between children and teachers,

not a silent one; sometimes they are instructed to work in pairs.

The lighting conditions and the relaxed atmosphere related to the internet use, reflect that in the school environment this medium is perceived as an interactive tool which requires children active involvement, contrasting with the physical passiveness related to TV viewing.

The Media Space in First School

In contrast with the two well defined and separated spaces for TV and the internet in Middle School, for younger children there is only one media space and that is the classroom. There is one screen for viewing videos, playing games and exploring websites, and that is the whiteboard. By turns and under adult supervision, young children use their hands on the big interactive screen to drag objects and activate links. For theorists who understand convergence as the confluence of content on one screen, this is it. Young children are capable of making distinctions between different types of content: a video, a game, a text, a slide show. However, there is no differentiation in the source: Is it an old VHS, a DVD, a CD ROM, something online or a PowerPoint prepared by their teacher? That kind of distinction does not exist in the First School's classrooms observed and does not seem relevant to pupils. The platform becomes the medium.

For this age cohort, individual experience with computers is either direct interactive contact on the whiteboard for the younger (Year 1) or by turns on a desktop computer (Year 3). Most groups in First School have few desktop computers in the classroom which are used by turns. These desktops are generally shared by pairs and in the observed sessions the computers were mainly used for exploring educational websites chosen by the teacher. However, there was one session with Year 3 when they explored a BBC website as a group, using the whiteboard as the amplified screen of the teacher's desktop; in this session the teacher chose by turn one child to control the mouse in her desktop. Since all the eyeballs were focused on the big common screen, the child in turn used the whiteboard as his/her interface, instead of the computer's monitor.

Thus, young children have a dual experience with computers: a) mentally active but physically passive, when they watch the whiteboard screen but do not participate, which is similar to the televisual experience described before or b) mentally and physically active, when they take turns to touch the whiteboard or to use a desktop, either with the small or the big screen as interface.

Convergent or Divergent Media Spaces

The settings and practices described above reflect different concepts described below:

If analysed from a *technological* point of view, First School children are closer to the *unimedia* experience defined by Pierre Lévy as "...the confluence of separate media within the same integrated digital network" (1997, pp. 44-45). Inglis *et al.* understand *unimedia* as the "combination of several functions in a single medium" (1999, p. 14); in this case, it would be a single platform which is the whiteboard. On the other hand, Middle School children are closer to the *multimedia* experience which implies the use of several media. McCormick describes it as a "multimedia approach, where television broadcasts [in this case videos] and software [in this case websites] are designed and developed together towards common goals with each medium making a unique contribution to the learning environment" (1986, p. 17).

However, from a *learning* point of view, *multimedia* refers to the combined comprehension of text and pictures, and this does not necessarily require high technology. Multimedia learning is also possible with printed books or blackboards instead of computer screens and with the human voice instead of loudspeakers (Schnotz, 2005, p. 50). Referring to this understanding, Pierre Lévy (1997, pp. 44-45) argues that "...linguistically,

it would be much more accurate to speak of multimodal information or messages, since they incorporate several sensory modes (sight, hearing, touch, proprioceptive sensation)".

Moreover, when analysed from a *cultural* perspective, media convergence (named *unimedia*, *multimedia* or *multimodal* by different authors) is more visible in the First School classroom, which is an environment where digital and online media converge with print, analog and non-interactive media types (Ito et al., 2008, p. 8).

The separated spaces and differentiated cultures of media use that establish a divergence between TV and the internet in Middle School make it more difficult for children to experience the transmedia navigation. As mentioned before we are not focusing on media convergence as a technological phenomenon, and therefore it is not relevant if contents are accessed through one single screen or via different platforms. However, given convergence culture consists of *flowing* through different media contents and experiences, it can be said that the flow is not being facilitated by the divergent physical settings described before.

Media Practices in School: The Media Session

In this section, media practices in school are explored through the media session as a learning experience integrated by three essential moments: before, during and after the media use. The media session is conceived as the whole set of practices that encompass the convergent use of educational TV and related websites. Most media sessions observed in this study started with the TV (or video) experience and the internet was usually the second medium to be used.

Before TV Viewing

The teacher announces they are going to view a video and the children are instructed to proceed to the corresponding sitting arrangement. Before the lights are switched off, the teacher gives an introduction to the video. Sometimes these are very brief and almost limited to subject and topic, but others are quite detailed. Some teachers write the learning objective on the board. In one class, the Year 4 teacher wrote the following learning objective: "I can use a TV programme and a website to find out more about the Romans", which integrates both media as part of the learning experience.

There are some cases when the children are instructed to do something specific during the video viewing: the Year 3 teacher distributed blank sheets and told them to take notes or make drawings of whatever they found interesting. With this instruction, she was acknowledging the different learning styles and the difficulties that writing represented to some of her students. This was also a very open task, because children could find very different things interesting. On the other hand, the Year 4 teacher distributed printed 'charts' with boxes and questions for noting and writing down particular aspects to be included in the programme.

Even though within the observed sessions note-taking during the video viewing was not the established practice, some of our observations are similar to those of Laurillard (1994), where teachers using interactive video had prepared questions on worksheets which required the children to pay careful attention to what they saw on the video. Pre-viewing discussion and note-taking, as part of an 'active viewing' strategy, are also suggested by Hobbs (2006, p. 49) as ways of improving media literacy.

Before Web Navigation

The 'before' moment of the internet session is more about practical information, from URL correct typing to specific instructions for playing a game or completing a challenge. In some cases children receive a piece of paper, blank or printed for note-taking. When Year 5 group first played the *Spellits* challenge, their teacher gave each one

a printed "Clue list" and explained it was to be completed during three sessions.

For one of the *Romans in Britain* sessions the Year 4 teacher prepared a *Word* "writing frame" and organised the children in pairs. For this particular session the instructions she gave were very detailed. The objective was to produce evidence of having used and understood information in the website. The instructions were written on the board: 1) Find Romans website; 2) Find the writing frame (*Microsoft Word*); 3) Skim and scan the web text for information (use the key words); 4) When the work is complete, print (with adult check, one per person). The same teacher, during the India sessions gave each child a printed list of tasks and a chart with boxes for handwriting their findings.

Once again, even when the preparation of writing frames or charts were not the common practice within the observed groups, their use and results are coincident with the findings of Laurillard (1994, p. 10) who noticed "Careful design of worksheets […] requiring pupils to attend to the material and answer questions, not just follow instructions, makes it more likely that they will make thorough use of the material". Reynolds & Anderson (1982) found that providing college students with questions before they read a text results in more time spent on passages related to those questions.

However, even in the few cases where writing frames or charts were prepared by the teacher for either the TV viewing of the web navigation, only one of them was conceived as a transmedia navigation tool for helping children to connect contents from different media sources: the Year 4 teacher asked the children to try to identify which web sections were related to the TV programme they had previously watched. She instructed them to find interesting facts and write them down in the provided sheet (printed fact chart). According to the instructions given by the teacher, the task was not only to learn about Romans, but also to learn to use a website and to connect information delivered by different media:

I don't expect you to read everything... use your skimming and scanning skills and 'zoom in' on the bits and facts you find interesting... We are doing two things: learning to explore a website and learning to make connections between what we've seen in the TV and what we are looking at in the website. (Video recorded session, November 23, 2006)

During TV Viewing

In most sessions observed children watch the videos in silence with occasional reactions to the content being presented. If they become too noisy or unsettled they are called to order by the teacher.

For viewing a video the most common practice in the observed sessions was to play it without pauses. Some teachers made occasional comments during the video without pausing. One exception was a session with Year 5 where the first viewing was without pauses and when the children were asked about the content (spelling strategies) they showed a poor retention. The teacher was not satisfied with this result and proposed a second viewing later that day. During the second viewing she made several pauses for explanations, questions and further examples.

The Year 4 teacher also used the pausing strategy when showing the video about India and turned on the lights for the children to take notes. During these pauses she made comments, asked questions and helped them to focus, turning the individual note-taking into a group collaborative activity. This is closer to the idea of socialized or communalized media that is central to the culture of media convergence (Jenkins, 2006).

Adult intervention is mentioned in previous examples not only for its value in terms of children comprehension (Collins, Sobol and Westby, 1981; Fisch, 2004), but mainly because of the role of teacher as *mediator* within the media experience,

which is one of the characteristics of convergence culture as understood from a New Media Studies perspective.

The pausing (or not-pausing) practice is also related to the content's nature itself; McCormick (1986, p. 23) comments:

Even with the use of pre-recorded material, teachers tend to expect to show the video as a whole and make limited use of the control features that are available. Indeed the design of most broadcasts as linear sequential material with carefully prepared linking sections to maintain continuity, encourages this, and does not provide the level of versatility often required.

Regarding the previous statement, still applicable to some of *BBC Schools'* materials, it is important to point out that the modular approach to BBC's science and mathematics programmes was introduced since the 80s (Tan, 1989, p. 90) and recent productions, such as the *Science Clips* series, as its name suggests, are produced with a "clipping" strategy in mind, which offers smaller pieces of content with 'transition curtains' for convenient pausing, responding precisely to concerns expressed by teachers. Most BBC Active DVD packs also break the programmes into pieces for customized viewing options and one of the most recent services offered by the BBC, the online *Learning Zone Clip Library*, is based on the video clipping principle.

The practice of playing the video without pauses (or rewinding) is included in Hobbs' typology of non-optimal uses of video in the classroom (2006). In a research project also implemented in Norwich, Tan (1989, p. 313) noted that during the observed sessions "the VCR was never paused nor rewound for a more detailed study though two of the teachers mentioned that they did use such facilities". In this project one teacher mentioned she did not like pausing because it "breaks the flow of the video". The previous statement implies essential distinctions between different-length contents, where clips may represent simple messages and longer segments or complete programmes are perceived as multilevel more complex systems of meanings.

The only time I observed the 'rewind' control being used was in one session with Year 6 when the children were in charge of the video playing. They were using *Knowledge Box*, an on-line subscription service; they viewed a video about mountains on the ICT room's whiteboard, first as a group and then individually on the computers. Some children viewed it more than twice and used the 'Pause' and 'Rewind' controls.

During Web Navigation

The "during" part of the observed internet sessions showed a wide variety of practices. Here are some examples:

Year 1 used an online simulator to do science experiments collectively on the whiteboard. The teacher controlled the mouse and used a voting system (thumbs up and thumbs down) to predict the experiment results. In another experiment, they were allowed to participate by taking turns to touch the interactive whiteboard screen.

Year 3 used the website collectively through the whiteboard, but instead of the teacher being in charge of the mouse, one child per turn controlled it for exploring the different sections. The rest of the class 'watched' the website and took notes. Simultaneously, selected pupils used desktop computers by pairs and took notes on paper while exploring websites chosen by the teacher.

Year 4 was supposed to complete a list of tasks and fill a chart with boxes, but the teacher detected that there was a generalised failure to explore the slide presentations included in the website. Therefore, she interrupted the web activity, brought back the children to the carpet and with the aid of the whiteboard offered a detailed explanation of how to access the necessary information for completing the task.

There was a session when Year 4 children worked by pairs using two computers: one with *Explorer*, for browsing the website and one with *Microsoft Word*, for filling a writing frame previously prepared by the teacher. In the writing frame there were several sentences taken from the website and the children had to complete them.

Year 5 worked in pairs to solve spelling challenges. In some cases they finished the 3 challenges that corresponded to that particular session and continued playing, solving other clues. In other cases, they solved the challenges of their choice without noticing they were supposed to solve only the first three. Some of them copied the clues from a neighbour and did not bother to solve the challenges. Their gaming experience was very uneven: some finished fast, others took longer and there were some children that could not make progress: even when they listened to the words, they simply had no idea how to spell them. There was one boy who discovered he could access the correct spelling by opening the dictionary included in the game. During the third session they finished the maze and had their "virtual reward", which was a short silly animation, which was a disappointing reward for most of them considering they had spent three sessions solving the challenges.

When Year 5 explored two Ancient Greece websites, in each session they were instructed to visit specific sections related to the video they had just watched. Each selection of sections included different types of content (written texts, interactive activities, animations, games, challenges, quizzes). Some children did not follow the instructions and explored non-selected sections: a war game in the British Museum site was particularly popular among boys, even when it was not included in the selected resources. Children who restricted their exploration to the required sections tended to spend more time in the games, challenges and activities, than reading the information. If a challenge required previous reading for it to be successfully solved, they preferred to approach it by guessing, even if that led to poor scores at the end. In other cases, the intuitive clicking approach of this group prevented them from exploring the whole experience; for example, by not reading the instructions they missed "hidden objects", not knowing they had to click on them to find more information. However, there were some interesting situations when a child found the "hidden" things (by following the instructions or by chance) and the neighbour saw and asked how she/he had done it, and then there was peer sharing and the information about how to do it spread around.

Year 6 did science experiments with an online simulator but many of them did not follow the teacher's instructions about prognosticating and discussing *a priori* the results of each experiment; they just rushed to the interactive experience with the simulator, without the offline previous discussion proposed by the teacher. When they finished the experiments, they did the quiz. Some of them wanted to solve the quiz quickly and tended to "guess" the answers, instead of reasoning and discussing them.

Again, some of these observations are coincident with those of Laurillard (1994, p. 11): "Free exploration was rarely successful. Pupils would too easily sample, and hurry on, seeking something more exciting, anxious not to miss anything." In her study, about the use of interactive media in schools, structured usage was apparently more successful.

The 'clicking around' practice has also been identified by other authors. Desmond (2001, p. 42) observed that "children immediately understand how to navigate hypertexts and that they are willing to use them". Buckingham (2003, p. 175) says that "children learn to use the media largely through trial and error – through exploration, experimentation and play – [...] much of the learning is carried out without explicit teaching: it involves active exploration, 'learning by doing', apprenticeship rather than direct instruction."

The observation *during* media sessions again confirmed how incipient media convergence culture in the classroom is. However, it is important to point out two of its manifestation in the observed sessions: a) the notion of socialized or communalized medium expressed through collective web navigation or shared information for solving a quiz; b) the mediation role, not of only of the teacher (as pauser or non-pauser of videos), but also of peers, as observed in an internet session when one child shared information with other about how to find "hidden" objects.

In these sessions we also observed unexploited potential for transmedia connections: a) In the Year 3 session where some children were navigating selected websites in the desktop computers, different from the one collectively explored in the whiteboard, a well planned integration activity would have embodied what Pierre Lévy (1997) defines as *collective intelligence*, through group sharing of information provided by different media sources. b) It was also observed that children doing intuitive web navigation were not using information they had from the previous video viewing to solve some of the quizzes. In terms of transmedia navigation, this was an excellent opportunity for them to understand, with the appropriate guidance, how to use information from one medium to solve a problem in a different media environment.

After TV Viewing
The general practice after viewing a video consists of oral comments and questions. The children share what they learned or discovered and the teacher summarises and complements the learning experience. Apparently, this has been the common practice for a long time:

After viewing the programme, very often there would be what is commonly termed 'discussions'. The 'discussions' are a form of oral comprehension sessions, often very brief, where teachers would question the pupils orally on the contents of the programmes viewed. (Tan, 1989, p. 171)

The nature of these discussions, as observed by Tan (1989, p. 508), consists mainly of a question-answer dynamic.

Almost twenty years after Tan's research, the use of discussions after the video viewing continues to be the norm; however, the nature of these conversations differs from teacher to teacher and from group to group and the number and variety of associated activities has considerably increased, including the use of related websites.

The Year 3 teacher organised small-group discussions after the video viewing and went around chatting with the children to assess their learning, to enquire about what they found interesting, explaining, clarifying and reinforcing core aspects. She also asked them to make extra notes or drawings (additional to the ones made during the video viewing) to remember the relevant information.

Although the discussions after the video viewing are interesting and reflect the children's retention and understanding of the contents presented, they constitute only the first of a number of extra activities which might include the use of the internet.

Regarding these extra activities, Tan (1989, p. 136) wrote: "The need for follow-up activities has never been under-emphasized ever since school television first began. However, there are reasons for teachers not doing follow-up. Often, the viewing place is not the classroom".

The first interesting issue to notice in Tan's account is the labelling of these learning activities as "follow-up". It clearly indicates the place of television as a point of entry. In this arena things have not changed considerably, since the televisual resource continues to be used invariably as the opening resource. However things are gradually changing and the pre-eminence of TV over other media is dissolving.

Secondly, the nature of the "follow-up" activities has changed and widened during the past twenty years, having evolved from group discussion and occasional work-sheets or activities taken from the teachers' notes provided by the producers into a richer mix of possibilities which includes: a) A variety of suggested activities (also photocopiable material) through the teacher's book when the programmes are bought by the school as a video or DVD packs. The packs also include posters, maps, charts and photographs. b) Accompanying websites designed as intertextual resources which offer different contents for reinforcement and/or further exploration of the topic; websites include printable worksheets and activities, both online and offline. c) The availability of other educational websites related to the topic, like the British Museum's site used for the *Ancient Greece* BBC TV series or the Snaith Primary's *Welcome to India* website used for the BBC *India* TV series; d) Extra activities and/or resources developed by the teacher.

However, according to the interviews with teachers, combining the use of videos and websites is not a common practice, even with the availability of websites developed as accompanying materials for the TV series; this is mainly due to time limitations and lack of information. Different teachers expressed that a usual thing for them to do was to use the video and the related website in different days, although close in time. Other teachers admitted it was their first time using both media in combination, since they would usually use one or the other as stand-alone resources; however, most of them expressed positive views about combining media and said they would continue to use them as complementary resources in the future.

After Web Navigation
Most participant teachers did not incorporate a specific 'after' website activity, but some of them made questions after its use. The Year 3 teacher, for example, asked the children what new things

(extra things) they learned in the website (not included in the video). The Year 6 teacher, after the children's work on online science experiments asked some questions: "Was the result what you expected? Did unexpected things happen? What did you discover?"

Nevertheless, most participant teachers implemented extra activities after the TV-internet sessions, all different in nature. Here are some examples:

The Year 1 teacher dedicated a whole day to offline activities based on the ones suggested in the *Science Clips* website. The post-media activities represented 80% of the class time; media were used only as 'detonators' for a variety of further activities.

The Year 3 teacher used not only the BBC accompanying website, but also a selection of other related websites, which were explored both collectively and individually. She included also a visit to the school library and 'the suitcase', which contained old nineteenth century objects for the children to see, touch and draw. All these activities – video, websites, library and suitcase – were intended to feed the children with information for them to write and illustrate their own 'books' about children working in Victorian Britain. The book was an integrating activity that helped children to connect information from a variety of sources (transmedia navigation).

The Year 6 teacher, after the video viewing and the web experiments and quizzes, went back to the classroom and with the aid of the chart stand and through questioning the children, wrote down a chart to summarize the main aspects about reversible and irreversible changes learned during the session. This was also an integrating activity that helped children to connect information from the TV programme and the website.

The Year 5 teacher closed the *Ancient Greece* cycle with a mini-museum, showing postcards and mini-replicas of ancient Greek objects to the children. She also linked the History *Ancient Greece* sessions with a following Art unit, where she used the British Museum website which includes models of Greek pottery for the children to copy using clay.

Year 4 teacher closed her *India* cycle with an Indian day which included music, regional food and a traditional Indian clothing trying-on for the girls.

The first thing to notice after describing the different moments of media sessions, is that there is a *before*, a *during* and an *after* for each medium, as separate entities, and not for an integrated transmedia experience as a whole. A *before* moment for the convergent media session would integrate both media in the lesson objectives. A *during* moment, would consider related activities explicitly connected to both media, taking in account that the entry point does not always have to be the television. An *after* moment, as observed in some of the media sessions described before, would be to follow-up the transmedia experience with offline related activities, creating a flowing continuum of connections even beyond media.

Underlying Concepts: Pedagogical Model, Roles Assigned to Teacher, Pupils and Media and Types of Users

The observed sessions reflect different teaching and learning styles, embody a pedagogical model and also constitute a blueprint for the roles assigned to teacher, pupils and media in the classroom.

Pedagogical Model

From the observations described it can be inferred that the lesson, at least when using media, is generally divided in three learning moments: the exposition (assigned in most cases to the video and complemented by the teacher), the activity (covered by the use of the website) and the assessment, through general discussion and/or and online quiz. It is important to notice that these three

Table 1. Instructional design of a Video-Web media session

Instructional component	Instructional resources and/or activities
Presentation of concepts and information	Video
Communication between teacher and student or between student and student about the learning content.	Teacher and students discussion
Self-study, primarily involving reading	Website
Individual practice and consolidation activities, such as exercises or essays, with some form of feedback	Website
Group activities	Teacher and students doing offline activities
Assessment and testing activities	Online quiz and/or teacher and students discussion

Based on Collis (1996: 14-15)

learning moments are components of the lesson as a whole and do not correspond to the *before*, *during* and *after* moments of the media sessions previously explored, given those are categories used to describe the cultural practices of using media as educational resources.

The previous description is very simplified and fails to fully acknowledge particular "moments" documented by the fieldwork like the teacher's explanations and questions after viewing the video, the in-depth exploration of online written texts or the extra off-line activities after using media. It was decided to compress the description to these three moments because this reflects the basic understanding of a lesson, as the Year 6 teacher explained in one of our conversations. She said that the 'three part lesson' is a common practice in England which includes: a) main input (video in the case of media sessions); b) group activity (website) and plenary to discuss what children learned (collective quiz or general discussion). She also explained that these three parts could be covered through different activities and using a variety of resources, not necessarily videos and/or websites.

The list of instructional components proposed by Collis (1996, pp. 14-15) is wider than the 'three part lesson' and from the researcher's point of view better reflects the different 'moments' that conform a media session in the primary classroom. The following list, based and adapted from Col-

lis', is the researcher's proposal of the underlying instructional design of convergent media sessions, according to what fieldwork revealed (Table 1).

Further research is needed to propose an instructional design for an authentic *convergent transmedia session*.

The Roles

Teachers and pupils are defined by other actors, like the media producers and the head teachers, but also by themselves reflexively and reciprocally.

Educational media are defined through their production and consumption (use) dynamics. Tyner (1998, p. 69) defines educational media as:

...[an array of] information resources [defined] by their purpose and audience in a euphemistic and arbitrary genre known as 'educational' media - educational television, educational software, textbooks, and so on. By separating itself into a narrowly defined category of educational resources, the genre of educational media implies that the selection and organizational function traditionally done by the teacher has been prefiltered by the producers of educational products.

However, according to information gathered through interviews with BBC media producers (Zorrilla, 2008), they do listen to teachers' opinions and incorporate their views to make their products as teacher-friendly as possible. Producers also conceive the primary teacher as a figure of power who has the authority to decide whether to use media or not, which resources, when and how. Also, the main guideline for developing educational resources is the National Curriculum, which places it as a supra-authority above teachers and producers. The Year 3 teacher expressed it this way: "TV makers tend to stick with QCA[5] units because that's what most people use" (Personal communication, November 21, 2006).

Thus, within this project and extending Cohen's definition (2001, p. 572) of educational television, *educational media resources* are understood as those created with formally articulated, explicit curricular goals.

It is important to notice that even when most educational media contents are intended to be curriculum relevant, they are not necessarily considered by the curriculum authorities. In the lesson-plans prepared by the Year 5 teacher for the *Ancient Greece* topic, which included copies of the QCA (1998) corresponding unit, it was found that in the "Resources" section for Unit 14, postcards, maps, stories and books were mentioned, but not videos or websites. In spite of this absence, in her lesson plans she included the BBC TV series as an important component. Teachers do not like to feel bounded by the QCA-defined units.

Teachers continue to operate as gatekeepers for media access; they still decide whether to use media or not, which media, when and how; they decide which is the function of each medium in relation with the lesson plan as a whole.

Educational television has many roles which depend on the teacher, the pupils and the teaching moment: an 'enriching' element (Fawdry, 1967, p. 23); a 'curriculum component' (Choat, 1982); a 'window to/on the world', for having a glimpse of different times and places (a common understanding in literature about educational TV); a curriculum-driven 'dictator' who would assume

the instructional role if left by the teacher (Tan, 1989, p. 513).

The internet has many faces too: a 'dangerous gateway' to the world (most techno-apocalyptics); 'peripheral to the core curriculum' (Ward Schofield, 2006, p. 532); "an 'extra' rather than something I would build into a lesson" (Year 5 teacher); a 'fun environment' for practicing skills, experimenting, looking for information and even creating (most participant teachers in this project); a game-console, a video-player, a giant encyclopaedia (participant children in this project).

Within this project the most relevant aspect of the roles' definition is not only how producers, teachers and children understand media, and therefore create and use them, but how they understand convergence and if they 'connect' media contents while developing and using them.

Producers develop their contents to operate as stand-alone and/or related products according to this project's findings, but at the end of the day it is teachers who decide to use them as stand-alone or convergent resources. It is teachers who guide the children to find those connections, even with apparently unrelated resources. It is teachers who ask "What has this website to do with the video we just viewed?" or "What is the relation of this video with the online experiment we made yesterday?" The teacher not only decides whether to use these contents as isolated resources or in combination, but also which the entry point for the transmedia experience is. It is the teacher who decides the temporal proximity between different media and what comes before, in-between and after the media.

However, 'almighty' visions of the teachers should be critically appraised, since there are issues to consider that are beyond their control, such as: a) Technical limitations and problems; b) Availability and opportunity (or lack of them) of information generated by the producers about the existing resources and how to make the best use of them, including the non-existence – based on the analysed resources – of explicit information about how to combine the use of TV series and accompanying website; c) Occasional practices of 'personal video-libraries' which prevent teachers from knowing what resources are available in school.

Active or Passive Users: Clicking Around, Reading and Interactivity

The convergent use of educational television and the internet in schools reflects the teachers' understanding of the televisual experience as the entry point, an introduction, and the internet as the practice, the hands-on experience for children. These basic assumptions lead to concepts and issues to be explored in this segment: particularly the idea of active/passive users.

Active or Passive Users
There are no media passive users: the user can be mentally and/or physically active, but never passive, unless he or she is totally disengaged and even in that case, the user would be mentally active, probably thinking about other things different from the content being presented by the medium, but marginally registering some of it. "Research on learning shows that meaningful learning depends on the learner's cognitive activity during learning rather than on the learner's behavioural activity during learning" (Mayer, 2005, p. 14).

Therefore, discussions about television viewers perceived as 'couch potatoes' and computer users as 'empowered agents' or distinctions of television as a 'sit back' technology and computers as a 'lean forward' technology (Uricchio, 2004, p. 171) are not ideas taken up in this chapter. Rather than adopting simple binary distinctions, the levels of activity and/or engagement of the two key users in the classroom, the teacher and the pupils, are the issues explored through this segment.

When viewing a video the teacher is mentally active in most cases, unless he or she has viewed it several times before. What was found from interviews with teachers, it is not uncommon for them to view the video for the first time with the children (and the reasons for this will be explored later in this chapter); therefore, teachers have to pay attention to the video in order to be able to guide the after-viewing discussion. This is why teachers read the programme's synopsis included in the teacher's book, when available, to have an idea before the viewing, and would welcome the inclusion of such information in the accompanying websites, which as a norm do not include information about the series. The next step in teacher's involvement would include pausing the video at strategic points and introducing explanations, examples or questions, but this would require, for an optimal application, familiarity with the resource. A further level of engagement would require the teacher to develop materials (questions, charts, quizzes) for the children to use during and/ or after the media activity. Again, for doing so, a previous familiarity with the material is necessary.

Pupils viewing a video are more likely to focus or sharpen their attention on core aspects if they are instructed before the viewing to take notes or look for specific information. However, note-taking should be considered carefully because it can distract them from the viewing activity, especially because of the dynamic pace of most series and the cognitive demands it implies. This obstacle could easily be solved by using the pausing and rewinding controls while viewing the programme; unfortunately, as commented before, these are hardly ever used. Yet, the trend of viewing online videos, if generalised within the educational sphere, would allow pupils to take control of their viewing and self-pace it, giving them time to process the information and, if necessary, take notes.

The website use requires the teacher to be involved in supervisor, assistant and guide capacities throughout the whole session. Younger children make more use of the assistant capacity and older ones require more supervision. Teachers' assistance ranges from helping the children to access the website to explaining how to interact with a specific game or tool. The supervision role is mainly about keeping the children within the selected website and/or sections doing the activities they were instructed to do.

Some teachers delegate the guiding role to the website design, counting on the menus and audio/written instructions for the children to move around; however, as mentioned before, there are teachers who decide *a priori* which web sections are going to be used and how. For the later to happen, familiarity with the website and identification of sections or features to be used during the media session are necessary, especially because the websites, even the ones developed by the BBC to accompany TV series, do not include guidance for teachers on how to combine its use with video resources. However, most teachers do not browse thoroughly the websites they use.

Clicking Around and Superficial Reading

For the children, using a website is a self-paced experience and they should take advantage of that possibility to explore in detail the available information or activities. Paradoxically, many of them rush around the website and, if instructed to take-notes, tend to copy the texts literally, a practice that is believed to be drawn on extensively in later stages of their educational life, if we consider the challenges of cyber-plagiarism in middle and higher education. Note-taking remains as a standard practice for retrieving information from any source and it was observed in several sessions how children struggled to handwrite, pushing the keyboard aside while exploring a website. Few teachers in primary school open the option for electronic note-taking and seem cautious of introducing the copying-pasting facilities.

Tuman (1992, p. 69) claims that hypertext discourages deep reading and encourages superficial reading, skimming, and frenetic motion.

Doing research about how students use a novel in CD-ROM, Jewitt (2002) found that they all chose to use the visual option, which included video clips, still images and written text screens. This is particularly interesting because it is not like a book adapted to film; even with the video component it maintains the presence of the original text. However, some students she observed located the video clips and *sat back*, hands off the mouse and keyboard, and watched the videos. These students by-passed the novel as a written text and engaged with it as a multi-modal video text (p. 185). She also observed the frenetic clicking-around phenomenon: "Student 3 clicks on the forward icon every two seconds and moves through the next 14 screens. [...] The students' 'flicking' movement through the still images of the chapter 'animates' the text like a cartoon" (pp. 185-186).

The Year 5 teacher commented about the British Museum site regarding the researcher's observations of superficial reading:

I could totally understand why the children just click, click, click and don't read things in depth... because there's lots and lots of information in there and yes, you do need to read it in order to do the challenge, but it's not very exciting...The children only find appealing the challenges and they prefer to face them intuitively and not going through the information. (Personal communication, February 8, 2007)

Considering the previous point of view, some questions that arise are: if they don't read and learn, what is the purpose of using the website? Are they 'reading' in a different way? Why does learning have to be fun? Rey Valzacchi (2007) says: Learning is not always fun or light. There is no magical learning and even Harry Potter and friends need to read a pile of books and practice their spells until they get them right.

The Year 4 teacher commented:

Only few children are capable of exploring a website... others just waste their time or can get hooked with distracting links... I thought it was better if I guided them through, so they've had a structure to work with... We were learning also to use a text... read the texts and find info to do a task... in a sense that's what most adults use internet for. (Personal communication, November 23, 2006)

It appears then that activities designed to challenge the children and 'force' them to read and think, like the popular Web Quest can be a way for improving children's involvement, consequently enhancing their learning experience. In designing these activities, the role of the teacher as mentor (mediator) is crucial. However there are two problems with this approach: a) these activities are mainly focused on informative sites, such as the ones designed for subjects like History or Geography; and b) they require more time from the teachers, a resource that is limited according to those who were interviewed. Laurillard (1994) reports similar findings: resource-based learning allows pupils to explore and discover information for themselves, although this only works well when the activity is properly supported.

Interactivity
Websites are not only written, visual or audio texts (or a combination of them), interactive features, such as activities, games and quizzes need to be very well designed in order to cognitively involve children; otherwise they tend to approach these by 'guessing' and 'trial-error' without gaining skills, new knowledge or comprehension of the educational content. In other cases, because progress in some interactive resources depends on user input, they fail to advance and opt for 'jumping' to another section instead of getting involved and seriously try to solve the problem.

Fisch (2005, p. 58) argues that the key is to "place the educational content at the heart of engaging game play, so that children employ the targeted academic skills and knowledge as an integral part of playing the game", however this is not easy to accomplish. Challenges and quizzes based on previous reading are not very well accepted by children. On the other hand, if the knowledge to be tested is obtained through virtual experiences (as in the *Science Clips* – now *Revision* site) the quiz is more successful and they are more likely to approach it based on the knowledge and experience acquired, rather than guessing. One resource for offering information without too much reading (written text) is the interactive exploratory activity, based on animated graphical representations, like those offered by the British Museum's *Ancient Greece* site or the *Science Clips* experiments. In these, if their "guess" is incorrect the feedback tools tell them what is not allowed, or why they are doing something wrong; even when the guessing is correct they receive extra information and therefore the learning is more likely to be accomplished.

The mentioned resources all have in common one feature: *interactivity*. In this project, interactivity is understood as the user-machine interaction; although the social dimensions user-machine-user and user-machine-community are acknowledged, these are not present in the primary educational sites developed by *BBC Schools* to accompany TV series. However, it is important to notice that BBC resources for secondary students do include tools based on social online interactions.

In the sites children used, the different interactive features were based on real time responses to user's input, going from the basic active link, or 'play' button in a video or audio player, to more sophisticated forms of response such as the changing results in science experiments when the variables were modified.

Interactive features *per se* are not the answer to online learning challenges; the way they are designed and how they are integrated within the learning experience yield very different outcomes.

Laurillard (1994, p. 15), reporting on her findings on multimedia learning, argues that "new features of interactive video systems (moving video, interaction with video, high quality sound and visuals, high-capacity information storage) only achieve their potential when on-line work is combined with off-line work, when interactivity is used to support pupils with meaningful feedback, and when pupils are helped to develop their information-handling skills".

Moreover, her analysis "suggests that the interactive capability of new technology does have a disadvantage. The immediacy of its response and the pull of its attendance on the user's next action conspire to reduce attention to the outcome of the previous action" (Ibid., p. 14). This is a good explanation for the *clicking around* practice commented before.

In addition to the previous considerations, Richards (2006) and Fisch (2004) both argue that interactivity is also about the content generation possibilities offered by the media. For Richards (2006, 537), "both interactivity and user production can occur outside of 'screen-based media'", but he also recognizes that this generation can be "facilitated by the package, in the package, and through the package". Fisch (2004, p. 107) comments that "interactive authoring tools provide children with the opportunity to incorporate a broader range of media in their creations". From the researcher's point of view, even when generation can occur online or offline, the medium resource can only be credited for promoting it when it offers the space or the tools for it to happen.

User activity (or passivity), practices like clicking around or superficial reading and different understandings of interactivity are covered in this section because all them are related directly or indirectly to convergent media. Transmedia navigation, for instance, requires cognitively active users all the way through the convergent media experience, since they need to make connections across information presented by different media.

Intuitive navigation (instead of reading) presents an excellent area of opportunity for transmedia activity designing, given video clips are easier deliverers of key information for young users than written text. Interactivity understood as the possibility for users to author content is a way of developing new media skills, described in detail by Jenkins et al. (2009).

Provisional Conclusions

Before moving on to the opinions and perceptions part of these findings, which draws on the teachers' interviews and questionnaires responses by the children, it is important to round-up some provisional conclusions.

At present, educational televisual resources and related websites are separate worlds, not only from a consumption (or use) point of view, but also from a cultural perspective. Despite the convergence or intertextual contents due to production strategies and/or the centrality of the National Curriculum, teachers tend to isolate each medium from the other or to choose only one of them as a teaching tool.

However, this is changing as: a) teachers are discovering how to combine these resources and are gradually moving from the activities suggested by the teacher's books that accompanied the TV series to richer related resources such as websites; b) convergent technologies are defusing the borders between different media: the whiteboard, where contents can smoothly flow from DVD to website; the laptop trolleys, which bring the ICT suite to the classroom; or the increasing availability of on-line videos, including educational ones, which allow individual experiences of video reproduction.

Does this mean convergence is at last happening? If yes, is it really happening in the school context? Or is the internet just the new educational medium which will eventually replace (or absorb) television? How do teachers and pupils perceive the confluence of the two media within the classroom?

Opinions and Perceptions from Teachers and Children Regarding the Convergent Use of Educational Media and Learning Outcomes

The Teachers

About Educational TV Series Having their Own Websites

All interviewed teachers expressed positive views about TV programmes having their own websites. However, some of their comments reflected particular views and uses of these resources:

When a website's main purpose is to deliver information, as in the History sites, it is important that it offers different or deeper information from the one presented on the video. The Year 3 teacher noticed the 'official' website was reiterative – talking about the *Children in Victorian Britain* site regarding its related video – and thus opted to use different websites to complement and/or enrich the video content.

On the other hand, when the purpose was to reinforce a skill, like spelling strategies, teachers welcomed the availability of websites which included opportunities for the children to engage in activities and exercises.

How They Perceive Each Medium

As a means of retrieving their ideas and perceptions of each medium, the teachers were asked about their preferences. The majority expressed no preference; they said they were happy working with either or both (video and internet) and that their choice was mostly based on the subject, the topic and the availability of resources. One teacher mentioned that the ethos of the class was also a point to consider when selecting resources. Two teachers mentioned that websites are particularly

useful for History and Geography and a third one added Science.

Two teachers said they preferred the internet because children have access to more hands-on activities and so are more involved. On the other hand, one teacher mentioned she prefers videos because she feels more in control having all the class doing one thing.

However, research in multimedia learning theory contradicts some of the teachers' views about 'doing' as the best way to accomplish learning:

You might suppose that the best way to promote meaningful learning is through hands-on activity, such as a highly interactive multimedia program. However, behavioral activity per se does not guarantee cognitively active learning. It is possible to engage in hands-on activities that do not promote active cognitive processing... in other situations... learners can achieve meaningful learning in a behaviorally inactive environment such as a multimedia instructional message. (Mayer 2005, 14-15)

About the Combined Use of Media

Teachers reported that they liked using TV series and websites in an integrated way; nevertheless, they expressed some critical views:

- The website should include information and activities for being used in combination with the TV series, and not only related to the website contents. In the same way, the teacher's books accompanying the DVD should include activities for using the DVD with its website. However, they both need to be designed to be used as stand-alone resources.

Bates, back in the early 80's previewed the need for a rich back-up system for teachers when using integrated media based on his experience with the Open University:

...there needs to be an extensive system of back-up facilities for programmes, not only in terms of notes, cassettes, books, but also in terms of local organizers and teachers, and that efforts must be made to clarify the different roles to be played by each 'component' of the system. (Bates, 1980, p. 399)

- It is not advisable to use the whole thing when websites contain a lot of information. It works better to select only some sections.
- If the website does not offer different ability levels, it is good idea to use mixed-ability groups.
- The biggest problem for the integrated use of media is lack of time; both within the lesson time-slot and for pre-exploring the resources. Regarding the first, the Year 6 teacher explained:

I tend to use one or the other, mostly because of the time constraints... I've got only an hour (two at the most), normally only one hour... so by the time we finish the video, which is normally 20 minutes long, you've only got 40 minutes left, so in that time you need to do some active teaching as well, not just let the video do the teaching, so it would not be practical to use both in the same lesson. (Personal communication, December 18, 2006)

Lack of time is also an issue regarding pre-viewing programmes and pre-browsing websites, not to mention developing transmedia activities or doing curriculum integration. Most participant teachers said that they would consider using new resources if a variety of rich back-up materials was readily available (organised lists of resources, summaries of programmes' and websites, curriculum relevance, suggestions for on-line and off-line activities). Tan (1989), Wragg (1993) and Dirr (2001) report similar findings.

About Learning and Fun

Among the interviewed teachers, there is a generalised impression that children have more fun using the website than watching videos and therefore teachers perceive this as an advantage of the internet.

However, in the session where the *Children in Victorian Britain* resources were used, the Year 3 teacher commented that even when *Magic Grandad* was more fun for learning History, she thought children learnt more with materials that delivered information in a more direct way, like the series *Children in Victorian Britain*, and not through a story, where the information is incidental. "Some people think that children have to be older to be given direct information and I think that is not true" (Personal communication, November 21, 2006).

The contrasting learning results from direct to indirect delivery of information might be related to what Fisch (2004) says about comprehension of media content being enhanced when the educational content is integral, rather than tangential, to the narrative: "When the two are closely intertwined, the narrative draws viewers' attention toward the educational content, but when they are only tangentially related, the narrative can pull attention away from the content instead" (Ibid., 108).

About one of the *Spellits* videos, the Year 5 teacher expressed her concerns about them being too much fun. "They put a lot of comedy in it, and yes, it is important, but you have to get the balance right, because with too much fun, the children can lose the point of the teaching activities" (Personal communication, November 28, 2006).

Individual or Collective

As previously discussed, it was found out that collective use of a website is a more common practice in First School and individual use is the

generalised practice in Middle School. These are some teachers' views about this particular issue:
Year 5 teacher:

Most sites are designed for individual children to work on them, but if you had more elements, perhaps of some kind of competition within the site, so that it was actually designed for more than one child to use it at a time it could work equally well... there is no chance for different people to input different ideas into the site, if there was, I think it would be quite successful, but I haven't come across one yet that does. (Personal communication, November 28, 2006).

Related to the previous idea, it is important to mention that the cancelled *BBC Jam* actually included multi-user educational games and registered users were able to create or join existing groups and make playlists.

The Year 6 teacher commented also about this topic:

We do the quiz collectively at the beginning of the lesson, to check what we already know... and then we would investigate the ones we had wrong... I tend to use it a lot like that because you start it off and you can go back to it at the end and get all them right, it's like a checklist I'd say... I do use it with the whole class as well as individually. (Personal communication, December 18, 2006)

About Available Resources

All participant teachers tend to use only the available videos at school, when they are aware of their existence.

It is important to point out that even though the contents are still available on a regular basis on open television, recording broadcasting television is not a common practice anymore. Apparently, the generalised practice within schools consists of buying BBC products from BBC Active, both DVD packages and interactive resources to be used with the Whiteboard.

About Media Literacies

Some teachers think that through teaching *with* media they offer the children an opportunity for learning *about* media, and that is not always true: "...media literacy necessarily involves 'reading' and 'writing' media. Media education therefore aims to develop *both* critical understanding *and* active participation" (Buckingham, 2003, p. 4)

A problem when using media resources for teaching-learning is that some teachers assume children are already media literate. Watching television is a daily experience for most children and thanks to DVD extra features many children are very well informed about media production (behind the scenes). Nevertheless, the critical understanding of media does not develop spontaneously and it is not proportionally related to the number of hours exposed to a medium. Similarly, knowing how to click around a website does not mean the child is really exploring its contents and moreover, understanding them. In many cases, children approach their internet experiences retrieving their competences as videogame players or TV zappers, more than their written-word-reader abilities, performing a *clicking around navigation*, a superficial scanning of the web pages with an almost anxious need to click on every active element. This could be a successful strategy for approaching certain interactive games and activities, but not for written text websites.

Two important things to notice about media literacies are: a) that familiarity with the 'old' TV does not mean we are already TV literate and critical appraisals of educational programmes, especially from the teachers, would be an ingredient that could add value to media sessions; b) that the novelty of the internet unveils new competences to develop, listed by different scholars, including nonlinear reading, manipulation of different types of texts, and more complex skills like creative and critical browsing, researching, organising, selecting and producing a variety of communication forms.

The Children

About Educational TV Series Having Their Own Websites and the Combined Use of Media
Most children said they liked TV series having websites. However, they were not very eloquent about their reasons, which are summarized through a selection of quotes:

"I think it was very fun and interesting. I really had a great time and I think that it is very nice to watch a programme like that and then finish going to the ICT room". (Year 5)

Talking about the websites they expressed:

"It is quite fun". (Year 3 and Year 5)

"You can go places and find lots of information". (Year 4)

"I like the quizzes because you can find out if you are right or wrong"; other child thought that they were useful for knowing "how good you are". (Year 4 and Year 6)

"You can do stuff... like games" (Year 5)

"It's good in case you did not understand the TV programme". (Year 6)

"You can experiment yourself". (Year 6)

"You can re-visit content you did not understand or questions you had wrong in the quiz". (Year 6)

How They Perceive Each Medium
TV is interesting, but the internet is fun. Most children say that they like using websites more than watching videos. Considering the social dynamics involved, it is understandable that some of the aspects they like about using the web are the freedom to choose, either to do the quiz or click around and eventually find a game to play, the relaxed individual supervision, the changing of physical space (when they use the ICT suite), the possibility of some chatting and giggling with peers. On the other hand, while the videos might be funny sometimes, and children's laughter confirms this, they generally have to behave and keep quiet while they watch, not their idea of having fun.

Most of the website "likers" mentioned the words "fun", "game" or "play" related to the website... also "doing stuff", "joining in" (being active) or having freedom ("doing what you want") versus "just watching" (being passive) in the case of TV.

However, it is important to mention that about 30% of the participant children preferred television and some of the reasons they expressed were: "because it is fun", "because I learn", "because it explains things in a way I understand".

Regarding modalities they seem to have very specific ideas about each medium: television "tells" you things and the website has pictures you can print and games you can play, so they identify the TV more like an "audio" medium and the web as a "visual" and "interactive" one.

About Teachers' and Children's Opinions and Perceptions
Even though educational TV series and related websites are designed as stand alone resources, media producers and also teachers can design transmedia activities to create connections between them, in a similar way as Web Quests create connections between unrelated websites. The different perceptions of each medium's ethos are a useful guidance to define their role in the transmedia experience. In this line of thought, the researcher developed ideas for some convergent media activities such as the *Media Quest*, the

Media Review, the *Media Journal* and the *Media Make-Over* (Zorrilla, 2008).

Transmedia experiences can be understood by media producers and teachers also as transcurricular adventures which do not need to be constrained to the time limits of an ordinary lesson.

The socialized or communalized use of media can be understood from a wide perspective, from sharing transmedia activities between teachers, in a similar way as Web Quests and PowerPoint presentations are shared, to the collective approach of media activities, especially online, not only within the group limits, but also seeking for sharing and collaborating with peer groups in other geographical locations.

CONCLUSION

In the United Kingdom, convergent production of educational media is a reality and the trend is to integrate different media into one rich medium, which is the internet, to be used both collectively (whiteboard) and individually (ICT rooms, laptop trolleys and mobile devices). However, convergent use of educational media at school is still a practice under construction and it will not establish itself as an integrated resource in the classroom unless users, especially teachers, embrace media convergence as an enriching possibility for teaching and learning. Whatever happens in the entertainment industry, and no matter how often 'convergence' is used to name technical achievements such as being able to download your favourite TV series to your mobile phone, convergence in the classroom will only be a reality when contents from different media converge not only on the screens, but also in the minds of teachers and children. For this to happen, a strong back-up system for teachers is needed, given their strategic role as mediators, at least at primary level.

However, there might be an alternative opportunity for educational media convergence beyond the classroom, considering that teenagers are perceived by producers as direct users who don't need teachers as gatekeepers (mediators) anymore. The profile of the teenager is particularly interesting, because he/she is considered as representative of the Net Generation, which is defined by John Millner in the following terms:

Secondary children are the Net Generation... for them the web is totally normal, like the TV, they don't see it as anything special... By the time UK children hit secondary school something like 90% have mobile phone and they are extremely web literate... We started [innovative web services] at the secondary end (KS4)... but actually the net generation gets younger and younger, now most kids at the top of primary school have mobile phones... we will need to rethink that, and increasingly the kind of innovative methods of distribution that we are using for GSCE bitesize will be used for lower levels. (J. Millner, BBC Schools Online Editor, personal communication, June 8, 2007)

Kristin Mason described how *BBC Jam* perceived young users:

... to get teenagers involved in a subject, inspired by that subject, you need to provide an experience which encourages them to seek more and to take things further and take that quest for information, into finding out more, in pursuing acquiring knowledge and learning... BBC Jam didn't assume that they were supported by an adult... it assumed that they could well be working on their own... (Kristin Mason, Commissioner for BBC Jam, personal communication, April 26, 2007)

If children are capable of developing by themselves (including peer mediation) new media literacies such as transmedia navigation, and furthermore, use those skills for learning, then convergence culture in education will be a reality, but not in classroom, which continues to be the teacher's dominium. The innovative and challenging resources developed by media producers, at the moment mainly targeted to teenagers, might be the key to hook children into educational convergence culture.

FUTURE RESEARCH DIRECTIONS

The production phase of this project, not reported in this chapter, explored what is done by educational media developers and emerging trends, such as the online *Rich Media* model, which consists of a combination of all media experiences –televisual, audio, internet and games– merged into one rich medium and delivered online.

Being the *Rich Media* model the latest trend form a production perspective, it is paradoxical how the industry, apparently more worried about its profits than about education, has exerted great pressure on the BBC to close some of its newest educational services, all representative of the *Rich Media* model: first, it was the *BBC Jam*, the digital online curriculum, which was forced to close on March 2007 and more recently, the BBC Trust froze the budgets of three online learning services (*Bitesize*, *Learning Zone Broadband* and the *Learning Portal*) pending a review of their market impact. "The investment freeze follows a complaint from the British Educational Suppliers Association (BESA)…" (The Guardian, October 8, 2009).

The new BBC's *Rich Media* model, still under construction and strongly challenged by the industry, is resulting in new content and services, but also in re-versioned, repurposed, recycled, chopped and up-dated versions of the resources created under previous models. But, will these contents reach the students? It seems that the BBC is struggling to generate innovative contents and services for the net generation within a hostile competitive environment.

Thus, considering the undeniable impact of production and market dynamics in the users' end of the media flow, it is suggested that future research on educational media and educational contents, should follow, as this research project does, a wide vision that encompasses production, contents and users, since these three aspects are closely related and what is observed in the classroom is only a fraction of what it is really happening around educational media.

REFERENCES

Bates, A. W. (1980). Towards a Better Theoretical Framework for Studying Learning from Educational Television. *Instructional Science*, *9*, 393–415. doi:10.1007/BF00121771

Bennett, M., & Smith, D. (1988). Evaluating Television-Linked Computer Software. *Computers & Education*, *12*(1), 133–139. doi:10.1016/0360-1315(88)90068-1

Buckingham, D. (2003). *Media education: literacy, learning and contemporary culture*. Cambridge, UK: Polity.

Choat, E. (1982). Teachers' use of Educational Television in Infants' Schools. *Educational Studies*, *8*(3), 185–207. doi:10.1080/0305569820080302

Cohen, M. (2001). The Role of Research in Educational Television. In Singer, D. G., & Singer, J. L. (Eds.), *Handbook of Children and the Media* (pp. 571–586). Thousand Oaks, CA: Sage Publications Inc.

Collins, W. A., Sobol, B. L., & Westby, S. (1981). Effects of adult commentary on children's comprehension and inferences about a televised aggressive portrayal. *Child Development*, *52*(1), 158–163. doi:10.2307/1129225

Collis, B. (1996). *Tele-learning in a Digital World. The Future of Distance Learning*. London: International Thomson Computer Press.

Crook, D. (2007). School Broadcasting in the United Kingdom: An Exploratory History. *Journal of Educational Administration and History, 39*(3), 217–226. doi:10.1080/00220620701698341

Department for Education and Skills. (2004). *Information and Communications Technology in Schools in England: 2004 (Provisional)*. London, U.K. Retrieved April 2008 from http://www.dfes. gov.uk/rsgateway/DB/SFR/s000480/index.shtml

Desmond, R. (2001). Free Reading: Implications for Child Development. In Singer, D. G., & Singer, J. L. (Eds.), *Handbook of Children and Media* (pp. 29–46). Thousand Oaks, CA: Sage Publications, Inc.

Dirr, P. J. (2001). Cable Television. Gateway to Educational Resources for Development at All Ages. In Singer, D. G., & Singer, J. L. (Eds.), *Handbook of Children and the Media* (pp. 533–545). Thousand Oaks, CA: Sage Publications, Inc.

Fawdry, K. (1967). School Television in the BBC. In Moir, G. (Ed.), *Teaching and Television: ETV explained* (pp. 13–30). London: Pergamon Press.

Fisch, S. M. (2000). A Capacity Model of Children's Comprehension of Educational Content on Television. *Media Psychology, 2*(1), 63–91. doi:10.1207/S1532785XMEP0201_4

Fisch, S. M. (2004). What's so 'new' about 'new media'?: Comparing effective features of children's educational software, television, and magazines. *IDC, 1*(3), 105–111. doi:10.1145/1017833.1017847

Fisch, S. M. (2005). Making Educational Computer Games 'Educational'. *IDC* June, 56-61.

Freedman, D. (2006). Internet transformations: 'old' media resilience in the 'new media' revolution. In Curran, J., & Morley, D. (Eds.), *Media and Cultural Theory* (pp. 275–290). London: Routledge.

Hobbs, R. (2006). Non-optimal uses of video in the classroom. *Learning, Media and Technology, 31*(1), 35–50. doi:10.1080/17439880500515457

Inglis, A., Ling, P., & Joosten, V. (1999). *Delivering Digitally. Managing the Transition to the Knowledge Media*. London: Kogan Page Limited.

Ito, M., Horst, H., Bittanti, M., Boyd, D., Herr-Stephenson, B., Lange, P. G., et al. with Baumer, S., Cody, R., Mahendran, D., Martínez, K., Perkel, D., Sims, C. and Tripp, L. (2008). *Living and Learning with New Media: Summary of Findings from the Digital Youth Project*. The John D. and Catherine T. MacArtur Foundation Reports on Digital Media and Learning. Retrieved April 2010 from: www.macfound.org.

Jenkins, H. (2006). *Convergence Culture: Where Old and New Media Collide*. New York: New York University Press.

Jenkins, H., Purushotma, R., Wigel, M., Clinton, K., & Robinson, A. J. (2009). *Confronting the Challenges of Participatory Culture: Media Education for the 21st Century. The John D. and Catherine T. MacArtur Foundation Reports on Digital Media and Learning*. Cambridge, MA: MIT Press.

Jewitt, C. (2002). The move from page to screen: the multimodal reshaping of school English. *Visual Communication, 1*(2), 171–195. doi:10.1177/147035720200100203

Kompare, D. (2006). Publishing Flow. DVD Box Sets and the Reconception of Television. *Television & New Media, 7*(4), 335–360. doi:10.1177/1527476404270609

Kress, G. (2003). *Literacy in the New Media Age*. New York: Routledge. doi:10.4324/9780203164754

Laurillard, D., & Taylor, J. (1994). Designing the stepping stones: An evaluation of interactive media in the classroom. *Journal of Educational Television, 20*(3), 169, 16 p. Retrieved as Microsoft Word document on April 2010 from: http://kn.open.ac.uk/public/document.cfm?docid=944

Lévy, P. (1997). *Cyberculture*. Minneapollis, MN: University of Minnesota Press.

Mayer, R. E. (2005). Introduction to Multimedia Learning. In Mayer, R. E. (Ed.), *The Cambridge Handbook of Multimedia Learning* (pp. 1–16). Cambridge, UK: Cambridge University Press.

Mayer, R. E. (Ed.). (2005). *The Cambridge Handbook of Multimedia Learning*. Cambridge, UK: Cambridge University Press.

McCormick, S. (1986). Software and Television - A New Approach. *Computers & Education, 10*(1), 17–24. doi:10.1016/0360-1315(86)90046-1

Miles, M. B., & Huberman, A. M. (1994). *Qualitative Data Analysis: an expanded sourcebook*. Thousand Oaks, CA: Sage Publications.

Moss, R., & Gunter, B. (1991). Teachers using Television. *Journal of Educational Television, 17*(2), 109.

Pérez de Silva, J. (2000). *La televisión ha muerto*. Barcelona: Gedisa.

Rantanen, T. (2005). The message is the medium. An interview with Manuel Castells. *Global Media and Communication, 1*(2), 135–147. doi:10.1177/1742766505054629

Rey Valzacchi, J. (2007). 'Novedosismo' educativo, o ¿por qué Harry Potter no aprende 'por arte de magia'? *El Magazine de Horizonte Informática Educativa, 88*. Retrieved March 2008 from: http://www.horizonteweb.com/magazine/Numero88.htm

Reynolds, R. E., & Anderson, R. C. (1982). Influence of Questions on the Allocation of Attention during Reading. *Journal of Educational Psychology, 74*(5), 623–632. doi:10.1037/0022-0663.74.5.623

Richards, R. (2006). Users, Interactivity and Generation. *New Media & Society, 8*(4), 531–550. doi:10.1177/1461444806064485

Schnotz, W. (2005). An Integrated Model of Text and Picture Comprehension. In Mayer, R. E. (Ed.), *The Cambridge Handbook of Multimedia Learning* (pp. 49–70). Cambridge, UK: Cambridge University Press.

Scott, K. D., & White, A. M. (2003). Unnatural history? Deconstructing the Walking with Dinosaurs phenomenon. *Media Culture & Society, 25*(3), 315–332.

Silverstone, R. (2005). Mediation and communication. In Calhoun, C., Rojek, C., & Turner, B. (Eds.), *International Handbook of Sociology*. London: Sage.

Tan, K.-S. (1989). *The uses of television in primary schools. Case studies in Malaysia and England*. Unpublished PhD thesis, School of Education, University of East Anglia. Norwich, U.K.

Tuman, M. (1992). *Word Perfect: Literacy in the Computer Age*. London: The Falmer Press.

Tyner, K. (1998). *Literacy in a Digital World*. Mahwah, NJ: Lawrence Erlbaum Associates.

Uricchio, W. (2004). Television's Next Generation: Technology/Interface Culture/Flow. In Spigel, L., & Olsson, J. (Eds.), *Television After TV. Essays on a Medium in Transition* (pp. 232–261). Durham, London: Duke University Press.

Ward Schofield, J. (2006). Internet Use in Schools. In Sawyer, R. K. (Ed.), *The Cambridge Handbook of the Learning Sciences* (pp. 521–534). Cambridge, UK: Cambridge University Press.

Wragg, E. C. (1993). Multi-media in education: Bane or boon? *Journal of Educational Television, 19*(2), 73–79.

Zorrilla Abascal, M. L. (2008). *Educational Television Beyond the TV Set: Educational Media Convergence in UK and a Proposal for the Mexican Model.* Unpublished PhD Thesis, School of Education and Lifelong Learning, University of East Anglia, Norwich, U.K.

ADDITIONAL READING

Ancient Greece. in BBC Schools.(n.d.). Multiple dates of access from February 2006 to October 2007, URL: http://www.bbc.co.uk/schools/ancientgreece/

Ancient Greece. in The British Museum. (n.d.). Multiple dates of access from February 2006 to October 2007, URL: http://www.ancientgreece.co.uk/

BBC Learning Zone Broadband Clips Library. in BBC website.(n.d.). Multiple dates of access from November 2007 to May 2008, URL: http://www.bbc.co.uk/learningzone/clips/

Children in Victorian Britain. in BBC Schools. (n.d.). Multiple dates of access from February 2006 to October 2007, URL: http://www.bbc.co.uk/schools/victorians/

Gibson, O. Media correspondent (2008, February 28). No relaunch for £150m BBC Jam. *The Guardian.* Retrieved February 29, 2008 from http://www.guardian.co.uk/theguardian

Jam, B. B. C. in BBC website. (n.d.). Multiple dates of access from February-November 2006, URL: http://www.bbc.co.uk/jam

Johnson, B. (2007, December 3). Channel 4 axes TV schools programmes. *The Guardian.* Retrieved December 4, 2007 from http://www.guardian.co.uk/theguardian

KS2 Bitesize Revision. in BBC website. (n.d.). Multiple dates of access from May 2006 to November 2007, URL: http://www.bbc.co.uk/schools/ks2bitesize/index.shtml

KnowledgeBox Primary Learning Environment website.(n.d.). Date of access: May 2007, URL: www.uk.knowledgebox.com

Mason, Kristin – Producer (2003). *Science Clips.* London: BBC Schools.

Nott, Sue – Executive Producer (2001). *Spell it out.* London: BBC Schools.

Nott, Sue – Executive Producer (2003). *Romans in Britain* (2003) London: BBC Schools.

Nott, Sue – Executive Producer (2005). *India* (2005) London: BBC Schools.

Plunkett, J. (2009, October 8). BBC freezes budgets of three online learning services after review. *The Guardian.* Retrieved December 5, 2009 from http://www.guardian.co.uk/theguardian

Romans in Britain. in BBC Schools. (n.d.). Multiple dates of access from February 2006 to October 2007, URL: http://www.bbc.co.uk/schools/romans/

Schools, B. B. C. in BBC website. (n.d.). Multiple dates of access from October 2005-May 2008, URL: (http://www.bbc.co.uk/schools/)

Science Clips. in BBC Schools. (n.d.). Multiple dates of access from February 2006 to October 2007, URL: http://www.bbc.co.uk/schools/scienceclips/

Scott, Moira – Executive Producer (2001). *Children in Victorian Britain.* Scotland: BBC Schools Scotland.

Scott, Moira – Executive Producer (2004). *Ancient Greece.* Scotland: BBC Schools Scotland.

Spelling with the Spellits. in BBC Schools. (n.d.). Multiple dates of access from February 2006 to October 2007, URL: http://www.bbc.co.uk/schools/spellits/

Welcome to India. in Snaith Primary website. (n.d.). Multiple dates of access from February 2006 to September 2006, URL: http://home.freeuk.net/elloughton13/india.htm

KEY TERMS AND DEFINITIONS

BBC Schools: Educational media products and services provided by the BBC to basic schools in Britain. Includes radio, print, television and web resources.

Media Convergence: The confluence of two or more media from the phase of production to the phase of consumption or use.

Convergence Culture: The cultural practice of following, integrating and combining contents across different media.

Educational Media: Media resources created with formally articulated explicit curricular goals.

Educational Television: Television resources created with formally articulated explicit curricular goals.

Educational Web: Web resources created with formally articulated explicit curricular goals.

Schools TV: Television resources generated within BBC Schools.

Schools Online: Web resources generated within BBC Schools.

Transmedia Navigation: The ability to follow the flow of stories and information across multiple modalities

ENDNOTES

[1] Research project supported by the Programme Alβan, the European Union Programme of High Level Scholarships for Latin America, scholarship No. E05D057899MX.

[2] Convergence possibilities summarised according to the concepts presented by Javier Pérez de Silva (2000) and Henry Jenkins (2006) in their respective books.

[3] First School: An organisational figure in the English educational system that comprehends Preschool and the first three years of primary education (children from 3 to 7 years old).

[4] Middle School: An organisational figure in the English educational system that comprehends the upper years of primary education and the first year of secondary educations (Years 4 to 7 – children from 8 to 12 years old).

[5] QCA: Qualifications and Curriculum Authority in the UK (www.qca.org.uk)

Chapter 9
The Modes of Governmentality in Language Education:
Blog Activities in a Japanese-as-a-Foreign-Language Classroom

Neriko Doerr
Ramapo College, USA

Shinji Sato
Columbia University, USA

ABSTRACT

This chapter discusses the validity of incorporating blog activities in language education classes as an equalizing practice. The authors examine blog activities aimed at providing a way for foreign language learners to communicate in a space free from any teacher-student hierarchy as part of a Japanese-as-a-Foreign-Language class at a university in the United States. The authors show that a teacher-student hierarchy still seeps into the blog space, albeit in a different form. Using Michel Foucault's notion of modes of governmentality, they analyze how the blog's postings and readers' comments define the space of a particular blog by evoking modes of governmentality of schooling and of "native" vs. "non-native" speakers. They suggest the importance of acknowledging the existence of relations of dominance in what was initially perceived to be a power-free online space and encourage educators who use blogs in classes to involve learners in the understanding and transformation of such relations of dominance.

DOI: 10.4018/978-1-60960-206-2.ch009

INTRODUCTION

New communication technologies such as the Internet have changed language use and foreign language pedagogy, enabling new ways to engage, create, and participate in communities (Cope and Kalantzis, 2000; Kern, 2006; Kern, Ware, and Warschauer, 2004; New London Group, 1996). However, some second-language education theorists consider these technologies as mere tools and focus on how teachers and researchers can implement the options that they already have for developing second-language tasks for learners (Blake, 2007; Chapelle, 2007). These studies tend to neglect the impact these technologies have on teaching practices. Other researchers situate the effects of online communication within larger contexts of power relations and broader social hierarchies. They argue that the difference between a face-to-face or verbal communication and online communication is the absence of physical self, thus of visual and aural markers (Flanagan and Booth, 2002; Harcourt, 1999; Kolko, Nakamura, and Rodman, 2000; O'Farell & Vallone, 1999).

In such critical cyber studies, many researchers' analyses of power relations have focused on gender, race, and class (Silver, 2000). While other kinds of power relations, such as that between "native" and "non-native" speakers in the online space have arisen (Lam, 2000; 2003; Sato, 2009), many researchers' studies tend to focus on the positive side of online learning without fully examining the power relations that exist in the online space. By investigating blog activities for a Japanese-as-a-foreign–language class, we will show in this chapter that the online space can be defined and redefined variously through postings, and that power relations such as "native speaker" vs. "non-native speaker" can emerge.

A blog is an electronic journal shared by many users and upkept by one or more assigned persons (Ducate & Lomicka, 2005). Blog users can easily publish a short entry for other people to read. This feature enables users to express their emotions, exchange opinions, and participate in or create a community. These characteristics of blogs provide foreign language learners with more exposure to language in action and more venues to use language with people outside the classroom.

In this chapter, we examine a foreign language classroom activity of blogging in terms of its specific mode of governmentality. Michel Foucault's (1991) analysis of governmentality, or the "conduct of conduct",—"how to govern oneself, how to be governed, how to govern others, by whom the people will accept being governed, how to become the best possible governor" (Foucault, 1991, p. 87)—led many scholars to examine "practices that try to shape, sculpt, mobilize, and work through the choices, desires, aspirations, needs, wants and lifestyles of individuals and groups" (Dean, 1999, p. 12). Dean (1999) argues that understanding modes of governmentality is a starting point to transform and be more responsible for one's actions and craft ways to counter such modes.

The classroom has its own mode of governmentality. As schooling developed for the masses, practices at school were governed by the mode of governmentality of discipline which "compares, differentiates, hierarchizes, homogeneizes, and excludes [students]. In short, it normalizes [them]" (Foucault, 1977, p. 183). This normalizing judgement is combined with observing hierarchy in the technique of examination (Foucault, 1977). Some aspects of such a mode of governmentality of schooling still exist in practice (Gore, 1998; Green, 1998).

The classroom blog project was an attempt to leave this mode of governmentality and let students learn Japanese in "communities of practice." There students are no longer deficient Japanese language speakers but novices participating in the practices of the community (Lave and Wenger, 1991). While research on blogging is often perceived in this way (Lam, 2000), we argue that the blog itself has its own governmentality, which needs to be investigated, as one can never be truly outside of power relations (Foucault, 1977). Our aim in this chapter is not to discredit the blog as a practice in language education but to alert one to the importance of acknowledging the existence of a mode of governmentality and therefore urge researchers and educators to be aware of the power relations that exist in the space of blogging. This article is part of a wider work in which Doerr analyzed blog projects Sato designed and implemented along with his co-instructors (also, see Doerr, forthcoming; Doerr and Sato, under review; Sato, forthcoming). This chapter specifically deals with cases from the course taught by Sato and his colleague, Tomo.

In what follows we will review discussions regarding the notion of governmentality, introduce the blog activities, and examine the blog postings by the students and comments for these postings from a beginner-level Japanese class in spring 2008 at a university in the northeastern United States. We identify the mode of governmentality that became apparent and suggest incorporating its awareness into the classroom blog practices.

MODES OF GOVERNMENTALITY

Michel Foucault (1991) uses the notion of governmentality in two ways. First, as a way to analyze the development of an "art of government" begun in sixteenth century Europe, when feudalism began to give way to territorially-based nation-states and how to govern the soul became a topic of discussion due to the religious Reformation and Counter-Reformation. What was at issue was "how we govern and how we are governed, and with the relation between the government of ourselves, the government of others, and the government of the state" (Dean, 1999, p. 2). Second, the notion of governmentality is used as "any more or less calculated and rational activity, undertaken by a multiplicity of authorities and agencies, employing

a variety of techniques and forms of knowledge, that seeks to shape conduct by working through our desires, aspirations, interests and beliefs, for definite but shifting ends and with a diverse set of relatively unpredictable consequences, effects and outcomes" (Dean, 1999, p. 11). It is the "conduct of conduct."

The second way is highly relevant to this study. We suggest that the analytical framework of governmentality allows us to connect micro-level, shifting power relationships created by each posting in the online space to wider fields of power relations and specific workings of domination in these fields. Within a society, many intermeshing modes of governmentality co-exist—that of punishing, curing, treating mental illness, etc. Even the practices aimed at the emancipation of certain groups take the form of "conduct of conduct," thus unable to escape the relations of dominance, as even the notion of liberty presupposes forms of the conduct of conduct (Dean, 1999; Foucault, 1991). We investigate modes of governmentality that are evoked in the blog space, bringing in this framework to the study of online space.

Existing studies (Hall, 1996; Poster, 1997; Turkle, 1995) suggest how on-line communication technologies reconfigure notions of "identity" and social relations within larger contexts of power relations. Those researchers argue that the absence of visual and aural markers of race, gender, and class influences online communication: the Internet detaches individual subjects' performance from the perceived bodies and places those performances within the text on the computer monitor. Here what Lam (2000) calls "textual identity" becomes more important. Textual identity is "the discursive strategies that a learner uses to articulate and position himself/herself in written texts as he/she negotiates diverse discourses on the Internet" (Lam, 2000, p. 464).

In these researches, differences of gender, race, and class have received attention (Flanagan and Booth, 2002; Harcourt, 1999; Kolko, Nakamura, and Rodman, 2000; O'Farell & Vallone, 1999). Little research has focused on revealing the relationship between "native" and "non-native" speakers online. Most studies of language acquisition in cyberspace treat the learners as imperfect and underdeveloped users of the language and discuss how teachers can help improve the learners' target language and culture skills online (Chapelle, 2007). Such an approach has not explored how inequitable relations of power between "native" and "non-native" speakers expand or limit opportunities that learners encounter outside the classroom (Norton, 2000).

One exception is the work of Lam (2000), who presented an ethnographic case study of Almon, a Chinese immigrant youth. Lam examined Almon's language use in both school and online settings and revealed how he described identities (e.g., a person who loves Japanese pop culture) that were not available in school. The online space allowed him to explore varieties of discourses and express his identities more freely. However, Lam's research tends to focus on the positive side of online communication and does not fully examine the power relations that exist within the online space.

In this chapter, we illustrate the ways in which power relations—teachers over student and "native" speakers over "non-native" speakers—emerge through participants' postings. We examine four postings and comments and analyze how they *cite* certain social relations among those involved. Judith Butler (1993) discusses how various acts can cite matrices of difference performatively, making them a meaningful grid to understand the relationships among people and making certain subject positions intelligible (Butler, 1993). We go a step further and view various postings as evoking modes of governmentality. In the cases we examine, two modes of governmentality were evoked. One is the mode of governmentality of schooling, in which the teacher occupies the place of authority, based on his/her possession

of knowledge of particular subjects and pedagogy, invested in sculpting students' behavior, thinking, perspective, expression, etc. (Gore, 1998; Green, 1998). Another mode of governmentality is that of language education, in which the "native" speaker occupies the space of authority based on his/her possession of knowledge of the language, often viewed as innate and complete (for critiques see Canagarajah, 1999; Doerr, 2009; Firth and Wagner, 2007; Pennycook, 1994; Philipson, 1992).

In the typical foreign language classroom, these two modes of governmentality are intertwined and place teacher and "native speakers" as authority figures, molding the practices, perspectives, and expressions of language learners (Braine, 1999; Canagarajah, 1999). The blog activity is an attempt to leave the mode of governmentality of schooling for an online space where a student can participate as just another language user. However, these two modes of governmentality are evoked in blog postings. Here, we view blog postings not so much as a reflection of the personality of the person posting comments but as reflection of existing and emerging discourses, which produce certain effects in the specific online space of the blog.

BLOG PROJECTS UNDER DISCUSSION

The blog activity presented here was a part of the course requirements for a beginner- Japanese class co-author Sato taught in the spring semester of 2008 at a university in the northeastern United States. The purpose of this project was to provide students with more opportunities to communicate using Japanese and learn about topics related to Japan using English outside the classroom. The students were able to communicate with a variety of people as well as with their classmates and teacher. For example, they were able to communicate with learners of Japanese language from different language levels, from different institutions, and with Japanese "native Japanese speakers" from all over the world. The variety of people whom learners met through blogging enabled the students to examine different perspectives by participating in a community that they elected to engage in, such as those interested in Japanese cuisine or cartoons. While blog activities were incorporated in Japanese classes of various levels, in the beginner-Japanese class, the focus was 1) to encourage the students to use Japanese in a "real-life" context and 2) to build a classroom or beginner-level Japanese language learners' community[1].

For this blog project, the students first learned about blogs. Then, each student created his/her own blog. Each student blog was linked to a class blog by the instructor. Students posted entries on their blogs on a regular basis. For the beginner Japanese class, the blog was used in composition assignments. The students were asked to write about a certain topic and post the final composition on their blogs. As for evaluation, in the beginning of the semester, the students and instructors discussed and created evaluation criteria together. Based on the criteria, students evaluated classmates' as well as their own blogs at the end of the semester.

It often takes some time to receive comments on a blog posting. Therefore, the instructors encouraged (and sometime required) students to exchange comments on each other's blogs. The instructors also asked their Japanese-speaking friends to leave comments on students' blogs. Besides these commentators, there were others whom were not known to the instructors or to the students.

Since the focus of the project was not the grammatical "correctness" of learners' Japanese but communication with other Japanese speakers, the instructors did not correct grammatical mistakes on the students' blog. However, if the students felt uncomfortable about posting their entry on the blog before the instructors looked at it, the students were encouraged to visit the instructors during their office hours to talk about their entry.

In the beginners' class, the blog activity was viewed as a practice of constructing sentences more than it was in advanced classes, where the blog activity was viewed as an opportunity for sending messages and communicating (see Doerr and Sato under review). For example, students responded in groups to the question of how to go about navigating blog activities as follows: for difficult vocabulary, add an English explanation (Anna-Marie, Fritz, Hans-Peter, Sayo, Li), put reading of difficult *kanji* (Chinese characters used in Japanese written script) (Anna-Marie, Fritz, Hans-Peter), use only kanjis that we learned in class (Josephina, Vanessa, Maikeru, Matthew, Emma, Jose), use both Japanese and English in posting (Jing, Thomas, Peter, J), use grammar that they learned in class only (Paul, Joan), and keep the topic to Japan-related issues (Manuel, Mary, Alex, Lilly, Paul, Joan). Amy, Johanna, M. Gabriel had the following positive comments about the blog activity: they can do it anytime they want, they can use whatever Japanese they want, express Japanese proficiency in various ways, and everyone can participate regardless of their proficiency in Japanese.

Among diverse kinds of blog spaces that appeared in the blog activities in this class (Doerr forthcoming; Motobayashi forthcoming; Sato forthcoming), we introduce below the space that is defined as a language learning space in two ways: by the posting and by the comments by others.[2]

USING BLOG SPACE AS LANGUAGE LEARNING SPACE: DEFINED BY POSTINGS

Some blog space is defined by those who created the blog as a space of learning language. We examine below blogs by Daniela and Tony that highlight this.

Case 1: Asking for Advice

<posting>

Thursday, February 7, 2008

How did you study Japanese? I remember that it is very difficult. I don't have much time, so any advice is welcome!³

Posted by Daniela at 12:54 pm.

<comment 1> Tomo February 7, 2008 4:49pm

Get a lot of advice from many people! My advice is "write words."⁴

<comment 2> Jule February 9, 2008 8:20pm

Yes, it is very difficult sometimes. There are many rules (rules). And I don't understand kanji. I am sorry, but I don't have any advice. Is Seattle a good town? I've never been there.⁵

<comment 3> Jerry February 12, 2008 11:15 AM

Is it Wat? It is very close. I study Japanese with Flash Cards.⁶

<comment 4> Junko February 18, 2008 1:55 AM

Japanese is difficult, isn't it? I am Japanese, so I am proficient in Japanese. I am learning English. I think speaking with Japanese people is good practice in learning Japanese.⁷

<comment 7> terry February 21, 2008 1:45 PM

Is kanji difficult? I practice kanji in small pieces of paper. It is more difficult to learn it in big pieces of paper than small pieces of paper. And I use Flash Cards!⁸

<comment 8> Sri February 24, 2008 3:04 PM

Flash Cards best, and then rewrite on paper a hundred times. You'll never forget.

This posting derives from a suggestion by the teacher when Daniela asked her for some advice. The comment by Tomo (the teacher) reflects this exchange. Comments by Jule and Jerry (classmates) focus on learning Japanese, but also include something else, such as comments on Seattle. There were comments (comments 5 and 6) that refer only to Seattle, which we omitted. Junko (stranger) mentioned learning Japanese and gave advice. Terry and Sri (classmates) responded to the Japanese-learning questions and gave advice.

As mentioned earlier, some "strangers" are instructors' friends. Students were not aware that these "strangers" were actually instructors' friends. Also, there are "true strangers" whose identities instructors were not aware of. For such "true strangers," it may or may not have been obvious that these blog postings were done by Japanese language learners. If they had taken the time to look at the older postings or follow the links, they could have found the composition entries that teachers assigned or the class site that indicates that these blog activities are part of a class project. What matters for this chapter, however, is not whether the commentators knew that these blog entries were posted by language learners; what matters is how commentators responded to those who made "grammatical mistakes" in their postings.

Let us focus on the comment by Junko, who took the blog space to a level different from the space of language learning Dianiela defined it to be. She shows sympathy to Daniela by stating, "Japanese is difficult, isn't it?", but continues to say "I am Japanese so I am proficient in Japanese." This suggests that Junko is proficient in "difficult" Japanese because she is Japanese. Here, Junko connects being a Japanese person and proficiency in Japanese as natural, thus, connecting ethnicity and language. In this process of connecting ethnicity and language, established is a hierarchical relationship between Junko, who is proficient in "difficult" Japanese because of her ethnicity, and Daniela, a non-Japanese (as defined by Junko) who is learning Japanese and in need of receiving advice. What is invoked and reinforced here is the ideology of "native speaker" that connects language and ethnicity and attributes mythical complete competence of "native speakers" in their "native language" (Canagarajah, 1999; Doerr, 2009; Firth and Wagner, 2007; Pennycook, 1994).

However, right after that statement, Junko states that "I am learning English" which implies that English is not easy for Junko because she is Japanese and that she needs to study. This can be seen as an attempt, by putting herself in a similar position to Daniela as a language learner, to soften the hierarchical relationship established previously. This implies that Daniela can be a teacher when it comes to English, and thus the existence of a possible hierarchy in which Daniela is positioned higher than Junko. This softening allows Junko to state and legitimize the last sentence, "I think speaking with Japanese people is good practice in learning Japanese" that puts Junko as a Japanese person in the position of the authority in Japanese. Authority is not something someone owns but emerges relationally and contextually (Mollooly and Varenne, 2006). We can see Junko's establishing her authority in relation to Daniela through these comments to Daniela's blog entry.

Case 2: Providing Vocabulary List

In his blog posting, Tony introduces a joke[9] about a saxophone teacher and provides a vocabulary list as below.

<post>

ongakuka:musician

tobu: jump

ijiwaruna:mean spirited

aruhi: one day

kyukyusha: ambulance

Posted by Tony Sullivan at 8:34 PM

This posting was made in response to the teacher's instruction to post drafts for the in-class speech assignment. This vocabulary list reflects Tony's understanding that blog activity is part of language learning and that the main audience of his blog postings are his classmates, thus learners of Japanese language. In other words, Tony understood blogs as part of Japanese language class. Here, despite the fact that the blog is open to the public, Tony defines the mode of governmentality to be that of language learning.

Cases of Daniela and Tony are examples of blog posting in which those posting the blog define it as language-learning space. This creates a contrast to blog postings in a more advanced class, in which the postings tended to define the blog space less as a language-learning space than a space for communication of ideas (see Doerr and Sato under review; Doerr forthcoming; Sato forthcoming).

When the creator of the blog defines the blog space as language-learning, comments made in the blog can support such a definition and the blog space can serve as an extension of the classroom. It would be a positive and effective use of blog space. However, it would have different implications and consequences if, even when those posting the blog do not define their blog as a language-learning space, those who make comments on them define it as such. What we see next are such examples.

TURNING BLOG SPACE INTO LANGUAGE LEARNING SPACE: DEFINED BY COMMENTS

Two examples below, that of Tony and EastWest, show cases in which commentators define the blog to be a space of language learning.

Case 3: Commenting on the Japanese Skill When the Topic is not Japanese Language Skill

<post>

Tuesday, November 13, 2007

I went to a good concert. Last Friday, I went to Suffan Stenvens concert in Brooklyn with my girl-friend. It was very good. It was also very beautiful. This is Suffan Stenvens's music. Let's listen to it.[10]

Posted by Tony Sullivan at 12:42 PM

<comment 1> Tomo November 13, 2007 4:36 PM

I listened to the music. Is it classical music? But, the photo does not look "classical"... A little bit mysterious (mysterious). Who is it in the photo?[11]

<comment 2> Yumi November 16, 2007 10:24 PM

How do you do? Your Japanese is very good!! I'm Japanese. I'm also studying English. It's difficult to learn different language. The difference between English and Japanese is grammar. I sometimes confuse.

*iideshitane→ yokattadesu[12]

Here, while Tomo, the teacher, is not correcting grammatical mistakes, Yumi, an outside writer, is pointing out Tony's grammatical mistakes and correcting them. This contrast shows that it is not a matter of whether or not the reader noticed the grammatical mistake, but of how to define the blog space. As mentioned, the teacher, Tomo, views the blog as a space of communication rather than paying attention to grammatical details, therefore does not point out and correct grammatical mistakes. Her comments are on the content of the posting, although she provides an English translation to a word, defining Tony as someone who may not know some Japanese words.

In contrast, Yumi positions the blog space not so much as a space for communicating a topic content but a space that displays the degree of one's competence in Japanese. Yumi at first greets Tony and then comments on Tony's Japanese proficiency. There is no mention of the content of Tony's posting. Yumi then positions herself as an expert in Japanese language by stating that "I'm Japanese" In a similar manner to Junko, connecting ethnicity and linguistic proficiency. Here, she switches from Japanese to English. If this switch implies that what comes after will be too difficult for Tony to understand in Japanese, her initial comment, "Your Japanese is very good!!" appears as hollow praise. Yumi's correction of Tony's Japanese at the end seems to point to that hollowness also. There, while she did understand what Tony meant as apparent from her rephrasing his word with correct word, she went out of her way to correct it. Judging and correcting Tony's posting, Yumi defined this space to be a lesson of Japanese language, probably from her kindness to teach Tony correct forms.

In a very similar way to Junko that we saw earlier, Yumi first positions herself as Japanese and thus an authority figure. Yumi positions herself as an English learner, which puts her on the same level to Tony as a language learner. Then she repositions herself as an authority figure by correcting his Japanese. In contrast to Tomo, Yumi defined the space of blog as a space of language learning, regardless of Tony's intention in this particular blog, and evoked the mode of governmentality of language learning in which relationships between the participants are arranged hierarchically as teachers/"native" speakers and students/"non-native" speakers.

Case 4: Commenting on Japanese Proficiency, not on Content

EastWest posted a comment on Kanye West's music, without commenting on learning Japanese language.[13] This posting received four comments, two of which are introduced below.

<comment 1>Tomo 2007/10/19 8:47

I listened to the song by Kanye West on YouTube. The video of "Can't Tell Me Nothing" was strange (strange), but the song is great. What part of this song makes you think that it's a good example of Kanye West? I'm just curious...[14]

<comment 4> Yumi 2007/11/16 20:12

How do you do? Your Japanese is very good!! I'm Japanese. I'm also studying English. It's difficult to learn different language. The difference between English and Japanese is grammar. I sometimes confuse. (^^) Can I write in English? I cracked up! I know your feeling.:) Good luck with your study of Japanese.[15]

Out of four comments, the first three talked about Kanye West's music (comments 2 and 3 are omitted here). The last comment was on the Japanese proficiency of EastWest. Here, Yumi left a similar comment as she did for Tony: Yumi praised EastWest's Japanese, positions herself as another foreign language learner, and commented

on EastWest's Japanese proficiency with little mention of the content of his posting.

The above two cases indicate how a space of blog can become a space for communicating a certain message or a space to judge others' Japanese proficiency, depending on how those who post or comment define the space. In these cases, those who post the blog here came to be positioned as student/"non-native" speakers, a subordinate position in language-learning context. This was common practice in the blog space of the beginners' lever JFL classes (Doerr forthcoming; Sato forthcoming) but less so in advanced classes (Doerr and Sato under review; Doerr forthcoming; Sato forthcoming). As sometimes those who were positioned as subordinate cannot escape such positionings, whether online or offline, it can have strong negative effects on their self-esteem (Lam 2000).

BLOG ACTIVITIES, LANGUAGE IDEOLOGIES, AND MODES OF GOVERNMENTALITY

The first two cases above show that, despite the intention of the teacher to offer a space of content-oriented communication, students often still chose to define the space of blog as a space for language learning. For example, Daniela asked for advice regarding how to study Japanese and Tony created a list of vocabulary for the readers. Teachers' blog entries also are accompanied by vocabulary lists, modeling this aspect of the blog space, despite their original intention. However, if students wished to use blog space as such an extension of classroom, there is a positive addition to students' language learning space.

The last two cases show that even when the blog posting itself does not evoke language learning, comments to the posting can define it as a space of language learning where the grammatical correctness of the posting is deemed more important than the content. We do not intend to argue that comments by Junko (case 1) and Yumi (cases 3 and 4) indicate an arrogant and/or malicious attitude. Their similarity indicates the existence of a discourse that frames social relations. Our aim is to point out and analyze discourses that become apparent in these comments so that we can understand their effects.

Two related language ideologies appear in the above cases.First, comments by Junko and Yumi indicate the language ideology that connects ethnicity and language, which is a constitutive part of the mode of governmentality of language learning. Researchers have been challenging this ideology by arguing that there is no obvious link between being Japanese and being a "native speaker" of Japanese. There are those whose parents are Japanese but cannot speak Japanese because they grew up in a linguistic environment other than Japanese. Also, there is a question of who is Japanese. Is a person of Japanese descent who grew up in Brazil a Japanese? Is a person one of whose parents is Japanese and one of whose parents is a non-Japanese a Japanese? Is a person of Chinese descent who grew up in Japan a Japanese?

Even though there is much criticism on it, Nihonjinron, which literally means "theories on the Japanese," has been popular since the 1960s in Japan, perpetuating this ideology. In this literature scholars write about the sociological, psychological, and linguistic uniqueness of the Japanese people (e.g., Doi, 1971; Nakane, 1967; Vogel, 1979) and tend to promote racial, ethnic, and class uniformity and harmony (Dale, 1986; Sugimoto and Mouer, 1982). Japanese people are often equated with people who speak Japanese language (Miller, 1982).

The ideology of "native speaker" is also part of this ideology, often connecting ethnicity and language proficiency. The ideology of "native speaker" is based on the assumptions that there exist a homogeneous and bounded community that shares one homogeneous language and that the native speakers have complete proficiency in their language, rendering "native speaker" as the ideal model to be emulated by the language learners (Doerr, 2009; Pennycook, 1994). The ideology of "native speaker" has been critiqued from various angles regarding the homogeneous notion of language and "linguistic community," its link to particular ethnic groups, hierarchy between "native" and "non-native" speakers, political nature of setting the standard of the language native speakers supposed to have mastered, and so on (Cook, 1999; Firth and Wagner, 2007; Leung, Harris, and Rampton, 1997; Pennycook, 1994; Phllipson, 1992). Despite this, the ideology of "native speaker" persists in foreign language education (Braine, 1999; Canagarajah, 1999).

The second language ideology appears when Junko and Yumi treated learning Japanese and learning English as the same kind of activity; suggested was a language ideology that separates sociocultural issues from language uses, thus masking the political nature of language (Calvert, 1998; Woolard 1998). They may have mentioned English because the blogger speaks English or because they study English. However, there is no mention of different meanings and contexts that involve the act of learning Japanese and learning English. Linguistically speaking, knowledge of Japanese and English are at the same level. However, the social positions of these bodies of knowledge differ significantly between Japanese, which is spoken mainly in Japan, and English, which is considered as an "international language" (Pennycook, 1994; 2007) or "hypercenral language" (de Swaan, 2001). To ignore these social positions of the languages and to compare learners of Japanese and learners of English are to separate language from the social realm, masking and naturalizing power relations manifested in relations between various linguistic varieties and thus prevent people from critically investigating such relations. One negative effect of such an ideology is that language teachers often separate these domains—the linguistics and the political—consciously in efforts to avoid "difficult questions," such as power relations in terms of race, gender, and class reflected in language uses (see Kumagai, 2008).

In the above cases, once the mode of governmentality of language learning was evoked, the blog space became a space of language learning. Without institutional assignment, such evocation positioned some as teachers and others as students, suggesting among them power relationships similar to teacher vs. students or "native" speaker vs. "non-native" speakers and manners of behavior associated with them. Although without official sanctions of credentials and disciplining, such temporal construction of relationships does affect subject positions of individuals involved (Lam 2000; Sato 2009, Takamori 2010).

BLOG ACTIVITIES AND RAISING AWARENESS OF POWER RELATIONS

The blog activity we examined in this chapter aimed at changing the position of language learners from passive "imperfect users of language" in need of assistance to active users of language. This is based on the understanding that the online space can provide a kind of space different from the classroom governed by the mode of governmentality of language learning (Lam 2000). To some degree, this aim was reached, as communication between the language learners and outside commentators on an equal footing emerged. However, we also saw the language learners being positioned as "imperfect users of language" sometimes by their own initiative and other times by commentators. In such cases, the mode of government of education and that of "native" vs. "non-native" speakers emerged.

We argue however that it is not to say that the blog activity failed to put language learners "outside-the-classroom" and in "more real" situations. In fact, the blog activity did put them in a context close to what they may encounter outside the classroom. It is because, in daily interaction outside classroom, language learners are also positioned as "non-native speakers" often (Braine, 1999; Canagarajah, 1999; Firth and Wagner, 2007) and commented more on their language proficiency than the content. The difference from "more real situations" is that the marker is not physical appearance but language use. That is, the mode of governmentality of schooling and that of language learning do exist outside the classroom in the online space.

What we call for is that language teachers use blog activities as opportunities to critically examine, with students, such modes of governmentality, analyze the ideologies behind them, and discuss possible ways to counter them. While the blog activities we analyzed in this chapter fell short of involving students in analyzing the power relations in the blog interactions, they do provide a useful resource to begin thinking about such actions.

CONCLUSION

In sum, in this chapter, we suggested the importance of acknowledging the existence of relations of dominance in an online space which are constructed and maintained by members of the online community through written text. In order to counter such relations of dominance, we encourage educators who incorporate blog activities in language learning to investigate and involve language learners in understanding and transforming such relations of dominance.

ACKNOWLEDGMENT

This chapter was developed from a book project in which experimental language teaching methods were introduced and discussed (Sato and Kumagai forthcoming). We would like to thank Miyuki Fukai, Hideki Hamada, Noriko Hanabusa, Yuri Kumagai, Kyoko Motobayashi, and Kazuaki Nakazawa for commenting on earlier versions of this chapter. We also thank students who participated to this project, anonymous reviewers, and Christopher Doerr for proofreading the final draft. All the deficiency in the chapter is our responsibility.

REFERENCES

Blake, R. (2007). New trends in using technology in the language curriculum. *Annual Review of Applied Linguistics, 27*, 76–97. doi:10.1017/S0267190508070049

Braine, G. (1999). Introduction. In Braine, G. (Ed.), *Non-native educators in English language teaching* (pp. viii–xx). Mahwah, NJ: Lawrence Erlbaum.

Butler, J. (1993). *Bodies that matter: On the discursive limits of "sex.".* New York: Routledge.

Calvet, L.-J. (1998). *Language wars and linguistic politics.* Oxford, UK: Oxford University Press.

Canagarajah, A. S. (1999). Interrogating the "native speaker fallacy": Non-linguistic roots, non-pedagogical results. In Braine, G. (Ed.), *Non-native educators in English language teaching* (pp. 77–92). Mahwah, NJ: Lawrence Erlbaum.

Chapelle, C. (2007). Technology and second language acquisition. *Annual Review of Applied Linguistics, 27*, 98–114. doi:10.1017/S0267190508070050

Cook, V. (1999). Going beyond the native speaker in language teaching. *TESOL Quarterly, 33*(2), 185–209. doi:10.2307/3587717

Cope, B., & Kalantzis, M. (Eds.). (2000). *Multiliteracies: Literacy learning and the design of social futures.* London: Routledge.

Dale, P. (1986). *The myth of Japanese uniqueness.* New York: St. Martin's Press.

de Swaan, A. (2001). *Words of the world: The global language system.* Cambridge, UK: Polity.

Dean, M. (1999). *Governmentality: Power and rule in modern society.* London: Sage Publications.

Doerr, N. (2009). Investigating "native speaker effects": Toward a new model of analyzing "native speaker" ideologies. In Doerr, N. (Ed.), *The native speaker concept: Ethnographic investigations of native speaker effects* (pp. 15–46). Berlin: Mouton de Gruyter.

Doerr, N. (forthcoming). Burogu no gabamentarity: Saibasupesu no Nihongo kyouiku. [Governmentality in Blog Activities: Japanese Language Education in the Cyberspace] In Sato, S., & Kumagai, Y. (Eds.), *Shakai ni sanka shiteiku shimin toshiteno gengo kyouiku* [Language education for the global citizen]. Tokyo: Hitsuji Shobo.

Doerr, N., & Sato, S. (Manuscript submitted for publication). The Regime of Governmentality in Language Education: A Case of Blog Activities in Japanese-as-a-Foreign-Language Classroom. *Learning, Media and Technology.*

Doi, T. (1971). *Amae no kôzo* [The structure of amae]. Tokyo: Kobundo.

Ducate, L., & Lomicka, L. (2005). Exploring the blogsphere: Use of web logs in the foreign language classroom. *Foreign Language Annals, 38*, 410–421. doi:10.1111/j.1944-9720.2005.tb02227.x

Firth, A., & Wagner, J. (2007). On discourse, communication, and (some) fundamental concepts in SLA research. *Modern Language Journal, 91,* 757–772.

Flanagan, M., & Booth, A. (2002). *Reload: Rethinking women + cyberpunk.* Cambridge, MA: MIT Press.

Foucault, M. (1977). *Discipline and punish: The birth of the prison.* New York: Vintage Books.

Foucault, M. (1991). Governmentality. In Burchell, G., Gordon, C., & Miller, P. (Eds.), *The Foucault effect: Studies in governmentality* (pp. 87–104). Chicago: University of Chicago Press.

Gordon, C. (1991). Governmental rationality: An introduction. In Burchell, G., Gordon, C., & Miller, P. (Eds.), *The Foucault effect: Studies in governmentality* (pp. 1–54). Chicago: University of Chicago Press.

Hall, S. (1996). Introduction: Who needs "identity"? In Hall, S., & du Gay, P. (Eds.), *Questions of cultural identity* (pp. 1–17). London: Sage.

Harcourt, W. (1999). *Women@internet: Creating new cultures in cyberspace.* London: Zed Books.

Kern, R. (2006). Perspectives on technology in learning and teaching languages. *TESOL Quarterly, 40*(1), 183–210. doi:10.2307/40264516

Kern, R., Ware, P., & Warschauer, M. (2004). Crossing frontiers: New directions in online pedagogy and research. *Annual Review of Applied Linguistics, 24,* 243–260. doi:10.1017/S0267190504000091

Kolko, B., Nakamura, L., & Rodman, G. (2000). *Race in cyberspace.* New York: Routledge.

Kramsch, C., A'Ness, F., & Lam, E. (2000). Authenticity and authorship in the computer-mediated acquisition of literacy. *Language Learning & Technology, 4*(2), 78–104.

Kramsch, C., & Lam, E. (1999). Textual identities: The importance of being non-native. In Braine, G. (Ed.), *Non-native educators in English language teaching* (pp. 57–72). Mahwah, NJ: Lawrence Erlbaum.

Kumagai, Y. (2008). Nihongo kyoushitsu ni okeru kotoba, bunka no hyoujunka katei: Kyoushi, gakusei kan no sougo koui no bunseki kara. [Standardization processes of language and culture in a Japanese language classroom: From the analyses of the interactions between the teacher and students] In Sato, S., & Doerr, N. (Eds.), *Bunka, kotoba, kyoiku: Nihongo/Nihon no kyoiku no "hyoujun" wo koete* [Culture, language, education: Beyond the "standard" in Japanese/Japan's education]. Tokyo: Akashi Shoten.

Lam, E. (2000). L2 Literacy and the Design of the Self: A Case Study of a Teenager Writing on the Internet. *TESOL Quarterly, 34*(3), 457–482. doi:10.2307/3587739

Lave, J., & Wenger, E. (1991). *Situated learning: Legitimate, peripheral, participation.* New York: Cambridge University Press.

Leung, C., Harris, R., & Rampton, B. (1997). The idealized native speaker, reified ethnicities, and classroom realities. *TESOL Quarterly, 31*(3), 543–560. doi:10.2307/3587837

Miller, R. A. (1982). *Japan's modern myth: The language and beyond.* New York: Weather Hill.

Motobayashi, K. (forthcoming). Burogu wo shiyou shita Nihongo kyouiku ni okeru "Nihongo" siyou to "gakushusha": Ta to "tsunagaru" tame no "Nihongo" jissen wo kangaeru. [The Use of "Japanese" and "Learner" in the Japanese language education using blog: Discussion of teaching "Japanese" in order to "connect" with others] In Sato, S., & Kumagai, Y. (Eds.), *Shakai ni sanka shiteiku shimin toshiteno gengo kyouiku* [Language education for the global citizen]. Tokyo: Hitsuji Shobo.

Mouer, R., & Sugimoto, Y. (1986). *Images of Japanese Society*. London: KPI.

Mullooly, J., & Varenne, H. (2006). Playing with pedagogical authority. In Pace, J., & Hemmings, A. (Eds.), *Classroom authority: Theory, research, and practice* (pp. 62–86). Mahwah, NJ: Lawrence Erlbaum.

Nakane, C. (1967). *Tateshakai no ningenkankei: Tanitsushakai no riron* [Human relations in a vertical society: a theory of a homogeneous society]. Tokyo: Kodansha.

New London Group. (1998). A pedagogy of multiliteracies: Designing social futures. *Harvard Educational Review, 66*(1), 60–92.

Norton, B. (2000). *Identity and language learning: Gender, ethnicity and educational change*. Harlow, Essex: Pearson Education.

O'Farell, M., & Vallone, L. (Eds.). (1999). *Virtual gender: Fantasies of subjectivity and embodiment*. Ann Arbor, MI: University of Michigan Press.

Pennycook, A. (1994). *The cultural politics of English as an international language*. London: Longman.

Pennycook, A. (2007). The myth of English as an international language. In Makoni, S., & Pennycook, A. (Eds.), *Disinventing and reconstituting languages* (pp. 90–115). Clevedon: Multilingual Matters.

Phillipson, R. (1992). *Linguistic imperialism*. Oxford, UK: Oxford University Press.

Poster, M. (1996). *The second media age*. Cambridge, UK: Polity Press.

Sato, S. (2009). Communication as Intersubjective Activity: When Native/Non-Native Speaker's Identity Appears in Computer-Mediated Communication. In Doerr, N. (Ed.), *The Native Speaker Concept: Ethnographic Investigations of Native Speaker Effects* (pp. 277–293). Berlin: Mouton de Gruyter. doi:10.1515/9783110220957.277

Sato, S. (forthcoming). Burogu purojekuto. [Blog Project] In Sato, S., & Kumagai, Y. (Eds.), *Shakai ni sanka suru shimin toshiteno gengo kyouiku* [Language education for the global citizen]. Tokyo: Hitsuji Shobo.

Sato, S., & Kumagai, Y. (Eds.). (forthcoming). *Shakai ni sanka suru shimin toshiteno gengo kyouiku* [Language education for the global citizen]. Tokyo: Hitsuji Shobo.

Silver, D., & Massanari, A. (Eds.). (2006). *Critical cyberculture studies*. New York: New York University Press.

Turkles, S. (1995). *Life on the screen: Identity in the age of internet*. New York: Simon & Schuster.

Vogel, E. (1979). *Japan as number one: Lesson for America*. Cambridge, MA: Harvard University Press.

Woolard, K. (1998). Introduction: Language Ideology as a field of inquiry. In Schieffelin, B., Woolard, K., & Kroskrity, P. (Eds.), *Language ideologies: Practice and theory* (pp. 3–50). New York: Oxford University Press.

ADDITIONAL READING

Bakhtin, M. (1981). *The dialogic imagination: Four essays*. Austin, TX: University of Texas Press.

Balibar, E. (1988). The nation form: History and ideology. In Balibar, E., & Wallerstein, I. (Eds.), *Race, nation, class: Ambiguous identities* (pp. 86–106). London: Verso.

Bauman, R., & Briggs, C. L. (2000). Language philosophy as language ideology: John Locke and Johann Gottfried Herder. In Kroskrity, P. V. (Ed.), *Regimes of language: Ideologies, polities, and identities* (pp. 139–204). Santa Fe, NM: School of American Research Press.

Bell, D., & Kennedy, B. M. (2000). *The cyber-cultures reader*. London: Routledge.

Bhatt, R. M. (2001). World Englishes. *Annual Review of Anthropology, 30*, 527–550. doi:10.1146/annurev.anthro.30.1.527

Bourdieu, P. (1991). *Language and symbolic power*. Cambridge, MA: Harvard University Press.

Burchell, G., Gordon, C., & Miller, P. (Eds.). (1999). *The Foucault effect: Studies in governmentality*. Chicago: University of Chicago Press.

Canagarajah, A. S. (2007). Lingua franca English, multilingual communities, and language acquisition. *Modern Language Journal, 91*, 923–939.

Davies, A. (2003). *The native speaker: Myth and reality*. Clevdon: Multilingual Matters.

Doerr, N. (2009). Uncovering another "native speaker myth": Juxtaposing standardization processes in First and Second Languages of English-as-a-Second-Language learners. In Doerr, N. (Ed.), *The native speaker concept: Ethnographic investigations of native speaker effects* (pp. 185–208). Berlin: Mouton de Gruyter. doi:10.1515/9783110220957.185

Firth, A., & Wagner, J. (2007). Second/Foreign Language learning as a social accomplishment: Elaborations on a reconceptualized SLA. *Modern Language Journal, 91*, 800–819.

Friedman, J. (2003). Globalizing languages: Ideologies and realities of the Contemporary global system. *American Anthropologist, 105*(4), 744–752. doi:10.1525/aa.2003.105.4.744

Hawisher, G., & Selfe, C. (2000). *Global literacies and world wide web*. New York: Routldge.

Hine, C. (2000). *Virtual ethnography*. London: SAGE.

Hine, C. (2005). *Virtual method*. London: Berg.

Irvine, J. T., & Gal, S. (2000). Language ideology and linguistic differentiation. In Kroskrity, P. V. (Ed.), *Regimes of language: Ideologies, polities, and identities* (pp. 35–83). Santa Fe, NM: School of American Research Press.

Jenkins, J. (2006). Current perspectives on teaching World Englishes and English as a Lingua Franca. *TESOL Quarterly, 40*(1), 157–181. doi:10.2307/40264515

Kachru, B. (1992). Models for non-native Englishes. In Kachru, B. (Ed.), *The other tongue: English across cultures* (pp. 48–74). Urbana: University of Illinois Press.

Kachru, B. (1997). Past imperfect: The other side of English in Asia. In Smith, L. E., & Forman, M. L. (Eds.), *World Englishes 2000* (pp. 68–89). Honolulu: University of Hawaii.

Kellock, P., & Smith, M. (1999). *Communities in cyberspace*. London: Rutledge.

Kroskrity, P. V. (2000). Regimenting languages: Language ideological perspective. In Kroskrity, P. V. (Ed.), *Regimes of Language: Ideologies, polities, and identities* (pp. 1–34). Santa Fe: School of American Research Press.

Kubota, R. (1998). Ideoloiges of English in Japan. *World Englishes, 17*(3), 295–306. doi:10.1111/1467-971X.00105

Lee, Y. (1996). *Ideology of Kokugo: Nationalizing language in modern Japan*. Honolulu: University of Hawaii Press.

Liu, J. (1999). From their own perspectives: The impact of non-native ESL professionals on their students. In Braine, G. (Ed.), *Non-native educators in English language teaching* (pp. 159–176). Mahwah, NJ: Lawrence Erlbaum.

Mashiko, H. (2003). *Ideologii to shite no "Nihon": "Kokugo," "Nihonshi" no chishiki shakaigaku* ["Japan" as an ideology: Sociology of knowledge of "national language," "Japanese history"]. Tokyo: Sangensha.

Milroy, J., & Milroy, L. (1991). *Authority in language: Investigating language prescription and standardization.* London: Routledge.

Nelson, C. (1992). My language, your culture: Whose communicative competence? In Kachru, B. (Ed.), *The other tongue: English across cultures* (pp. 327–339). Urbana, IL: University of Illinois Press.

Nero, S. J. (2006). Introduction. In Nero, S. J. (Ed.), *Dialects, Englishes, creoles, and education* (pp. 1–18). New York: Lawrence Erlbaum Associates.

Pennycook, A. (2004). Perfoamtivity and language studies. *Critical inquiry in language studies. International Journal (Toronto, Ont.)*, *1*(1), 1–19.

Pennycook, A. (2007). *Global Englishes and transcultural flows.* London: Routledge.

Popkewitz, T., & Brennan, M. (Eds.). (1998). *Foucault's challenge: Discourse, knowledge, and power in education.* New York: Teachers College Press.

Rampton, B. (1995). *Crossing: Language and ethnicity among adolescents.* London: Longman.

Sakai, N. (1996). *Shizan sareru nihongo, nihonjin: Nihon no rekishi – chisaiteki haichi* [Japanese language and Japanese people that are being stillborn: History and geopolitical location of "Japan."]. Tokyo: Shinyosha.

Sakai, N. (1997). *Translation and subjectivity: On "Japan" and cultural nationalism.* Minneapolis, MN: University of Minnesota Press.

Sato, S., & Doerr, N. (Eds.). (2008). *Bunka, kotoba kyoiku: Nihongo/nihon no kyôiku no "hyôjun" o koete* [Culture, language, education: Beyond the "standard" in Japanese/Japan's education]. Tokyo: Akashi Shoten.

Seidlhofer, B. (2001). Closing a conceptual gap: The case for a description of English as a lingua franca. *International Journal of Applied Linguistics*, *11*(2), 133–158. doi:10.1111/1473-4192.00011

Skutnabb-Kangas, T., & Phillipson, R. (1989). "Mother tongue": The theoreitcal and sociopoliical construction of a concept. In Ammon, U. (Ed.), *Status and function of languages and language varieties* (pp. 450–477). Berlin: Walter de Gruyter.

Smith, L. E. (1992). Spread of English and issues of intelligibility. In Kachru, B. (Ed.), *The other tongue: English across cultures* (pp. 75–90). Urbana, IL: University of Illinois Press.

Urciuoli, B. (1995). Language and borders. *Annual Review of Anthropology*, *24*, 525–546. doi:10.1146/annurev.an.24.100195.002521

Varenne, H., & McDermott, R. (1999). *Successful failure: The school America builds.* Boulder, CO: Westview Press.

Voloshinov, V. (1973). *Marxism and the philosophy of language.* New York: Seminar Press.

Wellman, B. (1999). *Networks in the global village: Life in contemporary communities.* Boulder, CO: Westview Press.

Widdowson, H. (1994). The ownership of English. *TESOL Quarterly*, *28*(2), 377–389. doi:10.2307/3587438

Willson, S., & Peterson, L. (2002). The anthropology of online communities. *Annual Review of Anthropology*, *31*, 449–467. doi:10.1146/annurev.anthro.31.040402.085436

Yasuda, T. (1999). *"Kokugo" to "hogen" no aida: Gengo kochiku no seijigaku* [Between "national language" and "dialects": Politics of language construction]. Tokyo: Jinbun Shoin.

Yasuda, T. (2003). *Datsu "Nihongo" eno shiza* [Perspectives towards post "Japanese language"]. Tokyo: Sangensha.

KEY TERMS AND DEFINITIONS

Blog: Web log journal shared by many users and upkept by one or more assigned person.

Japanese-as-a-Foreign-Language Education: Education of Japanese language for "non-native speaker" of Japanese.

Language Ideologies: Ideas that inform discourses and practices regarding language. Language ideologies reflect viewpoints of certain groups.

Mode of Governmentality: Practices that shape and mold individuals' activities, desires, and aspirations.

Native Speaker: A group of people imagined to have complete competence in a particular language that is considered as their first language. They are considered to form a homogeneous linguistic community with special cultural connection to the language in question.

Textual Identity: the discursive strategies that a learner uses to articulate and position himself/herself in written texts as he/she negotiates diverse discourses on the Internet" (Lam 2000: 464).

ENDNOTES

1   For the beginning-level Japanese the following goals were stated: (1) To share/express your happiness, surprise, excitement, and/or frustration, as well as any questions you might have, while learning the Japanese language (or any other topics). (2) To communicate with your classmates and other people outside of class. (3) To reflect (or evaluate) what you have done so far.

2   In all of the blogs below, we translate the Japanese posting in English and mark the part that was originally written in English in italics.

3   どう日本語べんきょしましたか。わたしはおぼえていますがとてもむずかしですね。わたしはあもりじかんがありませんからANY Adviceはとてもいいですよ!

4   いろいろな人から、たくさんアドバイスをもらってください!私のアドバイスは、「ことばをかきましょう」です。

5   はい、ときどきとてもむずかしいですよ。たくさんルール(rules)があります。そしてかんじがぜんぜんわかりません。すみませんが、アドバイスがありませんよ。 Seattleはいいまちですか。I've never been there.

6   ワットですか。とてもちかいですね。私はFlash Cardsで日本ごをべんきょうします

7   にほんごってむずかしいですね。わたしは日本人なので日本ごができます。いま、英語をべんきょうしています。日本人とはなすことがいいれんしゅうになるとおもいます。

8   かんじはむずかしですか。ちいさいかみにかんじをれんしゅうします。おおきいかみはちいさいかみよりむずかしですね。そして、Flash Cards をつかいます!

9   saxophoneの先生のおはなしです。今日は、私のおもいではsaxophoneの先生のおはなしです。高校生の時、saxophoneをいつもふきました。だい好きでした。わたしのsaxophoneの先生はとてもよかったですよ。先生はおしえてくれた時、よくおはなしをしました。ひととぅおはなしはたのし

くて、おもしろいでした。このおはなしはsaxophoneおんがくかのことです。昔々、saxophoneおんがくかがいました。毎日、saxophoneおんがくかのうちのまどでふきました。うちのそとに　いろいろな人がいました。ときどきそのsaxophoneのうたがきこえました。saxophoneおんがくかをふいた時、うたをひとつだけふきました。(melody from "Somewhere over the rainbow")。まず、いろいろな人はうたが好きでした。人は　もう一どふいてください　と言いました。(same melody again)。でも、おなじうたをたくさんきてから、好きじゃありませんでした。人は　好きじゃありません　と言いました。saxophoneおんがくかはうちをそんあにでますから、とてもさびしでした。もう、うたをたぶんふきたいでしたが、うたをひとつだけふきました。(melody again)。まどでふいた時、いろいろな人がいじわるになりました。人は　ふかないでください　と言いました。ある日、saxophoneおんがくかはとてもさびしでした。しにたいでしたから　saxophoneおんがくかはとぶでまどからみちまででした。きゅきゅしゃがついた時、きゅきゅしゃはおとをつくりました。(play next melody from somewhere over the rainbow. (it's funny because it sounds like an ambulance!)) saxophoneおんがくかのうたがみちました。

10　いいコンサトへいきました。せんしゅうのきんょうびにbrooklynでわたしのかのじょと　Sufjan Stenvens　コンサトへいきました。いいでしたね。そしてとてもきれいでしたね。_これはsufjan stevensのおんがくです。ききましょう。

11　おんがくをききました。クラシックですか。でも、しゃしんはあまり「クラシック」じゃありませんね...。ちょっとふしぎ (mysterious) です。しゃしんの中のひとは、だれですか.

12　はじめまして。にほんご、じょうずですね!! I'm Japanese. I'm also studying English. It's difficult to learn different language. The difference between English and Japanese is grammar. I sometimes confuse. *いいでしたね→よかったです。

13　カヌイェウェストのアルバムカンイェウェストのアルバムは"Graduation"です。このあたらしいアルバムはいいです。そうぞうてきです。アルバムのいちばんいいうたは"Can't Tell Me Nothing"。このうたはカンイェウェストのおんがくのみほんです。えいごでいいですか...."Can't Tell Me Nothing" exemplifies Kanye West for a couple of reasons. First, the verses on the song are not meant to be lyrical gems like those of his other chi-town natives Common or Lupe Fiasco. In fact, the verses only truly flourish because of Ye's charismatic flow and egomaniacal, I-don't-care-what-you-think swagger. Kanye has developed these characteristics since before his first album and they are show-cased in this song. However, putting aside the stylistic issues, the content of the song is also exemplary West. Centered around his uncontrollable persona, materialistic inclinations, and of course almost comically large ego, the song paints the picture of West probably better than even he could have imagined. "Let up the suicide doors / this is my life homie you decide yours/... / So I parallel double parked that m***** f***** sideways/ old folks talkin bout back in my days/ but homie this is my day / class started two hours ago, 'Oh am I late'." His self-centered and frankly a**hole tendencies, which would probably make you hate him in person, are exactly what makes his music so addictive. On a whole, Kanye is unwilling to do what many people, especially hip-hop heads, would want him to do; instead he chooses to make much more pop-inspired and generally simple-themed music, and that is exactly what makes it so good. "Don't ever fix your lips like collagen / and say somethin' when you gonna end up apologin' / Let me know if it's a problem then / alright man holla then."

14 カニエ・ウェストのうたをYouTubeでききました。"Can't Tell Me Nothing"のビデオは、ちょっとへん(strange)ですが、

いいうたですね. What part of this song makes you think that it's a good example of Kanye West? I'm just curious...

15 はじめまして。にほんご、じょうず!!I'm Japanese. I'm also studying English. It's difficult to learn different language. The difference between English and Japanese is grammar. I sometimes confuse. (^^) えいごでいいですか.... わらっちゃいました!I know your feeling.:) がんばって、日本語。

Chapter 10
Designing Web–Facilitated Learning Strategy Guidance System:
Based on Young Learners' Learning Styles

Wu Liwei
Xiamen University, China

Fan Yihong
Umeå University, Sweden & Xiamen University, China

Yang Sujuan
South China Normal University, China

ABSTRACT

This chapter elaborates on the research the authors engaged in for improving young learners learning competence and effectiveness. This research investigates learning styles and learning strategies, based on which comes up with principles, contents and activities for the design and development of a Web-Facilitated Learning Strategy Guidance System (WFLSGS). A Quisi-Experiment is designed to test the function and implementation of WFLSGS and 3 distinctive findings comes out from the experiment: the research subjects' learning strategy level is generally low, thus learning strategies guidance is needed for improving learners learning effectiveness; the learning strategy guidance based on learning styles is effective for improving learning strategies, especially cognitive strategies and meta-cognitive strategies; the application of learning strategies is influenced by many factors such as teaching environment, learning content and learner self and so on. By designing and developing learning strategy guidance system, this study enriches the research of learning strategy and provides the teachers and young learners with operational advices and approaches to impoproving individualized learning competence and effectiveness.

DOI: 10.4018/978-1-60960-206-2.ch010

INTRODUCTION

This chapter demonstrates the research the authors engaged in for improving young learners learning competence and effectiveness. The research was carried out at South China Normal University from 2007-2009, targeted at undergraduate learners. The objective of the research is designing an operable web-facilitated system to help young learners develop competences and effectiveness through understanding their individualized learning styles and guiding them to internalize learning strategies, thus they could learn a more efficient way to learn rather than only learning knowledge.

This research investigates learning styles and learning strategies as the underpinning philosophy, based on which comes up with principles, contents and activities for the design and development of Web-Facilitated Learning Strategy Guidance System (WFLSGS). A Quisi-Experiment was designed to test the function and implementation of WFLSGS at two sets of web-based courses at South China Normal University. As a result, 3 distinctive findings come out from the experiment: the research subjects' learning strategy level is generally low, thus learning strategies guidance is needed for improving learners learning effectiveness; the learning strategy guidance based on learning styles is effective for improving learning strategies, especially cognitive strategies and meta-cognitive strategies; the application of learning strategies is influenced by many factors such as teaching environment, learning content and learner self and so on.

By designing and developing a learning strategy guidance system based on learning styles, this research enriches the study of learning strategy and provides the teachers and young learners with operational advices and approaches to improving individualized learning competence and effectiveness. This chapter introduces the research by giving a snap shot of the context, literature review,

system design and development, as well as the test results of the research.

CONTEXT OF THIS RESEARCH

One of the important goals of education is to help learners "Learning to Learn", the ability of students to become independent learners. On April 11, 1996, UNESCO issued the report "Learning—the Treasure Within" which placed "Learning to Learn" as the core concept of education in the 21st century. Learning strategy is a measure and distinctive symbol of learners competence to learn and to think (Gao, 2000). Adequate use of learning strategies can improve student learning outcomes (Weinstein & Alexander, 1998). Modern scientific research results showed that: learning effect = 50% Learning Strategy + 40% effort + 10% intelligence. Learning strategies, to a large extent, determine the learning outcomes so the approaches to helping learners grasp effective learning strategies will improve their learning results.

Good teaching includes teaching the student how to learn, to memorize, to think and to motivate oneself (Weinstein & Mayer, 1983). Winogrand (1989) maintains that the purpose of teaching learning strategy is to help students actively engage in self-learning, information processing, problem solving, making good use of the brains, and actively choose strategies for effective learning, so that students in the process of learning have always been filled with selective options and of high level of thinking. There is a Chinese ancient saying that "Give a man a fish is not as good as delegating him how to do fishing." China has always attached great importance to the learner's learning ability. The core of learning ability are comprised of self-regulation, self-regulation is, in turn, the core concept of learning strategies that learners need to master in the process of grasping learning strategies.

Since the 70s of the 20th century, researchers at home and abroad have always highly valued learning strategies. Domestic learning strategy research started late, but the development is relatively fast. The content of learning strategy research has focused on the concept of multi-definition, system construction and functional analysis, as well as cognitive strategies. In general, the domestic scope of the study of learning strategies is rather narrow, confined to cognitive strategies and meta-cognitive strategies, relatively neglected of the resource management strategies and emotional strategies. Learning strategy training or training materials are largely learned or borrowed from foreign countries, there is a lack of influential, better-prepared scholars to lead the development of domestic scholars in promoting the study and research in learning strategies.

To provide students with personalized learning strategies must pay attention to individual characteristics of learners. Learning style is personalized feature of an important aspect of learner learning behavior based on which teachers could analyze and help learners identify problems in their learning. Studies have shown that, in the last few decades, the study of learning style abroad gains increasing influence for curriculum and instructional design(An Huiyun, Lv Lin & Shang Xiaojing, 2005).

Knowledge includes declarative knowledge (answering the question "what is"), procedural knowledge (solve the "why") and strategic knowledge (explore "how to do"). The three elements are indispensable, but in actual classroom teaching, teachers usually pay attention to the first and the second aspects, rather than the third. In the information age, self-learning ability of learners to learn more demands more attention, which is also reflected in China's new curriculum reform, which requires that new teachers should be provided with strategic advice and guidance, and in turn they could provide those advice and guidance to learners. But most teachers have neither the awareness nor the experiences in teaching learning strategy.

Looking at domestic learning strategies research, it is still in the exploratory stage. Researchers understand the concept of learning styles, but the theory and practice of research has yet to be enriched. Overall, more emphasis has been put on theoretical research, little attention has been placed on empirical research.

All in all, we understand very well that the developing of learning society requires the next generation of learners equipped with high learning ability, which means that young learners should not only learn knowledge, but also master skills for effective learning. Learning strategy is an important scale to measure learners' learning skills and can be a road map directing learners to learn more effectively. So acquiring and improving learning strategies become a critical engagement for young learners. It is necessary to give individualized learning strategy guidance to improve learners' learning ability if we would like to see young learners develop to be life-long learners.

The development of information technology makes internet not only an important individual learning environment but also an important way to develop learning interests and independent learning abilities. The Web is distributed and can be powerful in facilitating interaction, which can satisfy learners' personalized learning needs. To give individualized learning strategy guidance, we need to concern learner's personalization characteristics. Learning styles, as one of the most important aspects of personalization characteristics, influences learning procedures and have attracted pedagogical attention since they were first put forward (Tan,1999). As the research deepening, the research objective and scope is being expanded. Only when we know learners' learning styles, could we make individualized instruction come true. Developing learning strategy guidance based on the understanding of learning styles is an important embodiment of the learning-centered principle. However the research of instructional design in China hasn't connected it organically with the study of learning styles, so learning strategies guidance based on learning styles is worth of in-depth research.

By actually designing and developing learning strategy guidance system based on the study of learning styles, this research enriches the study of learning strategy and provides the teachers and young learners with operational advices and approaches to improving individualized learning competence and effectiveness.

LITERATURE REVIEW

Through reviewing literature from home and abroad for references, this research investigates the study on learners' learning styles and learning strategies, based on which come up with the ideas for the design and development of web-facilitated learning strategy guidance system. This section gives an overview of relevant literature based on which the WFLSGS was designed.

Study on Learning Styles

Ever since Herbert Thelon (1954) presented his study on learning styles, there are numerous studies going on in the past half century. As De Bello, T.C (1990) maintained, there are as many definitions of learning styles as the studies on learning styles. Keefe (1979) defines learning styles as the "composite of cognitive, affective, and physiological factors that serve as relatively stable indicators of how a learner perceives, interacts with, and responds to the learning environment" .Dunn and Dun (1993) define that learning style is the way in which each learner begins to concentrate on, process, absorb, and retain new and difficult information. Stewart and Felicetti (1992) define learning styles as those "educational conditions under which a student is most likely to learn".

Tan (1999) summarizes learning styles as the continuous and individualized learning approach of learners, integrating learning orientation and strategy.

Despite the fact that there are many definitions and various studies on learning styles, there are some aspects that pertinent. As Oxford pointed out, learning styles and individual characteristics in learning is hard to change. This research take the study of learning styles as one of the underpinning pillars, based on which embark on the journey of designing and developing WFLSGS. Also, this research takes Kang's more practical view of learning styles, cf. learning styles is the accustomed approach and tendency to learning that learner engaged in their learning process (Kang, 2003).

Index of Learning Styles (ILS)

Just as there are many opinions on definitions of learning styles, there is also disagreement on how to best measure learning styles (Coffield, et. al., 2004). There have been more than 30 kinds of learning styles inventory used in the teaching practices. The situation calls for a summary of the different models. Richard Riding and Stephen Rayner (1998) organized the learning styles models into four groups as follows: models based on learning process; models based on learning tendency; models based on teaching preference and models based on the development of cognitive skills. Each model contains several dimensions, for example, the model based on learning process includes learning perception consisting of concrete experiential feeling and abstract conceptual thinking. Different styles have been applied in different contexts, and no model of learning styles is universally accepted. Researches on the application of learning styles have done a lot in the educational field. For example, Dunn et al. (1989) indicates that the achievement of college students could be improved by providing instruction in a manner consistent with each student's learning style. Practically, educators select the model depending on teaching or research objectives. Teachers implementing individualized classroom teaching may consider Kolb's model to match teaching styles with learner's learning styles. A quantitative research done by Desmedt and Valcke (2004) found that Kolb's and Dunn's model have been used far more than others.

Riding and Rayner's (1998) research shows that different learning styles models describe learners' learning tendency or characteristics from different points of view. Of all the models in the category they described, the models based on learning process and teaching preference describe learning styles which are likely to change with teachers' teaching methods and learning materials. These learning styles are changeable factors as they are likely to change over time, if affected by teachers' teaching strategies and learning materials. The model selected in the research must be relatively stable as well as measurable.

Many of the learning style theories have spawned assessment tools that can be used to categorize learners learning styles. But which learning style theory is the best one to apply in the web context? Jasna Kuljis and Fang Liu (2005) did a preliminary study which suggests that Felder-Silverman's model is the most appropriate candidate to take in respect to e-learning. In this research, we chose Felder-Soloman Index of Learning Styles (ILS) to measure the research objects' learning styles. The Index of Learning Styles (ILS) is an index developed for college students, which has been proved to be a reliable and valid instrument and is widely used to diagnose how students learn as well as a tool to encourage self-development (Litzinger et. al, 2005). Since it was first published in 1996, it has been translated into many languages. The Web-based version of the ILS is used over 100,000 times per year and has been used in a number of published studies. The ILS consists of four scales, sensing-intuitive,

visual-verbal, active-reflective, and sequential-global. Within each scale, there are 11 items. Felder and Spurlin summarize the four scales as follows:

- Sensing (concrete, practical, oriented toward facts and procedures)or intuitive (conceptual, innovative, oriented toward theories and underlying meanings);
- Visual (prefer visual representations of presented material, such as pictures, diagrams and flow charts) or verbal (prefer written and spoken explanations);
- Active (learn by trying things out, enjoy working in groups) or reflective (learn by thinking things through and prefer working alone or with one or two familiar partners);
- Sequential (linear thinking process and learning in incremental steps) or global (holistic thinking process, learn in large perspectives).

In the online ILS, there is learning strategies guidance for learners of each style. For example, active learners are encouraged to study in group in which the members take turns explaining different topics to each other and reflective learners are indicated not to simply read or memorize the material and so on.

Study on Learning Strategies

The study on learning strategies (goal-directed learning) started in the post World War II era and developed into wide scope in the 1970s. At its first stage, it was influenced by behaviorist view and later was influenced by cognitive view. Dansereau proposed general learning strategies and then Weinstein came up with cognitive learning strategies (Dansereau,1975; Weinstein,1985). Oxford (1990) expanded on the definition by stating that "learning strategies are specific actions taken by the learners to make learning easier, faster, more enjoyable, more self-directed, more effective and transferable to new situations." Researchers have given many definitions to learning strategies ever since it was first put forward. Some takes the view of learning methods but some goes deeply to information processing. From the different definitions given by researchers in the area of learning strategies, it would be appropriate to state that learning strategies have characteristics as follows:

- It illustrates specific actions taken by the learners but also points to the thoughts that a learner engages in during learning.
- It develops with learning environment and could be improved by teaching.

Various researches define learning strategies as the rules, the methods, the skills and other actions learners take to make effective learning. It includes the actions learners take but also learners' thinking process. There is an agreement on the saying "Good teaching includes teaching students how to learn, how to remember, how to think, and how to motivate themselves," but the question is which learning strategies should be taught?

According to Pintrich (1988), a variety of taxonomies are available for describing and classifying students' learning strategies including those developed by Dansereau, Pressley, and Weinstain and Mayer (Dansereau,1985; Pressley 1986; Weinstain and Mayer 1986; and Pintrich,1988). Dansereau (1985) developed a theoretical framework for learning strategies that emphasized primary and support strategies. The primary strategies focused on learning strategies needed for text-based materials and support strategies targeted at developing a mental environment. Pressley (1986) examined goal-specific, monitoring and higher order learning strategies. The taxonomy developed by Weinstein and Mayer (1986) outlined learning strategies from a cognitive perspective. In 1986, McKeachie et al. incorporated elements of several learning models, including the cognitive approach established by Weinstein and Mayer (1986), into

a taxonomy of learning strategies. The taxonomy proposed by McKeachie and others contains three components, cognitive strategies, meta-cognitive strategies and resource management (McKeachie et al,1990).

Cognitive Strategies

The cognitive component of McKeachie's taxonomy focuses on the methods by which students actively process information and structure this information into memory (Weinstein & Mayer,1986). This active constructive process allows the learner to interpret information and connect it to existing cognitive structures (Schuemer,1993). Specific cognitive strategies, in the model proposed by McKeachie et al.(1986), include rehearsal, elaboration, and organization.

Rehearsal strategies are tactics employed by learners to remember material using repetition aloud, copying the material, taking selective verbatim notes and underlining the most important parts of the material (Weinstein & Mayer,1986, p.3 18) Elaboration is the process by which the learner builds an internal connection between what is being learned and previous knowledge. Specific tactics include paraphrasing, summarizing, creating analogies, generative note-taking, and question answering (McKeachie et al.1986; Weinstein & Mayer,1986). Organization is the process by which the learner organizes and builds connections with the information received in the learning environment (Olgren, 1998). Specific tactics associated with the process of selecting the main ideas through outlining, networking, and diagramming the information (McKeachie et al.1986; Weinstein & Mayer, 1986).

Meta-Cognitive Strategies

The meta-cognitive component of the theoretical model focuses on the skills students use to plan their strategies for learning, to monitor their present learning, and to estimate their knowledge in a variety of domains (Everson, Tobias, & Laitusis, 1997). The purpose of such strategies is to improve self-regulation by encouraging students to test their understanding (Pace, 1985, as cited in Jonassen, 1985). The meta-cognitive strategies outlined by McKeachie et al. (1986) are similar to those of Everson et al. (1997) and include planning, monitoring, and regulating.

Planning includes such tactics as setting goals, skimming the material, and generating questions (McKeachie et al., 1986). According to Bernt and Bugbee (1990) 89% of the high achieving students reported very frequently or almost always skimming each chapter before reading it. Conversely, only 35% of the failing students and 29% of the low achieving students reported using this tactic (Bernt and Bugbee, 1990). Regulating are activities that utilize self-regulation (McKeachie et al., 1986), while monitoring involves the process by which learners constantly check themselves for comprehension of knowledge or mastering skills (Weinstein & Mayer, 1986).

Resource Management Strategies

Resource management involves the process of developing well-defined goals and scheduling the course to obtain the best results. Scheduling is the process by which the student defines a specific time or creates a daily ritual, a weekly pattern, or some other type of arrangement devoted to learning (Eastmond,1995).

Study environment management is the development of a setting that is conducive to learning. According to McKeachie et al. "the nature of the setting is as important as the fact that the student recognizes that this particular location is set aside for studying" ((1986, p. 29).

Effort management is the process by which a learner utilizes tactics such as attribution to effort, mood, self-talk, persistence, and self-reinforcement (McKeachie et al., 1986).

Support of others is the final strategy associated with this taxonomy of learning strategies. Students must learn to utilize this support by seeking help from other students and the instructor (McKeachie et al., 1986).

The study on the literature of learning styles and learning strategies forms the theoretical underpinning of designing and developing the learning strategy guidance system of our research.

DEVELOPING LEARNING STRATEGY GUIDANCE SYSTEM IN LIGHT OF LEARNING STYLES

Based on the theory and principles of developing conscious learning strategies, as well as the understanding of learning styles the authors designed the learning strategy guidance system and guidance activities. Explanations of the principles, objectives, contents and activities of the system design are given below.

Principles of Learning Strategy Guidance

We took five principles into consideration before actually designing the learning guidance strategy system, including awareness-targeted, learner-oriented, diversity valued, activity enhanced and easily operable.

- Awareness-targeted: Young learners usually do not aware their learning style. The initial principle is targeted on drawing learners' attention to their own learning styles so they'll understand their own learning processes and gradually being able to find the most suitable approaches to his or her own learning.
- Learner-oriented: Teachers respect learners as independent learners who can take initiative and responsible for their own learn-

ing, encouraging learners to reflect on their learning, develop independent and critical thinking, and consciously apply learning strategies in their learning processes.

- Diversity valued: Teachers recognize and value that students learn differently and with diverse learning styles, thus offer different advice and guidance to students with different learning styles.
- Activity enhanced: Learners recognize their learning styles and consciously develop learning strategies through various activities, tasks and peer support.
- Easily operable: The learning guidance system should be easy to operate and naturally embedded in the learning process, not adding work load to either teachers or students.

Objectives of Learning Strategy Guidance

The objectives of developing this learning strategy guidance system are listed below, including understanding students' learning styles through learning style analysis.

- Understanding learners: This learning strategy guidance system aims at understanding learners through learning style analysis and learning strategy test.
- Understanding learning strategy guidance environment: This study uses two sets of web-based courses to analyze and understand learning strategy guidance environment, one set includes the courses offered through the Course Center of South China Normal University and the other is a web-based course on Contemporary Educational Technology. Both can be located via: http://202.116.47.190/course_center/index/..

- Specific learning strategy guidance objectives: This learning strategy guidance system uses McKeachie's category of learning strategies, e.g. cognitive strategy, meta-cognitive strategy and organizational level of learning resources. For the framework, please see Figure 2.

Contents of the Learning Strategy Guidance

This learning strategy guidance system is based on the understanding of learners learning styles and McKeachie's learning strategy category that clearly elaborated in the literature review of this research and demonstrated in Figure 1.

In preparing the design and development of the learning strategies guidance system, the learning strategies are sub-categorized into cognitive strategies, meta-cognitive strategies and resource management strategies, which are further sub-categorized mainly following McKeachie's taxonomy. The framework of the learning strategy guidance system includes the following parts as displayed in Figure 2.

Design of the Learning Strategy Guidance System

The function of the learning strategy guidance system

- Helping learners understand their learning style
- Providing advice and guidance to learners of different learning styles
- Providing knowledge of learning strategies

The content of the learning guidance system

- Understanding of learning style
- Learning style test
- Understanding learning strategies

Figure 1. Taxonomy of McKeachie's Learning Strategies (McKeachie et al., 1986)

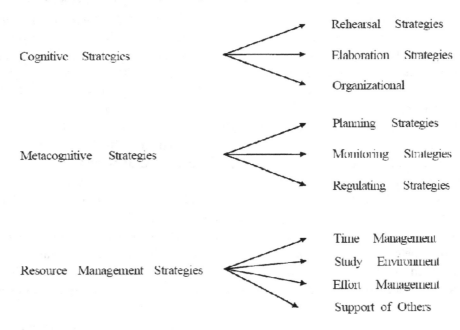

- Learning strategy guidance based on learning style

Design of the Learning Strategy Guidance Activities

Contents of learning strategy guidance activities

- Understanding learners learning style
- Testing learners learning style
- Group discussion on different learning styles and their significance to learning
- Provide knowledge of learning strategies
- Activities of learning strategy guidance based on learning style
- Practice learning strategies in learners learning process

Design of Tutor Guidance Activities

The main task of the tutor in the guidance activities is to help learners recognize their own learning styles, thus leading to more effective way of using learning strategies. Through group discussion, the tutor draws learners' attention to their own learning styles, and then direct them to more focused learning strategies appropriate to their own learning style. Then the tutor assigns learning tasks to the learners aiming at practicing learning strategies in their real learning circumstances, thus creates the opportunity for the learner to use learning strategies in their own learning processes.

- Directing learners to recognize their own learning styles through task design;
- Leading learners to reflect on their learning strategies through discussion;
- Design situations and tasks for learners to practice specific learning strategies.

Design of Learner Activities Applying Learning Strategy

- Autonomous learning: activities directed to understanding one's one learning style through learning style test, finding appro-

Figure 2. Framework of Learning Strategies organized in WFLSGS

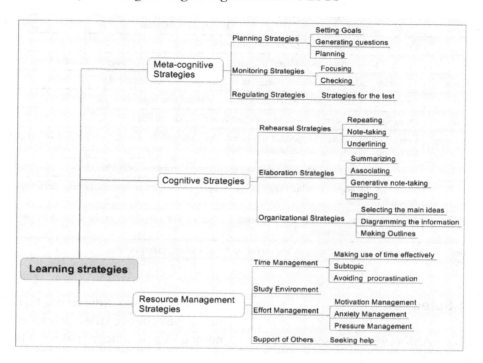

priate learning strategies suitable for one's own learning style and engaging in activities to practice using learning strategies.

- Peer discussion and reflection: activities targeted on using learning strategies that are appropriate for one's own learning style;
- Accomplishing learning strategies tasks: activities aiming at internalizing learning strategies assigned by the tutor.

QUASI-EXPERIMENT ON THE IMPLEMENTATION OF LEARNING STRATEGY GUIDANCE SYSTEM

After the learning strategy guidance system was developed the research team made a quasi-experiment (including questionnaire and interview) to test the effect of the guidance system. The experiment was implemented on the web-based curriculum platform of South China Normal University and carried out following two sets of courses. In the quasi-experiment, Weinstein's LASSI(1987) was chosen as the experimental tool to measure learners' learning strategies. A group of senior college students of 105 was chosen as subjects for pretest, within which we further chose experiment group of 36 and control group of 40 students. These students all majored in the course of "Modern Educational Technology" during the experiment time and were chosed because of their practises of computer technology. Using Weinstein's Learning and Study Strategies Inventory (LASSI) for the experiment and post-test, the results were analyzed using SPSS 11.0 to obtain frequency data on the responses. Z-test, single-variable analysis and paired-samples t-test were carried out on the qualitative data in the questionnaire. The experimental research of 2 months generated findings as detailed in the next section of this chapter.

Table 1. Descriptions of the 10 Scales from LASSI

Scale	Description of Scale
Attitude	Contains items addressing attitude and interest in college.
Motivation	The next scale, addresses students' diligence, self-discipline, and willingness to work hard.
Time Management	Examines students' use of time management principles for academic tasks
Anxiety	Items address the degree to which students worry about school and their performance
Concentration	Items focus on students' ability to pay close attention to academic tasks.
Information Processing	Contains items addressing several sub-areas. These include the use of imaginal and verbal elaboration, comprehension monitoring, and reasoning.
Selecting Main Ideas	Items address students' ability to pick out important information for further study.
Study Aids	Examines the degree to which students use support techniques or material to help them learn and remember new information.
Self Testing	Concentrates on reviewing and preparing for classes and tests. Most of the items deal with some aspect of comprehension monitoring.
Test Strategies	Focuses on students' approach to preparing for and taking examinations.

Instrument Selection

The Weinstein's LASSI(1987) was selected because it focus on both convert the overt thoughts, behaviors, attitudes, motivations and beliefs that relate to successful learning and training settings and that can be altered through educational interventions. Research has repeatedly demonstrated that these factors contribute significantly to success in college and that they can be learned or enhanced through educational interventions such as learning strategies and study skills courses. The LASSI is both diagnostic and prescriptive. For this experiment, LASSI 1st edition was chosen.

There are ten scales of the LASSI(1987): Anxiety, Attitude, Concentration, Information Processing, Motivation, Selecting Main Ideas, Self Testing, Study Aids, Test Strategies, and Time Management. It contains 77 items, and each scale has 8 items except the scale of Selecting Main Ideas which has only 5 items. Table 1 provides a description of each of the 10 scales measured. Students indicate the extent to which they agree or disagree with each item on a five-point Likert-type scale from strongly disagree to strongly agree.and the ratings were from 1 to 5, with equidistance between the values. After completing all the LASSI items, we compared the result score to a national norm group of college students and then get the measured score. Based on a student's scale scores. Eith in relation to the national norms included with the instrument or on a percentile cut-off(75% being a common cut-off used on many campuses), prescriptions can then be made. The Test-retest reliability for the instrument is .88.

EXPERIMENT FINDINGS AND ANALYSIS

Through the experimental research work described above, we obtain research findings as follows:

1. Research subjects' learning strategy level is generally low.

Table 2 shows the results of a descriptive analysis of the LASSI. Comparing with the national norm, we get the three highest score: Anxiety (61.5%), Concentration (54.7%) and Self Testing (61.4). The other seven scales are all below 50%, showing that learners in the experiment were doing

Table 2. Descriptive Statistics result of the LASSI

	N	Minimum	Maximum	Mean	Std. Deviation
PTOTAL	76	185.00	322.00	251.3026	22.01698
PATT	76	14.00	37.00	27.2895	4.03249
PMOT	76	14.00	36.00	27.8684	3.21804
PTMT	76	13.00	36.00	23.7763	3.81086
PANX	76	17.00	39.00	28.0526	4.39058
PCON	76	17.00	35.00	25.8947	3.50078
PINP	76	16.00	37.00	25.9342	4.29056
PSMI	76	10.00	23.00	17.0395	2.64041
PSTA	76	15.00	34.00	25.8158	4.21967
PSFT	76	11.00	30.00	21.3816	3.57012
PTST	76	19.00	36.00	28.3947	3.51029
Valid N (listwise)	76				

Table 3. ANOVA result of the LASSI

			Sum of Squares	df	Mean Square	F	Sig.
Between	(Combined)		1813.521	1	1813.521	4.140	.045
Groups	Linear Term	Unweighted	1813.521	1	1813.521	4.140	.045
		Weighted	1813.521	1	1813.521	4.140	.045
Within Groups			32415.15	74	438.043		
Total			34228.67	75			

poorly on most of the scales of LASSI. It calls for learning strategies improvement to make learning more effective. The result has been also proved by some other domestic researchers. Ma Ding and Zheng Lanqin (2008) made a questionnaire survey of four college students using Weinstein's LASSI questionnare, which found that students learning strategies level was low. The results of both our study and the Ma and Zheng's study alert educators' attention. So we should pay more attention to giving learning strategies guidance to improve learners' learning strategies and then improve their learning effect.

In the interview with learners' taking part in the experiment, we found that learners favor face-to-face teaching more than learning by themselves, and are accustomed to letting teachers decide learning content. They are more motivated by external factors such as learning environment, showing some kind of lack of the ability of self-learning. That may explain the pre-test result to some extent.

2. The quasi-experiment shows that learning strategy guidance based on learning styles is effective in improving learning strategies, especially cognitive strategies and meta-cognitive strategies. Teachers could make use of the guidance system to help young learners know their learning styles and instruct studying knowledge of learning

Table 4. ANOVA result of the LASSI

				Sum of Squares	Df	Mean Square	F	Sig.
AATT	Between	(Combined)		34.532	1	34.532	3.476	.066
	Groups	Linear Term	Unweighted	34.532	1	34.532	3.476	.066
			Weighted	34.532	1	34.532	3.476	.066
	Within Groups			735.100	74	9.934		
	Total			769.632	75			
AMOT	Between	(Combined)		8.992	1	8.992	.650	.423
	Groups	Linear Term	Unweighted	8.992	1	8.992	.650	.423
			Weighted	8.992	1	8.992	.650	.423
	Within Groups			1023.956	74	13.837		
	Total			1032.947	75			
ATMT	Between	(Combined)		25.301	1	25.301	1.546	.218
	Groups	Linear Term	Unweighted	25.301	1	25.301	1.546	.218
			Weighted	25.301	1	25.301	1.546	.218
	Within Groups			1210.739	74	16.361		
	Total			1236.039	75			
AANX	Between	(Combined)		11.380	1	11.380	.682	.412
	Groups	Linear Term	Unweighted	11.380	1	11.380	.682	.412
			Weighted	11.380	1	11.380	.682	.412
	Within Groups			1234.614	74	16.689		
	Total			1246.355	75			
ACON	Between	(Combined)		5.333	1	5.333	.292	.590
	Groups	Linear Term	Unweighted	5.333	1	5.333	.292	.590
			Weighted	5.333	1	5.333	.292	.590
	Within Groups			1349.614	74	18.238		
	Total			1354.947	75			
ANIP	Between	(Combined)		120.801	1	120.801	7.084	.010
	Groups	Linear Term	Unweighted	120.801	1	120.801	7.084	.010
			Weighted	120.801	1	120.801	7.084	.010
	Within Groups			1261.975	74	17.054		
	Total			1382.776	75			
ASTA	Between	(Combined)		77.058	1	77.058	4.597	.035
	Groups	Linear Term	Unweighted	77.058	1	77.058	4.597	.035
			Weighted	77.058	1	77.058	4.597	.035
	Within Groups			1240.350	74	16.761		
	Total			1317.408	75			

continued on following page

Table 4. continued

				Sum of Squares	Df	Mean Square	F	Sig.
ASFT	Between	(Combined)		3.202	1	3.202	.212	.647
	Groups	Linear Term	Unweighted	3.202	1	3.202	.212	.647
			Weighted	3.202	1	3.202	.212	.647
	Within Groups			1117.956	74	15.108		
	Total			1121.158	75			
ASTS	Between	(Combined)		10.896	1	10.896	.797	.375
	Groups	Linear Term	Unweighted	10.896	1	10.896	.797	.375
			Weighted	10.896	1	10.896	.797	.375

Table 5. Paired Samples Test result of experiment group of the LASSI

	Paired Differences							Sig. (2-tailed)
				95% Confidence Interval of the Difference				
	Mean	Std. Deviation	Std. Error Mean	Lower	Upper	t	df	
Pair 1 PTOTAL – ATOTAL	-17.6667	14.17644	2.36274	-22.4633	-12.8700	-7.477	35	.000
Pair 2 PATT – AATT	-2.4167	4.63758	.77293	-3.9858	-.8475	-3.127	35	.004
Pair 3 PMOT – AMOT	-.9167	3.50000	.58333	-2.1009	.2676	-1.571	35	.125
Pair 4 PTMT – ATMT	-.8889	2.65951	.44325	-1.7887	.0110	-2.005	35	.053
Pair 5 PANX – AANX	.3056	3.17867	.52978	-.7700	1.3811	.577	35	.568
Pair 6 PCON – ACON	-1.3333	3.00476	.50079	-2.3500	-3.167	-2.662	35	.012
Pair 7 PINP – AINP	-3.4444	4.22540	.70423	-4.8741	-2.0148	-4.891	35	.000
Pair 8 PSMI – ASMI	-2.1944	2.20155	.36693	-2.9393	-1.4495	-5.981	35	.000
Pair 9 PSTA – ASTA	-3.444	4.68703	.78117	-5.0303	-1.8586	-4.409	35	.000
Pair 10 PSFT – ASFT	-1.7778	2.64155	.44026	-2.6715	-.8840	-4.038	35	.000
Pair 11 PSTS – ASTS	-1.2500	2.56766	.42794	-2.1188	-.3812	-2.921	35	.006

strategies without bothering the teaching plan.

Table 3 is the result of a one-way between-groups multivariate analysis of variance (ANOVA). The main effect for the experiment grout versus control group students was significant(sig.045).Table 4 shows the result of the each scale in LASSI, showing improvement in learning strategies of concentration and self-testing, indicating the improvement of cognitive strategies and meta-cognitive strategies. But there seems little influence on learners' learning strategies of organization, especially strategy of time management. That might be because of the emphasizing of the guidance of strategies on making notes and concept maps in the experiment. Learning knowledge of organization strategies hasn't brought improvement to the general learning strategies. So the experiment proves the effectiveness of teaching learning strategies and at the same time calling for the development of

Table 6. Paired Samples Test result of control group of the LASSI

	Paired Differences						df	Sig. (2-tailed)
	Mean	Std. Deviation	Std. Error Mean	95% Confidence Interval of the Difference		t		
				Lower	Upper			
PATT – AATT	-1.5500	2.35285	.37202	-2.3025	-.7975	-4.166	39	.000
PMOT – AMOT	-4.250	3.23354	.51127	-1.4591	.6091	-.831	39	.411
PTMT – ATMT	.0000	3.25813	.51515	-1.0420	1.0420	.000	39	1.000
PANX – AANX	.8000	3.04833	.48198	-.1749	1.7749	1.600	39	.105
PCON – ACON	.0000	4.71223	.74507	-1.5070	1.5070	.000	39	1.000
PINP – AINP	-2.0000	2.73814	.43294	-1.0757	.6757	-.462	39	.647
PSMI – ASMI	-.5750	3.05411	.48290	-1.5518	.4018	-1.191	39	.241
PSTA – ASTA	-.7000	2.95435	.46712	-1.6448	.2448	-1.499	39	.142
PSFT – ASFT	-1.2750	4.37351	.69151	-2.6737	.1237	-1.844	39	.073
PSTS – ASTS	.5750	1.87955	.29718	-.0261	1.1761	1.935	39	.060
PTOTAL – ATOTAL	-3.3500	16.60483	2.62545	-8.6605	1.9605	-1.276	39	.210

reflective practice and communication. It is very important for learners to apply learning strategies they learn in the learning process.

3. The application of learning strategies is influenced by many factors such as teaching environment, learner self and so on, so teachers should consider the other factors such as courses' content and provide learners with abundant learning materials and useful learning content to inspire learners' learning interests.

Table 5 gives the result of paired samples test of the experiment group(sig.006), showing the improvement of their cognitive, meta-cognitive and organization learning strategies. Table 6 is the result of control group(sig.21), which doesn't show remarkable changes in the general level, but still comes a change of the level of attitude and motivation. It shows that there are other factors affecting learners' learning strategies as well as learning strategies guidance in the experiment. Individual interview after the experiment sug-

gests that the reason might be the course itself and the web-based teaching environment. The course included the teaching of the use of some useful software like Cool-Edit which interested and motivated learners a lot. Another factor might be that the teacher uploaded many resources to learners through internet which helped to arouse learners' attention and interests.

CONCLUSION

The study demonstrated in this chapter enriches the research of learning strategy by designing and developing a learning strategy guidance system, which provided the teachers and learners with operational advices and web-facilitated guidance system to develop personalized learning strategies.

A Quisi-Experiment was designed to test the function and implementation of WFLSGS and 3 distinctive findings comes out from the experiment: the research subjects' learning strategy level is generally low, thus learning strategies guidance is needed for improving learners learning effectiveness; the learning strategy guidance based on learning styles is effective for improving learning strategies, especially cognitive strategies and meta-cognitive strategies; the application of learning strategies is influenced by many factors such as teaching environment, learning content and learner self and so on.

The experiment proved the effectiveness of teaching normal learning strategy under the web context, but it also showed that mastering the knowledge of learning strategies could not bring about the improvement of the level of learning strategies. So teachers should design activities for learners to apply the learning strategies to facilitate improvement. However the findings comes from the study of Chinese objects, whether it is proper for learners from other culture needs more data to prove it.

FUTURE RESEARCH DIRECTIONS

Since the experiment done in the research only targets college students, whether the learning strategies guidance designed is fit for learners of other backgrounds, such as adult distance learners needs be further studied. So, exploring the application of the guidance system with different learners might be our future work.

REFERENCES

An, H., Lv, L & Shang, X. (2005). A review of learning strategies studies. *Mordern Primary and Secondary Education,. 134* (4).

Bernt, F. M., & Bugbee, A. C. (1990). *Study practices of adult learners in distance education: Frequency of use and effectiveness.* Paper presented at the Annual Meeting of the American Educational Research Association, Boston, MA. ERIC Document Reproduction Service No. ED 323 385.

Coffield, F., et al. (2004), *Learning styles and pedagogy in post-16 learning,* Learning and Skills Research Centre. from the World Wide Web: http://www.lsda.org.uk/files/PDF/1543.pdf

De Bello, T. C. (1990) Comparison of Eleven Major Learning Styles Models: Variables, Appropriate Populations, Validity of Instrumentation and The Research Behind Them. In *Reading, Writing, and Learning Disabilities*, 6,203-222. Retrieved from http://www.ldrc.ca/projects/atutor/content/7/debello.htm

Dunn, R., Beautry, J., & Klavas, A. (1989). Survey of research on learning styles. *Educational Leadership, 47*(7).

Dunn, R., & Dunn, K. (1992). *Teaching Elementary Students Through Their Individual Learning Styles.* Boston: Allyn & Bacon.

Dunn, R., & Dunn, K. (1993). *Teaching secondary students through their individual learning styles: Practical approaches for grades.* Boston: Allyn & Bacon.

Eastmond, D. V. (1995). *Alone but together: Adult distance study through computer conferencing.* Cresskill, NJ: Hampton Press, Inc.

Everson, H. T., Tobias, S., & Laitusis, V. (1997). *Do meta-cognitive skills and learning strategies transfer across domains?* Paper presented at the Annual Meeting of the American Educational Research Association, Chicago, IL. ERIC Document Reproduction Service No. ED 410 262.

Felder, R. M., & Spurlin, J. (2005). Reliability and Validity of the Index of Learning Styles: A Meta-analysis. *International Journal of Engineering Education, 21*(1), 103–112.

Gao, W. (2000). Learning how to learn and learning strategies. *Foreign Education Research, 1*, 48–52.

Kang, S. (2003). A review of abroad studies. *Shandong Foreign Language Teaching Journal, 47*, (3).

Keefe, J. W. (1979). Learning style: An overview. In *NASSP's Student learning styles: Diagnosing and proscribing programs* (pp. 1–17). Reston, VA: National Association of Secondary School Principles.

Kuljis, J., & Liu, F. (2005). *A Comparison of Learning Style Theories on the Suitability for E-learning*. IASTED International Conference on Web Technologies, Applications, and Services, Calgary, Alberta, Canada, July 4-6, 2005.

Ma, D., & Zheng, L. (2008). Research of the status quo of college students' learning strategies and its cultivation strategies. In *China. Educational Technology, 258*(7), 40–44.

McKeachie, W. J., Pintrich, P. R., Lin, Y., & Smith, D. (1986). *Teaching and learning in the college classroom: A review of the research literature*. Ann Arbor, MI: National Center for Research to Improve Postsecondary Teaching and Learning, University of Michigan.

Rebecca, L. Oxford. (1990). *Language Learning Strategies: What Every Teacher Should Know*. New York: Newbury House Publishers. Retrieved from http://www.pdf-search-engine.com/language-learning-strategies-what-every-teacher-should-know-pdf.html

Riding, R. J., & Rayner, S. G. (1998). *Cognitive Styles and Learning Strategies: Understanding Style Differences in Learning and Behaviour*. London: David Fulton Publishers.

Schuemer, R. (1993). *Some psychological aspects of distance education*. Fern University, Hagen (Germany): Institute for Research into Distance Education. ERIC Document Reproduction Service No. ED 357 266.

Stewart, K. L., & Felicetti, L. A. (1992). Learning styles of marketing majors. *Educational Research Quarterly, 15*(2), 15–23.

Tan, D. (1999). *Theories of Learning Styles*. Jiangsu: Jiangsu Education Press.

Thomas, A. Litzinger., et al. (2005). *A Study of the Reliability and Validity of the Felder-Soloman Index of Learning Styles*. Presented at the Proceedings of the 2005 American Society for Engineering Education Annual Conference & Exposition. Portland, Oregon, June 12-15.

Weinstein, C. E. (1987). *LASSI user's manual*. Clearwater, FL: H & H Publishing LASSI User's Manual [DB/OL] http://www.hhpublishing.com/_onlinecourses/study_strategies/BSL/admin/usersmanual.html

Weinstein, C. E., Goetz, E. T., & Alexander, P. A. (1998). *Learning and study strategies: Issues in assessment, instruction, and evaluation*. New York: Academic Press.

Weinstein, C. E., & Mayer, R. E. (1986). The teaching of learning strategies. In M. Wittrock (Ed.). *Handbook of research on teaching* (pp. 3 15-327). New York: Macmillan Publishers.

Weinstein, C.E., & Richard E.M. (1983) The teaching of learning strategies. *Innovation Abstracts*, 5 (32).

Wingrand, P., Scoff, G., & Paris, A. (1989). A Cognitive and Motivational Agenda for Reading Instruction. *Educational Leadership, 46*(4), 30–36.

Section 4
Contemporary Challenges

Chapter 11
Political Dropouts and the Internet Generation

Henry Milner
University of Montreal, Canada & Umeå University, Sweden

ABSTRACT

Daunting obstacles remain to the Internet's becoming a source of political information for a segment of the population as wide as there was for newspapers and television during their heydays – obstacles not in the form of access but rather of skills. With increasing dependence on digital information and tools, citizens are expected to exercise independent, informed judgments in order to make use of the information and tools, but the skills involved in those judgments are very unequally distributed. This unequal distribution, as in other domains, reflects class differences, but also generational ones. These are different cross-nationally and for the generation that grew up with the Internet due especially to differences in efforts to narrow the gap through policies designed to disseminate the needed knowledge and skills.

INTRODUCTION

Recent transformations in the family and community have made the young citizen's civic duty to vote and otherwise participate politically less compelling. The same is true of voluntary associations. Membership in traditional groups that teach young people what it means to be part of a community are being replaced by electronically-linked peer groups that more readily bypass traditional information gatekeepers and authorities.

This places more of a burden on the schools and the information media. Informed political participation, especially when the sense of civic duty to vote is weak, is dependent on a politically literate citizenry. Political literacy entails a minimal familiarity with the relevant institutions of decision making, combined with a basic knowledge of the key positions on relevant issues and some ability to distinguish the key political

DOI: 10.4018/978-1-60960-206-2.ch011

actors holding them. The crucial characteristic is attentiveness to the political world. The key means of doing so is via the information media, while it is the schools that must increasingly develop the habits and skills needed for effective media attentiveness.

Young people reaching adulthood after 1990 entered a world fundamentally transformed by the revolution in communications technology from that of earlier generations. The revolution in information and communications technology (ICT), combining the home computer, digitalization, and the high-speed Internet, has radically transformed the patterns of media use. Following upon the multichannel, remote-controlled television universe, this latest transformation is unique, indeed revolutionary, in its comprehensive and multidimensional character, in its simultaneous and integrated transformation of the medium of communication and the nature of the content, and in its interactivity.

Given the complexity and recentness of the transformation, there is no consensus about its effects. For every observer who is persuaded that the unlimited information and increased intensity of communication will foster an increase in political communication and political knowledge, and, therefore, political participation, there is another observer who fears that its effect will be to reinforce the participation gap between the politically engaged and the dropouts. Indeed, both are right: there will be heightened political communication and knowledge will widen the gap between the engaged and the dropouts.[1]

In this chapter I set out the arguments on both sides and cite several important cases from the literature they are based on. I find that daunting obstacles remain to the Internet's becoming a source of political information for as wide a segment of the population as were newspapers and (pre multichannel) television, obstacles not in the form of access but rather of skills. The skills involved in making judgments using digital information and

tools are unequally distributed along the usual class lines but also generational ones. Moreover, there appear to be important cross-national differences, which are largely based on efforts to narrow the gap through policies designed to disseminate the needed knowledge and skills.

What is not in question is that the Internet is here to stay as the basic media information environment for emerging generations. During the 2008 US elections, the Internet displaced newspapers as the second source – after television – for national and international news, while among young people it even rivaled television as the leading source.[2]

For good or bad, as a way of becoming informed and communicating about politics and public affairs, the Internet is here to stay. There are some grounds for expecting the new digital technologies to boost civic literacy (the proportion of citizens with the knowledge and skills to be effective citizens) but even stronger grounds for anticipating them to exacerbate class-based gaps in such knowledge and skills. If so, the fundamental challenge is to assure that those lacking an information-rich family or community environment – the potential political dropouts – gain the skills appropriate to that environment.

THE INTERNET AND MEDIA CONSUMPTION

The Internet (shorthand for the combination of the personal computer, digitalization, wireless links, PDAs and the high-speed Internet) is a new medium of information alongside newspapers, radio and television – but it is also a new medium of communication that has transformed every existing form of communication. Its arrival signals a simultaneous and integrated transformation of the very nature of the content (which is not merely sound, as in the telephone, or text and graphics as in the newspaper, or pictures and video – but all of them together, and in much higher resolution). As a medium of information, it is sometimes compared to television, but the analogy only begins to hold at all with the arrival of the remote control device and the expansion of viewing options through cable and, then, satellite transmission. And when it comes to political information, the analogy is not a comforting one. Prior (2007, p.126) shows that the choice presented by cable fundamentally altered the effect of TV watching on political knowledge and political participation. While he finds no link between the political knowledge of respondents without access to cable or Internet and their degree of preference for entertainment, "for those with access to cable television…moving from low to high entertainment preference corresponds to a 20 percent drop in political knowledge."[3]

The arrival of the remote control, video recorders, and the channel repertoires offered by cable and satellite providers allowed viewers, with minimal or no effort, to avoid political news. The result was a deeper political knowledge gap between those who follow news and those who avoid it, a gap that could only grow with the arrival with the Internet. With the remote control you can easily exit, i.e., leave the "boring" news program; with the Internet you have the ready option of flipping to a wide range of "less boring" ones. The externally imposed order (within which, in a democratic society, the individual can exercise choice) of the old media thus gives way to one where the content is internally selected, ordered and, potentially, created.

While the Internet has not yet replaced television consumption in general nor as a source of public affairs information, it has replaced printed sources. In the US, the biggest single-decade drop in reported regular newspaper reading was not in TV's heyday, but in the decade the Internet emerged, the 1990s, when readership declined from approximately 50 to 40 percent (Wattenberg, 2007, p.14). In the first decade of the new century

the Internet, especially in the replacement of paid newspaper classified ads by free interactive listings on craigslist.com and similar sites, began seriously to undermine the newspapers' revenue stream,[4] with newspapers laying off journalists, and many shutting down.[5] But the Internet is also a print medium,[6] one that has transformed the very nature and content of print journalism.[7]

There is a wide diversity of views on where these trends will lead. Keen (2007) argues that "the new democratic internet" that was supposed to replace the "dictatorship of expertise" in the old media with podcasts and streamed videos is in reality a "dictatorship of idiots." These unaccountable blogs and "news" sites, he contends, are often just fronts for public relations machines, or other forces with hidden agendas. Once dismantled, the institutions sustaining professional media can never be put back together. A politician refuses calls from representatives of the press and TV news at his peril. When they are gone, he asks, who will hold politicians to account? Or as another observer puts it, if newspapers go bust there will be nobody covering city hall, corruption will rise, and legislation more easily captured by vested interests.[8]

On the other hand, the addition of Internet sources has undeniably resulted in an explosion in the quantity of accessible information, which leads some to the conclusion that while average quality of information may decline in the short term, heightened competition among so many competing sources will result in good quality winning out over time. This is the position of optimists like Colville, for whom "the Internet will bring a far greater openness to politics….

The power of search will enforce consistency and depth in both policy and communication of policy. And the tone of debate will, at least in many cases, remain lively, anti-establishment and original. For the activist and the citizen, the internet will increas-

ingly be used to hold politicians to account and to enable like-minded groups ... to develop potent single-issue campaigns.... For policy development, the internet will bring greater scrutiny; and greater access to official government data could revolutionise the way policy-making works.... The most subtle, but perhaps most powerful, change, will be to the public's mindset. As we grow used to the instant availability of information online, we will no longer tolerate delay and obfuscation in getting similar information from government. The individual, and not the state, will be the master in the digital age (Colville, 2008, p.i-ii)

Evidence that this is taking place is nevertheless scarce. And it does not all point in the same direction. For example, a study which compared campaign coverage of candidates in the 2007 Australian election in the "old" media and the various Internet sources, found the latter more skewed toward the major candidates and parties. "Far from re-ordering old hierarchies, the Internet news may have made the election a less even contest" (Goot, 2008, p.99).

More profoundly, the optimistic interpretation presumes that the individual is capable of good judgement as master in the digital age. Increasingly freed of the "gatekeepers" in the professional media, what will enable ordinary Web users to distinguish the "facts" that the many conspiracy theorists purvey on the Web from real facts? And even if they can distinguish such reporting, can we expect a generation that has learned to expect to be able to download free its music and other media content to pay for professional news reporting? No one has yet come up with a formula under which third parties replace the income from lost readers, as well as advertisers, of printed newspapers.

The danger is that professional news reporting to continues to recede, creating a kind of vicious circle. Consumers of information are flooded with content produced by amateurs, much of

consciously blurring the line between news and opinion. Newspapers know that they can be sued for libel for printing false information; these is nothing comparable to sanction, and discourage, doing the same on the Internet. Bauerlein (2008) goes even further, arguing that the Internet has engendered a brazen disregard of books and reading. This corresponds to a report in fall 2007 by the US National Endowment for the Arts that linked low national reading test scores among young people with the decline in reading "for fun". Despite an explosion of time spent on the Internet by children,[9] it has not enhanced reading achievement. Yet the results are ambiguous, since it does appear to have improved standardized reading test scores and school grades among low-income students (Jackson et al., 2006).

The evidence is far from conclusive. Anecdotal evidence suggests that the Internet is less reliable than that from other media. One Finnish study (Carlson, 2008) showed that YouTube uploads intensify negative aspects as they are circulated and picked up by media. For example, Donald J. Leu, asked 48 students at the University of Connecticut, to look at a spoof website about a mythical species that was called the 'Pacific Northwest tree octopus.' Nearly 90 percent of them, when further question, assessed the site to be a reliable source.[10] In a similar vein, a 2008 *Economist* article described how easy it is to propagate hatred and lies through messages amplified with blogs, online maps and text messaging;[11]

As a campaign migrates from medium to medium, fresh layers of falsehood can be created. Drawing examples from a crisis that engulfed Kenya, a crazy theory about Koreans having a genetic vulnerability to mad-cow disease, and faked video-clips of dark-skinned teenagers beating up ethnic Russians, the article concludes that a "a decade ago, a zealot seeking to prove some absurd proposition – such as the denial of the Nazi

Holocaust, or the Ukrainian famine – might spend days of research in the library looking for obscure works of propaganda. Today, digital versions of these books, even those out of press for decades, are accessible in dedicated online libraries. [12]

Can we assume that resources can and will be marshaled to counter such nasty rumors and claims? In principle, yes: it is far easier to check facts in newspaper stories than in television reports, and even easier to verify ICT information. Digital media files persist over time in ways that analog files of the same types do not. Their being indexed, stored, and readily accessible facilitates assembling and comparing information. Hence the Internet provides easy means of testing what appear to be dubious assertions, making every consumer of information a potential fact-checker through Google, Wikipedia, etc.). Access to high speed Internet brings information costs toward the heretofore mythical zero built into the economists' model of the market. There can be no doubt that many, including professional researchers like this author benefit greatly from easy access to limitless information.[13] And the generation born into this medium naturally develops a level of savvy earlier generations cannot aspire to.

Still, the storing and ready accessibility of digitalized information is a two-edged sword. Users leave traces of data that sophisticated Web companies can follow, which enables them to target users with advertising tailored to their tastes and proclivities. And files – sometimes bogus files – may follow individuals through their lives, and reappear at inopportune moments. Young people, though increasingly sophisticated as to the Internet's potential uses and abuses, run the risk of their normal youthful experimentation becoming embedded into digital media.[14]

We cannot at this point count on the "average" citizen to be sufficiently motivated to check assumptions against facts, even if the "user friendliness" and reliability of Internet information sources like Wikipedia are increasing. The Internet makes it easier than do even television or radio to emulate the prototypical Fox news watcher and talk-show listener, selecting online sources that skew information so as to reinforce assumptions and prejudices. A study cited by Sunstein (2007) revealed that Web political bloggers rarely highlight opposing opinions: of 1,400 blogs surveyed, 91 percent of links were to like-minded sites.[15]

As far as the relationship between Internet use and political participation is concerned, the findings are still tentative. When asked (in the 2000 Canadian Election Study) if they ever used the Internet to inform themselves about politics, by far the most important discriminating factor was education, with income second (Gidengil et al, 2004, p.33). Moreover, studies in the United States confirm that not only is socioeconomic class an important determinant of quantity and quality of Internet use, but that, as in other aspects of informed political participation, race matters – even when controlling for education and Income (Mossberger, Tolbert, and McNeal, 2008.)

The authors found that reading online news tends to lead to an increase in the level of interest in politics, political knowledge and political discussion. But another study using results of the Maxwell poll found that while moderate and occasional users of the Internet are more likely than non-users to participate politically, frequent users are generally less likely be involved in outside activities (Reeher, 2006). This suggests a parallel to Prior's above-noted finding of the effects of the widened choice provided by cable television: increased Internet access may widen the gap in informed political participation between people looking for news and those looking for other things.

When we set our findings about North America against a study of Finland, a society with very high Internet usage and high civic literacy, we find a somewhat different situation: while highly motivated Finns do make use of the Internet to obtain political information, the overall relationship between such use and level of political knowledge is still quite weak (Grönlund, 2007).

A useful Spanish survey investigated this phenomenon. A 2007 survey (Anduiza et al., 2009) of 3700 respondents used three political knowledge items and found the expected strong, positive and linear relationship between level of education and of political interest with political knowledge. The highly educated and highly interested in politics averaged twice the correct answers of the least educated and interested, with the political knowledge gap between the well educated and the poorly educated larger for Internet users than for non-Internet users.

While their finding supports the pessimistic interpretation, they also tested an alternative and more positive interpretation, namely, the possibility that the Internet could also have an effect comparable to the pre-cable days of television when entertainment TV watchers stayed on the same channel and thus "accidentally" watched the news. Was there a similar accidental effect due, say, to use of email servers and other webpages that contain news portals, or to uninvited receipt of electronic correspondence with political content? While they could find no direct evidence of this, they did find that, controlling for education, Internet use raised political knowledge more among the politically uninterested than the politically interested. Somehow, it appears, Internet use compensates for low interest in politics.

Whatever distinguishes the effects of the Internet from those of television, it is less and less that of access. By 2004 three out of four Americans under the age of 18 had access to a computer, which, on average, they used 30 minutes every day.[16] Table 1 shows that Europe also is close to having universal access to the Internet.

Table 1. Home Internet Access in Europe: 2008

Iceland	88
Netherlands	86
Norway	84
Sweden	84
Denmark	82
Luxembourg	80
Germany	75
Finland	72
United Kingdom	71
Austria	69
Belgium	64
Ireland	63
France	62
Malta	59
Slovenia	59
Estonia	58
Slovakia	58
Latvia	53
Lithuania	51
Spain	51
Hungary	48
Poland	48
Italy	47
Czech Republic	46
Portugal	46
Cyprus	43
Greece	31
Romania	30
Bulgaria	25

Source: Eurostat

IS THE INTERNET GENERATION DIFFERENT? MOBILIZING YOUNG PEOPLE POLITICALLY ON THE INTERNET

The above numbers would be quite a bit higher if respondents were limited to the Internet generation. A recent comparative study in which this author participated surveyed a representative

Table 2. Media use and political knowledge in Americans and Canadians aged 15–25

Over the past 7 days, on how many days did you:		Political knowledge (sum of 7 answers)
Read a newspaper?	r*	.145****
	sig.	.000
	N	1,993
Watch national news on television?	r	.085**
	sig.	.000
	N	1,999
Listen to the news on the radio?	r	.026
	sig.	.242
	N	1,988
Read news on the Internet?	r	.269**
	sig.	.000
	N	1,988

*r=pearson correlation

**sig= *statistical significance*

***N=number of respondents

**** correlation is significant at the 0.01 level.

sample of 15 to 25 year-olds from both the US and Canada, and a smaller sample of those 26 plus. One question asked about Internet use revealed that only 8 percent of the young American respondents and 10 percent of the young Canadians reported never using the Internet.[17] The respondents also answered a set of questions testing their political knowledge, plus 55-odd questions designed to test out possible sources or consequences of political knowledge (Milner, 2007). The first of these, the Civic and Political Health Telephone Survey, was undertaken by CIRCLE, and conducted in May 2006 with a representative sample of 1765 people[18] living in the continental United States, of whom 1209 were aged 15 to 25.[19] The Canadian survey was conducted by the author using similar methodology[20] in September 2006 with 877 respondents aged 15 to 25 and 477 aged 26 plus. Just over one-third (451) of the interviews were conducted in French.

CIRCLE's earlier US survey (Keeter et al., 2002) had posed three political knowledge questions. For this, second, round, five questions were added (chosen from among those proposed by the author). The resulting questionnaires allowed for 8 possible correct political knowledge answers for the American respondents and 10 for the Canadians, 7 of which are common to both. It is this combined score out of 7 that serves as our main indicator of political knowledge (Table 2).

For the young Americans, Internet use was significantly related to political knowledge, as well as intention to vote (among those not having had a chance to do so), while for the young Canadians it was significantly related to having voted in the last election (for those eligible), and, slightly more weakly, with political discussion at home. Added insight is provided by a study by Kidd and Phillips (2007) that surveyed 664 18-25 year-olds on different forms of Internet-based communications. They found that the Internet as an information source can be clearly a significant and positive influence on youth political engagement, but only when it takes an appropriate form. In fact, the only form that positively and significantly influenced youth participation were irregular e-mails with information about important issues. This insight helps explain an unexpected finding in an experiment by Sherr (2005), in which the young participants learned less from the more youthful and dynamic websites that they preferred than from the standard sites from which they retained more.[21]

Indeed, it is not higher levels of Internet use per se that is the main distinguishing characteristic of the Internet generation. Those who see a generational transformation due to the Internet, emphasize not the information but rather the communication side. Unlike for other media, Internet users can be producers as well as consumers of content. And according to a recent study (Jenkins 2006), more than half of all teenagers have created media content in some form, and roughly one-third of those who use the Internet have shared content they produced. It is here that the digital divide is most apparent. A study by Hargittai and Walejko (2008) explored the extent to which young adults create and share video, music, writing and artistic photography online. They found that despite the new opportunities, it is largely confined to a relatively small minority of young adults with well-educated parents.

One popular characterization of this development is the Internet as a participatory Web, having moved into a new phase called "Web 2.0.," a "user-driven platform" providing "an architecture of participation": the Web shifts from a publishing medium to a platform for social participation and interaction based around social networking activities (Carlson, 2008). As such, it raises the practical possibility of the attainment of what we might term "netizenship", effective citizenship through interactive communication and the distribution and sharing of political content.[22]

As the cost of high-speed access declines, the physical capacity to retrieve and exchange digital content as text, sounds, still and moving pictures, and various types of graphics – anytime, anywhere and with anyone – will become standard. But standard only for those with the requisite skills. Beyond emails and SMS messaging, netizenship entails skills to manoeuvre effectively through blogs, podcasts, social networking services, digital petitions, and wikis (online documents written and edited by volunteers). Informed choices must be made as to membership in online communities, message boards, etc. And skills must be upgraded to keep up with new forms of expression.

Closing this skill-based digital divide will entail attaining an ICT form of literacy akin to – and comprising – print literacy. Yet, it bears remembering that universal print literacy has yet to be attained in North America, in which over 20 percent of adults are below minimal levels of functional literacy. This is a situation quite different from that found in high-civic literacy

countries of Northern Europe where state agencies are directly involved in promoting adult literacy and where we can see parallel efforts to promote literacy and new media access (see Milner, 2002). In North America such efforts are largely in the hands of private foundations, some of which have poured large sums of money into new initiatives to teach young people the skills to express themselves through digital media links. In a sense, the outcome of the debate between pessimists and optimists over the capacity of the new ICT media to foster a generation of netizens hinges on the potential effectiveness of these initiatives to close the new digital divide. The evidence is contradictory, and opinions vary. Optimists like Krueger (2002) argue that, given equalized access, the Internet shows genuine potential to bring individuals into the political process. But more pessimistic observers interpret the data to show that online activities reinforce the established patterns of inequality between the participants and dropouts (see Gibson, Lusoli and Ward, 2005).

One study shows that Britain, where Internet use is comparatively low, is a long way from attaining desired levels of netizenship. Using evidence from the 2005 Oxford Internet Survey, Di Gennaro and Dutton (2006) found that Internet experience and proficiency had a significant impact on whether one becomes politically engaged online, but that online political participation reinforced and in some cases exacerbated existing social inequalities in offline political participation. Similarly, Australian data assembled by Vromen (2008) shows that Internet use facilitates participation by already politically engaged 18 to 34 year-olds, but in so doing exacerbates the digital divide due to geography, education level, income level and occupational classification.

It is undeniable that the Internet opens an extraordinary new space for political interaction and organization. In the above cited article, Vromen describes how information sharing and organizing on the Internet facilitates young Australians' involvement in activist and community groups. There is a growing number of such non-partisan resources, e.g., TakingITGlobal/ www.tigweb.org (see Raynes-Goldie and Walker, 2007), oriented towards enhancing youth participation. Offering a variety of interactive resources, such sites often seek not only to encourage young people's interest, but also to convey young people's views and concerns to policy makers and enhance two-way communication between them (Xenos, Bennett and Loader, 2007). Indymedia, for example, had its origins in 1999 in the lead-up to the protests against the World Trade Organization meetings in Seattle. It grew to become a global network of over 135 news websites where volunteer contributors post news with local, regional, and international content (Chadwick, 2006).

Some such sites encourage social networking: for example, essembly.com where young people can find others with similar political interests, vote on posted 'resolutions', and engage in online discussion of political issues. Yet despite the multiplicity of such more targeted sites, they are dwarfed as forums for political organizing by the social network, Facebook. Originally, political organizing on Facebook was limited to unconventional forms of involvement. However, its overwhelming success[23] attracted the attention of mainstream political parties, which are increasing efforts to use Facebook and similar networks for recruitment purposes (Schifferes, Ward and Lusoli, 2007).

The Internet facilitates the ability of politically-oriented organizations to petition online. Earl and Schussman (2007) analyzed online petitions, hosted on the PetitionsOnline website, and focused on those that address entertainment and the media, the most important of eight categories in which the host site classifies the petitions. The 14,395 petitions with over 10 signatures in the month of November 2006 in this category roughly equalled the total of the other 7 categories (environment, technology and business, religion, and

international, national, state, and local politics and government). Their study of a large sample of those addressing entertainment and the media (with a median of 143 participants), revealed that these typically focus on products and industries associated with youth culture, and often represent consumer contestation of decisions about the scheduling (or cancelling) of entertainment programs or events. Of course, the fact that ICT technology makes petitioning easy no doubt makes the targets of online petitions sceptical as to the commitment of the signers.[24] Yet some are clearly effective in getting results when addressing matters of concern to young people.

But to what extent are these political? In what ways do protests in gaming communities, music file sharing, or fan petitioning of music companies constitute political behaviours?" The answer, Earl and Schussman suggest, lies in evidence that may show that the communication skills and actions in these areas of online life are being transferred to more familiar political realms such as voting and public protest. Calenda and Mosca (2007) argue that this is only natural since the Internet is perceived by young people as the appropriate medium for discussing political matters, via new and more creative forms of communication and participation. Yet the evidence is spotty. In carrying out "sophisticated electronic content analysis," Wilhelm (1999, p.175) found that "political forums do not provide virtual sounding boards for signalling and thematising issues to be processed by the political system."

In sum, while Internet idealists (e.g., Trippi, 2004) envisage a universal electronic public sphere for debate and deliberation, this aspiration appears, at best, "premature [since] the web does not lead to objectively measurable changes in political involvement or information" (Scheufele and Nisbet, 2002, p.68). Though younger citizens seem to increasingly expect "e-engagement" possibilities and are encouraged to make use of "e-services" from government, a survey of concrete initiatives suggests that actual exercise of these possibilities is limited to those already interested (see Gibson and Ward, 2008).

The question thus remains: to what extent do Internet-based social networking sites such as Facebook, in transcending the social limits of the geographic community and bypassing traditional information gatekeepers and authorities, also provide forums for communicating, organizing and socializing for young people without face-to-face contact? So far, cross-national research suggests that the hopes of the creators of youth-oriented civic and political sites that the Internet would reengage the young in the public sphere have not been realized (Livingstone and Dahlgren, 2007). Hindman (2009), tracking nearly three million websites, finds that the Internet in fact empowers a small set of mainly familiar elites, and that online organizing is dominated by a few powerful interest groups, concluding that the Internet has neither diminished the audience share of corporate media nor given greater voice to ordinary citizens. Faced with such facts, even the optimists insist on the necessity of profound educational and political change in order to fulfill the potential of ICTs (Ferguson, 2007).

A parallel finding at the micro level emerges from a case study (Kavanaugh et al., 2008) of local political participation recently conducted in Virginia in a community with a mature computer network (the Blacksburg Electronic Village). The authors found that it fostered more ad hoc political talk and knowledge sharing among the citizens. But "little evidence that the Internet (including blogs) helps bring these individuals into community or political decision-making spheres." They concluded that although "these communication technologies add voices from engaged segments of the population, voices from passive-apathetic and apathetic groups largely remain silent.... If we are to broaden enfranchisement, it seems powerful social and technological interventions remain needed."

This is indeed the lesson I draw from what we know at this point. The Internet is not a technological fix to the problem of political abstention – but, conversely, any such fix cannot but incorporate ICT technology.

THE INTERNET AND POLITICAL CAMPAIGNS: THE OBAMA EFFECT

We noted above that the 2008 US election campaign was when young people came to use the Internet as much as television for political information. It started when seven of the 16 presidential aspirants in 2008 announced their candidacies on YouTube. It culminated in the victorious Obama campaign, which has been heralded as ushering in a new era in online (and offline) youth civic engagement and two-way communication between citizens and political decision makers.[25] The Obama campaign perfected techniques developed by various politically-motivated organizations, but it went further. Its campaign infrastructure "became, to a significant degree, self-organizing ... [using] its website to disseminate tools for grass-roots organizing and made its campaign infrastructure infinitely expandable as groups replicated over and over, learning from and copying one another".[26] With an email list of some 13,000,000, Obama was able to come seemingly from nowhere to vanquish the powerful Clinton organization and then win the presidency.[27]

It remains to be seen if this can be replicated: it could indeed be that there is something unique in the Obama 2008 phenomenon. This raises a more prosaic question: for how many of those who watched the videos on the Web was Obama in effect the electronic celebrity of the moment? While a political figure can become "hot" under extraordinary circumstances, political realities, such as those faced by Obama in office, quickly take their toll. Many young people were happy to invite Obama into their virtual space – but for how long? It remains to be seen how successful will prove to be the efforts of the Obama organization to convert the campaign's success with social networking technologies into a tool for good governance: "to remake the tools of factional organization as instruments of broad, cross-partisan and respectful public engagement."[28]

In observing this process, we should note that the Obama campaign mobilization among young white Americans did not reach political dropouts. It was in 2004, as casualties from the Iraq war mounted, that US voter turnout abruptly reversed its decline, with those 18-24 voting at a level more than 9 percentage points higher than in 2000. The further rise in youth voting in 2008 was due to additional African-American (and, though less so, Hispanic) voters, with turnout by African-Americans under 30 increased by 9 percentage points.[29] Few of these can be expected to turn out to vote in the mid-term 2010 Congressional elections when Obama's name is not on the ballot.

The Obama phenomenon thus leaves us with our question unanswered: will the emerging generations be able to participate politically as informed citizens? Those lacking the skills to make sense of what is happening in the political world cannot be counted on to participate meaningfully. There is an as yet unrealized potential in the digital technologies to boost civic literacy, i.e., to disseminate those skills beyond the already informed. In the final part of this paper we briefly address that potential, setting out some promising examples of ICT technology being used to foster new forms of political participation.

SOME PROMISING INITIATIVES

There are myriad efforts by public agencies around the world to use web-based techniques of e-voting, e-consultation, e-petitioning and e-discussion forums. Typically, they engage the already involved rather than those on the sidelines,

both among citizens and citizens to be. We cannot expect those lacking an information-rich family or community environment to be in a position to adequately make use of them. How then can we change this? A priority on my current research agenda (see Milner 2009) is thus to identify and assess cases of concrete efforts to meet this challenge through Internet-based non-partisan, non-commercial instruments of political information and political participation, targeting potential political dropouts in the schools and beyond. Typically these are produced by voluntary associations or state agencies, (though in some cases interest groups, political parties, and the news media have set up sites that meet the criteria).

One type of such initiatives take the form of online vote selectors (voting aid applications, i.e., VAAs) found in many European countries. VAAs provide the voter with an objective individualized comparison between her or his own policy preferences and those of candidates or parties in upcoming elections, by having both complete the same questionnaires. Some operate independently of government, e.g., *Smartvote* in Switzerland, as opposed to others, e.g., *Wahlomat* in Germany, which is operated by the BPB (*Bundeszentrale für politische Bildung),* the federal agency responsible for civic education materials (Marschall and Schmidt, 2008).

Understandably, thus, though intended for the entire electorate, young voters are a particular target of the *Wahlomat.* In the most recent (2009) election, in cooperation with local educational authorities, the BPB organized public question-and-answer assemblies in a score of upper-secondary schools in two provinces (Saarland and Rhineland-Palatinate). But S*martvote* too has sought to reach out to the young, with a shorter, more simply-worded version known as *Myvote.* To spread the word, its designers collaborated with a textbook publisher, teachers' associations, and youth organizations, and provided a training course to give teachers an overview and explain how the site could be used for civic education. To reach first-time voters who did not attend an educational institution offering civic education, *Myvote* joined forces with *20 Minuten*, Switzerland's most widely read free daily newspaper, and owner of the largest Swiss online community information platform targeted at those under thirty-five. The combined platform and website accounted for 8 percent of the total *Smartvote* use (Ladner et al., 2009). Still, neither has so far matched the Dutch VAA, *Stemwijzer*. According to Ruusuvirta, and Rosema (2008), in the most recent Dutch election, 75 percent of 18-24 year-olds used *Stemweiser*.

Turning more directly to the schools, we find in Norway an especially promising case of using such instruments in civic education. In the case of Norway, it is the news media that run the VAAs. The curriculum of civic education for the last two years of compulsory school, roughly for 15 and 16 year-olds, is structured in such a way as to facilitate teachers incorporating into the coursework the issues and events of campaigns for elections that always take place in mid-September. From my in-the-field observations, teachers made available party literature and drew attention to the VAAs, as well as other media and party websites. They also were involved with the student vote, which in Norway, as in a number of other countries, allowed students to participate in a mock campaign and vote electronically. Recent modifications in the organization of the Norwegian student vote have been designed to integrate it into civic education in and beyond the classroom by giving students and teachers easy access to results by school, allowing them to compare themselves to their peers. In one Oslo school that I visited, civic education students attended as a group a debate among spokespersons from the party youth organization a week before the vote and acted as poll clerks during the student vote.

Such activities allow for hands-on use of electronic sources of relevant political information by young people. Moreover, they are not limited to the already politicized minority, but encourage the participation even of potential political dropouts. Most interesting in this regard, again in Norway, are model parliamentary committees. In recent years, the parliaments of Sweden, Norway and Denmark created and funded interactive centers, called Democracy Workshops or Mini-Parliaments, which offer students in their last two years of compulsory school the opportunity to experience, through role-playing, the parliamentary committee decision-making process. Unlike model parliaments, these are not targeted at the already politically aware, but to all students in the age group. While there are only sufficient places for a minority of civic education classes in Denmark and Sweden, the set-up and funding in Norway is such that most can participate.

The centers are located next to the parliaments, with space divided to provide places for party caucus meetings, committee rooms, and plenary meetings. (In Oslo, there are also rooms for press conferences, in which students have to defend their positions in response to questions from real journalists.)[30] Trained animators, who also work as parliamentary information officers, guide the students through the process.[31] The students are assigned to a particular committee and then go to their parties' caucus rooms, where they work out a position on the legislative issue under consideration. They are guided in their deliberations by instructions they receive on a computer screen in the booth, with access to relevant newspaper articles and excerpts from TV and radio coverage. An added twist interrupts their deliberations with telephone calls and computer screen messages from interested persons, such as lobbyists, constituents, party activists.

Debate over the bills is carried out alternatively in party caucuses and in committee meetings where the students try to form alliances or compromises in order to win majority support. When the bills come to the plenary floor, in a mock session of Parliament, there are speeches for and against each measure, and a vote is taken. Finally, the students are asked to vote again, this time based on their own views on the issue, and to reflect on whether and how their positions changed during the simulation. Through role-playing, the students come to appreciate that politicians are subject to conflicting influences and constraints, requiring making alliances and arriving at compromises through a long, but nevertheless comprehensible, legislative process.

CONCLUSION AND FUTURE RESEARCH

These are but a few examples. There are undoubtedly many other interesting innovations taking place "under the radar" of comparative research in different countries and at other levels of political activity. It is difficult thus to evaluate their effect and thus potential when it comes to turning political dropouts into participating citizens. The first challenge is simply to exchange information so that both those involved in such projects and those conducting the relevant research can collaborate to spread the word. Only in this way will "best practices" be identified and, developed and adopted. And only in this way can ICT begin to live up to its potential when it comes to fostering engaged citizens. The mere availability of Internet technology is no panacea. While it is not the immediate threat to civic literacy that some make it out to be, the Internet is also no more a technological fix to the problem of political dropouts than it is to school dropouts.[32] The choice is ours.

REFERENCES

Althaus, S. L. & David Tewksbury. (2002). Agenda Setting and the 'New' News: Patterns of Issue Importance among Readers of the Paper and Online Versions of the New York Times. *Communication Research 29* (2), 180–207.

Bauerlein, M. (2008). *The Dumbest Generation: How the Digital Age Stupefies Young Americans and Jeopardizes Our Future*. New York: Jeremy P. Tarcher/Penguin.

Bellamy, R. V., & Walker, J. R. (1996). *Television and the Remote Control: Grazing on a Vast Wasteland*. New York: Guilford.

Calenda, D., & Mosca, L. (2007). Logged On and Engaged? The Experience of Italian Young People. In Loader, B. D. (Ed.), *Young Citizens in the Digital Age: Political Engagement, Young People, and New Media*. New York: Routledge.

Carlson, T. (2008). *Riding the Web 2.0 Wave: Candidates on YouTube in the Finnish 2007 Election*. Unpublished paper.

Chadwick, A. (2006). *Internet Politics: States, Citizens and New Communication Technologies*. Oxford, UK: Oxford University Press.

Colville, R. (2008). *Politics, Policy and the Internet*. London: Centre for Policy Studies.

Di Gennaro, C., & Dutton, W. (2006). The Internet and the Public: Online and Offline Political Participation in the United Kingdom. *Parliamentary Affairs, 59*(2), 299–313. doi:10.1093/pa/gsl004

Earl, J., & Schussman, A. (2008). Contesting Cultural Control: Youth Culture and Online Petitioning. In Bennett, W. Lance (ed). *Civic Life Online: Learning How Digital Media Can Engage Youth* Cambridge, MA: MIT Press.

Ferguson, R. (2007). Politics: Young People and Policy Deliberation Online. In Loader, B. D. (Ed.), *Young Citizens in the Digital Age: Political Engagement, Young People, and New Media*. (p. 2P). New York: Routledge.

Fuchs, T., & Woessmann, L. (2004). Computers and Student Learning: Bivariate and Multivariate Evidence on the Availability and Use of Computers at Home and at School. CESifo Working Paper Series 1321.

Gibson, R., Lusoli, W., & Ward, S. (2005). Online Participation in the UK: Testing a 'Contextualised' Model of Internet Effects. *British Journal of Politics and International Relations, 7*, 561–583. doi:10.1111/j.1467-856X.2005.00209.x

Gibson, R., & Ward, S. (2008). E-Politics: The Australian Experience. [REMOVED HYPERLINK FIELD]. *Australian Journal of Political Science, 43*(1), 111–131. doi:10.1080/10361140701842607

Gidengil, E., Blais, A., Nevitte, N., & Nadeau, R. (2008). *(2004.) Citizens.* Vancouver: University of British Columbia Press. Gibson and Ward.

Goot, M. (2008). Is the News on the Internet Different? Leaders, Frontbenchers and Other Candidates in the (2007 Australian Election. *Australian Journal of Political Science, 43*(1), 99–110. doi:10.1080/10361140701851939

Grönlund, K. (2007). Knowing and Not Knowing: The Internet and Political Information. *Scandinavian Political Studies, 30*(3), 397–418. doi:10.1111/j.1467-9477.2007.00186.x

Hargittai, E., & Walejko, G. (2008). The Participation Divide: Content Creation and Sharing in the Digital Age. *Information Communication and Society, 11*(2), 239–256. doi:10.1080/13691180801946150

Hindman, M. (2009). *The Myth of Digital Democracy.* Princeton, N.J.: Princeton University Press.

Iyengar, S., & Jackman, S. (2004). Technology and Politics: Incentives for Youth Participation. *Center for Information and Research on Civic Learning and Engagement (CIRCLE)* Working Paper 24, http://www.civicyouth.org/PopUps/WorkingPapers/WP24Iyengar.pdf (retrieved 25 September (2009).

Jackson, L. A., von Eye, A., Biocca, F. A., Barbatsis, G., Zhao, Y., & Fitzgerald, H. E. (2006). Does Home Internet Use Influence the Academic Performance of Low-income Children? *Developmental Psychology, 24*, 413–437.

Jenkins, H. (2006). *Confronting the Challenges of Participatory Culture: Media Education for the 21st Century.* Occasional Paper. Chicago: MacArthur Foundation.

Kavanaugh, A. B. Joon Kim, Manuel A. Prez-Quiones, Joseph Schmitz, & Philip Isenhour. (2008). Net Gains in Political Participation: Secondary Effects of Internet on community. *Information, Communication & Society 11* (7), 933–63. http://www.informaworld.com/smpp/content~db=all~content=a904084056 (retrieved 5 October 2009).

Keen, A. (2007). *The Cult of the Amateur.* New York: Random House.

Keeter, S., Zukin, C., Andolina, M., & Jenkins, K. (2002). The Civic and Political Health of the Nation: A Generational Portrait. *Center for Information and Research on Civic Learning and Engagement (CIRCLE),* http://www.eric.ed.gov/ERICDocs/data/ericdocs2sql/content_storage_01/0000019b/80/36/2c/9f.pdf (retrieved 24 September (2009).

Kidd, Q., & Phillips, E. (2007, September). *Does the Internet Matter? Examining the Effects of the Internet on Young Adults' Political Participation.* Paper presented at the annual meeting of the American Political Science Association, Chicago.

Krueger, B. S. (2002). Assessing the Potential of Internet Political Participation in the United States: A Resource Approach. *American Politics Research, 30*(5), 476–498. doi:10.1177/1532673X02030005002

Ladner, A., Nadig, G., & Fivaz, J. (2009). Voting Assistance Applications as Tools to Increase Political Participation and Improve Civic Education. In Print, M., & Milner, H. (Eds.), *Civic Education and Youth Political Participation.* Rotterdam, the Netherlands: Sense.

Livingstone, S., & Dahlgren, P. (2007). Interactivity and Participation on the Internet: Young People's Response to the Civic Sphere. In Livingstone, S., & Dahlgren, P. (Eds.), *Young Citizens and New Media.*London: Routledge.

Marschall, S., & Schmidt, C. K. (2008). Preaching to the Converted or Making a Difference? Mobilizing Effects of an Internet Application at the German General Election 2005. In Farrell, D. M., & Schmitt-Beck, R. (Eds.), *Non-Party Actors in Electoral Politics. Baden-Baden: Nomos.*

Milner, H. (2002). *Civic Literacy: How Informed Citizens Make Democracy Work.* Hanover, N.H.: University Press of New England.

Milner, H. (2007). *Political Knowledge and Political Participation among Young Canadians and Americans.* Montreal: Institute for Research in Public Policy.

Milner, H. (2009). *The Internet Generation: Engaged Citizens or Political Dropout.* Hanover, N.H.: University Press of New England.

Morris, Jonathan S., & Richard Forgette. (2004). News Grazers, Television News, Political Knowledge, and Engagement. *Press/Politics 12* (1), 91–107.

Mossberger, K., Tolbert, C. J., & McNeal, R. S. (2008). *Digital Citizenship: The Internet, Society, and Participation.* Cambridge, MA: MIT Press.

Perea, A., Eva, A. G. D., & Jorba, L. (2009, April). *New Media Exposure, Knowledge and Issue Polarization.* Paper presented at the European Consortium for Political Research (ECPR) Joint Sessions of Workshops, University of Lisbon.

Prior, M. (2007). *Post-broadcast Democracy: How Media Choice Increases Inequality in Political Involvement and Polarizes Elections.* New York: Cambridge University Press.

Raynes-Goldie, K., & Walker, L. (2007). Taking IT Global: Online Community to Create Real World Change; A Case Study. In Bennett, L. (Ed.), *Civic Engagement.* Cambridge, MA: MIT Press.

Reeher, G. (2006). *Log On, Tune Off? The Complex Relationship between Internet Use and Political Activism.* Retrieved from Http://www.personaldemocracy.com (retrieved 5 October (2009).

Robinson, M. J. (1974). The Impact of the Televised Watergate Hearings. *The Journal of Communication, 24*(2), 17–30. doi:10.1111/j.1460-2466.1974.tb00365.x

Ruusuvirta, O., & Rosema, M. (2009, September). *Do Online Selectors Influence the Direction and Quality of the Vote?* Paper presented at the European Consortium of Political Research (ECPR) biennial conference, University of Potsdam, Germany.

Scheufele, D. A., & Nisbet, M. C. (2002). Being a Citizen On-line: New Opportunities and Dead Ends. *The Harvard International Journal of Press/Politics, 7*(3), 53–73.

Schifferes, W., & Lusoli, W. (2007.) *What's The Story. . .? Online News Consumption in the (2005 UK Election.* Unpublished manuscript. Sherr, Susan. (2005). *News for a New Generation: Can It Be Fun and Functional?* Center for Information and Research on Civic Learning and Engagement (CIRCLE) Working Paper 29, http://www.civicyouth.org/PopUps/WorkingPapers/WP29Sherr.pdf (retrieved 24 September 2009).

Sunstein, C. R. (2007). *Republic.com 2.0.* Princeton, N.J.: Princeton University Press.

Trippi, J. (2004). *The Revolution Will Not Be Televised: Democracy, the Internet, and the Overthrow of Everything.* New York: Regan.

Wilhelm, A. (1999). Virtual Sounding Boards: How Deliberative Is Online Political Discussion? In Barry, N. (Ed.), *Hague & Brian D. Loader Digital Democracy: Discourse and Decision Making in the Information Age.* London: Routledge.

Xenos, M. A., & Bennett, W. L. (2007). Young Voters and the Web of Politics: The Promise and Problems of Youth-oriented Political Content on the Web. In Loader, B. D. (Ed.), *Young Citizens in the Digital Age: Political Engagement, Young People, and New Media.* New York: Routledge.

ADDITIONAL READING

Bauerlein, M. (2008). *The Dumbest Generation: How the Digital Age Stupefies Young Americans and Jeopardizes Our Future.* New York: Jeremy P. Tarcher/Penguin.

Bennett, L. (2008). *Civic Life Online: Learning How Digital Media Can Engage Youth.* Cambridge, MA: MIT Press.

Gidengil, E., Blais, A., Nevitte, N., & Nadeau, R. (2008). *(2004). Citizens.* Vancouver: University of British Columbia Press. Gibson and Ward.

Grönlund, K. (2007). Knowing and Not Knowing: The Internet and Political Information. *Scandinavian Political Studies, 30*(3), 397–418. doi:10.1111/j.1467-9477.2007.00186.x

Hindman, M. (2009). *The Myth of Digital Democracy.* Princeton, N.J.: Princeton University Press.

Keen, A. (2007). *The Cult of the Amateur.* New York: Random House.

Ladner, A., Nadig, G., & Fivaz, J. (2009). Voting Assistance Applications as Tools to Increase Political Participation and Improve Civic Education. In Print, M., & Milner, H. (Eds.), *Civic Education and Youth Political Participation.* Rotterdam, the Netherlands: Sense.

Livingstone, S., & Dahlgren, P. (2007). *Young Citizens and New Media.* London: Routledge.

Loader, B. D. (2007). *Young Citizens in the Digital Age: Political Engagement, Young People, and New Media.* New York: Routledge.

Milner, H. (2002). *Civic Literacy: How Informed Citizens Make Democracy Work.* Hanover, N.H.: University Press of New England.

Mossberger, K., Tolbert, C. J., & McNeal, R. S. (2008). *Digital Citizenship: The Internet, Society, and Participation.* Cambridge, MA: MIT Press.

Prior, M. (2007). *Post-broadcast Democracy: How Media Choice Increases Inequality in Political Involvement and Polarizes Elections.* New York: Cambridge University Press.

Sunstein, C. R. (2007). *Republic.com 2.0.* Princeton, N.J.: Princeton University Press.

ENDNOTES

[1] A parallel concern emerges from a survey conducted early in 2007 of some 1200 Internet specialists, many "hand-picked due to their positions as stakeholders in the development of the Internet or they were reached through the leadership listservs of top technology organizations.... Respondents were asked if people will be more tolerant in 2020 than they are today. Some 56% of the expert respondents disagreed with a scenario positing that social tolerance will advance significantly by then.... Some 32% predicted tolerance will grow. A number of the survey participants indicated that the divide between the tolerant and intolerant could possibly be deepened because of information-sharing tactics people use on the Internet." (Pew Foundation: The future of the Internet III: Internet ill online

survey (p.7). http://www.pewinternet.org/Reports/2008/The-Future-of-the-Internet-III.aspx (retrieved 22 September 2009).

2   "Internet Overtakes Newspapers as News Outlet," *News Interest Index*, 23 December 2008, http://people-press.org/report/479/internet-overtakes-newspapers-as-news-source (retrieved 23 September 2009). The Obama effect seems to have sped this process along.

3   Observers have found that pre-remote control generations are more deliberate when they choose what to watch, typically tuning in with a specific programming goal in mind. In a process analogous to newspaper readers interested in sports or entertainment being exposed to news, earlier generations developed TV watching habits that made them close to m – if not indeed – captive audiences for the network news telecast. Many television watchers were thus exposed to coverage of political news and events because they simply did not wish to switch the channel (Bellamy and Walker, 1996; see also Morris and Forgette, 2007; Robinson, 1974).

4   In 2005 US newspaper advertising reached its peak.... Online ads produced $2 billion and $11 billion came from 54 million daily readers. "Since then, it has been downhill.... Ad revenues declined to $45.4 billion in 2007, followed by quarter-by-quarter falls of 12 percent to 20 percent during the catastrophes of 2008.... The most immediate threat from the Internet is classified ads ... vulnerable to complete cannibalization by the Internet.... Losing up to 30 percent of the revenues in a leveraged model is not good, but the real fear is that the rest of the advertisers will also leave." James V. DeLong, ("Preparing the Obituary," *The American*, March 3, 2009, http://american.com/archive/2009/february-2009/preparing-

the-obituary/?searchterm=Preparing%20the%20Obituary (retrieved 22 September 2009).

5   See John Nichols & Robert W. McChesney, "The Death and Life of Great American Newspapers."*The Nation*, April 6, 2009.

6   We do not know the effects of switching from print-on-paper to print-on–the-screen. Some research suggests that such a shift may be more significant than it appears. Althaus and Tewksbury (2002) conducted an experiment in which subjects read either the print or online version of the New York Times for a week, finding online readers less likely to follow the cues of news editors and producers, which meant that they read fewer public affairs stories.

7   For example, old-style reporters are giving way to the "mojos," mobile journalists who have smart phones, laptops, digital audio recorders and cameras, but no office and no landline telephone. They send their material electronically, directly to their newspaper's website, material which may also find its way into print in the newspaper's hard copy – if there still is one. The text can be readily complemented by pictures, graphics, and videos, with sound added. The original source of that content can be a report prepared by a New York Times or BBC News reporter. But it can be many other things: blogs, podcasts, etc., produced under a very different cost structure.

8   Porter rejects the idea that the Internet and Cable TV will fill the gap: "Cash-strapped TV stations depend on newspapers for much of their local news coverage. Cable news is increasingly commentary. And rather than a citizen reporter, the Internet has given us the citizen pundit, who comments on: newspaper articles. Reporting the news in far-flung countries, spending weeks on investigations of uncertain payoff, fighting for freedom

of information in court — is expensive. Virtually the only entities still doing it on the necessary scale are newspapers. Letting them go on the expectation that the Internet will enable a better-informed citizenry seems like a risky bet" ("Newspapers, It matters." *New York Times*. February 12, 2008: A18).

[9] In a study of 2,032 representative 8 to 18-year-olds, the Kaiser Family Foundation found that nearly half used the Internet on a typical day in 2004, up from just under a quarter in 1999. The average time these children spent online on a typical day rose to one hour and 41 minutes in 2004, from 46 minutes in 1999. See Motoko Rich, "Literacy Debate: Online, R U Really Reading?" *New York Times*, July 27, 2008.

[10] The site is at http://zapatopi.net/treeoctopus. Motoko Rich, "Literacy Debate: Online, R U Really Reading?" *New York Times*, July 27, 2008.

[11] In the US, "more than 75 billion text messages are sent a month, and the most avid texters are 13 to 17, say researchers. Teens with cell phones average 2,272 text messages a month, compared with 203 calls, according to the Nielsen Co". (Donna St. George "6,473 Texts a Month, But at What Cost? Constant Cell phone Messaging Keeps Kids Connected, Parents Concerned" *Washington Post*, February 22, 2009; Page A01.

[12] "The Brave New World of E-hatred: Social Networks and Video-sharing Sites don't always Bring People Closer Together." *The Economist*, July 24th 2008.

[13] A positive example of real potential benefits of this technology is the case of John Philip Neufeld, a 21-year-old music student at Concordia University in Montreal, who sometimes acts as moderator on a site where people can upload computer-generated animation. When surfing the web just before dawn on March 17 2009, Nuefield "stumbled

on a fresh posting that made him nervous. 'It said: 'Today at 11:30, I am going to blow up my school. Those bastards are going to pay,' [along with] a photograph of himself holding a gasoline canister.... Having spotted a link on the posting to a news site in England's Norfolk region, Mr. Neufeld tracked down the phone number for police in the area.... Mr. Neufeld said police, who had received another warning from a British web surfer, took the tip seriously.... Police were waiting at Attleborough High School when a 16-year-old boy arrived around 11:30 a.m. armed with a knife, matches and a canister of what appeared to be flammable liquid." ("Montreal student helps avert British school attack" Peggy Curran, Canwest News Service Published: Friday, March 20, 2009.

[14] See Louise Story, "To aim ads, Web is Keeping Closer Eye on you," New York Times, March 10, 2008. Another disturbing element emerges from a Canadian survey of 308 Facebook users found the more time they spent on the site, the more suspicious they became of their partners. The researchers argue that the social-networking site provides a vast catalogue of potentially painful artefacts.... The site gives people unprecedented access to the "off hours" of their significant others. 'You get a news feed telling you who posted on your partner's wall, who said what, what friends have been added." Even those who refrain from spying on their partners are not immune. "Friends end up providing you with information that 10, 15 years ago you would never have found out about.... And suddenly you're exposed to everybody else's misattribution of what's going on in the pictures and comments" (Zosia Bielski "Facebook is ... breeding spying, jealous lovers" *Globe and Mail*, February 12, 2009). Another study, reported in Montreal's La Presse on April 21 2009, found that users

of Facebook studied less than half as many hours as non-Facebook users.

15 In an interview with salon.com, Sunstein expresses the fear that "when it comes to the Internet, we demand the right to reinforce our own beliefs without embracing the responsibility to challenge them." He found a danger to democratic discourse in "all the excitement about personalization and customization, hearing people saying "this is unbelievably great that we can just include what we like and exclude what we dislike," when his research into jury behavior was finding "that like-minded jurors, when they talk to one another, tend to get more extreme." (http://www.salon.com/news/feature/2007/11/07/sunstein, (retrieved 22 September 2009). In a similar analysis, Manjoo (2008) describes Americans organizing themselves into "echo chambers." The earliest thinker along these lines was MIT Media Lab founder Nicholas Negroponte, who coined the term "the Daily Me" to describe a virtual daily-newspaper customized for an individual's tastes.

16 "In the words of a 17 year-old respondent in a recent Pew Internet and American Life survey, 'I multi-task every single second I am online. At this very moment I am watching TV, checking my email every two minutes, reading a newsgroup about who shot JFK, burning some music to a CD, and writing this message'" (Iyengar and Jackman, 2004, p.3).

17 The questions are not identical since American respondents had 8 possible answers based on reported number of days the Internet was used in the last week, while Canadian respondents cast an either-or choice on at least occasional use.

18 The number surveyed was actually higher but I do not include the data from the survey of over-sampled African-Americans, Latinos and Asian-Americans aged 15 to 25

carried on via the web. No such effort was undertaken in Canada, both because there is no comparable population, and also because there is reason to suspect that Internet survey respondents act differently. Responses are drawn from a list of persons who have expressed initial interest in participating in surveys, and the methodology used to create Internet samples in Canada is more problematic than that used by Knowledge Networks which carried out the American Internet survey.

19 The sample was drawn using standard list-assisted random digit dialing (RDD) methodology. The telephone interviewing over-sampled 15-to-25-year-olds by setting a maximum quota for respondents 26 and older. After that quota was filled, all remaining interviews were conducted with 15 to 25 year-olds. Interviews were conducted with 15 year-olds only after getting parental consent.

20 The US survey, which had greater financial resources available, made a greater effort to track down difficult to reach potential respondents. In the end, the response rate for 15 to 25 year-olds was 24.7 percent; while that in Canada it was only 9.7 percent. It is clearly becoming extremely difficult to carry on telephone surveys, especially of young people. For Canada especially, this is evidenced in that reported voting was much higher than that found by elections Canada -- another reason I give little weight to reported voting. In many instances low response rates make conclusions dubious, since those not responding are likely to differ from those responding on the attitudes being surveyed. A glaring example of this is a survey headlined in Montreal`s *La Presse* (4 July, 2007) stating that 86% of young Quebeckers were happy. As far as political knowledge is concerned, if the low response

rate skewed the outcome, it most likely did so in the direction of higher levels of political knowledge. Hence there is no reason to see it affecting the basic findings -- except that the differential in response rate could account in part for the lower level of knowledge of the Americans.

21   Sherr suggests that the latter had greater credibility, which is a significant factor in determining the degree to which subjects retain the information provided. Another experiment showed that providing young people with a CD with useful political information gave them a meaningful opportunity to engage in the world of politics (Iyengar and Jackman 2004).

22   The term 'netizen' was coined in 1992 by computer specialist Michael Hauben, to refer to an Internet user with a sense of civic responsibility to the online community corresponding to a citizen's duty to his country. The expression 'netizenship' refers to the extension of participatory citizenship into the virtual space of the internet.

23   According to Advertising Age, 90 per cent of Canadian undergraduate students report using Facebook daily (Zosia Bielski, *Globe and Mail*, February 12, 2009; *op. cit.*).

24   Here is a story that suggests that people put very little weight on their online commitments. "One day this past summer, I logged on to Facebook and realized that I was very close to having 700 online 'friends.' ... So I decided to have a Facebook party. I used Facebook to create an 'event' and invite my digital chums.... Facebook gives people the option of RSVP'ing in three categories — 'attending,' 'maybe attending' and 'not attending.' .... Fifteen people said they were attending, and 60 said maybe; .... one person showed up. I would learn, when I asked some people who didn't show up the next day, that 'definitely attending' on Facebook

means 'maybe' and 'maybe attending' means 'likely not'" (Hal Niedzviecki "Facebook in a Crowd," *New York Times*, October 26, 2008).

25   Many candidates ... uploaded ads and permitted freewheeling — sometimes ferocious — discussion of them.... Candidates virtually forfeited control over the context of their videos and allowed them to be embedded, critiqued, recut and satirized.... Some candidates also discovered, to their surprise, that they could upload vanity videos (or ones that seemed fairly parody-proof) and supporters would circulate them on social networks, amateurs would use them to make ads and they would get influential, focused advertising for nothing. Early on, the musician will.i.am used film of an Obama speech to make his "Yes We Can" music video. That video, in multiple versions, has become the most-watched political entry on the site, having been seen around 15 million times. (The campaign's upload of the actual "Yes We Can" speech has fewer than two million views.) Heffernan, Virginia, "The Medium: Clicking and Choosing", *New York Times Magazine,* November 16, 2008.

26   Allen, Danielle, "Citizenship 2.0" *Washington Post*, November 25, 2008; A15.

27   In the primaries, Obama racked up huge scores in college towns, especially in states that require greater efforts at participation by choosing delegates through caucuses – rather than primaries -- a result in good part of the use of sophisticated electronic mobilization techniques to capitalize on Obama's attractiveness. At the end of February 2008, when his campaign really took off, Obama had 300,000 "friends" on Facebook (to Hillary Clinton's 85,000). On both MySpace and Youtube there were almost three times as many sites for Obama as Clinton. Among the Youtube election-related clips, the five

most popular Clinton ones were seen by an average of 383,000 compared to 847,000 for Obama's top 5. (*La Presse*, "L'Internet favorise Obama, Karine Prémont." February 22: A17).

28   Allen, Danielle, *op. cit.*

29   Analysis of the 2008 Current Population Survey (CPS), Voter and Registration Supplement (downloaded from www.projectvote. org April 20 2008).

30   For the case of Norway, see http://www. tinget.no/minitinget/minitinget.aspx>.

31   The details here are derived from an observation of the Swedish Democracy workshop. Here, each student is given a card with the first name of an individual MP and his or her party, and placed on a committee responsible for dealing with one or two issues. The card gives information about the legislator's party affiliation, age, gender, professional back-

ground, etc. The five parties are fictitious, but their positions and names are based on those of existing parties. The party groups vary in size to reflect the actual composition of legislature. During my visit in spring 2008, one committee was considering whether the punishment for graffiti should be made harsher, and another whether boxing should be outlawed. Both matters had come up in Parliament.

32   Using the international student-level PISA (Programme for International Student Assessment) database, Fuchs and Woessmann (2004) show that the positive correlation between student achievement and the availability of computers both at home and at school becomes negative for home computers, and insignificant for school computers, once they control for family background and school characteristics.

Chapter 12
Predicting the Participation in Information Society

Sheila Zimic
Mid Sweden University, Sweden

ABSTRACT

The approach in this chapter is to recognize what is said to be important regarding the feeling of participation in the information society. The perceived feeling of participation is assumed to be an important indicator for young people's online experiences. In previous research, digital skills and other related concepts such as self-efficacy and a relationship with technology are shown to be important in order to be able to participate in the information society. In this case, there is an exploration into the amount that social factors, digital skills, self-efficacy and a relationship with technology are able to explain the variance in perceived feelings regarding participation. It has been determined that education, self-efficacy, instrumental computer skills, information skills and strategic skills can explain 22 percent of the variance in the perceived feeling of participation. This implies that young people themselves might define other factors as being more important with regards to participation in the information society.

INTRODUCTION

15 years have passed since the start of use of the internet within Swedish society (Findahl, 2009). At the outset, only a few, technologically interested people, engaged with the internet. As time has passed more and more people have adopted

it and today 83 percent of Swedish people use it. The majority (85 percent) of those who do not use the internet are 60 or over (Findahl, 2009). Because the internet has become highly adopted in the industrialized part of the world, the focus has shifted from the classical 'digital divide' in explaining the divide between those who have and those who do not have access to the internet to a more explorative focus on social divides (Peter

DOI: 10.4018/978-1-60960-206-2.ch012

& Valkenburg, 2006). With respect to the digital divide, the importance of digital literacy has been discussed where an attempt has been made to explain what it is that is important to know regarding the use of information and communication technology in order to not become disadvantaged within the information society (Hargittai, 2005; Livingstone, Bober, & Helsper, 2005; Van Dijk & Hacker, 2003). As stated previously, it is the elderly people in Sweden who pose the highest risk of not being a part of the information society. Young people's involvement in the information society is on the other hand taken for granted since very few are non-users. However, in the case of digital literacy, previous studies have shown that it is not necessarily the young who have the highest digital skills (Duimel & deHaan, 2009). In accordance with Duimel & de Haan (2009), some of the results from my previous study have indicated that young people (12-16 years) tend to rate their competence in using computers as fairly or very high which does not entirely correspond to the rates scored in the so called internet skills (Zimic, 2009). I had come to the conclusion that it was probable that it had not proved possible to measure their skills in using the internet. Often, when measuring digital skills, the focus lies on the "instrumental skills" – what people know in relation to operating hardware and software when using both the internet and a computer. The question then becomes what skills are expected from people in order to participate in the information society? In this chapter the concept of digital skills by van Dijk and Hacker (2003) has been used because they measured different levels of skills which are defined to be important in order to participate in the information society. The questions representing the different digital skills in this chapter are not identical to the original model for digital skills (van Deursen & van Dijk, 2009; Van Dijk & Hacker, 2003) so they can be viewed more as indicators of digital skills rather than the actual skills. The questions are used as an inspiration to

explore young people's perceived feeling of participation in order to answer the general research questions – 1) which skills do young people think are important for participation? and 2) who are those at risk of being disadvantaged because of the lack of skills?

The aim is not to explain how young people participate online but the focus is rather on young people's perceived feelings of participation within the information society. It provides us with important information concerning young people's online experience and what participation in the information society could mean to them because the feeling of participation is assumed to be consensually related to actual participation. Peoples' perceived participation affects how much they actually participate online and the actual participation affects how they perceive their participation. It is important to investigate how young people perceive their feelings of participation because there are many stereotypical images regarding young people's internet usage (Tapscott, 1998; Tapscott & Dawsonera, 2009). Being active online does not however necessarily have to mean participating in a way that is expected of citizens in the information society. In accordance with other studies which have critically explored the notion of 'Net geners' (S. Bennett, Maton, & Kervin, 2008; Cheong, 2008; Facer & Furlong, 2001; Livingstone & Helsper, 2007; Sherry & Fielden, 2005) this study explores what is said to be important for participation online by placing the focus on the perspective of young people. The approach is to recognize what is said to be important regarding being a part of the information society by linking the social factors, digital skills, self-efficacy in using computers and attitude towards using new technology (relation with technology) in order to explore how much they affect the feeling of participation in the information society.

WHAT IS MEANT BY YOUNG PEOPLE'S PARTICIPATION?

Being a part of the information society does not have to mean active participation in the information society. There is however reason to believe that participation merits the perceived feeling of taking part in the information society and that the same factors that explain the variations in participation should also explain the perceived feeling of being a part of the information society. But what is meant by children's and young people´s participation? In article 12 of the Convention on the Rights of the Child the following statement has pointed out that children and young people are independent subjects and have their rights to participate:

"State Parties shall assure to the child who is capable of forming his or her own views the right to express those views freely in all matters affecting the child, the views of the child being given due weight in accordance with the age and maturity of the child."

With this as the focus Roger Hart developed a model called *"the ladder of participation"* which has been greatly influential for research and practice regarding young people's participation. The model illustrates a ladder with eight steps in which the first three steps consider the non-participation and steps four to eight are different degrees of participation. The first step is called *manipulation* and suggests that children act as the adults tell them to act without having any understanding of why they should act in that certain way and what influence their acts have had on the final decision. The second step on the ladder is *decoration*. It refers to events in which children take part by performing (singing, dancing) or wearing T-shirts with logos but do not really understand the cause. They are there for other reasons, such as refreshments, an interesting performance etc.

Adults organize the whole occasion and use the children to support the cause in an indirect way. The third step is *tokenism* which is used to describe occasions when young people are asked to say what they think about an issue but have little or no choice about the way they express their views. The fourth step is called *assigned but informed* and means that children understand the intentions of the project; they know who made the decisions concerning the involvement and why; they have a meaningful rather than 'decorative' role and they volunteer for the project after the project has been made clear to them. The fifth step of participation is *consulted and informed*. It means that the project is designed and run by adults but children are consulted. Children understand the process and their opinions are treated seriously. *Adult-initiated, shared decisions with children* is the sixth step in the ladder. Hart states that at this level true participation takes place since decision making is shared with the young people. However, the projects at this level are still initiated by adults. The next, seventh level, is *child-initiated and directed*. Children have the initial idea and decide how the project should be carried out. The adults are available for support but they do not take charge of the project. The final step in the ladder of participation is *child-initiated shared decisions with adults*. At this level young people have the initial idea, set up a project and finally invite adults to join them in making decisions (Hart, 1992).

The internet is considered to possess great potentials for making participation possible, especially for young people (Loader & Hague, 1999). The often used terms 'digital natives' (Prensky, 2001) and 'Net generation' (Tapscott, 1998) refer to young people as being born into the information society and where the use of the internet is integrated into their everyday lives. Children and young people are considered to be more skilled and knowledgeable than adults in relation to the use of the internet and other

information and communication technologies. ·
For the first time, young people are placed in a
higher power position (Prensky, 2001; Tapscott,
1998). The implication of this is that they have
more say and are being listened to.

There are a wide range of examples of children's and young people's participation online.
Montgomery (2008) has investigated the "youth
civic web" – platforms built for young people in
order to invite them to participate. This has, according to Montgomery, shown to be promising
in expanding the opportunities for young people
to connect, engage and create. She concludes that
the interactive media is helping to provide young
people with some of the essential skills for civic
and political engagement by: learning about the
critical issues of the day; inserting their own voices
into the public discourse; and actively participating
in a range of political issues. The possibilities of
web 2.0 activities online are considered by many
to be arenas for young people's participation (L.
W. Bennett, Wells, & Rank, 2009; Livingstone,
Bober, et al., 2005; Montgomery, 2008). According
to Bennett, Wells and Rank (2009) "good citizenship" could be practiced within the internet's
interactive opportunities and not only as traditional
government-centered activities.

Livingstone, Bober and Helsper (2005)
examined young people's take-up of a range
of internet activities broadly falling under the
umbrella of 'participation'. They examined what
kind of activities young people engage in, what
civic possibilities these sites offer, whether or not
young people embrace all of the activities, and
if so, why. However, the question in relation to
which activities merit the label of 'participation'
remained unresolved. In general, Livingstone
et. al.(2005), found that young people do take
part of a range of online opportunities and gain
new experiences when it comes to participating.
However, not all young people are engaged and
they do not engage in the same way.

In accordance with Livingstone, Bober and
Helsper (2005) there are critical voices regarding
young people's participation online (S. Bennett, et
al., 2008; Cheong, 2008; Facer & Furlong, 2001;
Herring, 2008; Sherry & Fielden, 2005). Herring
(2008) questioned the existence of the 'Net generation' which is said to be creating content online.
She suggested that the real 'Net generation' has
not yet been born. The present young people are
not driven by their own interests in constructing
the content online. Instead the content online is
still managed by corporate interests and adults
are in fact thus constructing the 'Net generation'.

Lindgren (2009) states that young people often
symbolize new elements in society and that often
leads to presupposing that young people are more
progressive than their parents and other adults.
The discourse concerning young people in the
digital landscape often takes its starting point in
technology deterministic views, meaning that the
generational differences are seen to be produced
by technology, rather than being as the result of
social, historical and cultural factors (Buckingham
& Willett, 2006). Buckingham (2006) states that
it is important to consider what children or young
people really are instead of ascribing them a set of
imperatives about what they should be and what
they need to become.

On the one hand children and young people are
considered to be participating online but on the
other hand there are critical voices with regards
to the aims and form of their participation. The
aim of this chapter is not to explain how young
people participate online. However, by analyzing
the perceived feeling of participation among young
people important information about participation
is provided. The perceived feeling of participation
indicates something about the actual participation and is, I would argue, equally important in
order to learn more about young people's online
experiences. In this chapter it is assumed that
digital skills and other related concepts such as
self-efficacy and relationships with technology

are important for people in order to be able to participate and hence to feel that they are a part of the information society.

ANALYTICAL FRAMES

To be able to participate one must have certain skills such as being able to understand important information in order to make good decisions. In the digital era it is important to know how to use the information and communication technologies in order to participate. These skills and knowledge are often referred to as *media literacy* and *digital literacy*. Livingstone et. al. (2005) pointed out three aims for media literacy. The first one is a citizen's democratic participation in which the literate citizen can obtain information concerning what is happening in society and participate in the formation of opinion. The second aim is that economic stability should build on knowledge and in which the literate citizen has more to offer and more to achieve in work which makes the society more innovative and competitive. The third aim is lifelong learning, cultural expression and the possibility for personal achievement. Being media literate means having the skills to critically examine the flow of information and make choices that lead to a meaningful life and to an informed, creative and ethical society (Livingstone, Van Couvering, et al., 2005).

One attempt to define and measure the skills required in the digital era has been conducted by van Dijk and Hacker (2003). Their model describes three different levels of so called digital skills: i) instrumental skills, ii) informational skills, iii) strategic skills. The instrumental skills refer to being able to operate hardware and software while informational skills refer to a slightly more advanced type of internet use involving being able to search, select, process, and apply information using the hardware and software. The strategic skills are on the highest skill level and they refer

to being able to use the information discovered in order to improve one's own social position in society (Van Dijk & Hacker, 2003). However, to achieve the informational skills one must master the instrumental skills, and to achieve the strategic skills both the instrumental and the informational skills are necessary. van Deursen and van Dijk (2009) developed the model further by specifically examining internet skills. These internet skills include operational, formal, information and strategic skills. In this chapter the former classification of digital skills will be used merely to obtain an indication of the skills at the instrumental, information and strategic level. By relating the level of skills to the previous definition of media literacy it can be argued that a high level of strategic skills entails a high level of media literacy.

Another way of describing the skills and competencies necessary in order to participate in the information society is described by Sharkey and Brandt (2008) as the *information literacy* and *technology literacy*. They define technology literacy as skills required in order to use the technical tools while information literacy involves skills for locating and using the information in addition to the knowledge for interpreting and evaluating it. The authors argue that information and technology literacy are complementary, meaning that the technologies are the tools, but it is the result of using them that is important which means that both technological and information literacy are required in the information society (Sharkey & Brandt, 2008, p. 86). Figure 1 illustrates how the different concepts of digital skills, media literacy, technology literacy and information literacy relate to each other. The digital skills are illustrated by the figure which appears to be a staircase since the different skills are considered to be at different levels. The line illustrates the continuum for media literacy; higher up along the line corresponds to a higher level of media literacy.

Figure 1. The relationship between media literacy, digital skills, technology literacy and information literacy

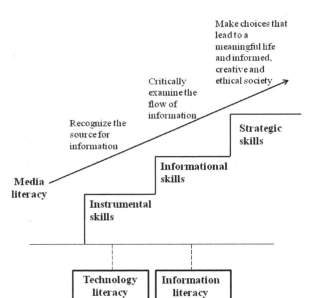

In relation to the model of digital skills, in this paper it is interpreted as technology literacy corresponding to instrumental skills and the information literacy corresponding to information skills.

Regardless of the manner in which the necessary competence is viewed in the information society, either as a staircase or a continuum, the highest level is considered to be a consciousness about a wider understanding of one's own relationship to the information society. It is about an individual's ability to grasp the whole picture – seeing how the information society could be used to make wise decisions for oneself and what he or she can do to contribute to a more informed and ethical society. In this manner, the values embedded in the definitions of high levels of media literacy and digital skills could also define what is considered to be "good citizenship" in terms of participation in the information society. In this chapter the basics from van Dijk and Hackers model (2003) were used to construct an analytical framework regarding the digital skills in order to determine whether they are able to explain the

variance in the perceived feeling of participation in the information society (Figure 2).

H1: Instrumental, information and strategic skills have a positive relationship with the perceived feeling of participation. From the three levels it is the strategic skills that have the strongest correlation with the perceived feeling of participation since these skills are at the highest skill level. They entail a high degree of media literacy and support the participation in the information society.

In a similar manner to that with which the perceived feeling of participation in information society is approached in this chapter, several studies have approached the perceived feeling of the ability to use computers and the internet (Torkzadeh & Van Dyke, 2002). The perceived feeling of one's own ability to perform is called *self-efficacy* (Bandura, 1997). In this study the self-efficacy in using computers is examined. Among others Torkzadeh et. al. (2002) found that self-efficacy is very important for an individual's performance in computer and internet use. They studied a group of students before and after

Figure 2. Illustration of relationships between digital skills, self-efficacy, relation with technology, age, gender, education with the perceived feeling of participation

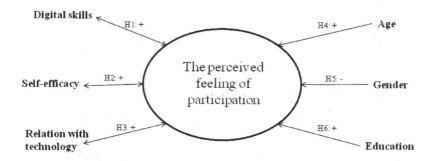

computer training course and they found that all the participants benefited from the training and improved their self-efficacy in using computers.

H2: There is a positive effect between self-efficacy in using computers and the perceived feeling of participation in the information society.

Self-efficacy in using computers is closely related to the relation with technology, referring to how people's attitudes towards technology affect their engagement with technology (Lindblad-Gidlund, 2005).

H3: There is a positive relationship between the relation with technology and the perceived feeling of participation, meaning that more positive attitudes entail a higher feeling of participation.

Further, it is expected that the feeling of participation varies among internet users regarding demographic factors. Livingstone, Bober and Helsper (2005) found that in general boys, middle class children and older teenagers are more likely than girls, working class children and younger teenagers to engage in online communication, information-seeking and peer to peer connection. Age is the most important factor when it comes to skills and the variety of ways young people participate online. It is the older children who make the most of their online experience, because they have been online for longer and have therefore gained more skills (Livingstone, Bober, et al., 2005; Livingstone & Helsper, 2007).

H4: Age has a positive effect on the perceived feeling of participation, meaning that the perceived feeling increases as does the age.

H5: Girls/women perceive their feeling of participation lower than boys/men.

H6: Education has a positive effect on the perceived feeling of participation. Higher levels of education entail a higher feeling of participation.

METHOD

This study is based on data collected in an annual Swedish national survey about Swedish peoples' internet use which is a part of the international World Internet Project (www.worldinternetproject.net). The survey was conducted between February and May 2009. A random sample of 2,063 people from all around Sweden from 12 years and older answered a wide range of questions about their internet use. Initially the survey was conducted as a panel study and through the years the "drop offs" where compensated for by a stratified random sample by age. Two different surveys were conducted, one with respondents of 16 years and older and one with young people from 12 (born in 1997) to 16 years (born in 1993). The main reasons for conducting two different surveys were that those under 16 required the permission from a parent/guardian to participate

Table 1. Sample sizes for different age groups

Age	N	Percent
12-16	143	7
17-19	116	6
20-29	258	12
30-39	285	14
40-49	321	16
50-59	298	14
60 +	642	31
Total	2063	100

Table 2. Sample sizes for 12-31 year olds

Age	N	Percent
12-16	286	33
17-19	231	27
20-25	173	20
26-31	168	20
Total	858	100

but also to obtain a larger sample of young people in order to be able to perform statistical analyses when the youngest groups are studied separately. Table 1 shows how the different age groups are distributed within the sample. The age groups 12-16 and 17-19 years are weighted by 0.5 to match the proportions within the Swedish population.

In this chapter young people between 12 and 31 years are the focus and thus the cases were not given any weight. This group is somewhat over-represented in relation to the entire sample of Swedish population. However, the aim in this chapter is to explore the tendencies among 12-31 year olds in general and for that reason the larger sample is chosen. Table 2 shows the distribution of the sample 12-31 years.

The survey includes a range of questions about internet activities, attitude towards the internet and a set of questions about the so called digital skills. It is an extensive study concerning the internet usage of the Swedish people.

The digital skills – instrumental, information and strategic, in accordance with van Dijk and Hacker (2003) are defined by matching some of the questions from the data used in this paper by the questions regarding digital skills (van Deursen & van Dijk, 2009). In table 3, an overview of the questions included can be seen. The questions in table 3 are recognized as being similar to those used by van Dijk and van Deursen (2009) and the model should be interpreted as an indication of the skills defined by the authors. There is always

a risk for multi-collinearity when several similar factors are included in one model. By performing collinearity diagnostics the risk for high multi-collinearity could be excluded since the variance inflation factors were lower than 5 (Instrumental computer skills VIF=1,818; Instrumental internet skills VIF=1,917; Information skill VIF=1,235; Strategic skills VIF=1,381).

The *instrumental skills* are, in this case, divided into *internet* and *computer* related skills. Instrumental skills in using the internet relate to what people can or cannot do in relation to using the internet to download music, send an email, attach documents to email and make a voice call. The questions are simply asked: *Do you know how to do the following things on the internet? Send an email?* Etc. The *instrumental skills in using a computer* are constructed in the same way and the questions are: plug in and install new accessories to the computer such as a printer, an external hard drive etc.; install and configure a network to share files, printer or broadband at home; install a new program; install a new operating system. The *information skill* refers to people's estimation regarding the ease or difficulty in finding information online which they are interested in. *Strategic skills* are activities that are, in some way, strategies regarding, for instance, saving time or money. They are defined here by the questions: *How often do you use the internet to get information about a product?* and *How often do you use the internet to make price comparisons between products or services?*. As previously stated, the questions do not entirely corre-

Table 3. Digital skills defined from the questions in the survey 2009

Instrumental skills		Information skill	Strategic skills
Internet	**Computer**		
Do you know how to do the following things on the internet? Send email?	Do you know how to do following things with a computer and computer accessories? Plug in and install new computer accessories such as a printer, external hard drive etc.?	How difficult or easy would you say it is to do the following things online? Please answer on a scale from 1 to 5. 1 means it is very difficult and 5 means it is very easy. Search and find information you are interested in?	How often do you use the Internet to get information about a product?
Attach documents to your email?	Install or configure a network in order to share files, printer and broadband at home?		How often do you use the Internet to make price comparisons between products or services?
Download music?	Install a new computer program?		
Make voice-calls online?	Install a new operating system?		

*Note: Instrumental internet and computer skills – answers are coded: 0=No; 1=Yes. Information and strategic skills are measured on a five-point scale with the values 1 to 5 (1 means very difficult and 5 means very easy), never is coded as 0.

spond to the original model regarding digital skills (van Deursen & van Dijk, 2009; Van Dijk & Hacker, 2003) so the results should be interpreted with some caution, meaning that the relations between digital skills and the feeling of participation regards the digital skills as they are measured within this study. However, even though the digital skills within this study do not cover the entire concept of digital skills, some of the items or issues are still represented and can therefore be used in the sense of interpreting the effect of digital skills on the dependent variable – feeling of participation.

In addition, variables such as *relation with technology* and *self-efficacy* for this model were included in the analysis. Relationship with technology, which has to do with people's attitudes to technology, was measured by asking people to rate how much they agree or disagree with the statement "*I like to try out new technology*". It is measured on a five point Likert-scale in which 1 is *do not agree at all* and 5 is *totally agree*. *Self-efficacy* in computer use was measured by asking people to rate their competence in using computers from "not competent at all" to "very competent". Both self-efficacy and relationship with technology measured what was supposed

to be measured. However, self-efficacy is not measured as precisely as the relationship with technology since it is measured on a four-point scale instead of a five-point scale.

The dependent variable in the analysis is people's perceived feeling regarding being a part of the information society. In this study the perceived feeling of participation was analyzed by asking the question: *You have now answered a range of questions about different media and you have probably heard or read about surfing the internet, using email and information technology. Do you feel like a part of this new information society?* The answers are: *No, not at all, Yes, but only a little, Yes, for the most part, Yes, totally.* The question is not an attempt to measure actual participation in the information society but it is an indicator of people's subjective feelings which provides very useful information in order to explore what participation really is about.

The factor *gender* was coded 1 for woman and 0 for man. *Age* was divided into three groups 12-16, 17-19, 20-25 and 26-31 years. Finally *education* was divided into three levels – primary/secondary school, high-school and university.

Table 4. Do you feel that you are a part of the new information society?

	Frequency	Percent
No, not at all	61	8
Yes, but just a little	195	25
Yes, for the most part	345	44
Yes, totally	189	24
Total	**790**	**100**

RESULTS

Approximately 17 percent (n=332) of Swedish people do not feel that they are a part of the information society. 48 percent of them are men and 52 percent are women. The majority (66%) of those who feel disengaged with the information society are 60 or older, 11 percent are under 30 years of age and 23 percent are between 30 and 59. Even though there is an age difference among those who claim that they do not feel that they are part of the information society, the gender difference is not significant. In table 4 the distribution of the perceived feeling of participation in information society for 12-31 year olds can be seen.

It is not obvious that all young people feel engaged in the information society. In this case, 8 percent of the young population do not feel engaged at all and 25 percent say that they feel engaged to a small extent. It is interesting to find out what characterizes the two groups of young people answering "No, not at all" and "Yes, totally" for the question regarding being a part of the information society (Table 5). It is not possible to generalize the results but it is however possible to see tendencies or patterns. Among those who answered "No, not at all" there appears to be little gender difference since 34 percent are men and 27 percent are women. However among those feeling totally engaged in the information society, there is a significantly larger difference between men and women (61% men and 39% women). In relation to age, there is no clear tendency or pattern. It appears as if the feeling of engagement increases with age since the proportion of those answering "No, not at all" decreases with age. The factor of education appears to have a positive relationship with the feeling of participation since there are many more highly educated respondents in the group of totally engaged as compared to the group of disengaged (5% university educated people in the group of disengaged and 30% university educated people in the group of totally engaged). Comparing the means between the two groups it was discovered that only the level of education differed significantly (sig.=0.003). However there might be an interaction between age and education since the youngest are still attending primary and secondary school and those with a higher education are among the older age groups.

According to previous studies (Livingstone, Bober, et al., 2005) it has been shown that demographic factors, as well as internet expertise and confidence in using the internet can explain the variation in level and form of participation. Hence, it is assumed that these factors might also have an effect on the perceived feeling of participation. Table 6 shows how the variables in the model correlate.

As suggested in hypotheses 1 the digital skills - instrumental computer skills (r=.35; p≤.01), internet skills (r=.261; p≤.01), information skill (r=.275; p≤.01) and strategic skills (r=.188; p≤.01) are positively correlated with the feeling of participation. Five of the six hypotheses are supported when the binary correlations are investigated. Hypotheses 5 is not supported (r=-.056; p>.05) meaning that the differences between men and women in relation to the feeling of participation are only minimal. The relationships are not highly correlated and some of them might not be significant when included together in a model. In order to explore the differences and to attempt to discover which variables best explain the variance in the perceived feeling of participation, the variables were consequently included in a model. To

Table 5. Age, gender and education for 12-31 year olds that answered no, not at all and yes, totally on the question - Do you feel that you are a part of the new information society?

Do you feel that you are a part of the new information society	Frequency	Percent	Frequency	Percent
	No, not at all	No, not at all	Yes, totally	Yes, totally
Gender	34	56	116	61
Man	27	44	73	39
Women	**61**	**100**	**189**	**100**
Total	20	33	46	24
Age	16	26	45	24
12-16	14	23	45	24
17-19	**11**	18	53	28
20-2526-31	**61**	**100**	**189**	**100**
Total	38	62	88	47
Education	18	30	44	23
Primary/Secondary	5	8	56	30
High-school				
University				
Total	**61**	**100**	**188**	**100**

reduce the complexity some of the variables were revised by combining categories. For example the relationship with technology (RwT) ended up with two values, 0 and 1 where 0 represents a low interest in trying new technology and 1 represents a relatively high or high interest in trying out new technology. In a similar way the self-efficacy, instrumental computer and internet skills, information skill and strategic skills were reduced to two values.

By using the -2 log-likelihood to compare two models it was possible to reduce factors from the original model and ensure that the new model retained a good quality (the r^2 value was the same for the original and the final model). By reducing gender, age, relationship with technology and instrumental internet skills which were not significant for the perceived feeling of participation, the final model could explain 22 percent of the variance in the dependent variable.

The category *high-school* is not significant for the explanation of variance in participation in the information society. However, the highest level of education (university) has a strong statistical effect on participation (Exp(B)=2.658). Self-efficacy and the information skill are also shown to be important for the explanation in the variance of the perceived feeling of participation. People rating their competence in using computers as fairly or very competent (corresponding to self-efficacy(1)) are almost 2.6 times more likely to rate their feeling of participation higher when comparing to the people in the reference category. People who find it relatively easy to search and discover information online are almost 4 times more likely to rate their feeling of participation as higher in comparison to those in the reference category. This is somewhat surprising since according to hypothesis 1 the strategic skills, which are at the highest level of skills, should have the strongest effect on the perceived feeling of participation. Thus, hypothesis 1 could not be supported.

The value for internet users within the age range of 12-31 with a high level of education, high level of self-efficacy and high levels of information, strategic and instrumental computer skills to feel more engaged in the information society is approximately 15 which is much higher in comparison to the value of 0.13 for those with a low education, low interest in trying out new technology, low self-efficacy, low instrumental, information and strategic skills. The probability

Table 6. Correlations among variables in the model

	Gender	Age	Education	Relation with technology	Instrumental skills (Comp)	Instrumental skills (Int.)	Information skill	Strategic skills	Self efficacy
Gender	1.00								
Age	0.053	1.00							
Education	0.084*	0.739**	1.00						
Relation with technology	-0.353**	-0.015	0.017	1.00					
Instrumental skills (Comp)	-0.387**	-0.301**	0.227**	0.430**	1.00				
Instrumental skills (Int.)	-0.142**	-0.249**	0.205**	0.272**	0.588**	1.00			
Information skill	-0.068*	-0.147**	0.122**	0.202**	0.311**	0.365**	1.00		
Strategic skills	-0.203**	-0.091*	0.096*	0.308**	0.312**	0.251**	0.194**	1.00	
Self efficacy	-0.163**	-0.047	0.092*	0.352**	0.456**	0.393**	0.247**	0.269**	1.00
Participation in information society	-0.056	0.158**	0.204**	0.281**	0.350**	0.261**	0.275**	0.188**	0.267**

Note: **Relationships are significant at the p=0.01 level, *relationships are significant at the p= 0.05 level.

for a highly perceived feeling of participation is 0.94 if the person has a high level of skills, high self efficacy and high level of education (Table 7).

DISCUSSION AND CONCLUDING REMARKS

The approach in this chapter was to recognize what is said to be important regarding the feeling of being a part of the information society by linking the digital skills, self-efficacy in using computers and attitude towards using new technology (relationship with technology) in order to explore whether they can explain the variance in the perceived feeling of participation in the information society. It was found that the variables education, self-efficacy, instrumental computer skills, information skill and strategic skills are significant for providing an explanation regarding the variance in the perceived feeling of participation in information society. The results imply that the information skill has the strongest relationship with perceived feeling of participation in the information society, which is surprising considering that the strategic skills should have the strongest effect since being at the highest skill level (Van Dijk & Hacker, 2003). Surprisingly age and gender could not explain the variation in the perceived feeling of participation among 12-31 year olds. In other studies (Livingstone, Bober, et al., 2005) it was found that age best predicts the variation in participation online among young people. However, when it comes to gender there

Table 7. Binary logistic regression - Predicting the variation in perceived feeling of information society by the factors: Education, Self-efficacy, Instrumental computer skills, Information skill and Strategic skills

	B	SE	Wald	df	Sig.	Exp(B)
Education			10.788	2	.005	
Education(High school)	-.230	.257	.801	1	.371	.794
Education(University)	.978	.358	7.909	1	.006	2.658
Self-efficacy(1)	.941	.320	8.650	1	.003	2.563
Instrumental_computer(1)	.936	.248	14.233	1	.000	2.549
Information_skill(1)	1.344	.429	9.825	1	.002	3.835
Strategic_skills(1)	.552	.245	5.064	1	.024	1.737
Constant	-2.035	.501	16.507	1	.000	.131

appears to be a gender difference among those who answered "Yes, totally" on the question regarding being a part of the information society. High level of education (university) proved to be important in relation to explaining the variance in perceived feeling of participation.

The results show that the feeling of participation does not have a direct relationship with age but since those who are the most highly educated who are more likely to feel a higher degree of participation there is of course an indirect relationship with age because those with a university education are among the oldest age group in this sample (26-31 years). This means that it is not necessarily the young who perceive a high feeling of participation, something that is often assumed because they have been born in the presence of the internet and are very active online (Prensky, 2001; Tapscott, 1998). The results also indicate that young people primarily ascribe the skill of searching and finding information online to participation in the information society. This skill is practiced within higher levels of education which could explain the higher proportions of university educated people who have a perceived feeling as the participation increases. According to the importance of the information skill it can be argued that technical expertise is not considered to be so important since the variable 'relation with technology' did not have any significance in

the model and nor did the instrumental internet skills. As previously stated, the strategic skills did not have as strong an effect as was expected which additionally indicates the importance of the information skill when it comes to a feeling of participation in the information society. Self-efficacy is, as expected, very important for a feeling of participation which also implies that the feeling of participation is important for actual participation.

The limitation of this study is firstly with regards to its deductive way of constructing the variables which were tested in the model. The questions regarding the digital skills are not exhaustively representing what the different skills are all about. They are to be seen more as indicators of the different skills rather than the actual skills. Another problematic issue is the broad dependent variable regarding the feeling of participation. One issue is that the concept 'information society' might direct the respondents association to the importance of information. However, the introduction to the question is referring back to the questions asked at an earlier stage in the interview which mainly focus on the internet behaviour. The term participation is not predefined, which leaves the respondent to interpret the concept on their own. This issue might be problematic; however in this study the aim was to explore what young people define by the term on their own.

In several aspects this study shows the importance of exploring young people's own subjective feelings regarding participation in order to learn more about what participation means to them. This chapter indicates that the skills and attitudes considered as being important for participation actually were not rated as the most important among the young people themselves. It also shows that must pay attention and make efforts to increase the level regarding a feeling of participation among many young people. Clearly, there are young people who think that they are not a part of the information society but the feeling of participation increases with the level of education which means that the structural differences cannot be ignored. By placing the focus on the young people's perspectives we can learn more about what they think is important for participation and meet their requirements in an acceptable manner. In addition, the risk of making assumptions built on stereotypical images about young people's online world will decrease. In this chapter the feeling of participation was linked to digital skills and other factors related to competences in using computers and the internet. Further studies are required in relation to internet behaviour, what young people actually engage in and to explore what kind of internet activities merit the feeling of participation among young people.

REFERENCES

Bandura, A. (1997). *Self-efficacy: the exercise of control*. Basingstoke, UK: W. H. Freeman.

Bennett, L. W., Wells, C., & Rank, A. (2009). Young citizens and civic learning: two paradigms of citizenship in the digital age. *Citizenship Studies*, *13*(2), 105–120. doi:10.1080/13621020902731116

Bennett, S., Maton, K., & Kervin, L. (2008). The "Digital Natives" Debate: A Critical Review of the Evidence. *British Journal of Educational Technology*, *39*(5), 775–786. doi:10.1111/j.1467-8535.2007.00793.x

Buckingham, D., & Willett, R. (2006). *Digital generations: children, young people, and new media*. Mahwah, NJ: Lawrence Erlbaum Associates.

Cheong, P. H. (2008). The young and techless? Investigating internet use and problem-solving behaviors of young adults in Singapore. *New Media & Society*, *10*(5), 771–791. doi:10.1177/1461444808094356

Duimel, M., & deHaan, J. (2009). *Instrumental, information and strategic ICT skills of teenagers and their parents*. Paper presented at the EU Kids Online conference.

Facer, K., & Furlong, R. (2001). Beyond the Myth of the 'Cyberkid': Young People at the Margins of the Information revolution. *Journal of Youth Studies*, *4*(4), 451–469. doi:10.1080/13676260120101905

Findahl, O. (2009). *Svenskarna och Internet 2009 (Internet in Sweden 2009)*. Hudiksvall, Sweden: World Internet Institute.

Hargittai, E. (2005). Survey Measures of Web-Oriented Digital Literacy. *Social Science Computer Review*, *23*(3), 371–379. doi:10.1177/0894439305275911

Hart, R. A. (1992). Children's participation. From tokenism to citizenship. *Innocenti essays 4*.

Herring, C. S. (2008). Questioning the Generational Divide: Technological Exoticism and Adult Constructions of Online Youth Identity. In Buckingham, D. (Ed.), *Youth, Identity, and Digital Media (Vol. The John D. and Catherine T. Macarthur Foundation series on digital media and learning)*. Cambridge, MA: MIT Press.

Lindblad-Gidlund, K. (2005). *Techno Therapy: a relation with technology.* Umeå universitet. Institutionen för informatik Umeå.

Lindgren, S. (2009). *Ungdomskulturer* (1. uppl. ed.). Malmö, Sweden: Gleerup.

Livingstone, S., Bober, M., & Helsper, E. (2005). Active participation or just more information? *Information Communication and Society, 8*(3), 287–314. doi:10.1080/13691180500259103

Livingstone, S., & Helsper, E. (2007). Gradations in digital inclusion: Children, young people and the digital divide. *New Media & Society, 9*(4), 671–696. doi:10.1177/1461444807080335

Livingstone, S., Van Couvering, E., & Thumim, N. (2005). *Adult Media Literacy: A review of the research literature on behalf of Ofcom.* London: London School of Economics and Political Science.

Loader, B. D., & Hague, B. N. (Eds.). (1999). *Digital Democracy – Discourse and Decision making in the Information Age.* London, New York: Routledge.

Montgomery, K. C. (2008). Youth and digital democracy: Intersections of practice, policy, and the marketplace. In Bennett, *W* (pp. Lance (2008). *Civic life online: Learning how digital media can engage youth.* The John D. and Catherine T. MacArthur Foundation series on digital media and learning. (pp. 2025-2049). Cambridge, MA: MIT Press. ix, 2206.

Peter, J., & Valkenburg, P. M. (2006). Adolescents' internet use: Testing the "disappearing digital divide" versus the "emerging digital differentiation" approach. *Poetics, 34*(4-5), 293–305. doi:10.1016/j.poetic.2006.05.005

Prensky, M. (2001). Digital Natives, Digital Immigrants. *On the Horizon. NCB University Press, 9*(5), 1–10.

Sharkey, J., & Brandt, D. S. (2008). Integrating technology literacy and information literacy. In Rivoltella, P. C. (Ed.), *Digital Literacy: Tools and Methodologies for Information Society* (pp. 85–96). Hershey: IGI.

Sherry, C. A., & Fielden, K. A. (2005). *The millennials: Computer savvy (or not?).* Paper presented at the HERDSA Conference.

Tapscott, D. (1998). *Growing up digital: the rise of the Net generation.* London: McGraw-Hill.

Tapscott, D., & Dawsonera. (2009). *Grown up digital [Elektronisk resurs]: how the net generation is changing your world.* New York: McGraw-Hill: [Dawsonera [distributör]].

Torkzadeh, G., & Van Dyke, T. P. (2002). Effects of training on Internet self-efficacy and computer user attitudes. *Computers in Human Behavior, 18*(5), 479–494. doi:10.1016/S0747-5632(02)00010-9

van Deursen, A. J. A. M., & van Dijk, J. A. G. M. (2009). Improving Digital Skills for the Use of Online Public Information and Services. *Government Information Quarterly, 26*(2), 333–340. doi:10.1016/j.giq.2008.11.002

Van Dijk, J., & Hacker, K. (2003). The Digital Divide as a Complex and Dynamic Phenomenon. *The Information Society, 19*(4), 315–326. doi:10.1080/01972240309487

Zimic, S. (2009). Not so 'techno-savvy': Challenging the stereotypical images of the 'Net generation'. *Digital Culture & Education, 1*(2), 129–144.

Chapter 13
African Art Students and Digital Learning

Paula Uimonen
Stockholm University, Sweden

ABSTRACT

Imagine 120 students sharing 5 computers, yet feeling that they are part of an interconnected world. This is the social context framing digital learning for African art students, the material limitations and cultural imaginations of which this chapter is concerned with. Based on extensive ethnographic engagements at TaSUBa, a national institute for arts and culture in Tanzania, this chapter investigates the development of digital media skills. Using the concept of digital learning to cover the acquisition of ICT skills as well as the use of ICT as a learning tool, the analysis spans from early expectations of connectivity to current forms of media engagement. Focusing on the social and cultural aspects of digital learning, the concept hybrid media engagement is introduced to capture the creative ways in which African art students overcome limitations in infrastructure, while exploring new forms of cultural production.

INTRODUCTION

The students sit cramped together, two to three sharing each computer. Some are seated on the floor between the wooden tables, without access to computers, a few at the back of the room, with laptops of their own hoisted on chairs or low tables. The curtains are drawn, ceiling fans shifting the

DOI: 10.4018/978-1-60960-206-2.ch013

hot air around. The teacher stands at the front of the room, using a projector attached to his laptop. Images of his computer monitor are projected onto a worn-out screen that has been refastened to its frame with some string. The computer interface is in English, but his instructions are in *Kiswahili*. The students are in their final year of studies at Taasisi ya Sanaa na Utamaduni Bagamoyo (TaSUBa), a national arts and culture institute in Bagamoyo, Tanzania. Regardless of their major subject, in dance, drama, music, stage technology or fine arts, all students study ICT. But as much as they enjoy their ICT classes, they are also frustrated by the lack of facilities, the student population of 120 sharing 5 computers.

This chapter investigates the development of digital media skills at TaSUBa, from the initial introduction of computers and Internet access to current learning and user practices.[1] When computers and Internet were first introduced in 2004, most students had no or very limited ICT skills. In the absence of formal training, students employed various methods to acquire these skills, not least through peer-to-peer learning. Even so, a baseline ICT user study carried out the following year showed that the computers available for students were largely underused (Uimonen 2006). In the new curriculum that came into effect from academic year 2006/2007, ICT was made a compulsory subject, and is now taught throughout the 3-year diploma programme. A trained instructor gives students weekly classes in a variety of ICT skills. Unfortunately, the formalization of ICT training has not been accompanied by infrastructure development. This lack of facilities is not merely attributable to financial constraints, but is expressive of managerial priorities and strategies, factors that constitute the institutional setting in which digital learning is embedded. Even so, students find creative ways of bypassing the limitations posed by infrastructure, thus developing innovative forms of *hybrid media engagement*.

BACKGROUND: DIGITAL LEARNING, ACCESS, AND CULTURAL TRANSFORMATION

In this analysis, I am using the concept of digital learning to capture the acquisition of ICT skills as well as the use of ICT as a learning tool, focusing on computers and Internet. While a growing body of research is investigating new media skills among

youth, this work is mainly focused on high-tech societies, mostly in Europe and the United States. A growing number of projects and initiatives on ICT in education notwithstanding, very little empirical research has been carried out in African contexts.[2] Nonetheless, theoretical debates and empirical insights from digitally more advanced societies can be used to shed further light on digital learning among African youth, not least as a point of comparison on questions relating to social context (Livingstone 2006), genres of participation (Ito et al 2008), and variations in user patterns (Facer and Furlong 2001, Selwyn 2009).

In order to appreciate digital learning in the context of African "mediascapes" (Appadurai 1996), it is important to recognize the limitations in Internet access. In Tanzania, one of the poorest countries in Africa, the Internet is only used by 1.22% of the population, compared with 87.84% in Sweden and 74% in the United States, or 8.67% in neighbouring Kenya and 7.90% in Uganda.[3] This low level of Internet penetration is particularly evident in the education sector, with most primary and secondary schools having no Internet access (MOEVT 2007). While many institutes of higher education have Internet access, they do not have broadband, the subscription rate for which is a mere 0,02% in Tanzania. In the case of TaSUBa, Internet access is through a dedicated line at the speed of 128kbs, with a monthly data allocation of 40Gb. Questions of digital inclusion and exclusion are thus rather pertinent in this low-access context (Castells 2004, Ferguson 2006).

Since this chapter is concerned with an arts college, the analysis will focus on digital learning in relation to cultural production and transformation. The only institute for practical arts training in East Africa, TaSUBa attracts students who wish to develop their artistic talents. For about half the students, the experience of studying at TaSUBa coincides with their first introduction to digital media, the development of digital media skills thus forming part of their artistic training and their acculturation into artistic practice. Meanwhile, the institutional context framing digital learning is increasingly entangled in global forces and trends, the introduction and development of ICT coinciding with the College's transformation into an executive agency. In order to appreciate this transformation, digital learning will be analysed through anthropological theories on globalization in general (Appadurai 1996, Hannerz 1992, 1996) and new forms of governance in particular (Shore and Wright 2000, Ferguson 2006).

This chapter builds on ethnographic engagements at TaSUBa, formerly Bagamoyo College of Arts (BCA), from 2002 to 2009. Having first visited the College in 2002, I was contracted as an ICT Consultant by the Swedish International Development Cooperation Agency (Sida), to plan, initiate and monitor ICT-related activities at the College from 2004 to 2007. In 2009, I carried out ethnographic fieldwork at TaSUBa, from April to August and November to December, for a research project on Internet, Culture and Identity in Tanzania, supported by Sida's Department for Research Cooperation (SAREC). While elaborating on my earlier publications (Uimonen 2004, 2006, 2008, 2009), this chapter includes previously unpublished material, not least data gathered during my recently completed fieldwork, which has relied on participant observation and interviews, along with digital, visual and sensory research methods, to elicit empirical data. A more comprehensive analysis is in process (Uimonen 2011).

It should be noted from the outset that this text is anthropological and as such it represents an effort to convey the realities and aspirations of Tanzanian art students, from their point of view. While there is no shortage of ideas and projects for digital learning in Africa, the much flaunted One Laptop Per Child initiative being but one example, it is worth our while to pay more attention to the meanings, aspirations and challenges that frame digital practices and perceptions in contemporary real life settings. In a context of extremely limited material resources, any attempt to furnish African students with the resources and capacity required for digital inclusion need to be based on existing realities rather than eventual possibilities, paying close attention to the cultural meanings and structural conditions framing such efforts.

EXPECTATIONS OF CONNECTIVITY

Mussa had just completed his second year of study when he got an opportunity to visually express his expectations of global connectivity in the new computer room. Housed in a building that had been used for dance practice, the room was secured with iron grids, and fine art students were invited to paint murals on the walls, before ten brand new computers were installed. Mussa painted a large globe overlaid with a smiling face, a PC on top, with the Internet Explorer logo on the monitor, and traditional drums, *ngoma*, on the sides. This symbolic combination of African art and global connectivity was also the theme of his fellow student, who painted a computer with a peace dove below it, and images of an African man and woman next to it. On the opposite wall, another student depicted connectivity through four African dancers, their heads joined in a globe. In a visual way, these murals expressed the cultural identities of Tanzanian art students and their sense of belonging to an interconnected world of art, culture and peaceful coexistence.

When Internet access was first established at Bagamoyo College of Arts on 12 July 2004, it responded to a "desperate need" among teachers and students. At the time, teachers and students were using Internet cafés, which were located at some distance from the College. The most popular one was housed in a container, which had been converted into a make shift Internet café, offering computer and Internet services. There were no Internet Service Providers in town, and hotels and Internet cafés were relying on costly satellite connections (VSAT) for Internet access. The College had very few computers, which were mainly used for administration, or for playing solitary as I noted during early observations. In the absence of Internet access, the College had limited ability to communicate with the outside world. External relations were managed through mail and fax, which was felt to be particularly cumbersome in preparations of the annual Arts Festival, which attracted artists from different parts of the country, the region and the world at large.

For management, computers and Internet access represented critical components of the College's institutional reforms and its efforts to develop into a "regional centre of excellence". In 2002, a fire had ravaged the theatre building, a landmark of the college and the East African art world in general. The fire raised pertinent issues regarding the management of the college, and the Swedish International Development Cooperation Agency (Sida), which had supported the construction of the theatre, commissioned an external evaluation (COWI 2002), which identified a number of challenges for improved management and operations. The management of the College was changed, workshops were held to chart a suitable direction for the future and a Strategic Plan for 2003-2006 was developed (MOEC/BCA 2003). ICT formed part of these efforts to improve the capacity and quality of the College, and following a request to Sida, the College received some support for ICT facilities, starting with an ICT Strategy based on an on-site feasibility study in March 2004 (Uimonen 2004). With the stated vision *"BCA aspires to use state of the art information and communication technology (ICT) to become a dynamic, creative, innovative and transparent Institution for high quality training, research and professionalism in the Arts"* (Ibid.: 12), the ICT Strategy built on the College's Strategic Plan, while identifying concrete areas for ICT integration, through a phased approach, scheduled for 2004 to 2007 and onwards.

While all heads of department were keen on Internet access, expectations varied among teachers. Most teachers at BCA had little skills in using computers or Internet, and while some of them were keen on getting access at the College, others felt unsure of the benefits it might bring. Those who were ICT literate saw the benefits of producing teaching material and handouts for students on computers, and to download teaching and learning material from the Internet. In the absence of computers, teachers were preparing handouts for classes by hand, which were then photocopied or copied by hand. Tests were usually typed on a shared PC for general use, but little was done to save material for reuse. Teachers also felt limited in their ability to upgrade their skills or to exchange information and experiences with colleagues elsewhere, and the Internet was considered a useful tool for communication with colleagues and organizations, especially outside the country. Music and Fine Art teachers were eager to use computers for artistic production like music composition and graphic design, while a drama teacher saw the possibilities of using computers for experimental forms of performances.

Students were very enthusiastic about getting Internet access, which represented a means with which to "stay in tune with global developments", be able to "communicate" with the outside world, get more "exposure" to the work of others and facilitate "access" to and "awareness" of the College. Students were already relying on Internet cafés to get access to information not available at BCA, ranging from learning material to Web sites of artists and organizations for artists. Given the lack of material in the College library, the Internet was their primary tool for research. Communication was another important use, especially with people overseas, but increasingly in Tanzania as well. The Web was an important resource for information on other training institutions for further study and eventual scholarships. Aware that artists around the world were using computers for their art production, students were also keen to explore such applications.

I have argued elsewhere that this desire for connectivity exemplifies aspirations to become part of an *interconnected world* (Uimonen 2009). Reflecting on the "natural affinity" for the Internet they observed in Trinidad, anthropologists have proposed the terms "expansive realization" and "expansive potential" to capture Internet-mediated identity formation, allowing users to "become what one thinks one really is" as well as "what one could be" (Miller and Slater 2000: 10-11). In the case of BCA, expansive identity formation was related to becoming part of what could be conceptualized as a global art world, a world of art training and production linked together through the Internet (Uimonen 2009).

These expectations of global connectivity can be contrasted with the sense of isolation students felt, or as one student put it "the College is like an isolated island". This notion of being on an isolated island was not merely expressive of a digital divide, but a more profoundly felt sense of cultural exclusion. Not having Internet access represented exclusion from a world in which culture is increasingly organized in connec-tions between the local and the long-distance, a "global ecumene" structured as a "network of networks" (Hannerz 1992). In other words, lack of Internet access represented exclusion from the "operative infrastructure" as well as the "culture of communication" of the global network society (Castells 2004), reflecting the sense of marginal-ization stemming from the low "rank" of Africa's "place-in-the-world" in the neoliberal world order (Ferguson 2006).

Aspirations for connectivity were embedded in power relations and the political value of ICT was evident in the ceremonial inauguration of the ICT building during the 23rd Arts Festival in September 2004. The festival's theme *Be Proud of Your Cultural Identity*, was quite befitting, corresponding to the Board's preoccupation with

globalization, while coinciding with the launch of the College Web site (Uimonen 2009). To mark the festive occasion, the ICT building was adorned with colourful balloons, glossy plastic ribbons, and tall wreaths tied from banana leaves, decorated with bright, red bougainvillea flowers. The guest of honour, a high level Ministry representative, ceremoniously cut a bright red ribbon fastened to posts outside the main door, to the cheerful music of the College brass band. With deliberate steps she then entered the computer room, accompanied by the Principal of the College, VIP guests and a TV crew, all dressed up in colourful batik clothes, in tribute to their national identity. Representing far more than a spectacular show for the cameras, this deliberate ritual was a "dramatization of status" (Geertz 1971), an enactment of political status hierarchies as well as political aspirations, reflecting and at the same time reinforcing the political power and prestige embodied in digital technology.

EARLY USER PATTERNS

From the outset, Mussa became one of the most avid ICT users at the College, while completing his diploma programme, majoring in fine art, with music as minor. Only 21 years at the time, he used the computer room every day for a couple of hours. His first exposure to computers was at his uncle's home in 2000, and from 2001 he was using Internet cafés in Dar es Salaam. He joined BCA in 2002 to develop his talent in drawing and painting, and in the hope of learning modern design methods, for which TV had served as a source of inspiration. When BCA got computers and Internet access, Mussa was very enthusiastic, and the ICT building was one of his favourite places on campus.

Like his fellow students at the time, Mussa came to rely on other students and the ICT technical staff to learn how to use computers. Although ICT staff tried to organize training after school hours, it was difficult to implement due to the lack of time. The heavy schedule of classes kept students busy from early morning until late afternoon, leaving little time for extracurricular activities. Similarly, students had little time to practice on computers, as the computer room was closed during their off-hours. Instead, students learned with the help of friends, fellow students, Internet cafe staff, and on their own. In the absence of formal training, peer-to-peer learning became an important means of acquiring ICT skills, and students could often be observed sitting together, helping each other out.

A baseline ICT user study carried out August 2005 to February 2006 found that the ICT facilities were infrequently and ineffectively used (Uimonen 2006).[4] While Mussa and a few other students became avid users, most teachers and students were only using the facilities 2 to 3 times per week, in many cases only once a week. Quite a high proportion of the students in the study, 24%, had never used the Internet. The majority of users were external visitors, primarily foreign tourists and volunteers, who used the facilities as an Internet café. For example, the records for September 2005 showed 437 public user visits, compared to 69 BCA students and only 13 BCA staff visits. While external users served as a source of revenue with which to subsidize access, their frequency of use had the detrimental effect of curtailing BCA students' access to the facilities, thus excluding them from resources put in place to serve them. With time, external usage to the Internet café was curtailed, and eventually abandoned.

Lack of training and time were cited as the main factors for the relatively low use of computers among students, all of whom asked for more training. When responding to the user study, students added comments like "More training to the Student", "I like it then I have to know more about it by getting training", and "I would like to get training, thanks". Meanwhile, teachers were hesitant to use the common facilities of the ICT building, while the lack of computers in their own offices impeded them from using computers as part of their daily routines. The user study found no differences in skills acquisition according to gender, but age played a role, with younger users learning ICT skills more quickly than older ones. This age difference was particularly evident in comparisons between students and teachers, reflecting a digital divide between learners and tutors.

The correlation between lack of training and low levels of use corresponds to the findings of other researchers. Although it is true that "peer-based learning" offers a supportive network and dynamic learning environment for young people (Ito et al 2008: 11), peer-to-peer learning alone is not sufficient for the development of digital media skills (Uimonen 2006). As argued by Selwyn (2009), the idea that youth are "digital natives", talented, innate users of digital technology, is a myth. Not only do their skills vary tremendously, but they continue to need support from various "information professionals". Similarly, reflecting on the recent Digital Youth Project, Herr-Stephenson underlines the continued importance of "guided learning" for young people (2008). She concludes that "media literacy" is a "blind spot" for some young people, which needs to be addressed, along with disparities in access to digital media technology. Early user patterns at BCA demonstrate that access alone is not sufficient in ensuring adequate skills development, nor a stimulus for more frequent usage. If anything, not having training in basic ICT skills can be a deterrent for young people to use and explore digital media (Uimonen 2006). This observation is corroborated by an earlier study of children identified as "low or ambivalent users" of computers in UK, which found that while access was an important factor, questions of "anxiety" and "lack of confidence" were also influential, even when access was provided in school environments (Facer and Furlong 2001).

Somewhat surprisingly, the user study found that Internet had already become a taken for granted part of student life (Uimonen 2006). In response to the question "What would happen if you could not access the Internet?" students made it clear that the Internet had become an important part of their lives and their futures, without which they would "suffer", or as one student put it "I can't live without the Internet now". Despite their low levels of use and limited skills, students placed tremendous value on Internet. Statements like "I would be out of date", "I couldn't develop", "My understanding will be down", "I would miss a lot about my arts" and "I will miss a lot of things, there are other things I can't get in class" exemplified the extent to which students had come to rely on the Internet as a learning resource. Students were also placing great value on Internet-mediated communication "I would loose communication and news", "I could not have the friends I have now", and "I could have few material and lost my relatives".

This apparent contrast between social practice and cultural imagination is indicative of Tanzanian urban youth culture. Despite the material limitations of everyday life, urban popular culture is expressed through "imaginative fantasy", with social practices shaped by "imaginative links to 'elsewheres' near and far" (Weiss 2002: 101). Heavily influenced by global images distributed through mass media, young Tanzanians both "envision" and "act upon" an "imagined global totality", an integrated world that they feel both included in and excluded from (Ibid.). Thus, while their skills may have been limited due to lack of training and access, BCA students still envisioned the Internet in terms of being part of an interconnected world, a sense of inclusion that they found to be most meaningful to their very existence. In other words, the Internet was already firmly embedded in their "imagined selves" and "imagined worlds", demonstrating how digital media has become a "constitutive feature of modern subjectivity" through the "*work of the imagination*" (Appadurai 1996: 3, emphasis in original). Without access, the students felt their lives would be isolated and stagnant: "I will loose contact with the world", "Development will not improve", "I could not know a lot of things in the world", and "We could not know about other places".

Corresponding to this deeply felt desire to be part of an interconnected world, the ICT building quickly evolved into a social hub on campus. In the absence of collective social spaces, the computer room became a favourite place to hang around. While waiting for their turn at the computers, students lingered on, the room often getting noisy from the social interaction taking place. In addition to offering Internet access, the computer room was the only place on campus with a TV, broadcasting satellite channels. In this media-rich environment, students could thus act upon their cultural imagination of being part of an interconnected world, regardless of their actual level of ICT-literacy, and despite their limited access to the computers hosted in the room.

For Mussa, the ICT building had become such an important part of his life that he stayed on after graduation, to have access to the computers and Internet. In addition to learning as much as he could from ICT staff, Mussa used every opportunity he found to play around on the computers. He also volunteered at the College, passing on his newly acquired knowledge of computers to other students. Although his lack of basic training was evident in his troubles of saving and locating files, which to him was a recurring source of frustration, he did explore all kinds of functions in the applications available. Having assisted me with the user study, when Mussa prepared the survey results in Power Point, he used every imaginable function available, adding photos as backgrounds in graphs, inserting video clips and formatting the text in creative ways. Using Power Point as an outlet for his artistic formation, Mussa even incorporated a computer animation, based on his hand drawn pictures (Uimonen 2008).

ICT SYLLABUS AND AUDIT TECHNOLOGY

The students are carefully re-reading the printed instructions handed out by their tutor, as they create their files, adding and formatting the content. The sound of *ngoma*, traditional drums, seeps in through the windows, as dance students prepare their practical exams on a nearby stage. By contrast, the computer room is steeped in silence. Some extra computers have been brought in from nearby offices, to enable the students to do their practical exams in batches of ten. A few bring in their own laptops, which they use at the back of the room. A power outage delays one group, and one of the computers is malfunctioning. Appointed for his technical skills, the examination guard tries his best to manage these technical mishaps, while answering students' various queries. Throughout the week of practical exams, the computer room remains occupied, as groups of students complete their tests, typing at varying speeds, many with one finger at a time, constantly checking the monitor.

The following week, students take their theoretical exam, in an impressive assembly in the flexible hall, a large open construction near the beach. Mostly used for social and commercial functions, it is the only construction large enough to house desks and chairs for the whole student population, furniture that students return to the class rooms after completing their tests, carrying the wooden desks on their heads. Although scheduled to be carried out in batches according to year of study, the academic office has decided to do all ICT exams in one sitting. Consequentially, the majority of the student population is gathered in the flexible hall, supervised by half a dozen examination guards. The students work in silence, occasionally knocking their tables and raising their hands to get more writing paper from the examination guards. "Examination rules" are written on a flip chart at the front of the room, behind tables where students have deposited their mobile phones. As they hand in their completed exams, meticulously stapled by the examination guards, some students have problems locating their phones in the large pile of mostly basic, standard models.

The practical and theoretical exams represent the culmination of the ICT training that all students at TaSUBa undertake since the academic year 2006/2007, when ICT was introduced as a compulsory subject in the new curriculum. Forming part of the transformation into an executive agency, which is expected to deliver public services in a quasi-business manner (MOICS 2007), the new curriculum was an important development at the College, allowing it to acquire formal accreditation as a technical college according to the standards set by the National Council for Technical Education (NACTE), which included ICT facilities and Internet access. Tasked with "setting and maintaining standards and quality of technical education and training", NACTE covers tertiary education institutions "delivering courses at technician, semi-professional and professional levels leading to awards of certificates, diplomas, degrees and other related awards"[5]. Categorized under Planning and Welfare, TaSUBa is accredited under its former name Bagamoyo College of Arts with an approved programme in Performing Arts.

The new curriculum follows the formalized standards and measurable formats anthropologists refer to as "audit culture", a growing trend in higher education around the world (Shore and Wright 2000; Strathern 2000; Wright and Rabo 2010). In the case of TaSUBa, the new curriculum specifies measurable indicators in terms of course credits, modules, a six-level grading system and four-level diploma classification. Compulsory subjects are communication skills (English and Swahili), art management, art and society, research methods, field work and ICT, the latter being the only compulsory subject taught throughout the 3-year diploma programme. Elective subjects, depending on students' choice of major and minor subjects are dance, drama, fine art, music, and stage technology. Compulsory subjects correspond to 38.4 credits, major subject to 61.2 credits and minor subject to 20.4 credits per year, a total of 120.0 credits, while the whole diploma programme is 360 credits, or 3,600 hours of class work, out of which 49.92 credits are in ICT.

The TaSUBa ICT syllabus is partially modelled after the International Computer Driving License (ICDL), an international computer skills certification programme used in more than 100 countries around the world (see http://www.ecdl.com). The syllabus does, however, not lead to an official certification, the process and cost for which makes little sense at TaSUBa, which has its own certification system. The syllabus is taught all semesters, with one module per semester. In the first year, students learn Module PA 101: ICT 1 Introduction to Computers and Word Processing and Module PA 101: ICT 2 Email and Internet. In the second year, they take Module PA 201: ICT 1 Advanced Word Processing and Module PA 201: ICT 2 Excel Spreadsheet. In the third year, Module PA 301: ICT 1 Power Point and Desktop Publishing is followed by Module PA 301: ICT 2 Web Design. The module on web design is not part of ICDL, but has been developed by ICT staff at TaSUBa.

Reflecting the performance indicator-based format of the TaSUBa curriculum, each module in the ICT syllabus contains detailed outcomes and assessment criteria. For instance, Module PA 101, which is worth 9.6 credits, and with the stated objective "To enable the student to acquire knowledge and understanding of the basic concepts of computers, the management of files and folders and Word Processing application" enumerates detailed outcomes, divided into learning outcomes, enabling outcomes, and sub-enabling

outcomes. A detailed list of these outcomes is followed by a list of assessment criteria, categorized into sub-enabling outcomes, related tasks, assessment criteria and assessment instrument, the latter being classroom exercises, practical try outs, assignments and end of semester examinations. This is followed by a list of benchmarking of assessment criteria, divided into assessment criteria, and three assessment categories: satisfactory, good, and excellent. Containing more detail than any other syllabus, the ICT modules cover 4-7 pages in the curriculum, compared to 2-4 pages for other modules.

When put into practice, the ICT syllabus is taught for 2 hours per week, by an ICDL-certified tutor. The schedule is neatly posted on the notice board in the computer room, along with updated lists of classes. In order to circumscribe the limitations in infrastructure, each year is divided into three groups, with 12 to 16 students in each group. The classes are spread out over two days per week. All in all, the ICT teacher has a total of 18 classes per week, which is far more than the 4 to 6 or 12 to 14 hours taught by other teachers. The instructor uses the Internet, ICDL modules and different books for teaching materials, and a projector and screen, connected to one of the PCs in the computer room. In addition to the computers available to them, students get a summarized pamphlet prepared by the instructor as learning material.

In addition to imparting basic ICT skills, the syllabus offers a creative reproduction of overlapping, cultural identities. While building on international standard modules, the instructor contextualizes ICT in the everyday realities of TaSUBa students. In the practical exam for PA 101, Introduction to Computer and Word Processing, students are instructed to open a document called "TaSUBa", and fill it with content that reflects the locality of the College (physical address), as well as its cultural identity of art training (short courses to improve practical artistic skills) and art production (BCA multimedia theatre performance). Similarly, 3rd year students are instructed to create invitation cards for a graduation party in TaSUBa theatre hall, thus building on their cultural identity as art students, while displaying skills in Power Point and Desktop Publishing.

The ICT syllabus reflects the practical mandate and ethos of TaSUBa, at least in theory, if not in practice. In class, the time is split between lecturing and practice, although the time is rather short, leaving students with a mere half hour for practice each time. In reality, the shortage of computers means that students do not have individual access to computers in class, but share the machines available, sitting 2 to 3 at each computer. Similarly, the lack of ICT facilities prevents students from practicing as much as they would like to outside class, and their progress is rather slow.

The dissonance between the formalized curriculum and actual learning conditions is interesting in its own right, especially in relation to audit culture. Anthropologists have examined the spread of measurable performance-oriented "audit technology" in higher education in terms of "instruments for new forms of governance and power" (Shore and Wright 2000: 57). They analyse audit as a "technology of neo-liberal governance", which perpetuates "new managerialism" in higher education, with an emphasis on economy and efficiency, rather than effectiveness (Ibid.). Not only does audit culture command resource-intensive administrative processes, which can divert time and energy away from teaching and learning, but the audit technologies put in place do not necessarily improve accountability.

When measured in terms of accountability, it becomes quite clear that teaching and learning practices differ from TaSUBa's formal ICT syllabus, since the measurable performance indicators cannot be adequately materialized with the facilities made available. More importantly, the formal structure and format of the new curriculum, in which the ICT syllabus stands out as an exemplary form of audit technology, conceals a social reality of under-resourced facilities, unserviced infrastructure, and over-worked and under-paid staff. In other words, under the guise of new managerialism (Ibid.), mismanagement of human and technical resources are able to flourish, the audit technologies actually disguising the absence of accountability for actual teaching and learning conditions. In this regard, TaSUBa is not an isolated case. Based on his research at a South African university, Oxlund (2010: 40) concludes that the "semi-autonomous status of the institution" actually "makes a mess of accountability issues", since the University appears to be more accountable to the external 'assessor' and 'audit' than its 'core constituency' of students and academics.

In somewhat more theatrical terms, the ICT exams reproduce audit culture in the form of a *spectacle*, the performance indicators serving as props in a staged display of new forms of management. Like all spectacles, it serves to "reconstitute" a "community" (Beeman 1993: 380), in this case an arts college reconstituted in the form of an executive agency. The spectacle is performed by students and teachers for an audience of external auditors, scripted by TaSUBa management, and staged in a centrally located and publicly visible building, imaginatively decorated with the words Bagamoyo College of Arts, Internet Café. What is not accounted for in this spectacular display of new managerialism is a back stage of discarded computers and printers, the very lack of material resources rendering the spectacle somewhat meaningless in terms of the accountability it is meant to execute.

MATERIAL SCARCITY, VIRTUAL OPPORTUNITY

Seated at the computers and between the tables, the students occupy the room as they would during

ICT class. Although the group discussion is supposed to be for a total of fourteen students, three others join this 1st year ICT group. Eleven are male, and six are female, roughly corresponding to the average gender ratio of TaSUBa students. Ten are in their twenties, 21 to 26 years old, five are in their thirties, from 30 to 36 years old, one is 45 and another one is 54. Only seven of them have used computers or Internet before joining TaSUBa, and only four have laptops of their own. No one owns a USB memory stick, or flash disk as it is locally known, and only one student has a digital camera. All of them have mobile phones, ten have advanced models with cameras, music and VDO applications, and six can access the Internet through their phones. As I start my inquiry about their experience of learning ICT at TaSUBa, students point out that that the "learning is good", but there is a "scarcity of computers".

The "scarcity of computers" is repeated by 2nd and 3rd year students, all of whom identify the lack of computers to be the main challenge for their ICT training.[6] Although there are 5 computers in the room, students point out that only 2 to 3 are usually working. And they are very slow. The computers are "sick" a student notes, since there is no one to service them after the technician "escaped". Based on their experiences, students estimate that by the time they graduate from College there may only be one or two computers left. This is a far cry from the "fantasy" that some students entertained before joining the College. When they read about the courses and discovered they would study ICT, some students thought the College would have a big room with lots of computers, a "room of dreams". Management has told them the facilities will improve ever since they started the College, but nothing has happened yet, it is still a "fantasy" they conclude. Problems with electricity are cited as another challenge, with frequent power cuts cancelling all ICT activity. In my field notes, I have jotted "third attempt, previously power outage" next to the date for the group discussion

with 3rd year students, having rescheduled it due to power failure. Students also note that there are network problems, with no Internet access as a result. These are sometimes caused by technical failure at the Provider's end, other times due to delays in payment by the College.

Students emphasize that their time to use the ICT facilities is "minimum", due to the lack of computers. The computers tend to be busy throughout the day, and after classes, the building is closed. This leaves students little time to use the computers, let alone practice their ICT skills. During their free time, students use the computer room for half an hour or one hour per week, a few use it up to three hours per week. Some students use nearby Internet cafés, but the costs involved curtail their time of use. The nearest Internet café is at a hotel, which charges TSH 1,500 (USD 1,15) for half an hour, or TSH 3,000 (USD 3,30) for an hour. This can be compared to the cost of food at a nearby cafeteria, where students can have a meal for TSH 1,000 and a soft drink for TSH 500.

The computer room is not only used to learn and practice ICT skills, but also an important resource for other subjects. Although students use the College library, it holds very little material, not even course material and reference books listed in the curriculum. Rather than travelling to town for better stocked libraries, students use the Internet to find learning materials. My observations confirm this use of the Internet as a *global library* to be a significant part of students' use of the computer room, even more so than ICT practice. The computers are also used to do on-line research for their research projects and to present the research results. In their third year of study, students are required to do a field study, on a topic of their own choice. In preparation, students use the Internet and upon completion, they type their reports on computers. By then, they have acquired advanced word processing and Power Point skills, which they can be observed applying through creative formatting and advanced content management.

Searching for information and learning material is usually done through Google, or on-line encyclopaedias and dictionaries. When students receive an assignment from the teacher, such as "what is art", they often type the question into Google to find an answer. Or they visit the Q&A site www.answers.com or on-line dictionary www.definitions.net to find an answer to their query. Some students use Wikipedia, while others are unaware of its existence. Although they don't have training in source criticism, students recognize that on-line information is not altogether reliable, and they also note that the information tends to be short, especially when compared to books. The material they find about Africa, for instance on African Art, is in their view often wrong, and the information is mostly from European rather than African sources and perspectives.

The lack of culturally relevant content is but one aspect of the cultural challenges of ICT-mediated learning. Students acknowledge that language is somewhat a problem when using ICT. Although both English and Kiswahili are languages of instruction at TaSUBa, most teachers use Kiswahili, as do students. In the case of ICT, the instructor often has to translate computer terms into Kiswahili, since students are not altogether familiar with "English computer language". Assignments and hand-outs, however, are in English. When students go on-line, searching for learning material, they usually rely on English, even though they are not so fluent in it. Another challenge is the lack of a well-established reading culture, in a society which continues to be dominated by oral culture. Students are not used to reading a lot of text, especially on a screen, or to write, let alone type, long texts.

In addition to using computers for ICT training and practice and as a learning tool for their art subjects, students also use the Internet for communication and entertainment. When they arrive in the computer room, students often start by logging into their e-mail accounts, the most popular one being Yahoo, or as one student noted in the questionnaire I passed around during our group discussions "yahoo is our home". All students in the 2nd and 3rd year had email accounts, and all but three in the 1st year group, although one student signed up for a Yahoo account immediately after the group discussion. Not surprisingly, students cite "communication and e-mail", "communication with friends" and "contact with friends and world at large" to be important aspects of the Internet, reflecting their use of e-mail and chat to stay in touch with people at the College, in Tanzania and overseas. Students also use the Internet for entertainment, to access music videos, photos, magazines, news, sports, and religious sites, but not for online dating.

Facebook is an increasingly popular social network site in Tanzania, used by a growing number of TaSUBa students. The growing popularity of Facebook is exemplified by the increase in use among new generations of students: while only 4 out of 15 students in the 3rd year use Facebook, the figure grows to 4 out of 11 in the second year and 8 out of 17 in the 1st year. A few students also use Tagged, Hi5, MySpace and Netlog. Most of the students who use Facebook started using it while at TaSUBa, following recommendations from fellow students. Although they are unfamiliar with the concepts ´social network site´ or 'social media', they use Facebook to stay in touch with friends in Tanzania and overseas. Interestingly enough, after asking them about Facebook during group discussions, some students sign up immediately after, with the help of students who already have Facebook profiles. Keen to add a profile photo from the outset, they borrow my digital camera and photograph one another outside the ICT building. Not surprisingly, several also request my friendship, after searching for my name in Facebook.

Nina, a young 1st year student, majoring in fine art, minoring in drama, started actively using Facebook in 2008, a year before joining TaSUBa. Before she had been in Hi5, but one of her friends there migrated to Facebook, so Nina joined as well. Nina has 344 friends, mostly from her high school in Zambia, a large number from UK whom she met while living there for a while, and a rather small number, only half a dozen or so, from Tanzania, a couple of whom are young teachers at TaSUBa. She rarely updates her profile, but prefers to communicate through her own and her friends' walls, or through messages to them. Nina has three albums in her profile page, photos she took with her previous phone. It was a good phone, she notes, I could even edit photos on it, but it got lost. The photos show Nina in different social contexts, her friends, and places she has visited. Reflecting her talent, some of the photos are very artistic, showing that Nina also likes to explore digital media as a form of visual art.

These user patterns exemplify the social and cultural context framing digital learning at TaSUBa. As suggested by other researchers, young people's use of digital media is often "unspectacular" (Selwyn 2009), with "information searching" and "contacting friends" being more common than a sustained engagement with the more "interactive opportunities" offered by digital media (Livingstone 2006). By way of comparison, it is worth noting that most TaSUBa students don't even know what a blog is, let alone use them. This should, however, not be discarded as an expression of digital exclusion or digital divide, but shows that "social stratification...remains crucial", not in terms of a binary divide, but a "continuum of quality of access and use", reflecting "differentiation in both material and cultural resources" (Ibid.: 220). In the case of TaSUBa, students have very limited material resources, in the sense of computers, time and speed of access, and complementary digital media equipment such as cameras, video cameras or even storage devices. Even so, they make optimal use of the resources available to reproduce and reinforce their cultural resources, digital media being an integral part of their professional training in cultural production

and their cultural formation as artists. In this regard, digital media represent an outlet for creativity that needs to be better accounted for, even in the "global shadows" of the neoliberal world order (Ferguson 2006).

HYBRID MEDIA ENGAGEMENT

In terms of genres of participation, user patterns among TaSUBa students both concur with and differ from what has been observed among youth elsewhere. In the Digital Youth Project, the researchers use "genres of participation" to "describe different modes or conventions for engaging with new media" (Ito et al 2008: 9). The concept of genre or "mode of making meaning" focuses on practices rather than individual users (Herr-Stephenson 2008: 74). A distinction is made between "friendship-driven" and "interest-driven" genres, the former centring around relationships with friends and peers, with on-line activities closely resembling offline activities, while the latter is not determined by existing friendships but the ability to "practice or demonstrate a particular skill" or "dig into a particular interest" (Ibid: 75). Three additional genres of participation are used to describe levels of intensity, sophistication and commitment: hanging out, messing around, and geeking out (Ito et al 2008: 10).

For TaSUBa students, the use of e-mail, chat and social network sites like Facebook can be categorized as friendship-driven participation, the primary aim of which is communication and interaction with friends and other social relations. As mentioned above, this mediated form of social communication is an important motivation for their Internet use. Since on-line communication and interaction is restricted to the computer room, it also becomes part of hanging out, both in the sense of the computer room representing a social hub on campus, but also in the sense that students hang out at the computers, often two to three at each machine. Whether checking their e-mail or updating their Facebook profile, students sit together, the computer forming part of a social rather than individual space. But unlike their US counterparts, TaSUBa students are not able to integrate new media in the sense of "always-on communication", with computers and mobile phones allowing them to constantly stay in touch with their close friends (Ito et al 2008:15-16). In other words, while used in the form of hanging out, digital media are not an integral part of hanging out, most of which takes place in off-line environments, through face to face interaction.

The use of digital media as a learning tool can be categorized as interest-driven participation, along with ICT training. The training is clearly centred on the practice of particular skills, in this case ICT skills, while the use of ICT also allows students to dwell deeper into the art subjects they study. The interest-driven participation resembles the 'messing around' genre, which includes "looking around, searching for information online, and experimentation and play" (Ito et al 2008: 20). In some cases, such activities are undertaken as part of their formal ICT training, but most of the time, digital media are used in support of other subjects. As they browse through different sites in their search for information on African art, TaSUBa students also explore digital media, while their preparation of research reports, in Word and Power Point formats, gives them an opportunity to experiment with digital media, the messing around genre thus representing a form of "self-directed exploration" that also contributes to the development of computer skills (Ibid. 25). This exploratory form of learning is further reinforced through the use of multimedia sites like Facebook, where students can post photos and links, and the use of Internet for entertainment through music videos and other media. Meanwhile, the requirement of "ongoing access to digital media" hinders students from participating in the geeking out genre (Ibid. 28).

In order to account for the limitations posed by infrastructure and access, it may be worth exploring a fourth genre of participation, which I would like to term *hybrid media engagement*. Whether they are hanging out or messing around in friendship- or interest-driven modes of participation, TaSUBa students combine digital and analogue media, high-tech and low-tech modes of making meaning. These hybrid media engagements take different forms, from the copying of on-line information with pen and paper and typing of handwritten notes on computers to the scanning of drawings and paintings or digital recordings of traditional music. Such hybrid media engagements reflect a social and cultural context in which media engagements cannot be accounted for in terms of "networked publics," digital media-rich social environments where youth are able to actively participate in the production and circulation of culture and knowledge (Ibib. 10). Nor can it be analysed in terms of "recursive publics," the direct engagement and modification characteristic of free software developers (Kelty 2008). Nonetheless, rather than being completely excluded from digital media flows, Tanzanian youth are able to participate in digitally mediated culture and knowledge production, while finding creative ways of circumventing limitations in infrastructure and access by building on more traditional forms of cultural production. Hybrid media engagement is a form of cultural blending, or "creolization", which follows in the wake of " transnational connections" between cultural centres and peripheries, mediated by various media, or 'machineries of meaning' (Hannerz 1996). It is also a form of media engagement that is expressive of cultural variation in what has been defined as the age of "techne," an age of art and technology in which digital media allow people to craft new forms of human sociality within the neoliberal paradigms of "creationist capitalism" (Boellstorff 2008).

24-year old David is an example of the dynamic and innovative character of hybrid media engagements. Originally from Kilimanjaro region, David belongs to the *chagga* tribe, an ethnic identity that he reproduces in Facebook where he uses his clan name as surname. After completing his diploma programme at TaSUBa in June 2009, majoring in fine arts, with a minor in stage technology, David was recruited as an assistant teacher at the College. Thanks to his evolving digital media proficiency, David was also appointed Web Master, the skills for which he picked up quickly. Although he doesn't have a desk of his own, David works in the ICT building, where he has frequent access to a PC or laptop. When he is not assisting students or trying to fix smaller technical problems, David likes to draw on the computer or the drawing tablet he learned to use while participating in an extracurricular computer animation course led by student volunteers from Holland during his final year of studies. David combines art and technology in a way that he describes as traditional and modern, traditional referring to drawing or painting by hand, while modern is computer-based. Without his training in drawing, David figures he wouldn't be good in multimedia, but "combining the two makes one complete".

CONCLUSION

This chapter has investigated the social and cultural context framing digital learning at TaSUBa, a national arts training institute in Tanzania. In the first section, culturally informed expectations of connectivity were analysed in relation to the sense of cultural exclusion stemming from not having access. Building on a baseline ICT user study carried out a year after the College was connected, the second section investigated early user patterns and perceptions. While demonstrating the insufficiency of Internet access without training, the analysis also noted how access in itself served to stimulate cultural imaginations and aspirations. In the third section, the new ICT syllabus was

scrutinized and contrasted with actual teaching and learning practices. Representing a form of audit technology, the syllabus was analysed within the broader social context of new forms of management and neo-liberal governance. The fourth section took a closer look at contemporary user patterns and perceptions, elaborating on the frustrations over limitations in infrastructure as well as the creative ways in which students are overcoming such challenges. In the fifth section, user patterns were analysed in terms of genres of participation, and the concept *hybrid media engagement* was introduced as an analytical tool.

Far from merely articulating a state of digital exclusion or digital divide, digital learning in Africa is embedded in a complex web of social, cultural and political factors framing young people's development of digital media skills. Being able to use digital media is something that young people aspire to, both for their professional development and to enrich their social lives. Digital media are embedded in cultural imaginations of an interconnected world, providing access to social and cultural resources, while facilitating communication and interaction with social relations and the world at large. Digital media are also embedded in material realities characterized by scarcity and deficiency, the lack of facilities and access serving as a painful reminder of a state of partial inclusion in the contemporary world order. But rather than feeling victimized or bypassed by global forces, African art students find creative ways of circumventing the limitations posed by material and organizational constraints, while their verbalized frustrations also serve as a reminder that they have yet to materialize their imagined place in the world.

I have introduced the concept *hybrid media engagement* to capture this state of partial digital inclusion, to explain how African art students straddle the digital divide, with one foot in a state of digital inclusion, the other in digital exclusion, to use a figure of speech that springs to mind. This creolized form of media engagement combines digital and analogue forms of culture and knowledge production, mixing techniques and instruments that are high-tech and low-tech, electronic and acoustic, handmade and machine-made. It is a form of media engagement that reflects social transformations taking place at the intersection of traditional and modern cultural forms, cultural junctions that are articulated through hybrid forms of cultural production.

Future research on digital learning in different social and cultural contexts can hopefully provide more empirical, comparative material for a deeper understanding of the socioeconomic, cultural and political factors that influence the ways in which youth use interactive media. As more and more societies around the world come to rely on digital media, not least in the field of learning, it will be imperative to assure that future generations get a chance to develop the capacities required for meaningful inclusion in the global network society. More research is clearly required to understand what this means in real life settings around the interconnected world we live in.

REFERENCES

Appadurai, A. (1996). *Modernity at large. Cultural dimensions of globalization.* Minneapolis, MN: University of Minnesota Press.

Beeman, W. (1993). The anthropology of theater and spectacle. *Annual Review of Anthropology, 22,* 369–393. doi:10.1146/annurev.an.22.100193.002101

Boellstorff, T. (2008). *Coming of age in Second Life: An anthropologist explores the virtually human.* Princeton, NJ: Princeton University Press.

Castells, M. (2004). Informationalism, networks, and the network society: a theoretical blueprint. In Castells, M. (Ed.), *The network society. A cross-cultural perspective* (pp. 3–45). Cheltenham, UK: Edward Elgar.

COWI (2002). *Review of Bagamoyo College of Arts.* Final Report, prepared for Swedish Embassy in Dar es Salaam.

Facer, K., & Furlong, R. (2001). Beyond the myth of the 'cyberkid': Young people at the margins of the information revolution. *Journal of Youth Studies, 4*(4), 451–469. doi:10.1080/13676260120101905

Ferguson, J. (2006). *Global shadows. Africa in the neoliberal world order.* London: Duke University Press.

Geertz, C. (1971). Deep play: notes on the Balinese cockfight. *Daedalus, 101,* 1–37.

Hannerz, U. (1992). The global ecumene as a network of networks. In Kuper, A. (Ed.), *Conceptualizing Society* (pp. 34–55). London: Routledge.

Hannerz, U. (1996). *Transnational connections. Culture, people, places.* London: Routledge.

Herr-Stephenson, B. (2008). Youth media and genres of participation: Reflections on the Digital Youth Project. *Youth Media Reporter, 2,* (1-6), 73-79.

Ito, M. (2008). *Living and Learning with new media: Summary of findings from the Digital Youth Project.* Chicago: The MacArthur Foundation.

Kelty, C. (2008). *Two bits. The cultural significance of free software.* Durham, NC: Duke University Press.

Livingstone, S. (2006). Drawing conclusions from new media research: Reflections and puzzles regarding children's experience of the Internet. *The Information Society, 22,* 219–230. doi:10.1080/01972240600791358

Miller, D., & Slater, D. (2000). *The Internet: An ethnographic approach.* Oxford, UK: Berg.

MOEC/BCA. (2003). *Strategic plan for the development of the Bagamoyo College of Arts 2003-2006.* Dar es Salaam: Ministry of Education and Culture/Bagamoyo: Bagamoyo College of Arts.

MOEVT. (2007). *ICT policy for basic education*. Dar es Salaam: Ministry of Education and Vocational Training, The United Republic of Tanzania.

MOICS. (2007). *Taasisi ya Sanaa na Utamaduni Bagamoyo (TaSUBa) framework document*. Dar es Salaam: Ministry of Information, Culture and Sports, The United Republic of Tanzania.

Oxlund, B. (2010). Responding to university reform in South Africa: Student activism at the University of Limpopo. *Social Anthropology, 18*(1), 30–42. doi:10.1111/j.1469-8676.2009.00095.x

Selwyn, N. (2009). The digital native – myth and reality. *Aslib Proceedings, 61*(4), 364–379. doi:10.1108/00012530910973776

Shore, C., & Wright, S. (2000). Coercive accountability. The rise of audit culture in higher education. In Strathern, M. (Ed.), *Audit cultures: Anthropological studies in accountability, ethics and the academy* (pp. 57–89). London: Routledge.

Strathern, M. (2000). Introduction: new accountabilities. In Strathern, M. (Ed.), *Audit cultures: Anthropological studies in accountability, ethics and the academy* (pp. 1–18). London: Routledge.

Uimonen, P. (2004). *Information and communication technology (ICT) strategy for Bagamoyo College of Arts*. Bagamoyo College of Arts/Embassy of Sweden in Tanzania.

Uimonen, P. (2006). *ICT user study at Bagamoyo College of Arts*. Bagamoyo College of Arts and Sida/Embassy of Sweden Dar es Salaam.

Uimonen, P. (2008). Lärande i en digitaliserad värld. In Selander, S., & Svärdemo-Åberg, E. (Eds.), *Didaktisk design i digital miljö-nya möjligheter för lärande* (pp. 54–69). Stockholm: Liber.

Uimonen, P. (2009). Internet, arts and translocality in Tanzania. *Social Anthropology, 17*(3), 276–290. doi:10.1111/j.1469-8676.2009.00073.x

Uimonen, P. (2011). *Digital drama. Art, multimedia, and transcultural liminality in Tanzania*. New York: Routledge (in process)

Weiss, B. (2002). Thug realism: Inhabiting fantasy in urban Tanzania. *Cultural Anthropology, 17*(1), 93–124. doi:10.1525/can.2002.17.1.93

Wright, S., & Rabo, A. (2010). Introduction: Anthropologies of university reform. *Social Anthropology, 18*(1), 1–14. doi:10.1111/j.1469-8676.2009.00096.x

ENDNOTES

[1] I would like to thank the editors of this volume for their initiative to collect research from so many parts of the world and their supportive cooperation throughout the publication process. The constructive comments of two anonymous reviewers helped strengthen my arguments, which I am grateful for. I would also like to thank David, Nina and Mussa for their positive comments on a draft version of this chapter and enthusiasm in participating in this research project. Any shortcomings in this text are of course my sole responsibility.

[2] The annual *eLearning Africa* conference offers a comprehensive overview of ongoing ICT for education activities in Africa. See http://www.elearning-africa.com

[3] Statistics from International Telecommunication Union (ITU) for Internet access in 2008. Retrieved December 29, 2009, from http://www.itu.int/ITU-D/icteye/Indicators/Indicators.aspx#

[4] The study used questionnaire-based interviews with 50 students and 18 students, approximately half of the total number of 97 students and 35 teachers. This was supplemented with interviews with a select

number of students and staff as well as observations in the ICT building from May 2005 to February 2006.

[5] NACTE web site. Retrieved December 30, 2009, from http://www.nacte.go.tz

[6] Group discussions carried out in November 2009, with 17 first year students, 11 second year students and 15 third year students, 43 in total out of a student population of 120.

Chapter 14
Learning Competence for Youth in Digital Lifelong Learning Society

Sujuan Yang
South China Normal University, China

Yihong Fan
Xiamen University, China

ABSTRACT

The purpose of this chapter is to identify challenges and opportunities of learning in rapidly changing digital age, and to propose a theoretical framework of classifying potentially useful learning competences for youths in digital lifelong learning society. The rapid development of technology, economics and society have placed unprecedented challenges to people in all countries and all walks of life, thus demand new ways of learning, or lifelong learning to help people function in this ever changing world more successfully. The framework of learning competences proposed in this chapter encompasses meta-cognition, learning strategies, transfer of learning, and information literacy. All of them are discussed in details in the chapter. Although the framework has the function to help learners achieve learning success in digital environment, a further research involving youth on development and application of it in the digital lifelong learning environment is needed as a next step of research. Therefore, experimental research is needed to further test and adjust the proposed theoretical framework in a digital lifelong learning environment.

DOI: 10.4018/978-1-60960-206-2.ch014

INTRODUCTION

In the twenty first century new expectations and demands on education are mounting rapidly, as social and economic development becomes geared around the concept of constructing a Society of Knowledge. Citizens need strong, autonomous, responsive and inclusive educational institutions to provide them with research-based education and learning in order to meet with the many challenges facing them ahead. Lifelong learning is considered as a positive response to such a changing world (EAEA, 2006). In its Resolution of 27 June 2002 on Lifelong Learning, the Council of the European Union considered that Lifelong learning "facilitates free mobility for European citizens and allows the achievement of the goals and aspirations of European Union: to become more prosperous, competitive, tolerant and democratic".

It has become obvious that traditional teaching and learning are not adequate enough to meet the needs of learners in today's fast-paced, rapidly changing environment. Lifelong learning, flexible learning, mobile learning and online learning become necessary (EAEA, 2006). The implementation of these new learning models requires new learning competence and skills (DeSeCo, 2005). It is necessary to identify and develop new learning competence for youths and to facilitate their learning successfully in digital lifelong learning environment.

By identifying the challenges and opportunities of learning in rapidly changing digital age, this research proposes a theoretical framework to classify potentially useful learning competences for youths in digital lifelong learning society as deliberate response to the challenges of rapid development of technology, economics and society.

This research mainly used literature review and policy survey to obtain information. By using Internet search engines, such as Google Academic,

Educational Resources Information Center (ERIC) and Psychological Abstracts (PsychLit) databases literature searches were conducted to determine the pressing challenges and potential opportunities, and in turn came up with appropriate theoretical framework. By paying attention to how different countries are responding to the challenges, the research learned insights from different national or regional resources. When the theoretical framework was chosen, additional literature searches were conducted to identify studies that had determined the success of specific learning tactics.

As background of the study, this part of the Chapter illustrates the challenges of the rapidly changing world and the evolving significance of lifelong learning in responding to the changes.

Part one of the Chapter identifies the challenges and opportunities of learning in digital age and points out that in the new digital learning environment, teacher becomes a facilitator, a coach, a guide and co-learner, and the learner becomes an information seeker, an explorer, a problem solver and a co-teacher. The role change both for teachers and learners requires new competences to adapt to the new learning environment.

Part two discusses the study of competence conducted in different countries and regions, and a working definition of competence is provided as "abilities help individual be successful in the society, includes knowledge, skills and attitudes." Similarly, the concept of learning competence has been defined as abilities help individual be successful in a learning context.

Part three elaborates on the components of learning competence needed in the digital lifelong learning environment. They are divided into four aspects: meta-cognition, learning strategies, transfer of learning, and information literacy. Detailed discussion about the definition, components and relative knowledge, skills and attitudes has been offered to provide the readers with a broad outline of each component of learning competence.

BACKGROUND

Lifelong Learning as Response to the Challenges of a Changing Society

Growing globalization, the rapid pace of change, the continuous emergence of new technologies, and the quick expansion of the World Wide Web have convergently placed unprecedented challenges for people around the world. Creativity and the ability to continue to learn and to innovate will count as much as, if not more than, specific areas of knowledge liable to become obsolete. Lifelong learning should be the norm. (EC, 2008b). The term lifelong learning addresses the quality of life as well as economic growth (EAEA, 2006), and the strategy of lifelong learning has been taken by many countries as the most usefully thought of a positive response to such a changing world.

For example, in November 2000, based on the conclusions of the European Year of Lifelong Learning in 1996, the European Commission issued *A Memorandum on Lifelong Learning*. Later in November 2001, a plan of action entitled *Communication from the Commission - Making a European Area of Lifelong Learning a Reality* was issued. This report shows that the demand for skills and qualifications from employers and individuals is changing; education should be more flexible to meet the increasing demand on learning opportunities and on individual preferences for how, when and where learning is accessed. In October 2006, the European Commission issued *Adult learning: It is never too late to learn*, suggests that lifelong learning should be the core of the ambitious Lisbon 2010-process, in which the whole of the European Union should become a learning area. Later in December 2007, in the *Report on Adult learning: It is never too late to learn*, a number of related recommendations and resolutions were recognized, and further urged member states of European Commission

to establish a culture of lifelong learning (EC, 2001, 2006, 2007). Now on The European Commission website, lifelong learning is defined as "all learning activity undertaken throughout life, with the aim of improving knowledge, skills and competence, within a personal, civic, social and/or employment-related perspective."[1] Thus, the European Commission has integrated its various educational and training initiatives under a single umbrella, the Lifelong Learning Programme.

In the view of The Scottish Executive (2004), "Lifelong learning covers the whole range of learning. That includes formal and informal learning and workplace learning. It also includes the skills, knowledge, attitudes and behaviours that people acquire in their day-to-day experiences." They believe in investing public money in lifelong learning because investment in knowledge and skills brings direct economic benefits both to individuals and to society as a whole.

The Japanese Ministry of Education, Culture, Sports, Science and Technology pointed out as below:

Lifelong learning comprises two main aspects: the concept to comprehensively review various systems including education, in order to create a lifelong learning society; and the concept of learning at all stages of life. In other words, the concept of learning in the context of lifelong learning encompasses not only structured learning through school and social education but also learning through involvement in such areas as sports, cultural activities, hobbies, recreation and volunteer activities. The places for conducting learning activities are also diverse, including elementary and secondary schools, universities and other institutions of higher education, citizens' public halls, libraries, museums, cultural facilities, sports facilities, lifelong learning program facilities in the private sector, companies, and offices." — MEXT, 2004

Lifelong learning becomes an important means for preparing all Thai people for a learning society in a knowledge-based economy. According to the National Education Act B.E.2542 of Thai government (1999), "the Lifelong education means education resulting from integration of formal, non-formal, and informal education so as to create ability for continuous lifelong development of quality of life. Learning is therefore part of life which takes place at all times and in all places. It is a continuous lifelong process, going on from birth to the end of our life, beginning with learning from families, communities, schools, religious institutions, workplaces, etc."

By identify challenges and the significance of lifelong learning in responding to the challenges in rapidly changing digital age we need to come up with a theoretical framework classifying potentially useful learning competences for youths in digital lifelong learning society. In the main body of this Chapter, the research illustrates further the challenges and opportunities in the digital age; the definition and significance of competence and learning competence; and the framework of learning competences proposed in this chapter encompasses meta-cognition, learning strategies, transfer of learning, and information literacy.

MAIN FOCUS

I. Challenges and Opportunities for Learning in Digital Age

As a result of the information and communication technology revolution, more and more digital products are being introduced into nowadays education and training systems, from computers to networks to interactive electronic whiteboard, with the aim of enhancing teaching and learning and helping youths create ability for continuous lifelong individual development.

With these digital products, learning content is easier to find, to access, to manipulate and remix, and to disseminate. Nowadays learning not only takes place in a face to face classroom, but also in a digital or online environment. By digital learning, people are not confined with specific classroom learning. In stead, they can choose the courses they want, and learn in anytime and anywhere through digital materials; and we can share and integrate unlimited resources and provide unlimited learning opportunities to citizens. In some instances, traditional institutions are making their educational content available to the general public online. In other cases, individuals who may have no connection to formal academia can nevertheless engage in teaching and learning with one another through the use of new technology[2]. Thus, flexible learning, mobile learning, universal learning and lifelong learning can come true.

The application of digital technology also provides challenges to our education system. In response, education is undergoing a major paradigm shift from traditional learning environments focused on the teacher as the "deliverer" of knowledge to new open learning environments focused on the learner as information seeker. The classroom environment becomes less teacher-directed, but more learner-centred. Teachers shift their role from being "the sage on the stage" to being "the guide on the side," and learners become more independent in their learning. In the new digital learning environment, teacher becomes a facilitator, a coach, a guide and co-learner, and the learner becomes an information seeker, an explorer, a problem solver and a co-teacher (Turner, 2003). All these changes call for new competences and skills of teachers and learners to meet the need of teaching and learning in digital environment.

II. Definition and Significance of Competence and Learning Competence

There are many confusion and debate concerning the term competence and a range of terms is used in the broad field related to it, such as competencies, capabilities, ability and skills. Competence is important because it distinguishes what is necessary for exemplary performance and encompasses more than knowledge and skill.

According to Mulder (2001, quoted from Biemans et al., 2004): "Competence is the capability of a person (or an organisation) to reach specific achievements. Personal competencies comprise integrated performance-oriented capabilities, which consist of clusters of knowledge structures and also cognitive, interactive, affective and where necessary psychomotor capabilities, and attitudes and values, which are required for carrying out tasks, solving problems and more generally, effectively functioning in a certain profession, organisation, position or role."

The OECD DeSeCo (*Definition and Selection of Competences*) defined competency as "the ability to meet complex demands, by drawing on and mobilising psychosocial resources (including skills and attitudes) in a particular context." And key competences are classified in three broad categories: using tools interactively, interacting in heterogeneous groups and acting autonomously (DeSeCo, 2005). Tools here include physical ones such as information technology and socio-cultural ones such as the use of language. Because individuals will meet people from different backgrounds in an increasingly interdependent world, it is important for them to interact in heterogeneous groups. And acting autonomously means to be able to take responsibility for managing one's own lives, situate one's lives in the broader social context and act autonomously.

Similar to the definition of competence, there is still no standard definition of learning competence, despite a long history of research and debate on it.

People generally believe that intelligence is learning competence for a very long time. For example, W. F. Dearborn defined intelligence as "the capacity to learn or to profit by experience." (quoted from Sternberg, 2000).

The WCEFA (World Conference on Education for All) Declaration states that basic learning competencies (BLCs) "comprise both essential learning tools (such as literacy, oral expression, numeracy and problem solving) and the basic learning content (such as knowledge, skills, values, and attitudes) required by human beings..." (UNESCO, 1990)

In USA, the State Council of Higher Education for Virginia (SCHEV) classifies the learning competence in six categories: writing competence, critical thinking competence, oral communication competence, quantitative reasoning competence, scientific reasoning competence and information technology competence. (George Mason University, 2007)

By literature reviewing, Higgins et al (2007) founded that Learning skills is a very broad term used to describe the various skills needed to acquire new skills and knowledge. It is often broken down into sub-categories which commonly include the following:

- Information and communication skills: often including aspects of literacy or literacies;
- Thinking and problem-solving skills: particular the development of critical thinking;
- Interpersonal and self-management skills.

In 2008 document of European Commission *European Reference Framework- - key competences for lifelong learning*, the competence of learning to learn is defined as "the ability to pursue and persist in learning, to organize one's own learning, including effective management of time and information, both individually and in groups" (EC, 2008).

From the definitions mentioned above, we can conclude that **learning competence** is a set of capabilities helping individual be successful in a learning context. It includes cognitive capabilities such as literacy and numeracy, information technology capabilities, management capabilities on time and information, capabilities for transfer of learning such as problem-solving and reasoning, learning strategy such as organizing one's own learning, and so on.

III. Learning Competences for Youths in Digital Lifelong Learning Society

In a hyper-connected world, learning materials are available on the web, and the digital learning environment enable people to learn any time, any where. Furthermore, the web has expanded the possibilities for all of us to reach our full potential through lifelong learning. However, the successful implementation of these new learning possibilities requires new competencies which are central challenges both world-wide and regionally.

Digital learning usually takes place when teachers and student are separated by either time or physical distance. Students have to learn along via computer and Internet because teachers aren't there for one-on-one help. Thus, they require maturity of character along with a set of learning capabilities to be successful in their digital learning, and motivation and confidence are crucial in this context.

Learning in a digital lifelong learning environment stresses the capabilities to use information and knowledge that extend beyond the traditional base of reading, writing and math. They demand learners obtain basic skills such as literacy, numeracy and ICT skills, in order to be able to access,

gain, process and assimilate new knowledge and skills. And they also require learners be effective in management of their learning, career and work patterns, as well as be persevered with learning, be concentrated for extended periods and be critically when reflecting on the purposes and aims of learning. (EC, 2004, 2008a) In these contexts, "the competencies that individuals need to meet their goals have become more complex, requiring more than the mastery of certain narrowly defined skills." (DeSeCo, 2005) Therefore, young people need a wider range of competences than ever.

To acquire these competences, young people need to "learn to learn" by reflecting critically on their learning aims, managing their learning with self-discipline, working autonomously and collaboratively, drawing the benefits from a heterogeneous group and sharing what they have learnt, seeking advice, information and support when necessary, and using all the opportunities of new technologies (EC,2008b). With another words, learning competences facilitate young people to complete their schooling and prepare for lifelong learning, and contribute to a successful life for them.

According to the definitions of learning competence mentioned above and demands of digital learning and lifelong learning, we can conclude that competence for learning in a digital lifelong learning environment is more complex than those in a traditional environment. It is the comprehensive capabilities of individuals to conduct learning activities effectively. It include literacy, numeracy and ICT skills, thinking and problem-solving skills, abilities for effective management of time and information, quantitative reasoning competence, scientific reasoning, critical thinking competence, oral communication competence, and so on.

This long list of required competencies for learning competence can be categorized into 4 sub-competences:

- Meta-cognition,
- Learning strategies,
- Transfer of learning, and
- Information literacy.

1. Meta-Cognition

The term meta-cognition refers to learners' automatic awareness of their own knowledge and their ability to understand, control, and manipulate their own cognitive processes. Activities such as planning how to approach a given learning task, monitoring comprehension, and evaluating progress toward the completion of a task are meta-cognitive in nature (Livingston, 1997). It is often simply defined as "thinking about thinking." According to Flavell (1979), meta-cognition consists of both meta-cognitive knowledge and meta-cognitive experiences or regulation. Meta-cognitive knowledge refers to acquired knowledge about cognitive processes, knowledge that can be used to control cognitive processes. Flavell further divides meta-cognitive knowledge into three categories: knowledge of person variables, task variables and strategy variables.

- Knowledge of person variables refers to general knowledge about how human beings learn and process information, as well as individual knowledge of one's own learning processes.
- Knowledge of task variables includes knowledge about the nature of the task as well as the type of processing demands that it will place upon the individual.
- Knowledge about strategy variables include knowledge about both cognitive and meta-cognitive strategies, as well as conditional knowledge about when and where it is appropriate to use such strategies.

Meta-cognitive experiences involve the use of meta-cognitive strategies or meta-cognitive regulation (Brown, 1987, cited in Livingston, 1997). Meta-cognitive strategies or meta-cognitive regulations are sequential processes that one uses to control cognitive activities, and to ensure that a cognitive goal has been met. These processes help to regulate and oversee learning, and include planning, monitoring, and regulating (McKeachie et al. 1986, Everson et al. 1997). Planning includes such tactics as setting goals, skimming the material, and generating questions (McKeachie et al., 1986). Monitoring and regulating are activities that utilize self-regulation (McKeachie et al., 1986). Monitoring involves the process by which learners check themselves for comprehension of knowledge or skills (Weinstein & Mayer, 1986). Regulating involves such processes as adjusting reading rate, rereading, reviewing, or utilizing test-taking tactics (Filcher & Miller, 2000).

Meta-cognition enables students to benefit from instruction and influences the use and maintenance of cognitive strategies. Learners with good meta-cognitive skills are able to monitor and direct their own learning processes.

2. Learning Strategies

Learning strategies are procedures that facilitate a learning task. They are person's approaches to learning and using information, and tools to help learners understand information and solve problems. All learners use learning strategies either consciously or unconsciously when processing new information and performing tasks in the classroom. Studies have confirmed that good language learners are skilled at matching strategies to the task they were working on, whereas less successful language learners apparently do not have the meta-cognitive knowledge about task requirements needed to select appropriate strategies (Chamot, 2005).

The term learning strategy has been defined by many researchers. According to Oxford (1990)[3] "learning strategies are specific actions taken by the learner to make learning easier, faster, more enjoyable, more self-directed, more effective, and more transferable to new situations." Weinstein & Mayer (1986) stated that learning strategies are "thoughts and behaviors intended to influence the learner's ability to select, acquire, organize, and integrate new knowledge." Wenden and Rubin (1987) stressed that learning strategies are "any sets of operations, steps, plans, routines used by the learner to facilitate the obtaining, storage, retrieval, and use of information."

Learning Strategies have been classified by many scholars. Dansereau (1985, cited in Filcher & Miller, 2000) developed a theoretical framework for learning strategies that emphasized primary and support strategies. The primary strategies focused on learning strategies needed for text-based materials and support strategies are needed for developing a mental environment. According to Rubin (1987, cited in Hismanoglu, 2000), there are three types of strategies used by learners that contribute directly or indirectly. These are: learning strategies, communication strategies and social strategies. The taxonomy proposed by McKeachie encompasses the cognitive, meta-cognitive, and resource management aspects of learning. (McKeachie et al, 1986, cited in Filcher & Miller, 2000)

Learning strategies are important in today's lifelong learning environment. It is clearly that today's student must be equipped with knowledge and skills of learning strategies which enable him/her to deal with the vast amount of information. Making learners more aware of the importance of strategy use, and the broad range of strategy choices, helping learners to become an independent and effective learner by using appropriate strategies, developing effective learning strategies, all these can improve learners' learning efficiency and help them become effective and autonomous learners for their lifelong learning. Therefore, learning strategies should be received considerable attention.

3. Transfer of Learning

Learning is important because no one is born with the ability to function competently in society. The reason why we do teaching and training is to ensure learners to have knowledge and skill so that they can function well in the society. Educators hope that students will transfer learning from one problem to another within a course, from one year in school to another, between school and home, and from school to workplace. Jose Mestre (2002) defines transfer of learning broadly to mean the ability to apply knowledge or procedures learned in one context to new contexts (Mestre, 2002). Swinney calls it "that almost magical link between classroom performance and something which is supposed to happen in the real world" (Swinney, 1989, cited in Foxon, 1993). Baldwin & Ford consider transfer as the effective and continuing application in the job environment of the skills and knowledge gained in a training context (Baldwin & Ford, 1988, cited in Foxon, 1993).

A distinction is commonly made between near and far transfer. Near transfer refers to transfer between very similar contexts, and far transfer refers to transfer between contexts that, on appearance, seem remote and alien to one another (Perkins & Salomon, 1992). The training of near transfer is easier to train and the transfer of learning is usually a success, but the learner is unlikely to be able to adapt their skills and knowledge to changes. In contrast, the training of far transfer is more difficult to instruct, but it does allow the learner to adapt to new situations.

Information or skills related to one topic can sometimes either help or hinder the acquisition of information or skills related to another topic. Positive transfer occurs when learning in one context improves performance in some other context (Perkins & Salomon, 1992). It is a very important part of learning. In addition to helping learners acquire specific information more easily, positive transfer helps learners function effectively in situations for which they have no previously acquired information. It enables learners to solve problems they have never seen before. Negative transfer occurs when learning in one context impacts negatively on performance in another (Perkins & Salomon, 1992). This negative transfer is most likely to occur when the learner incorrectly believes there are common features, improperly links the information while encoding it, or incorrectly sees some value in using information from one setting in another.

Simons (1999) cataloged transfer into three kinds: from prior knowledge to learning, from learning to new learning, and from learning to application. In our everyday lives, prior learning is being transferred continuously to the development of new skills and knowledge.

Marguerite Foxon (1993) conceptualised transfer as a process with various stages through which transfer can be tracked. The five stages of the transfer process are: transfer intention, transfer initiation, partial transfer, transfer maintenance and transfer failure. She pointed out that the process approach reflects what actually happens as learners try out some of the skills, practise them, discontinue their use, or fail to use the skills. The process approach also enables practitioners to measure transfer at various points on the transfer time continuum, and the degree of transfer at those points. There is an acceptable degree of transfer, and an optimal degree of transfer (Marguerite Foxon, 1993).

Transfer of learning ensures the knowledge and skills acquired during a learning intervention are applied on the job. It is central to understanding how people develop important competencies. Evidence suggests that students possessing high knowledge in a domain do better at inference and problem solving after reading a passage related to that domain if the passage is sparse, requiring significant active processing of its meaning; this is in contrast to the poorer performance of students when the passage was much more complete,

requiring less processing of its deep meaning (McNamara, et al, 1996, cited in Mestre, 2002).

The research on transfer of learning to date has focused primarily on the transfer of skills learned during formal training (Rouiller & Goldstein, 1993). Because skills learned informally are likely to share similar features with transfer tasks in terms of context and content, the potential exists for skills learned informally to be more readily transferred than skills learned in formal training contexts. Yet the lack of research examining factors that influence the transfer of informal learning leaves human resource practitioners with unanswered questions about ways to ensure that managers apply what they learn informally.

Transfer of learning begins with the learning of a task in a unique situation and ends when we quit learning (experimenting) with that task. The power of varied context, examples, different practice scenarios, etc. cannot be overemphasized. No matter if you are learning simple discriminations or complex concepts, stimulus variations are helpful. Encouraging transfer of learning in the classroom provides the skills and knowledge for its successful implementation outside of the class.

4. Information Literacy

Information literacy is a prerequisite and essential enabler for lifelong learning. Lifelong learning in a digital environment relies on the information skills of learners.

The most generally accepted definition of information literacy is the one put forward by the American Library Association in 1989: "To be information literate, a person must be able to recognize when information is needed and have the ability to locate, evaluate and use effectively the needed information".

According to the Prague Declaration (2003) information literacy is a "key to social, cultural and economic development of nations and communities, institutions and individuals in the 21st century" and declared its acquisition as "part of the basic human right of lifelong learning"

In the 2008 document *European Reference Framework - - key competences for lifelong learning,* the European Commission use the term "digital competence" instead of "information literacy". Digital competence in this document involves the confident and critical use of Information Society Technology (IST) for work, leisure and communication. It is underpinned by basic skills in ICT: the use of computers to retrieve, assess, store, produce, present and exchange information, and to communicate and participate in collaborative networks via the Internet (EC, 2008a).

In 2000, the Association of College and Research Libraries (ACRL) released *Information Literacy Competency Standards for Higher Education,* describing five standards and numerous performance indicators for information literacy:

- **Standard One:** *The information literate student determines the nature and extent of the information needed.*
- **Standard Two:** *The information literate student accesses needed information effectively and efficiently.*
- **Standard Three:** *The information literate student evaluates information and its sources critically and incorporates selected information into his or her knowledge base and value system.*
- **Standard Four:** *The information literate student, individually or as a member of a group, uses information effectively to accomplish a specific purpose.*
- **Standard Five:** *The information literate student understands many of the economic, legal, and social issues surrounding the use of information and accesses and uses information ethically and legally.*

—ACRL, 2000

The Australian and New Zealand Information Literacy framework (Alan Bundy, 2004) lists six core standards which underpin information literacy acquisition, understanding and application by an individual. These standards identify that the information literate person:

- *recognizes the need for information and determines the nature and extent of the information needed*
- *finds needed information effectively and efficiently*
- *critically evaluates information and the information seeking process*
- *manages information collected or generated*
- *applies prior and new information to construct new concepts or create new understandings*
- *uses information with understanding and acknowledges cultural, ethical, economic, legal, and social issues surrounding the use of information*

—Alan Bundy, 2004

In China, Professor Zhong Zhixian proposes a framework for information literacy in 2001, which is widely recognized and applied in training programmes for information literacy development in China. The framework categorizes eight standards as the overall features of information literacy (Zhong, 2001):

- **using information tools:** *proficient use of information tools, in particular, the network communication tools*
- **accessing to information:** *Can effectively collect a variety of learning materials and information according to their own learning goals, can proficient obtain information by using skills such as reading, in-*

terviews, discussions, visits, experiments, retrieval

- **processing of information:** *the information collected can be summarized, classification, storage memory, identification, selection, analysis synthesis, abstraction and expression, etc.;*
- **generating information:** *based on the information collected, can accurate overview, integrate, perform and express information, to make it clear, concise, popular, smooth and full of personality characteristics;*
- **creating information:** *based on the interaction of a variety of collected information, generate new growth point of information, thereby creating new information to reach the ultimate purpose of collecting information;*
- **playing benefits of information:** *taking advantage of the received information to solve problems, maximizing the social and economic benefits of information;*
- **coordinating Information:** *to make information and information tools as a medium to across time and space;*
- **Information Immunization:** *consciously resisting and eliminating spam and harmful information, improving the Information Ethics literacy.*

—Zhong, 2001

Though the above mentioned definitions of information literacy are not the same, but they all relate, at their core, to an individuals' ability to use new media such as the Internet to access and communicate information effectively, and the ability to gather, organize and evaluate information, and to form valid opinions based on the results.

Only when young people master all four sub-competences as analyzed above, i.e. meta-cognition, learning strategies, transfer of learning, and information literacy, could they develop mature learning competences needed in the digital lifelong learning environment.

FUTURE RESEARCH DIRECTIONS

This review and synthesis of the literature indicates that there is a paucity of learning competence research involving youths in a digital lifelong learning environment. Although the European Commission (2008) has defined the competence of learning to learn and pointed out some essential knowledge, skills and attitudes related to this competence, but it is just a macro level approach to learning competence, short of a taxonomy and relevant specific knowledge, skills and attitudes, as well as strategies for developing these competences for youth.

Research is needed to reinforce the framework of learning competences and furthermore to provide specific knowledge, skills and attitudes subcategories to each component of the learning competence. It also needs to test experimentally the theoretical framework proposed by the authors in digital lifelong learning environment. Research in this area should strive to answer the following questions:

- Can the learning competence components proposed in this Chapter enhance the learning quality and learning outcomes in a digital lifelong learning environment?
- How to complete and refine the specific knowledge, skills and attitudes to each learning competence component?
- How to develop learning competence matching more closely to the characteristic to the youth's growing-up phases immersed in the digital world?

Answers to these questions may provide useful information on how to develop the learning competences for the youth, and how they might apply these competences in their own learning context. More practical help is needed for informing and teaching the learning competence strategies to youth in order to help them succeed in digital society. In this way, they could increase their satisfaction of learning at the same time while they improve their learning outcomes.

CONCLUSION

The roll-out of ICT has changed not only the way we work and live, but also the way we teach and learn. Lifelong learning has been emphasized as response to growing globalization and quick expansion of digital technology. Lifelong learning means all learning activities undertaken throughout life. It indicates that learning takes place at any time, anywhere and any place. Both lifelong learning and digital learning call for adequate learning competences. Competence means the abilities that help individual be successful learners in the society, including knowledge, skills and relevant attitudes. Similarly, learning competences can be defined as abilities that help individual be successful in learning context. It also includes knowledge, skills and attitudes that needed in lifelong learning context. To be successful in a digital lifelong learning environment, it is essential for learners to acquire a set of competences: meta-cognition, learning strategies, transfer of learning, and information literacy. These are the basic learning competences for learning in a digital lifelong learning environment. Each consists of relevant knowledge, skills and attitudes. It is necessary to prepare the youth with such basic learning competences for meeting with the current and future challenges.

REFERENCES

American Library Association Presidential Committee on Information Literacy. (1989). *Final report*. Chicago. (ED 315 074) Retrieved December 31, 2009, from http://www.ala.org/

Association of College and Research Libraries. (2000). *Information literacy competency standards for higher education*. Retrieved December 31, 2009, from http://www.ala.org/.

Baldwin, T. T., & Ford, J. K. (1988). Transfer of training: A review and directions for future research. *Personnel Psychology*, *41*, 63–105.. doi:10.1111/j.1744-6570.1988.tb00632.x

Bernt, F. M., & Bugbee, A. C. (1990). *Study practices of adult learners in distance education*. Paper presented at the Annual Meeting of the American Educational Research Association, Boston, MA. ERIC Document Reproduction Service No. ED 323 385.

Biemens., et al. (2004). Competence-based VET in the Netherlands: background and pitfalls. *Vocational Education and Training, 56* (4), pp. 523-538. Retrieved December 31, 2009, from http://www.bwpat.de/7eu

Brown, A. L. (1987). Metacognition, executive control, self-regulation, and other more mysterious mechanisms. In Weinert, F. E., & Kluwe, R. H. (Eds.), *Metacognition, motivation, and understanding* (pp. 65–116). Hillsdale, NJ: Lawrence Erlbaum Associates.

Bunk, G. P. (1994). Kompetenzvermittlung in der beruflichen Aus- und Weiterbildung in Deutschland. *Europäische Zeitschrift für Berufsbildung, 1*, 9–15.

Castells (1997). *The Information Age: Economy, Society, and Culture Vol 1The rise of the network society*, Oxford, and Malden, MA, 1996; Vol. 2 The power of identity,. Oxford, and Malden, MA, 1997.

Chamot, A. U. (2004). Issues in Language Learning Strategy Research and Teaching. *Electronic Journal of Foreign Language Teaching, 1*(1), 14-26. Retrieved December 31, 2009, from http://e-flt.nus.edu.sg/

Chamot, A. U. (2005). Language learning strategy instruction: Current issues and research. *Annual Review of Applied Linguistics* 25, 112-130. New York: Cambridge University Press. Retrieved December 31, 2009, from http:// journals.cambridge.org

Commission of the European Communities. (2006). *Adult learning: It is never too late to learn.* COM(2006) 614 final. Brussels, 23.10.2006.

Dansereau, D. (1985). Learning strategy research. In Segal, J., Chipman, S., & Glaser, R. (Eds.), *Thinking and learning skills: Relating instruction to research* (*Vol. 1*, pp. 209–239). Hillsdale, NJ: Erlbaum.

Definition and Selection of Competences (DeSeCo). (2005). *The definition and selection of key competencies- executive summary*, Retrieved December 18, 2006, from http://www.oecd.org/edu/statistics/deseco

Deist, F. D. L., & Winterton, J. (2005, March). What Is Competence? *Human Resource Development International, 8*(1), 27–46. doi:10.1080/1367886042000338227

European Association for the Education of Adults (EAEA). (2006). *Adult education trends and issues in Europe, 2006)* Retrieved December 31, 2009, from http://www.eaea.org/.

European Commission - Education and Culture (EC). (2006). *Adult learning: It is never too late to learn* (COM(2006) 614 final). Brussels, 23.10.2006.

European Commission -Education and Culture (EC). (2007). *Key competences for lifelong learning -European reference framework. Luxembourg.* 2007

European Commission -Education and Culture(EC). (2003). *What is lifelong learning?* Retrieved December 31, 2009, from http://europa.eu.int/.

European Commission-Education and Culture(EC). (2008a). *Education & Training 2010.* February 2008.Retrieved December 31, 2009, from http://europa.eu.int/

European Commission-Education and Culture(EC). (2008b). *Improving competences for the 21st Century: An Agenda for European Cooperation on Schools.* Brussels, 3.7.2008. Retrieved December 31, 2009, from http://europa.eu/

European Parliament: Committee on Culture and Education(EP) (2007). *Report on Adult learning: It is never too late to learn* (2007/2114(INI)). December 11, 2007.

Everson, H. T. Tobias, & S. Laitusis, V. (1997). *Do metacognitive skills and learning strategies transfer across domains?* Presented at the Annual Meeting of the American Educational Research Association, Chicago, IL. ERIC Document Reproduction Service No. ED 410 262.

Ficher, C., & Miller, G. (2000). Learning strategies for distance education students. *Journal of Agricultural Education, 41* (1),60-68. Press Retrieved December 31, 2009, from http://pubs.aged.tamu.edu

Foxon, M. (1993). A process approach to the transfer of training. *Australian Journal of Educational Technology, 9*(2), 130–143.

George Mason University. (2007). Assessing Competence in Six Areas at Mason: A Summary of the First Cycle: 2002-2006. *In Focus, 12* (1), February 2007. Retrieved December 31, 2009, from http://assessment.gmu.edu/

Higgins, S. (2007). Learning skills and the development of learning capabilities. Report. In *Research Evidence in Education Library*. London: EPPI-Centre, Social Science Research Unit, Institute of Education, University of London.

Hismanoglu, M. (2000). Language learning strategies in foreign language learning and teaching. *The Internet TESL Journal, VI*(8), August 2000. Retrieved December 31, 2009, from http://iteslj.org/

Jeris, L., & Johnson, K. (2004) *Speaking of competence: toward a cross-translation for human resource development (HRD) and continuing professional education (CPE)*. In Proceedings Academy of Human Resource Development Annual Conference,(Vol. 2, pp.1103-1110) Austin, TX, 4-7 March.

Livingston, J. A. (1997). *Metacognition: An Overview*. Retrieved December 31, 2009, from http://gse.buffalo.edu

McKeachie, W. J., Pintrich, P. R., Lin, Y., & Smith, D. (1986). *Teaching and learning in the college classroom: A review of the research literature*. Ann Arbor, MI: National Center for Research to Improve Postsecondary Teaching and Learning, University of Michigan.

McNamara, D. S., Kintsch, E., Songer, N. B., & Kintsch, W. (1996). Are good texts always better? Text coherence, background knowledge, and levels of understanding in learning from text. *Cognition and Instruction, 14*, 1–43. doi:10.1207/s1532690xci1401_1

Mestre, J. (2002).*Transfer of Learning: Issues and Research Agenda*. Presented at Workshop held at the National Science Foundation, March 21-22, 2002. Retrieved December 31, 2009, from: http://www.nsf.gov

Ministry of Education. Culture, Sports, Science and Technology (MEXT) [Japan] (2004). *Lifelong learning: What is lifelong learning?* Retrieved December 31, 2009, from http://www.mext.go.jp/.

Perkins, D. N., & Salomon, G. (1992). *Transfer of learning: Contribution to the international encyclopedia of education*. Second Edition Oxford, England: Pergamon Press. Retrieved December 31, 2009, from http://learnweb.harvard.edu/alps/

Rouiller, J. A., & Goldstein, I. L. (1993). The relationship between organizational transfer climate and positive transfer of training. *Human Resource Development Quarterly, 4*(4), 377–390. doi:10.1002/hrdq.3920040408

Scottish Executive. (2004). *Life through learning; learning through life*. The Lifelong Learning Strategy for Scotland: Summary Retrieved from http://www.scotland.gov.uk/.

Simons, P. R. J. (1999). Transfer of learning: paradoxes for learners. *International Journal of Educational Research, 31*(7), 577–589. Retrieved November 31, 2009..doi:10.1016/S0883-0355(99)00025-7

Sternberg, R. J. (2000). *Handbook of Intelligence*. New York: Cambridge University Press.

Transfer of Learning: Planning Workplace Education Programs.(2010). Retrieved November 31, 2009. from http://www.nald.ca/nls/inpub/transfer/Engish/page01.htm.

Turner, S. V. (2003). *Learning in a digital world: The role of technology as a catalyst for change*. Retrieved December 31, 2009, from www.neiu.edu/~ncaftori/sandy.doc

UNESCO. (1990). Final *Report on the World Conference on Education For All: Meeting basic learning needs*. Jomtien, Thailand. Paris: UNESCO. P.43

UNESCO. (1996), *Learning: the Treasure Within*. Report to UNESCO of the International Commission on Education for the twenty-first Century.Paris, France. Retrieved October 28, 2003. from http://unesdoc.unesco.org/images/0010/001095/109590ab.pdf

UNESCO. (2003), *The Prague Declaration – 'Toward an Information Literate Society'*. Prague, Czech Republic Sept 2003. Retrieved November 28, 2009. from http://portal.unesco.org/ci/en/

Weinert, F. E. (2001) Concept of competence: a conceptual clarification. In D. S. Rychen & L. H.Salganik (Eds).*Defining and Selecting key Competencies*, 45-66 Gooettingen: Hogrefe, Germany.

Weinstein, C. E., & Mayer, R. E. (1986). The teaching of learning strategies. In M. Wittrock (Ed.), *Handbook of research on teaching* (pp. 3 15-327). New York: Macmillan

Wenden, A., & Rubin, J. (1987). *Learner Strategies in Language Learning*. Upper Saddle River, NJ: Prentice Hall.

Zhong, Zh. X. (2001). Information literacy: build up eight competencies for you. *China education (Newspaper)*. 02.March.2001

ENDNOTES

[1] Retrieved November, 2009, from http://ec.europa.eu/dgs/education_culture,

[2] Retrieved November, 2009, from http://cyber.law.harvard.edu/media/files/copyrightandeducation.html#1_1

[3] Quoted in: Murat Hismanoglu (2000). Language Learning Strategies in Foreign Language Learning and Teaching. The Internet TESL Journal, Vol. VI, No. 8, August 2000. Retrieved December 31, 2009, from http://iteslj.org/

Compilation of References

Allen, G. (2000). *Intertextuality*. London, New York: Routledge.

Althaus, S. L. & David Tewksbury. (2002). Agenda Setting and the 'New' News: Patterns of Issue Importance among Readers of the Paper and Online Versions of the New York Times. *Communication Research 29* (2), 180–207.

American Decades. (2001). *Television's effect on education*. Retrieved April 5, 2010, from http://www.encyclopedia.com/doc/1G2-3468301851.html

American Library Association Presidential Committee on Information Literacy. (1989). *Final report*. Chicago. (ED 315 074) Retrieved December 31, 2009, from http://www.ala.org/

An, H., Lv, L & Shang, X. (2005). A review of learning strategies studies. *Mordern Primary and Secondary Education,. 134* (4).

Anderson, C. A., & Bushman, B. J. (2001). Effects of violent video games on aggressive behavior, aggressive affect, physiological arousal, and prosocial behavior: A meta-analytic review of the scientific literature. *Psychological Science, 12*(5). doi:10.1111/1467-9280.00366

Anderson, C. A., Sakamoto, A., Gentile, D. A., Ihori, N., Shibuyya, A., & Yukawa, S. (2008). Longitudinal effects of violent video games on aggression in Japan and the United States. *Pediatrics, 122*(5), 1067–1072. doi:10.1542/peds.2008-1425

Anderson, R. E., & Becker, H. J. (2001). School investments in instructional technology. *Teaching, Learning, and Computing, 8.* Retrieved March 15, 2010, from http://www.crito.uci.edu/tlc/findings/report_8/startpage.htm

Annetta, L. A., Murray, M. R., Laird, S. G., Bohr, S. C., & Park, J. C. (2006). Serious games: Incorporating video games in the classroom. *EDUCAUSE Quarterly, 29*(3), 16–22.

Appadurai, A. (1996). *Modernity at large. Cultural dimensions of globalization*. Minneapolis, MN: University of Minnesota Press.

Armstrong, A., & Casement, C. (1998). *The child and the machine: Why computers may put our children's education at risk*. Toronto, Canada: Key Porter Books.

Association of College and Research Libraries. (2000). *Information literacy competency standards for higher education*. Retrieved December 31, 2009, from http://www.ala.org/.Aufderheide, P. (2001). Media literacy: From a report of the national leadership conference on media literacy. In Kubey, R. (Ed.), *Media literacy in the information age: Current perspectives* (pp. 79–88). Piscataway, NJ: Transaction Books.

Baird, D. E., & Fisher, M. (2005-2006). Neomillennial user experience design strategies: Utilizing social networking media to support "Always on" learning styles. *Journal of Educational Technology Systems, 34*(1), 5–32. doi:10.2190/6WMW-47L0-M81Q-12G1

Bakhtin, M. M. (1986). *Speech Genres and Other Late Essays* (5th ed.). Austin, TX: University of Texas Press.

Baldwin, T. T., & Ford, J. K. (1988). Transfer of training: A review and directions for future research. *Personnel Psychology, 41*, 63–105. .doi:10.1111/j.1744-6570.1988.tb00632.x

Bamford, A. (2004, September). *Cyber-bullying*. Paper presented at the AHISA Pastoral Care National Conference, Melbourne, Australia.

Bandura, A. (1997). *Self-efficacy: the exercise of control.* Basingstoke, UK: W. H. Freeman.

Barab, S., Cherkes-Julkowski, M., Swenson, R., Garrett, S., Shaw, R., & Young, M. (1999). Principles of self-organization: Learning as participation in autocatakinetic systems. *Journal of the Learning Sciences, 8*(3&4), 349–390. doi:10.1207/s15327809jls0803&4_2

Barr, R., & Tagg, J. (1995). *From Teaching to Learning – A New Paradigm for Undergraduate Education.* Philadelphia, PA: Change Magazine.

Barton, D. (2007). *Literacy: an introduction to the ecology of written language* (2. ed.). Malden, MA: Blackwell.

Bates, A. W. (1980). Towards a Better Theoretical Framework for Studying Learning from Educational Television. *Instructional Science, 9*, 393–415. doi:10.1007/BF00121771

Bateson, G. (1972). *Steps to an ecology of mind.* San Francisco: Chandler.

Bauerlein, M. (2008). *The Dumbest Generation: How the Digital Age Stupefies Young Americans and Jeopardizes Our Future.* New York: Jeremy P. Tarcher/Penguin.

Bauman, Z. (2003). *Diogenes, 50.* Educational Challenges of the Liquid-Modern Era.

Beck, U. (2000). *The Risk Society and Beyond: Critical Issues for Social Theory.* London: Sage.Beck, U. (1998). *Democracy without enemies.* Cambridge, UK: Polity Press.Becker, K. (2007). Pedagogy in commercial video games. In Gibson, D., Aldrich, C., & Prensky, M. (Eds.), *Games and simulations in online learning. Research and development frameworks* (pp. 26–34). Hershey, PA: Information Science Publishing.

Beeman, W. (1993). The anthropology of theater and spectacle. *Annual Review of Anthropology, 22*, 369–393. doi:10.1146/annurev.an.22.100193.002101

Beggs, T. A. (2000). *Influences and barriers to the adoption of instructional technology.* In Proceedings of the Mid-South Instructional Technology Conference. Retrieved November 25, 2008, from http://frank.mtsu.edu/~itconf/proceed00/beggs/beggs.htm

Bellamy, R. V., & Walker, J. R. (1996). *Television and the Remote Control: Grazing on a Vast Wasteland.* New York: Guilford.

Bellotti, F., Berta, R., De Gloria, A., & Primavera, L. (2009). Enhancing the educational value of video games. *Computers in Entertainment (CIE), 7*(2).

Benkler, Y. (2006). *The Wealth of Networks: How social production transforms markets and freedom.* New Haven, CT: Yale University Press.

Bennett, M., & Smith, D. (1988). Evaluating Television-Linked Computer Software. *Computers & Education, 12*(1), 133–139. doi:10.1016/0360-1315(88)90068-1

Bennett, L. W., Wells, C., & Rank, A. (2009). Young citizens and civic learning: two paradigms of citizenship in the digital age. *Citizenship Studies, 13*(2), 105–120. doi:10.1080/13621020902731116

Bennett, S., Maton, K., & Kervin, L. (2008). The "Digital Natives" Debate: A Critical Review of the Evidence. *British Journal of Educational Technology, 39*(5), 775–786. doi:10.1111/j.1467-8535.2007.00793.x

Bennett, W. L. (2008). Changing citizenship in the digital age. In W. L. Bennett (Ed.), Civic life online: Learning how digital media can engage youth *(The John D. and Catherine T. MacArthur Foundation Series on Digital Media and Learning)* (pp. 1–24). Cambridge, MA: The MIT Press.

Bernt, F. M., & Bugbee, A. C. (1990). *Study practices of adult learners in distance education: Frequency of use and effectiveness.* Paper presented at the Annual Meeting of the American Educational Research Association, Boston, MA. ERIC Document Reproduction Service No. ED 323 385.

Biemens., et al. (2004). Competence-based VET in the Netherlands: background and pitfalls. *Vocational Education and Training, 56* (4), pp. 523-538. Retrieved December 31, 2009, from http://www.bwpat.de/7eu

Black, R. (2008). *Adolescents and Online Fan Fiction. New Literacies and Digital Epistemologies.* New York: Peter Lang Publishing Group.

Black, R. (2006). Digital Design: English Language Learners and Reder Reviews in Online Fiction. In M. Knobel & C. Lankshear (Eds.), *A New Literacies Sampler.* (pp115-136). Peter Lang. Retrieved December 18, 2009, from http://www.soe.jcu.edu.au/sampler/.

Blake, R. (2007). New trends in using technology in the language curriculum. *Annual Review of Applied Linguistics, 27,* 76–97. doi:10.1017/S0267190508070049

Bloom, D. E., & Canning, D. (2005). *Global Demographic Change: Dimensions and Economic Significance.* Boston: Harvard Initiative for Global Health.

Boellstorff, T. (2008). *Coming of age in Second Life: An anthropologist explores the virtually human.* Princeton, NJ: Princeton University Press.

Bourdieu, P. (1984). *Distinction: A Social Critique of the Judgement of Taste.* London: Routledge.

boyd, d. (2006). Friends, Friendsters, and MySpace Top 8: Writing Community Into Being on Social Network Sites. *First Monday, 2006*(11:12).

Boyse, K. (2009). Television and Children. *YourChild Development & Behavior Resources.* Retrieved April 1, 2010, from http://www.med.umich.edu/yourchild/topics/TV.htm

Braine, G. (1999). Introduction. In Braine, G. (Ed.), *Non-native educators in English language teaching* (pp. viii–xx). Mahwah, NJ: Lawrence Erlbaum.

Brown, A. L. (1987). Metacognition, executive control, self-regulation, and other more mysterious mechanisms. In Weinert, F. E., & Kluwe, R. H. (Eds.), *Metacognition, motivation, and understanding* (pp. 65–116). Hillsdale, NJ: Lawrence Erlbaum Associates.

Brown, T. H. (2006). *Beyond constructivism: navigationism in the knowledge era.* In On the Horizon, 3.

Bruner, J. S. (1996). *The culture of education.* Cambridge, MA: Harvard University Harper Perennial.

Bruun, H. (2002). Global Tv-genre og komplekse nærhedsoplevelser. *Dansk Sociologi, 2/13.*

Brynjolfsson, E., Hu, Y., & Smith, M. D. (2003). Consumer Surplus in the Digital Economy: Estimating the Value of Increased Product Variety at Online Booksellers. *Management Science, 49*(11), 1580–1596. doi:10.1287/mnsc.49.11.1580.20580

Buckingham, D. (2003). *Media Education: Literacy, Learning and Contemporary Culture.* Cambridge, UK: Polity Press.

Buckingham, D. (2000). *After the death of childhood: Growing up in the age of electronic media.* Cambridge, UK: Polity.

Buckingham, D. (2003). *Media education: Literacy, learning and contemporary culture.* Cambridge, UK: Polity.

Buckingham, D. (2007). *Beyond technology: Children's learning in the age of digital culture.* Cambridge, UK: Polity.

Buckingham, D., & Willett, R. (2006). *Digital generations: children, young people, and new media.* Mahwah, NJ: Lawrence Erlbaum Associates.

Buckingham, D. (2005). The Media Literacy of Children and Young People. A Review of the Literature. *Centre for the Study of Children Youth and Media Institute of Education,* London. Retrieved November 11, 2009, from http://www.ofcom.org.uk/advice/media_literacy/medlitpub/medlitpubrss/ml_children.pdf.

Bunk, G. P. (1994). Kompetenzvermittlung in der beruflichen Aus- und Weiterbildung in Deutschland. *Europäische Zeitschrift für Berufsbildung, 1,* 9–15.

Burniske, R. W., & Monke, L. (2001). *Breaking down the digital walls: Learning to teach in a post-modern world.* New York: State University of New York Press.

Butler, J. (1993). *Bodies that matter: On the discursive limits of "sex.".* New York: Routledge.

Calenda, D., & Mosca, L. (2007). Logged On and Engaged? The Experience of Italian Young People. In Loader, B. D. (Ed.), *Young Citizens in the Digital Age: Political Engagement, Young People, and New Media.* New York: Routledge.

Calongne, C. M. (2008, September/October). Educational frontiers: Learning in a virtual world. *Educause Review, 43*(5), 36-48. Retrieved April 3, 2010, from http://www.educause.edu/EDUCAUSE+Review/EDUCAUSEReviewMagazineVolume43/EducationalFrontiersLearningin/163163

Calvet, L.-J. (1998). *Language wars and linguistic politics.* Oxford, UK: Oxford University Press.

Campbell, A. J., Cumming, S. R., & Hughes, I. (2006). Internet use by the socially fearful: addiction or therapy? *Cyberpsychology & Behavior, 9*(1), 69–81. doi:10.1089/cpb.2006.9.69

Camtasia. (2008). Softwarecasa. Retrieved from http://www.softwarecasa.com/

Canagarajah, A. S. (1999). Interrogating the "native speaker fallacy": Non-linguistic roots, non-pedagogical results. In Braine, G. (Ed.), *Non-native educators in English language teaching* (pp. 77–92). Mahwah, NJ: Lawrence Erlbaum.

Carlson, T. (2008). *Riding the Web 2.0 Wave: Candidates on YouTube in the Finnish 2007 Election.* Unpublished paper.

Carlsson-Paige, N., & Lantieri, L. (2005). A changing vision of education. In Noddings, N. (Ed.), *Educating citizens for global awareness* (pp. 107–121). New York: Teachers College Press.

Castells, M. (2000). Materials for an exploratory theory of the network society. *The British Journal of Sociology, 51*(1), 5–24. doi:10.1080/000713100358408

Castells (1997). *The Information Age: Economy, Society, and Culture Vol 1 The rise of the network society*, Oxford, and Malden, MA, 1996; Vol. 2 The power of identity,. Oxford, and Malden, MA, 1997.

Castells, M. (2004). Informationalism, networks, and the network society: a theoretical blueprint. In Castells, M. (Ed.), *The network society. A cross-cultural perspective* (pp. 3–45). Cheltenham, UK: Edward Elgar.

Castells, M. (1996). *The rise of the network society*, Oxford, UK: Blackwell (2nd edition, 2000).

Cattuto, C., Loreto, V., & Pietronero, L. (2007). Semiotic dynamics and collaborative tagging. *Proceedings of the National Academy of Sciences of the United States of America, 104*(5), 1461–1464. doi:10.1073/pnas.0610487104

Chadwick, A. (2006). *Internet Politics: States, Citizens and New Communication Technologies.* Oxford, UK: Oxford University Press.

Chamot, A. U. (2004). Issues in Language Learning Strategy Research and Teaching. *Electronic Journal of Foreign Language Teaching, 1*(1), 14-26. Retrieved December 31, 2009, from http://e-flt.nus.edu.sg/

Chamot, A. U. (2005). Language learning strategy instruction: Current issues and research. *Annual Review of Applied Linguistics 25*, 112-130. New York: Cambridge University Press. Retrieved December 31, 2009, from http:// journals.cambridge.org

Chapelle, C. (2007). Technology and second language acquisition. *Annual Review of Applied Linguistics, 27*, 98–114. doi:10.1017/S0267190508070050

Chen, H. -H., & O'Neil, H. F. (April, 2005). *Training effectiveness of a computer game.* Paper presented in a symposium titled "Research Issues in Learning Environments" at the annual meeting of the American Educational Research Association, Montreal, Canada.

Cheng, X., Dale, C., & Liu, J. (2008). Statistics and social network of YouTube videos. In *Proceedings of the 16th International Workshop on Quality of Service* (pp. 229–238). Enschede: IWQoS.

Cheong, P. H. (2008). The young and techless? Investigating internet use and problem-solving behaviors of young adults in Singapore. *New Media & Society, 10*(5), 771–791. doi:10.1177/1461444808094356

Choat, E. (1982). Teachers' use of Educational Television in Infants' Schools. *Educational Studies, 8*(3), 185–207. doi:10.1080/0305569820080302

Chou, C., Condron, L., & Belland, J. C. (2005). A review of the research on Internet addiction. *Educational Psychology Review, 17*(4), 363–388. doi:10.1007/s10648-005-8138-1

Clark, R. E. (1983). Reconsidering research on learning from media. *Review of Educational Research, 53*(4), 445–459.

Clark, R. E. (Ed.). (2001). *Learning from media: arguments, analysis, and evidence*. Greenwich, CT: Information Age Publishing.

Clark, R. E. (2007). Learning from serious games? Arguments, evidence and research suggestions. *Educational Technology*, *47*(3), 56–59.

Clifford, P., & Friesen, S. (2001). The stewardship of the intellect: Classroom life, educational innovation and technology. In Barrell, B. (Ed.), *Technology, teaching and learning: Issues in the integration of technology* (pp. 31–42). Calgary, Alberta, Canada: Detselig.

Coffield, F., et al. (2004), *Learning styles and pedagogy in post-16 learning*, Learning and Skills Research Centre. from the World Wide Web: http://www.lsda.org.uk/files/PDF/1543.pdf

Cohen, M. (2001). The Role of Research in Educational Television. In Singer, D. G., & Singer, J. L. (Eds.), *Handbook of Children and the Media* (pp. 571–586). Thousand Oaks, CA: Sage Publications Inc.

Cohen, A. (Producer), & Capra, B. (Director). (1990). *Mindwalk* [motion picture]. America: Paramount.

Collins, A., & Halverson, R. (2009). *Rethinking Education in the Age of Technology: The Digital Revolution and Schooling in America*. New York: Teachers College.

Collins, W. A., Sobol, B. L., & Westby, S. (1981). Effects of adult commentary on children's comprehension and inferences about a televised aggressive portrayal. *Child Development*, *52*(1), 158–163. doi:10.2307/1129225

Collins, S., & Clarke, A. (2008). Activity frames and complexity thinking: Honouring both the public and personal agendas in an emergent curriculum. *Teaching and Teacher Education*, *24*, 1003–1014. doi:10.1016/j.tate.2007.11.002

Collis, B. (1996). *Tele-learning in a Digital World. The Future of Distance Learning*. London: International Thomson Computer Press.

Colville, R. (2008). *Politics, Policy and the Internet*. London: Centre for Policy Studies.

Commission of the European Communities. (2006). *Adult learning: It is never too late to learn*. COM(2006) 614 final. Brussels, 23.10.2006.

Cook, V. (1999). Going beyond the native speaker in language teaching. *TESOL Quarterly*, *33*(2), 185–209. doi:10.2307/3587717

Cope, B., & Kalantzis, M. (Eds.). (2000). *Multiliteracies: Literacy learning and the design of social futures*. London: Routledge.

COWI (2002). *Review of Bagamoyo College of Arts*. Final Report, prepared for Swedish Embassy in Dar es Salaam.

Crook, D. (2007). School Broadcasting in the United Kingdom: An Exploratory History. *Journal of Educational Administration and History*, *39*(3), 217–226. doi:10.1080/00220620701698341

Cuban, S., & Cuban, L. (2007). *Partners in literacy: Schools and libraries building communities through technology*. New York: Teachers College Press.

Cvetkovic, V. B., & Lackie, R. (Eds.). (2009). *Teaching generation M: A Handbook for Librarians and Educators*. New York: Neal-Schuman Publishers, Inc.

Czerniewicz, L., & Brown, C. (2010). Strengthening and weakening boundaries. Students negotiating technology mediated learning. In Sharpe, (Eds.), *Rethinking Learning for a Digital Age. How Learners are shaping their own Experiences*. Amsterdam: Routledge.

Dale, P. (1986). *The myth of Japanese uniqueness*. New York: St. Martin's Press.

Dansereau, D. (1985). Learning strategy research. In Segal, J., Chipman, S., & Glaser, R. (Eds.), *Thinking and learning skills: Relating instruction to research* (*Vol. 1*, pp. 209–239). Hillsdale, NJ: Erlbaum.

Davidson, C. (2009). *Game school opens in New York: Quest to learn. HASTAC*. Retrieved April 4, 2010, from http://www.hastac.org/node/1959

Davis, B., & Simmt, E. (2003). Understanding learning systems: Mathematics education and complexity Science. *Journal for Research in Mathematics Education*, *34*(2), 137–167. doi:10.2307/30034903

Davis, B., & Sumara, D. (2006). *Complexity and education*. Mahwah, NJ: Lawrence Erlbaum Associates, Inc.

Davis, B., Sumara, D., & Luce-Kapler, R. (2008). *Emerging minds: Changing teaching in complex times* (2nd ed.). New York: Routledge.

De Bello, T. C. (1990) Comparison of Eleven Major Learning Styles Models: Variables, Appropriate Populations, Validity of Instrumentation and The Research Behind Them. In *Reading, Writing, and Learning Disabilities*, 6, 203-222. Retrieved from http://www.ldrc.ca/projects/atutor/content/7/debello.htm

de Swaan, A. (2001). *Words of the world: The global language system*. Cambridge, UK: Polity.

Dean, M. (1999). *Governmentality: Power and rule in modern society*. London: Sage Publications.

Dede, C. (2000). Rethinking how to invest in technology. In *The Jossey-Bass reader on technology and learning* (pp. 184–191). San Francisco: Jossey-Bass.

Dede, C. (2005). Planning for neomillennial learning styles: Shifts in students' learning style will prompt a shift to active construction of knowledge through mediated immersion. *Educause Quarterly, 28*(1). Retrieved March 20, 2005, from http://www.educause.edu/apps/eq/eqm05/eqm0511.asp?bhcp=1

Definition and Selection of Competences (DeSeCo). (2005). *The definition and selection of key competencies-executive summary*, Retrieved December 18, 2006, from http://www.oecd.org/edu/statistics/deseco

Deist, F. D. L., & Winterton, J. (2005, March). What Is Competence? *Human Resource Development International, 8*(1), 27–46. doi:10.1080/1367886042000338227

Department for Education and Skills. (2004). *Information and Communications Technology in Schools in England: 2004 (Provisional)*. London, U.K. Retrieved April 2008 from http://www.dfes.gov.uk/rsgateway/DB/SFR/s000480/index.shtml

Desmond, R. (2001). Free Reading: Implications for Child Development. In Singer, D. G., & Singer, J. L. (Eds.), *Handbook of Children and Media* (pp. 29–46). Thousand Oaks, CA: Sage Publications, Inc.

Dewey, J. (1916). *Democracy and Education: an introduction to the philosophy of education*. New York: The Macmillan Company.

Di Gennaro, C., & Dutton, W. (2006). The Internet and the Public: Online and Offline Political Participation in the United Kingdom. *Parliamentary Affairs, 59*(2), 299–313. doi:10.1093/pa/gsl004

Dirr, P. J. (2001). Cable Television. Gateway to Educational Resources for Development at All Ages. In Singer, D. G., & Singer, J. L. (Eds.), *Handbook of Children and the Media* (pp. 533–545). Thousand Oaks, CA: Sage Publications, Inc.

Doerr, N. (2009). Investigating "native speaker effects": Toward a new model of analyzing "native speaker" ideologies. In Doerr, N. (Ed.), *The native speaker concept: Ethnographic investigations of native speaker effects* (pp. 15–46). Berlin: Mouton de Gruyter.

Doi, T. (1971). *Amae no kôzo* [The structure of *amae*]. Tokyo: Kobundo.

Doll, W. (2008). Complexity and the culture of curriculum. *Educational Philosophy and Theory, 40*(1), 191–212. doi:10.1111/j.1469-5812.2007.00404.x

Drotner, K. (2001). *Medier for fremtiden: børn, unge og det nye medielandskab*. København: Høst.

Ducate, L., & Lomicka, L. (2005). Exploring the blogsphere: Use of web logs in the foreign language classroom. *Foreign Language Annals, 38*, 410–421. doi:10.1111/j.1944-9720.2005.tb02227.x

Duffy, P. D., & Bruns, A. (2006, September 26). *The use of blogs, wikis and RSS in education: A conversation of possibilities*. Paper presented at Online Learning and Teaching Conference 2006, Brisbane, Australia.

Duimel, M., & deHaan, J. (2009). *Instrumental, information and strategic ICT skills of teenagers and their parents*. Paper presented at the EU Kids Online conference.

Dunkels, E., Frånberg, G.-M., & Hällgren, C. (2008). Young People and Contemporary Digital Arenas - Identity, Learning and Abusive Practices. In *Journal of Research in Teacher Education*.

Dunkels, E. (2007). *Bridging the Distance - Children's Strategies on the Internet*. Sweden:Umeå, Umeå universitet.

Dunn, R., Beautry, J., & Klavas, A. (1989). Survey of research on learning styles. *Educational Leadership, 47*(7).

Dunn, R., & Dunn, K. (1992). *Teaching Elementary Students Through Their Individual Learning Styles*. Boston: Allyn & Bacon.

Dunn, R., & Dunn, K. (1993). *Teaching secondary students through their individual learning styles: Practical approaches for grades*. Boston: Allyn & Bacon.

Durkheim, É. (1912). *The Elementary Forms of Religious Life*. New York: Free Press.

Earl, J., & Schussman, A. (2008).Contesting Cultural Control: Youth Culture and Online Petitioning. In Bennett, W. Lance (ed).*Civic Life Online: Learning How Digital Media Can Engage Youth* Cambridge, MA: MIT Press.

Eastmond, D. V. (1995). *Alone but together: Adult distance study through computer conferencing*. Cresskill, NJ: Hampton Press, Inc.

Efimova, L., Hendrick, S., & Anjewierden, A. (2005). *Finding 'the life between buildings': An approach for defining a weblog community*. Presented at the Internet Research 6.0: Internet Generations, Chicago. Retrieved from https://doc.telin.nl/dscgi/ds.py/Get/File-55092/AOIR_blog_communities.pdf.

E-learning Nordic. (2006). *Effekten af it i uddannelsessektoren*. Retrieved January 22,2010, from http://www.elearningeuropa.info/files/media/media10112.pdf

Ellison, N. B., & Boyd, D. (2007). Social Network Sites: Definition, History, and Scholarship. *Journal of Computer-Mediated Communication*, *13*(1), 210–230.

Erstad, O. (1997). *Mediebruk og medieundervisning. En evaluering av medieundervisningen i norsk skole:intensjoner ... elever på ungdomsskolen og videregående skol*. Oslo: NOVA Rapport 8/04.

Europa, E. (2005). *A European Framework for Digital Literacy*. Retrieved January 15,2010, from http://www.elearningeuropa.info/directory/index.php?page=doc&doc_id=6007&doclng=6).

European Association for the Education of Adults (EAEA). (2006). *Adult education trends and issues in Europe, 2006)* Retrieved December 31,2009, from http://www.eaea.org/.

European Commission - Education and Culture (EC). (2006). *Adult learning: It is never too late to learn* (COM(2006) 614 final). Brussels, 23.10.2006.

European Commission -Education and Culture (EC). (2007). *Key competences for lifelong learning -European reference framework. Luxembourg.* 2007

European Commission -Education and Culture(EC). (2003). *What is lifelong learning?* Retrieved December 31, 2009, from http://europa.eu.int/.

European Parliament: Committee on Culture and Education(EP) (2007). *Report on Adult learning: It is never too late to learn* (2007/2114(INI)). December 11, 2007.

Everson, H. T. Tobias, & S. Laitusis, V. (1997). *Do metacognitive skills and learning strategies transfer across domains?* Presented at the Annual Meeting of the American Educational Research Association, Chicago, IL. ERIC Document Reproduction Service No. ED 410 262.

Facer, K., & Sandford, R. (2010). The Next 25 Years?: Future Scenarios and Future Directions for Education and Technology. *Journal of Computer Assisted Learning*, *26*(1), 74–93. doi:10.1111/j.1365-2729.2009.00337.x

Facer, K., & Furlong, R. (2001). Beyond the Myth of the 'Cyberkid': Young People at the Margins of the Information revolution. *Journal of Youth Studies*, *4*(4), 451–469. doi:10.1080/13676260120101905

Fawdry, K. (1967). School Television in the BBC. In Moir, G. (Ed.), *Teaching and Television: ETV explained* (pp. 13–30). London: Pergamon Press.

Felder, R. M., & Spurlin, J. (2005). Reliability and Validity of the Index of Learning Styles: A Meta-analysis. *International Journal of Engineering Education*, *21*(1), 103–112.

Ferdig, R. E., & Trammell, K. D. (2004). *Content delivery in the 'Blogosphere'*. Technological Horizons in Education Journal, 31.

Ferguson, J. (2006). *Global shadows. Africa in the neoliberal world order*. London: Duke University Press.

Ferguson, R. (2007). Politics: Young People and Policy Deliberation Online. In Loader, B. D. (Ed.), *Young Citizens in the Digital Age: Political Engagement, Young People, and New Media.* (p. 2P). New York: Routledge.

Ficher, C., & Miller, G. (2000). Learning strategies for distance education students. *Journal of Agricultural Education, 41* (1), 60-68. Press Retrieved December 31, 2009, from http://pubs.aged.tamu.edu

Ficklen, E., & Muscara, C. (2001). Harnessing technology in the classroom. *American Education, 25*(3), 22–29.

Findahl, O. (2009). *Svenskarna och Internet 2009 (Internet in Sweden 2009)*. Hudiksvall, Sweden: World Internet Institute.

Findahl, O. & Zimic, S. (2008): *Unga svenskar och Internet 2008*. Gävle: WII.

Findahl, O., & Zimic, S. (2008). *Unga svenskar och Internet 2008 – en rapport som baseras på en pilotstudie av barn och ungdomars internetanvändning*. Hudiksvall: World Internet Institute. Retrieved February 20, 2010, from http://www.wii.se.

Fink, H., Harder, P., Holm, P., Sonne Jacobsen, K., Stjernfelt, F., & Pahuus, A. M. (Red.). (2004). *Humanistisk viden i et vidensamfund*. Temarapporter fra Forskningsrådet for kultur og kummunikation. København: Statens Humanistiske Forskningsråd

Firth, A., & Wagner, J. (2007). On discourse, communication, and (some) fundamental concepts in SLA research. *Modern Language Journal, 91*, 757–772.

Fisch, S. M. (2000). A Capacity Model of Children's Comprehension of Educational Content on Television. *Media Psychology, 2*(1), 63–91. doi:10.1207/S1532785X-MEP0201_4

Fisch, S. M. (2004). What's so 'new' about 'new media'?: Comparing effective features of children's educational software, television, and magazines. *IDC, 1*(3), 105–111. doi:10.1145/1017833.1017847

Fisch, S. M. (2005). Making Educational Computer Games 'Educational'. *IDC* June, 56-61.

Fish, S. E. (1993). Att tolka Variorumupplagan. In Entzenberg, C., & Hansson, C. (Eds.), *Modern litteraturteori* (pp. 164–190). Lund: Studentlitteratur.

Flanagan, M., & Booth, A. (2002). *Reload: Rethinking women + cyberpunk*. Cambridge, MA: MIT Press.

Flynn, W., & Vredevoogd, J. (2010). The Future of Learning: 12 Views of Emerging Trends in Higher Education. *Planning for Higher Education, 38*(2), 5–10.

Foxon, M. (1993). A process approach to the transfer of training. *Australian Journal of Educational Technology, 9*(2), 130–143.

Frånberg, G.-M., & Gill, P. (2009). *Vad är mobbning? I På tal om mobbning och vad som görs*. Stockholm: Skolverket.

Franklin, C. A. (2008). Factors determining elementary teachers' use of computers. *Principal Magazine, 87*, 54–55.

Frechette, J. D. (2002). *Developing media literacy in cyberspace: Pedagogy and critical learning for the twenty-first century classroom*. Westport, CT: Praeger.

Freedman, D. (2006). Internet transformations: 'old' media resilience in the 'new media' revolution. In Curran, J., & Morley, D. (Eds.), *Media and Cultural Theory* (pp. 275–290). London: Routledge.

Fuchs, C. (2008). *Internet and society: Social theory in the information age*. New York: Routledge.

Fuchs, T., & Woessmann, L. (2004). Computers and Student Learning: Bivariate and Multivariate Evidence on the Availability and Use of Computers at Home and at School. CESifo Working Paper Series 1321.

G8. (2006). *G8 Wold Summit in St.Petersburg*. July 16, 2006. Retrieved April 01, 2008 http://en.g8russia.ru/docs/12.html, Georgsen, M. & Konnerup, U. (2009). Mobil læring på Søndervangskolen, *Rapport nr. 1 fra følgeforskningen til projektet "Bæredygtighed i elevernes nærmiljø* Aalborg: Center for User-Driven Innovation, Learning & Design, 54 s.(eLearning Lab Publication Series; 18).

Gagné, R. M., Briggs, L. J., & Wager, W. W. (1992). *Principles of instructional design* (4th ed.). Fort Worth, TX: Harcourt Brace Jovanovich College Publishers.

Gamemaker 7.0. (2008). Yoyogames. Retrieved from http://glog.yoyogames.com/?p=535

Gao, W. (2000). Learning how to learn and learning strategies. *Foreign Education Research, 1*, 48–52.

Gee, J. P. (2003). *What video games have to teach us about learning and literacy* (2nd ed.). New York: Palgrave Macmillan.

Gee, J. P. (2004). *Situated language and learning: A critique of traditional schooling.* London: Routledge.

Gee, J. P. (2008). Learning and games. In Salen, K. (Ed.), *The ecology of games: Connecting youth, games, and learning* (pp. 21–40). Cambridge, MA: The MIT Press.

Geertz, C. (1971). Deep play: notes on the Balinese cockfight. *Daedalus, 101,* 1–37.

George Mason University. (2007). Assessing Competence in Six Areas at Mason: A Summary of the First Cycle: 2002-2006. *In Focus, 12* (1), February 2007. Retrieved December 31, 2009, from http://assessment.gmu.edu/

Gibson, J. J. (1979). *The Ecological Approach to Visual Perception.* Boston: Houghton Mifflin.

Gibson, R., Lusoli, W., & Ward, S. (2005). Online Participation in the UK: Testing a 'Contextualised' Model of Internet Effects. *British Journal of Politics and International Relations, 7,* 561–583. doi:10.1111/j.1467-856X.2005.00209.x

Gibson, T. G. (2009). *Plato on the Break Boundary: Implications for the Digital Revolution.* Paper presented at the meeting of the International Communication Association, Montreal, Quebec, Canada. Retrieved May 23, 2009, from http://www.allacademic.com/meta/p234593_index.html

Giddens, A. (1990). *The Consequences of Modernity.* Cambridge, UK: Polity Press.

Giddens, A. (1991). *Modernity and Self-Identity. Self and Society in the Late Modern Age.* Cambridge, UK: Polity Press.

Giddens, A. (2006). *Sociology.* Cambridge, UK: Polity Press.

Giddens, A. (2007). Living in a Post-Traditional Society. In U. Beck, A. Giddens & S. Lash, *Reflexive Modernization.* Cambridge, UK: Polity Press.

Gidengil, E., Blais, A., Nevitte, N., & Nadeau, R. (2008). *(2004.) Citizens.* Vancouver: University of British Columbia Press. Gibson and Ward.

Gilster, P. (2000). Digital literacy. In *The Jossey-Bass reader on technology and learning* (pp. 215–228). San Francisco: Jossey-Bass.

Goodson, I. F., Knobel, M., Lankshear, C., & Mangan, J. M. (2002). *Cyber spaces/Social spaces: Culture clash in computerized classrooms.* New York: Palgrave Macmillan.

Goot, M. (2008). Is the News on the Internet Different? Leaders, Frontbenchers and Other Candidates in the (2007 Australian Election. *Australian Journal of Political Science, 43*(1), 99–110. doi:10.1080/10361140701851939

Gordon, C. (1991). Governmental rationality: An introduction. In Burchell, G., Gordon, C., & Miller, P. (Eds.), *The Foucault effect: Studies in governmentality* (pp. 1–54). Chicago: University of Chicago Press.

Gray, L. (2008). A Fangirl's Crush. *Houston Chronicle.* Retrieved November 29, 2009, from http://www.chron.com/disp/story.mpl/moms/5611220.html.]

Gredler, M. E. (1996). Educational games and simulations: A technology in search of a research paradigm. In Jonassen, D. H. (Ed.), *Handbook of research for educational communications and technology* (pp. 521–540). New York: Simon & Schuster Macmillan.

Grönlund, K. (2007). Knowing and Not Knowing: The Internet and Political Information. *Scandinavian Political Studies, 30*(3), 397–418. doi:10.1111/j.1467-9477.2007.00186.x

Gynther, K. (2010). *Didaktik 2.0.* København: Akademisk Forlag.

Hall, S. (1996). Introduction: Who needs "identity"? In Hall, S., & du Gay, P. (Eds.), *Questions of cultural identity* (pp. 1–17). London: Sage.

Hällgren, C. (2006). *Researching and Developing Swedkid: A Swedish Case Study at the Intersection of the Web, Racism and Education.* Doktorsavhandlingar i Pedagogiskt arbete. Nr. 5. Fakultetsnämnden för lärarutbildning. Umeå universitet.

Hannerz, U. (1996). *Transnational connections. Culture, people, places.* London: Routledge.

Hannerz, U. (1992). The global ecumene as a network of networks. In Kuper, A. (Ed.), *Conceptualizing Society* (pp. 34–55). London: Routledge.

Harcourt, W. (1999). *Women@internet: Creating new cultures in cyberspace*. London: Zed Books.

Hargis, J. (2005). Collaboration, community and project-based learning? Does it still work online? *International Journal of Instructional Media, 32*(2), 157–161.

Hargittai, E., & Walejko, G. (2008). The Participation Divide: Content Creation and Sharing in the Digital Age. *Information Communication and Society, 11*(2), 239–256. doi:10.1080/13691180801946150

Hargittai, E. (2005). Survey Measures of Web-Oriented Digital Literacy. *Social Science Computer Review, 23*(3), 371–379. doi:10.1177/0894439305275911

Hart, R. A. (1992). Children's participation. From tokenism to citizenship. *Innocenti essays 4*.

Hastrup, K. (Ed.). (2003). *Ind i verden. En grundbog i Antropologisk metode*. København: Hans Reitzels Forlag.

Hayes, R. T. (2005, November). Effectiveness of instructional games: A literature review and discussion. *Technical Report 2005-004*. Retrieved April 3, 2010, from http://www.dtic.mil/cgi-bin/GetTRDoc?AD=ADA441935&Location=U2&doc=GetTRDoc.pdf

Heil, D. (2005). The Internet and student research: Teaching critical evaluation skills. *Teacher Librarian*, 26–29.

Hellekson, K., & Busse, K. (Eds.). (2006). *Fan Fiction and Fan Communities in the Age of the Internet: New Essays*. Jefferson: McFarland & Co.

Herman, A., Coombe, R. J., & Kaye, L. (2006, March/May). YOUR SECOND LIFE? Goodwill and the performativity of intellectual property in online digital gaming. *Cultural Studies, 20*(2-3), 184–210. doi:10.1080/09502380500495684

Herring, S. (2008). Questioning the Generational Divide: Technological Exoticism and Adult Construction of Youth Identity. In D. Buckingham (Ed.) *Youth, Identity and Digital Media*, Pp. 71-92. John D. and Catherine T. MacArthur Foundation Series on Digital Media and Learning. Cambridge, MA: MIT Press.

Herr-Stephenson, B. (2008). Youth media and genres of participation: Reflections on the Digital Youth Project. *Youth Media Reporter*, 2, (1-6), 73-79.

Higgins, S. (2007). Learning skills and the development of learning capabilities. Report. In *Research Evidence in Education Library*. London: EPPI-Centre, Social Science Research Unit, Institute of Education, University of London.

Hindman, M. (2009). *The Myth of Digital Democracy*. Princeton, N.J.: Princeton University Press.

Hismanoglu, M. (2000). Language learning strategies in foreign language learning and teaching. *The Internet TESL Journal, VI*(8), August 2000. Retrieved December 31, 2009, from http://iteslj.org/

Hobbs, R. (2006). Non-optimal uses of video in the classroom. *Learning, Media and Technology, 31*(1), 35–50. doi:10.1080/17439880500515457

Hoechsmann, M., & Low, B. E. (2008). *Reading youth writing: Literacies, cultural studies and education*. New York: Peter Lang.

Holgersen, S. (2002). *Mening og deltagelse: iagttagelse af 1-5 årige børns deltagelse i musikundervisning. Diss*. Diss. København: Danmarks Paedagogiske Universitet.

Holland, J. (1998). *Emergence: From chaos to order*. Reading, MA: Addison-Wesley.

Hopper, T. (In press). Complexity thinking and creative dance: Creating conditions for emergent learning in teacher education. *PHEnex, 1*(1).

Inglis, A., Ling, P., & Joosten, V. (1999). *Delivering Digitally. Managing the Transition to the Knowledge Media*. London: Kogan Page Limited.

Ito, M. (2008). *Living and Learning with new media: Summary of findings from the Digital Youth Project*. Chicago: The MacArthur Foundation.

Ito, M. (2008). Introduction. In Varnelis, K. (Ed.), *Networked publics* (pp. 1–14). Cambridge, MA: MIT Press.

Ito, M., Davidson, C., Jenkins, H., Lee, C., Eisenberg, M., & Weiss, J. (2008). Foreword. In W. L. Bennett (Ed.), Civic life online: Learning how digital media can engage youth *(The John D. and Catherine T. MacArthur Foundation Series on Digital Media and Learning)* (pp. vii–ix). Cambridge, MA: The MIT Press.

Ito, M., Horst, H., Bittanti, M., Boyd, D., Herr-Stephenson, B., Lange, P. G., et al. with Baumer, S., Cody, R., Mahendran, D., Martínez, K., Perkel, D., Sims, C. and Tripp, L. (2008). *Living and Learning with New Media: Summary of Findings from the Digital Youth Project.* The John D. and Catherine T. MacArtur Foundation Reports on Digital Media and Learning. Retrieved April 2010 from: www.macfound.org.

Iyengar, S., & Jackman, S. (2004). Technology and Politics: Incentives for Youth Participation. *Center for Information and Research on Civic Learning and Engagement (CIRCLE)* Working Paper 24, http://www.civicyouth.org/PopUps/WorkingPapers/WP24Iyengar.pdf (retrieved 25 September (2009).

Jackson, L. A., von Eye, A., Biocca, F. A., Barbatsis, G., Zhao, Y., & Fitzgerald, H. E. (2006). Does Home Internet Use Influence the Academic Performance of Low-income Children? *Developmental Psychology, 24,* 413–437.

Jacobsen, M., & Goldman, R. (2001). The hand-made's tail: A novel approach to educational technology. In Barrell, B. (Ed.), *Technology, teaching and learning: Issues in the integration of technology* (pp. 83–111). Calgary, Alberta, Canada: Detselig.

James, A., & Prout, A. (Eds.). (1997). *Constructing and Reconstructing Childhood: Contemporary Issues in the Sociological Study of Childhood.* London: Falmer Press.

Jarvis, P. (2003). *The Theory and Practice of Learning.* London: Kogan.

Jenkins, H. (2006). *Confronting the challenges of participatory culture: media education for the 21st century.* Chicago: The MacArthur Foundation.

Jenkins, H. (1992). *Textual poachers: Television fans & participatory culture.* New York: Routledge.

Jenkins, H. (2006). *Convergence culture: Where old and new media collide.* New York: New York University Press.

Jenkins, H., Purushotma, R., Clinton, K., Weigel, M., & Robinson, A. (2009). *Confronting the Challenges of Participatory Culture: Media Education for the 21st Century.* Cambridge, MA: MIT Press.

Jenkins, H. (1992). *Textual Poachers: Television Fans & Participatory Culture.* New York: Routledge.

Jenkins, H. (2006). *Convergence Culture: Where Old and New Media Collide.* New York: New York University Press.

Jenkins, H., Purushotma, R., Wigel, M., Clinton, K., & Robinson, A. J. (2009). *Confronting the Challenges of Participatory Culture: Media Education for the 21st Century. The John D. and Catherine T. MacArtur Foundation Reports on Digital Media and Learning.* Cambridge, MA: MIT Press.

Jenkins, H. (2006). *Confronting the Challenges of Participatory Culture: Media Education for the 21st Century.* Occasional Paper. Chicago: MacArthur Foundation.

Jenkins, H. (2007). Confronting the challenges of participatory culture: Media education for the 21st century. *MacArthur Foundation Website.* Retrieved October 27, 2009, from http://www.projectnml.org/files/working/NMLWhite Paper.html.

Jenkins, H. (2008). *Convergence Culture: Where Old and New Media Collide.* (New ed.). New York: New York University Press.

Jeris, L., & Johnson, K. (2004) *Speaking of competence: toward a cross-translation for human resource development (HRD) and continuing professional education (CPE).* In Proceedings Academy of Human Resource Development Annual Conference, (Vol. 2, pp. 1103-1110) Austin, TX, 4-7 March.

Jewitt, C. (2002). The move from page to screen: the multimodal reshaping of school English. *Visual Communication, 1*(2), 171–195. doi:10.1177/147035720200100203

Johnson, S. (2005). *Everything bad is good for you: How today's popular culture is actually making us smarter.* New York: Riverhead Books.

Johnson, L. L. (2001). *Media, education, and change.* New York: Peter Lang.

Johnson, S. (2001). *Emergence: The connected lives of ants, brains, cities and software.* New York: Simon & Schuster.

Jones, J. G., & Bronack, S. C. (2008). Rethinking cognition, representations, and processes in 3D online social learning environments. In Rivoltella, P. C. (Ed.), *Digital literacy: Tools and methodologies for information society* (pp. 176–206). Hershey, PA: Idea Group Inc.

Jones, S., & Fox, S. (2009). Pew Internet Project data memo. *Pew Internet and American Life Project.* Retrieved March 22, 2010, from http://www.pewinternet.org/~/media/Files/Reports/2009/PIP_Generations_2009.pdf

Kaiser Family Foundation. (2005). *Generation M: Media in the lives of 8-18 year olds.* Retrieved October 30, 2009, from http://www.kff.org/entmedia/entmedia030905pkg.cfm

Kang, S. (2003). A review of abroad studies. *Shandong Foreign Language Teaching Journal, 47*, (3).

Kaplan-Rakowski, R., & Loh, C. S. (2010). Modding and rezzing in games and virtual environments for education. In Baek, Y. K. (Ed.), *Gaming for classroom-based learning: Digital role playing as a motivator of study.* Hershey, PA: Information Science Reference. doi:10.4018/978-1-61520-713-8.ch012

Kaplan-Rakowski, R. (2010). Foreign language instruction in a virtual environment: An examination of potential activities. In Giovanni, V., & Braman, J. (Eds.), *Teaching through multi-user virtual environments: Applying dynamic elements to the modern classroom.* Hershey, PA: Information Science Reference.

Katz, J. (1997). *Virtuous reality: How America Surrendered Discussion of Moral Values to Opportunists, Nitwits and Blockheads like William Bennett.* New York: Random House.

Kavanaugh, A. B. Joon Kim, Manuel A. Prez-Quiones, Joseph Schmitz, & Philip Isenhour. (2008). Net Gains in Political Participation: Secondary Effects of Internet on community. *Information, Communication & Society 11* (7), 933–63. http://www.informaworld.com/smpp/content~db=all~content=a904084056 (retrieved 5 October 2009).

Keefe, J. W. (1979). Learning style: An overview. In *NASSP's Student learning styles: Diagnosing and proscribing programs* (pp. 1–17). Reston, VA: National Association of Secondary School Principles.

Keen, A. (2007). *The Cult of the Amateur.* New York: Random House.

Keeter, S., Zukin, C., Andolina, M., & Jenkins, K. (2002). The Civic and Political Health of the Nation: A Generational Portrait. *Center for Information and Research on Civic Learning and Engagement (CIRCLE),* http://www.eric.ed.gov/ERICDocs/data/ericdocs2sql/content_storage_01/0000019b/80/36/2c/9f.pdf (retrieved 24 September (2009).

Kelty, C. (2008). *Two bits. The cultural significance of free software.* Durham, NC: Duke University Press.

Kern, R. (2006). Perspectives on technology in learning and teaching languages. *TESOL Quarterly, 40*(1), 183–210. doi:10.2307/40264516

Kern, R., Ware, P., & Warschauer, M. (2004). Crossing frontiers: New directions in online pedagogy and research. *Annual Review of Applied Linguistics, 24*, 243–260. doi:10.1017/S0267190504000091

Kidd, Q., & Phillips, E. (2007, September). *Does the Internet Matter? Examining the Effects of the Internet on Young Adults' Political Participation.* Paper presented at the annual meeting of the American Political Science Association, Chicago.

Kleiman, G. (2000). Myths and realities about technology in K-12 schools. In Gordon, D. T. (Ed.), *The digital classroom: How technology is changing the way we teach and learn* (pp. 7–15). Cambridge, MA: Harvard Education Letter.

Kluge, S., & Riley, L. (2008). Teaching in virtual worlds: Opportunities and challenges. *Issues in Informing Science and Information Technology, 5.*

Kohut, A., Parker, K., Keeter, S., Doherty, C., & Dimock, M. (2007). How young people view their lives, futures and politics: A portrait of "Generation Next". *The Pew Research Center for the people and the press.* Retrieved March 28, 2010, from www.people-press.org

Kolko, B., Nakamura, L., & Rodman, G. (2000). *Race in cyberspace.* New York: Routledge.

Kompare, D. (2006). Publishing Flow. DVD Box Sets and the Reconception of Television. *Television & New Media, 7*(4), 335–360. doi:10.1177/1527476404270609

Koohang, A., & Durante, A. (2003). Learners' perceptions toward the web-based distance learning activities/assignments portion of an undergraduate hybrid instructional model. *Journal of Information Technology Education*, *2*, 105–113.

Kowalski, R. M., Limber, S. P., & Agatston, P. W. (2008). *Cyberbullying*. Oxford, UK: Blackwell.

Kozma, R. B. (1991). Learning with media. *Review of Educational Research*, *61*(2), 179–211.

Kozma, R. B. (1994). Will media influence learning? Reframing the debate. *Educational Technology Research and Development*, *42*(2). doi:10.1007/BF02299087

Kramsch, C., A'Ness, F., & Lam, E. (2000). Authenticity and authorship in the computer-mediated acquisition of literacy. *Language Learning & Technology*, *4*(2), 78–104.

Kramsch, C., & Lam, E. (1999). Textual identities: The importance of being non-native. In Braine, G. (Ed.), *Non-native educators in English language teaching* (pp. 57–72). Mahwah, NJ: Lawrence Erlbaum.

Kraut, R., Patterson, M., Lundmark, V., Kiesler, S., Mukopadhyay, T., & Scherlis, W. (1998). Internet paradox: A social technology that reduces social involvement and psychological well-being? *The American Psychologist*, *53*, 1017–1031. doi:10.1037/0003-066X.53.9.1017

Kress, G. R. (2003). *Literacy in the New Media Age*. London: Routledge. doi:10.4324/9780203164754

Kress, G. (2003). *Literacy in the New Media Age*. New York: Routledge. doi:10.4324/9780203164754

Krueger, B. S. (2002). Assessing the Potential of Internet Political Participation in the United States: A Resource Approach. *American Politics Research*, *30*(5), 476–498. doi:10.1177/1532673X02030005002

Kubey, R. (Ed.). (2001). *Media literacy in the information age: Current perspectives* (*Vol. 6*). Piscataway, NJ: Transaction Books.

Kuljis, J., & Liu, F. (2005). *A Comparison of Learning Style Theories on the Suitability for E-learning*. IASTED International Conference on Web Technologies, Applications, and Services, Calgary, Alberta, Canada, July 4-6, 2005.

Kumagai, Y. (2008). Nihongo kyoushitsu ni okeru kotoba, bunka no hyoujunka katei: Kyoushi, gakusei kan no sougo koui no bunseki kara. [Standardization processes of language and culture in a Japanese language classroom: From the analyses of the interactions between the teacher and students] In Sato, S., & Doerr, N. (Eds.), *Bunka, kotoba, kyoiku: Nihongo/Nihon no kyoiku no "hyoujun" wo koete* [Culture, language, education: Beyond the "standard" in Japanese/Japan's education]. Tokyo: Akashi Shoten.

Kurokawa, K. (1977). *Metabolism in Architecture. London: StudioVista. Catalogue to an exhibition at Cube Gallery London*. London: BookArt.

Kurzweil, R. (2005). *The singularity is near. When humans transcend biology*. New York: Penguin.

Ladner, A., Nadig, G., & Fivaz, J. (2009). Voting Assistance Applications as Tools to Increase Political Participation and Improve Civic Education. In Print, M., & Milner, H. (Eds.), *Civic Education and Youth Political Participation*. Rotterdam, the Netherlands: Sense.

Lam, E. (2000). L2 Literacy and the Design of the Self: A Case Study of a Teenager Writing on the Internet. *TESOL Quarterly*, *34*(3), 457–482. doi:10.2307/3587739

Lamb, B. (2004). Wide open spaces: Wikis, ready or not. *EDUCAUSE Review*, *39*(5).

Lange, P. G. (2008). Publicly private and privately public: Social networking on YouTube. *Journal of Computer-Mediated Communication*, *13*(1), 361–380. doi:10.1111/j.1083-6101.2007.00400.x

Lange, P. G. (2007). "The Vulnerable Video Blogger: Promoting Social Change Through Intimacy". *The Scholar & Feminist Online*, *5*(2).

Lankshear, C., & Knobel, M. (2006). *New Literacies: Everyday Practices and Classroom Learning*. London: Open University Press.

Lankshear, C., Snyder, I., & Green, B. (2000). *Teachers and techno-literacy: Managing literacy, technology and learning in schools*. St. Leonards, NSW, Australia: Allen & Unwin.

Laurillard, D., & Taylor, J. (1994). Designing the stepping stones: An evaluation of interactive media in the classroom. *Journal of Educational Television, 20*(3), 169, 16 p. Retrieved as Microsoft Word document on April 2010 from: http://kn.open.ac.uk/public/document.cfm?docid=944

Lave, J., & Wenger, E. (1991). *Situated learning: Legitimate, peripheral, participation*. New York: Cambridge University Press.

Lenhardt, A., & Madden, M. (2005). *Teen Content Creators and Consumers*. Washington, DC: PewInternet. Retrieved from http://www.pewInternet.org/PPF/r/166/report_display.asp

Lenhart, A., Madden, M., & Hitlin, P. (2005). *Teens and technology: Youth are leading the transition to a fully wired and mobile nation*. Washington, D.C.: Pew Internet & American Life Project.

Lenhart, A., Kahne, J., Middaugh, E., Macgill, A. R., Evans, C., & Vitak, J. (2008). Teens, video games, and civics: Teens' gaming experiences are diverse and include significant social interaction and civic engagement. *Pew Internet and American Life Project*. Retrieved January 1, 2010, from http://www.pewinternet.org/Reports/2008/Teens-Video-Games-and-Civics.aspx

Leppänen, S. (2007). Youth Language in Media Contexts: insights into the functions of English in Finland. In *Word Englishes, 26* (2), 149-169.

Leu, D. J., Kinzer, C. K., Coiro, J. L., & Cammack, D. W. (2008). Toward a theory of new literacies emerging from the Internet and other information and communication technologies. In Mackey, M. (Ed.), *Media literacies: Major themes in education* (*Vol. 2*, pp. 337–374). New York: Routledge.

Leung, C., Harris, R., & Rampton, B. (1997). The idealized native speaker, reified ethnicities, and classroom realities. *TESOL Quarterly, 31*(3), 543–560. doi:10.2307/3587837

Levinsen, K. & Sørensen, B.H. (2008). *It, faglig læring og pædagogisk videnledelse: rapport vedr. Projekt It læring*. Gentofte Kommune /DPU, AU.

Levinsen, K. (2010). Effective use of ICT for Inclusive Learning of Young Children with reading and writing Difficulties. In Mukerji & Tripathi (Eds.) *Cases on Interactive Technology Environments and Transnational Collaboration: Concerns and Perspectives,* pp.56-73. Hershey, PA: IGI-Global.

Levy, F. (2008). *15 Minutes of Fame: Becoming a Star in the YouTube Revolution*. New York: Alpha.

Lévy, P. (1999). *Collective intelligence: Mankind's emerging world in cyberspace*. Cambridge, MA: Perseus Books.

Lévy, P. (1997). *Cyberculture*. Minneapollis, MN: University of Minnesota Press.

Lickona, T. (2004). *Character matters*. New York: Touchstone.

Lindblad-Gidlund, K. (2005). *Techno Therapy: a relation with technology*. Umeå universitet. Institutionen för informatik Umeå.

Lindgren, S. (2009). *Ungdomskulturer* (1. uppl. ed.). Malmö, Sweden: Gleerup.

Livingston, J. A. (1997). *Metacognition: An Overview*. Retrieved December 31, 2009, from http://gse.buffalo.edu

Livingstone, S., & Bowill, M. (Eds.). (2001). *Children and their Changing Media Environment: A European Comparative Study*. New York: Erlbaum.

Livingstone, S., Bober, M., & Helsper, E. (2005). Active participation or just more information? *Information Communication and Society, 8*(3), 287–314. doi:10.1080/13691180500259103

Livingstone, S., & Helsper, E. (2007). Gradations in digital inclusion: Children, young people and the digital divide. *New Media & Society, 9*(4), 671–696. doi:10.1177/1461444807080335

Livingstone, S., Van Couvering, E., & Thumim, N. (2005). *Adult Media Literacy: A review of the research literature on behalf of Ofcom*. London: London School of Economics and Political Science.

Livingstone, S. (2006). Drawing conclusions from new media research: Reflections and puzzles regarding children's experience of the Internet. *The Information Society, 22*, 219–230. doi:10.1080/01972240600791358

Livingstone, S., & Dahlgren, P. (2007). Interactivity and Participation on the Internet: Young People's Response to the Civic Sphere. In Livingstone, S., & Dahlgren, P. (Eds.), *Young Citizens and New Media.* London: Routledge.

Livingstone, S. (2003). *The Changing Nature and Uses of Media Literacy.* Working paper. London: London School of Economics. http://www.lse.ac.uk/collections/media@lse/mediaWorkingPapers/ewpNumber4.htm

Livingstone, S., & Bober, M. (2005). *UK Children Go Online.* London: Economic and Social Research Council. Retrieved from http://personal.lse.ac.uk/bober/UKCGO-finalReport.pdf

Loader, B. D., & Hague, B. N. (Eds.). (1999). *Digital Democracy – Discourse and Decision making in the Information Age.* London, New York: Routledge.

Lovink, G., & Niederer, S. (2008). *Video vortex reader: responses to YouTube.* Amsterdam: Institute of Network Cultures.

Lund, T. & Almås, A.G. (2003). *På vei mot god praksis? En beskrivelse og analyse på tvers av ni skoler i PILOT.* Tromsø: Universitetet i Tromsø.

Lyman, P. with Billings, A., Ellinger, S., Finn, M., & Perkel, D. (2004). *Literature Review: Digital-Mediated Experiences and Kids' Informal Learning.* San Francisco: Exploratorium. Retrieved from http://www.exploratorium.edu/research/digitalkids/Lyman_DigitalKids.pdf

Ma, D., & Zheng, L. (2008). Research of the status quo of college students' learning strategies and its cultivation strategies. In *China. Educational Technology, 258*(7), 40–44.

Maia, M., Almeida, J., & Almeida, V. (2008). Identifying user behavior in online social networks. In *Proceedings of the 1st workshop on Social network systems* (pp. 1–6). New York: ACM.

Malyn-Smith, J. (2004). Power Users of Technology - Who are they? Where are they going? Why does it matter? *UN Chronicle Online Edition*, (2), pp 58 [online], http://www.un.org/ Pubs/chronicle/2004/issue2/0204p58.asp

Marschall, S., & Schmidt, C. K. (2008). Preaching to the Converted or Making a Difference? Mobilizing Effects of an Internet Application at the German General Election 2005. In Farrell, D. M., & Schmitt-Beck, R. (Eds.), *Non-Party Actors in Electoral Politics. Baden-Baden: Nomos.*

Masuda, Y. (1980). *The Information Society.* Tokyo: Institute for the Information Society.

Mayer, R. E. (Ed.). (2005). *The Cambridge Handbook of Multimedia Learning.* Cambridge, UK: Cambridge University Press.

McAdoo, M. (2003). The real digital divide: Quality not quantity. In Johnson, D. L., & Maddux, C. D. (Eds.), *Technology in education: A twenty-year retrospective* (pp. 35–48). New York: Haworth Press.

McCormick, S. (1986). Software and Television - A New Approach. *Computers & Education, 10*(1), 17–24. doi:10.1016/0360-1315(86)90046-1

McKeachie, W. J., Pintrich, P. R., Lin, Y., & Smith, D. (1986). *Teaching and learning in the college classroom: A review of the research literature.* Ann Arbor, MI: National Center for Research to Improve Postsecondary Teaching and Learning, University of Michigan.

McNamara, D. S., Kintsch, E., Songer, N. B., & Kintsch, W. (1996). Are good texts always better? Text coherence, background knowledge, and levels of understanding in learning from text. *Cognition and Instruction, 14*, 1–43. doi:10.1207/s1532690xci1401_1

Medierådet. (2008). *Ungar och medier 2008: fakta om barns och ungas användning och upplevelser av medier.* Retrieved January 15, 2010, from http://www.medieradet.se/upload/Rapporter_pdf/Ungar_&_Medier_2008.pdf.

Merrill, M. D. (2001). First principles of instruction. *Journal of Structural Learning and Intelligent Systems, 14*(4), 459–466.

Mestre, J. (2002). *Transfer of Learning: Issues and Research Agenda.* Presented at Workshop held at the National Science Foundation, March 21-22, 2002. Retrieved December 31, 2009, from: http://www.nsf.gov

Michael, D., & Chen, S. (2006). *Serious games: Games that educate, train, and inform.* Boston: Thomson Course Technology.

Miles, M. B., & Huberman, A. M. (1994). *Qualitative Data Analysis: an expanded sourcebook*. Thousand Oaks, CA: Sage Publications.

Miller, R. A. (1982). *Japan's modern myth: The language and beyond*. New York: Weather Hill.

Miller, D., & Slater, D. (2000). *The Internet: An ethnographic approach*. Oxford, UK: Berg.

Milner, H. (2002). *Civic Literacy: How Informed Citizens Make Democracy Work*. Hanover, N.H.: University Press of New England.

Milner, H. (2007). *Political Knowledge and Political Participation among Young Canadians and Americans*. Montreal: Institute for Research in Public Policy.

Milner, H. (2009). *The Internet Generation: Engaged Citizens or Political Dropout*. Hanover, N.H.: University Press of New England.

Ministry of Education. Culture, Sports, Science and Technology (MEXT) [Japan] (2004). *Lifelong learning: What is lifelong learning?* Retrieved December 31, 2009, from http://www.mext.go.jp/.

Mislove, A., Koppula, H. S., Gummadi, K. P., Druschel, P., & Bhattacharjee, B. (2008). Growth of the flickr social network. In *Proceedings of the first workshop on Online social networks* (pp. 25–30). New York: ACM.

MOEC/BCA. (2003). *Strategic plan for the development of the Bagamoyo College of Arts 2003-2006*. Dar es Salaam: Ministry of Education and Culture/Bagamoyo: Bagamoyo College of Arts.

MOEVT. (2007). *ICT policy for basic education*. Dar es Salaam: Ministry of Education and Vocational Training, The United Republic of Tanzania.

MOICS. (2007). *Taasisi ya Sanaa na Utamaduni Bagamoyo (TaSUBa) framework document*. Dar es Salaam: Ministry of Information, Culture and Sports, The United Republic of Tanzania.

Moinian, F. (2007). *Negotiating Identities: Exploring children's perspectives on themselves and their lives*. Dissertation, SU - Stockholms universitet.

Montgomery, K. C. (2008). Youth and digital democracy: Intersections of practice, policy, and the marketplace. In Bennett, W (pp. Lance (2008). *Civic life online: Learning how digital media can engage youth*. The John D. and Catherine T. MacArthur Foundation series on digital media and learning. (pp. 2025-2049). Cambridge, MA: MIT Press. ix, 2206.

Moreno-Ger, P., Burgos, D., & Torrente, J. (2009). Digital games in eLearning environments. *Simulation & Gaming, 40*(5), 669–687. doi:10.1177/1046878109340294

Morowitz, H. (2002). *The Emergence of everything: How the world became complex*. New York: Oxford.

Morris, Jonathan S., & Richard Forgette. (2004). News Grazers, Television News, Political Knowledge, and Engagement. *Press/Politics 12* (1), 91–107.

Moss, R., & Gunter, B. (1991). Teachers using Television. *Journal of Educational Television, 17*(2), 109.

Mossberger, K., Tolbert, C. J., & McNeal, R. S. (2008). *Digital Citizenship: The Internet, Society, and Participation*. Cambridge, MA: MIT Press.

Motobayashi, K. (forthcoming). Burogu wo shiyou shita Nihongo kyouiku ni okeru "Nihongo" siyou to "gakushu-sha": Ta to "tsunagaru" tame no "Nihongo" jissen wo kangaeru. [The Use of "Japanese" and "Learner" in the Japanese language education using blog: Discussion of teaching "Japanese" in order to "connect" with others] In Sato, S., & Kumagai, Y. (Eds.), *Shakai ni sanka shiteiku shimin toshiteno gengo kyouiku* [Language education for the global citizen]. Tokyo: Hitsuji Shobo.

Mouer, R., & Sugimoto, Y. (1986). *Images of Japanese Society*. London: KPI.

Mullooly, J., & Varenne, H. (2006). Playing with pedagogical authority. In Pace, J., & Hemmings, A. (Eds.), *Classroom authority: Theory, research, and practice* (pp. 62–86). Mahwah, NJ: Lawrence Erlbaum.

Murphy, E., & Laferrière, T. (2001). Classroom management in the networked classroom: New problems and possibilities. In Barrell, B. (Ed.), *Technology, teaching and learning: Issues in the integration of technology* (pp. 305–324). Calgary, Alberta, Canada: Detselig.

Murray, J. (1997). *Hamlet on the holodeck: The future of narrative in cyberspace*. Cambridge, MA: The MIT Press.

Nakane, C. (1967). *Tateshakai no ningenkankei: Tanitsushakai no riron* [Human relations in a vertical society: a theory of a homogeneous society]. Tokyo: Kodansha.

New London Group. (1998). A pedagogy of multiliteracies: Designing social futures. *Harvard Educational Review*, *66*(1), 60–92.

Newhouse, P. (1999). Examining how teachers adjust to the availability of portable computers. *Australian Journal of Educational Technology*, *14*(2), 148–166.

Norton, B. (2000). *Identity and language learning: Gender, ethnicity and educational change*. Harlow, Essex: Pearson Education.

Notari, M. (2006). How to use a Wiki in education: Wiki based effective constructive learning. *Proceedings of the 2006 international symposium on Wikis*, 131-132.

NSF [National Science Foundation] (2008). *Fostering Learning in the Networked World the Cyber Learning Opportunity*. Retrieved from 20080827: http://www.nsf.gov/pubs/2008/nsf08204/nsf08204.pdf

O'Farell, M., & Vallone, L. (Eds.). (1999). *Virtual gender: Fantasies of subjectivity and embodiment*. Ann Arbor, MI: University of Michigan Press.

O'Neil, H. F., Wainess, R., & Baker, E. (2005). Classification of learning outcomes: Evidence from the games literature. *Curriculum Journal*, *16*(4), 455–474. doi:10.1080/09585170500384529

Oblinger, D., & Oblinger, J. (2005). *Educating the Net Generation*. Boulder, CO: Educause.

Oblinger, D. (2003). Boomers & Gen-Xers Millennials: Understanding the "new students". *EDUCAUSE Review*, *38*(4).

Oblinger, D., & Oblinger, J. (Eds.). (2005). *Educating the Net Generation*. EDUCAUSE, [online], e-book, www.educause.edu/educatingthenetgen/

OECD. (2001). *Meeting of the OECD education ministers*, Paris, 3-4 April 2001. Retrieved April 01, 2008 http://www.oecd.org/dataoecd/40/8/1924078.pdf.

OECD. (2004). *OECD-rapport om grundskolen i Danmark – 2004*. http://pub.uvm.dk/2004/oecd/oecd.pdf

Olin-Scheller, C. (2008). Trollkarl eller mugglare? Tolkningsgemenskaper i ett nytt medielandskap. In *Didaktikens forum*, 3, pp. 44-58. Stockholm: Stockholms universitet.

Olin-Scheller, C. (fourthcoming). Förvärva, förvalta och förädla. Ungas läsande och skrivande av fanfiction. In Anne Banér (ed.), *Kulturarvingarna, typ. Vad ska barnen ärva – och varför?* Stockholm: Centrum för barnkulturforskning.

Olsson, T. (2005). *Alternativa resurser: om medier, IKT och lärande bland ungdomar i alternativa rörelser*. Rapport. Lund: Lunds universitet.

Oppenheimer, T. (1997, July). The computer delusion. *Atlantic Monthly*, *280*(1), 45–62.

Owings, W. A., & Kaplan, L. S. (Eds.). (2003). *Best practices, best thinking, and emerging issues in school leadership*. Thousand Oaks, CA: Corwin Press.

Oxlund, B. (2010). Responding to university reform in South Africa: Student activism at the University of Limpopo. *Social Anthropology*, *18*(1), 30–42. doi:10.1111/j.1469-8676.2009.00095.x

Papert, S. (1993). *The children's machine: rethinking school in the age of the computer*. New York: Basic Books.

Parrish, J. J. (2007). *Inventing a Universe: Reading and Writing Internet Fan Fiction*. Pittsburgh, PA: University of Pittsburgh. Retrieved November 14, 2009, from http://etd.library.pitt.edu/ETD/available/etd-08072007170133/unrestricted/Parrish2007.pdf

Paulsson, F. (2008). *Modularization of the learning architecture: supporting learning theories by learning technologies*. Stockholm: KTH.

Pedersen, S.G. & Hornskov, M.B. (2009). *It I skolen – erfaringer og perspektiver*. Købenahvn: EVA (English summary)

Pennycook, A. (1994). *The cultural politics of English as an international language*. London: Longman.

Pennycook, A. (2007). The myth of English as an international language. In Makoni, S., & Pennycook, A. (Eds.), *Disinventing and reconstituting languages* (pp. 90–115). Clevedon: Multilingual Matters.

Perea, A., Eva, A. G. D., & Jorba, L. (2009, April). *New Media Exposure, Knowledge and Issue Polarization.* Paper presented at the European Consortium for Political Research (ECPR) Joint Sessions of Workshops, University of Lisbon.

Pérez de Silva, J. (2000). *La televisión ha muerto.* Barcelona: Gedisa.

Perkins, D. N., & Salomon, G. (1992). *Transfer of learning: Contribution to the international encyclopedia of education.* Second Edition Oxford, England: Pergamon Press. Retrieved December 31, 2009, from http://learnweb.harvard.edu/alps/

Peter, J., & Valkenburg, P. M. (2006). Adolescents' internet use: Testing the "disappearing digital divide" versus the "emerging digital differentiation" approach. *Poetics, 34*(4-5), 293–305. doi:10.1016/j.poetic.2006.05.005

Phillipson, R. (1992). *Linguistic imperialism.* Oxford, UK: Oxford University Press.

Polka, W. (2001). Facilitating the transition from teacher centered to student centered instruction at the university level via constructivist principles and customized learning plans. *Educational Planning, 13*(3), 55–61.

Poster, M. (1996). *The second media age.* Cambridge, UK: Polity Press.

Postman, N. (1985). *Amusing ourselves to death: Public discourse in the age of show business.* New York: Penguin.

Potter, W. J. (2004). *Theory of media literacy: A cognitive approach.* Thousand Oaks, CA: Sage Publications.

Potter, W. J. (2008). *Media literacy* (4th ed.). Thousand Oaks, CA: Sage Publications.

Prensky, M. (2006). *Don't Bother Me Mom - I'm Learning!* St. Paul, MN: Paragon House.

Prensky, M. (2007). *Digital game-based learning.* St. Paul, MN: Paragon House.

Prensky, M. (2001). Digital Natives, Digital Immigrants. *On the Horizon. NCB University Press, 9*(5), 1–10.

Prior, M. (2007). *Post-broadcast Democracy: How Media Choice Increases Inequality in Political Involvement and Polarizes Elections.* New York: Cambridge University Press.

Pugh, S. (2005). *The Democratic Genre: Fan Fiction in a Literary Context.* Glasgow, UK: Seren.

Putman, R., & Borko, H. (2000). What do new views of knowledge and thinking have to say about research on teacher learning? *Educational Researcher, 29*(1), 4–15.

Qvortrup, L. (1998). *Det hyperkomplekse samfund. 14 fortællinger om informationssamfundet.* København: Gyldendal.

Qvortrup. L. (2002). *Samfundets uddannelsessystem.* Arbejdspapir, Kolding: Institut for Pædagogisk Forskning og Udvikling, Syddansk Universitet.

Raines, C. (2003). *Connecting generations: The Sourcebook.* Berkley, CA: Crisp Publications, Inc.

Rainie, L. (2009). Networked Learners. *Pew Internet & American Life Project.* Retrieved January 1, 2010, from http://www.authoring.pewinternet.org/Presentations/2009/52-Networked-Learners.aspx

Rantanen, T. (2005). The message is the medium. An interview with Manuel Castells. *Global Media and Communication, 1*(2), 135–147. doi:10.1177/1742766505054629

Raynes-Goldie, K., & Walker, L. (2007). Taking IT Global: Online Community to Create Real World Change; A Case Study. In Bennett, L. (Ed.), *Civic Engagement.* Cambridge, MA: MIT Press.

Rebecca, L. Oxford. (1990). *Language Learning Strategies: What Every Teacher Should Know.* New York: Newbury House Publishers. Retrieved from http://www.pdf-search-engine.com/language-learning-strategies-what-every-teacher-should-know-pdf.html

Reeher, G. (2006). *Log On, Tune Off? The Complex Relationship between Internet Use and Political Activism.* Retrieved from Http://www.personaldemocracy.com (retrieved 5 October (2009).

Reigeluth, C. M., Merrill, M. D., Wilson, B. G., & Spiller, R. T. (1980). The elaboration theory of instruction: A model for sequencing and synthesizing instruction. *Instructional Science, 9*(3), 195–219. doi:10.1007/BF00177327

Rey Valzacchi, J. (2007). 'Novedosismo' educativo, o ¿por qué Harry Potter no aprende 'por arte de magia'? *El Magazine de Horizonte Informática Educativa*, 88. Retrieved March 2008 from: http://www.horizonteweb.com/magazine/Numero88.htm

Reynolds, R. E., & Anderson, R. C. (1982). Influence of Questions on the Allocation of Attention during Reading. *Journal of Educational Psychology, 74*(5), 623–632. doi:10.1037/0022-0663.74.5.623

Rheingold, H. (1994). *The virtual community: finding connection in a computerized world.* London: Secker & Warburg.

Rheingold, H. (2002). *Smart Mobs: The Next Social Revolution.* Cambridge, MA: Perseus.

Richards, R. (2006). Users, Interactivity and Generation. *New Media & Society, 8*(4), 531–550. doi:10.1177/1461444806064485

Riding, R. J., & Rayner, S. G. (1998). *Cognitive Styles and Learning Strategies: Understanding Style Differences in Learning and Behaviour.* London: David Fulton Publishers.

Roberts, D. F., Foehr, U. G., & Rideout, V. (2005). *Generation M: Media in the lives of 8-18 year-olds.* Washington, DC: Henry J. Kaiser Family Foundation.

Robinson, M. J. (1974). The Impact of the Televised Watergate Hearings. *The Journal of Communication, 24*(2), 17–30. doi:10.1111/j.1460-2466.1974.tb00365.x

Rouiller, J. A., & Goldstein, I. L. (1993). The relationship between organizational transfer climate and positive transfer of training. *Human Resource Development Quarterly, 4*(4), 377–390. doi:10.1002/hrdq.3920040408

Rowling, J. K. (2005). *Harry Potter and the Half-Blood Prince.* London: Bloomsbury.

Ruusuvirta, O., & Rosema, M. (2009, September). *Do Online Selectors Influence the Direction and Quality of the Vote?* Paper presented at the European Consortium of Political Research (ECPR) biennial conference, University of Potsdam, Germany.

Ryberg, T. (2007). *Patchworking as a Metaphor for Learning: Understanding youth, learning and technology.* Aalborg University: e-Learning Lab Publication Series; 10.

SAFT. (2004). Retrieved July 07, 2004, http://www.medieraadet.dk/html/saft

Salen, K. (2008). Toward an ecology of gaming. In K. Salen (Ed.), The ecology of games: Connecting youth, games and learning *(The John D. and Catherine T. MacArthur Foundation Series on Digital Media and Learning)* (pp. 1–17). Cambridge, MA: MIT Press.

Säljö, R. (2005). *Lärande i praktiken: ett sociokulturellt perspektiv.* Stockholm: Nordstedts akademiska förlag.

Säljö, R. (2005). *Lärande i praktiken: ett sociokulturellt perspektiv.* (1. uppl. uppl.). Stockholm, Sweden: Norstedts akademiska förlag.

Sanford, K., & Hopper, T. (2009). Videogames and complexity theory: Learning through game play. *Loading...., 3*(4). Retrieved October 31, 2009, from http://journals.sfu.ca/loading/index.php/loading/article/view/62.

Sanford, K., & Madill, L. (2007). Understanding the power of new literacies through videogame play and design. *Canadian Journal of Education, 30*(2), 421–455. doi:10.2307/20466645

Santos, R. L., Rocha, B. P., Rezende, C. G., & Loureiro, A. A. (2007). *Characterizing the YouTube video-sharing community, (Technical report).* Retrieved from http://security1.win.tue.nl/~bpontes/pdf/yt.pdf.

Sato, S., & Kumagai, Y. (Eds.). (forthcoming). *Shakai ni sanka suru shimin toshiteno gengo kyouiku* [Language education for the global citizen]. Tokyo: Hitsuji Shobo.

Sato, S. (2009). Communication as Intersubjective Activity: When Native/Non-Native Speaker's Identity Appears in Computer-Mediated Communication. In Doerr, N. (Ed.), *The Native Speaker Concept: Ethnographic Investigations of Native Speaker Effects* (pp. 277–293). Berlin: Mouton de Gruyter. doi:10.1515/9783110220957.277

Sato, S. (forthcoming). Burogu purojekuto. [Blog Project] In Sato, S., & Kumagai, Y. (Eds.), *Shakai ni sanka suru shimin toshiteno gengo kyouiku* [Language education for the global citizen]. Tokyo: Hitsuji Shobo.

Scheufele, D. A., & Nisbet, M. C. (2002). Being a Citizen On-line: New Opportunities and Dead Ends. *The Harvard International Journal of Press/Politics, 7*(3), 53–73.

Schifferes, W., & Lusoli, W. (2007.) *What's The Story? Online News Consumption in the (2005 UK Election.* Unpublished manuscript. Sherr, Susan. (2005). *News for a New Generation: Can It Be Fun and Functional?* Center for Information and Research on Civic Learning and Engagement (CIRCLE) Working Paper 29, http://www.civicyouth.org/PopUps/WorkingPapers/WP29Sherr.pdf (retrieved 24 September 2009).

Schiro, M. S. (2008). *Curriculum theory. Conflicting visions and enduring concerns.* Los Angeles, CA: Sage Publications.

Schnotz, W. (2005). An Integrated Model of Text and Picture Comprehension. In Mayer, R. E. (Ed.), *The Cambridge Handbook of Multimedia Learning* (pp. 49–70). Cambridge, UK: Cambridge University Press.

Schuemer, R. (1993). *Some psychological aspects of distance education.* Fern University, Hagen (Germany): Institute for Research into Distance Education. ERIC Document Reproduction Service No. ED 357 266.

Schwarz, G. (2001). Literacy expanded: The role of media literacy in teacher education. *Teacher Education Quarterly, 28*(2), 111–119.

Scott, K. D., & White, A. M. (2003). Unnatural history? Deconstructing the Walking with Dinosaurs phenomenon. *Media Culture & Society, 25*(3), 315–332.

Scott, W. R. (2003). *Organizations: rational, natural and open systems.*(5 ed) Upper Saddle River, NJ: Prentice Hall.

Scottish Executive. (2004). *Life through learning; learning through life.* The Lifelong Learning Strategy for Scotland: Summary Retrieved from http://www.scotland.gov.uk/.

Seimens, G. (n.d.). Blended. *elearnspace.* Retrieved April 3, 2010, from http://www.elearnspace.org/doing/blended.htm

Selfton-Green, J. (1998). Introduction: Being Young in the Digital Age. In Selfton-Green, J. (Ed.), *Digital Diversions: Youth Culture in the Age of Multimedia* (pp. 1–20). London: UCL Press.

Selg, H., & Findahl, O. (2008). *InternetExplorers – Delrapport 6, Nya användarmönster. Jämförande analys av två användarstudier.* Uppsala, Sweden: Uppsala universitet. Retrieved January 25, 2010, from http://www.foruminternet.se/downloads/20081105-Forum-Internet-InternetExplorers-Delrapport-6-Nya-anvandarmonster.pdf.

Selwyn, N. (2009). The digital native – myth and reality. *Aslib Proceedings, 61*(4), 364–379. doi:10.1108/00012530910973776

Serafin, G. M. (2007). Media mindfulness. In Macedo, D., & Steinberg, S. R. (Eds.), *Media literacy: A reader* (pp. 178–186). New York: Peter Lang.

Shaffer, D. W., & Gee, J. P. (2005). *Before every child is left behind: How epistemic games can solve the coming crisis in education.* Manuscript submitted for publication.

Shaffer, D., Squire, K., Halverson, R., & Gee, J. (2005). Video games and the future of learning. *Phi Delta Kappan, 87*(2), 104–111.

Shariff, S. (2008). *Cyber-bullying: Issues and solutions for the school, the classroom and the home.* New York: Routledge.

Sharkey, J., & Brandt, D. S. (2008). Integrating technology literacy and information literacy. In Rivoltella, P. C. (Ed.), *Digital Literacy: Tools and Methodologies for Information Society* (pp. 85–96). Hershey: IGI.

Sharp, D. (2001). *Kisho Kurokawa. Metabolism + Recent Work. Catalogue to an exhibition at Cube Gallery London.* London: BookArt.

Sherry, C. A., & Fielden, K. A. (2005). *The millennials: Computer savvy (or not?).* Paper presented at the HERDSA Conference.

Shore, C., & Wright, S. (2000). Coercive accountability. The rise of audit culture in higher education. In Strathern, M. (Ed.), *Audit cultures: Anthropological studies in accountability, ethics and the academy* (pp. 57–89). London: Routledge.

Siemens, G. (2005). Connectivism: A learning Theory for the Digital Age. In Donald G. Perrin (EdInternational Journal of Instructional Technology and Distance Learning.2(1)Article 1.20081020: http://www.itdl.org/Journal/Jan_05/index.htm

Siemens, G. (2006). *Knowing Knowledge.* 20081020: http://www.knowingknowledge.com/book.php

Sigrell, A. (2008). Lärarens förebildlighet och elevens förmåga att efterbilda. In A. Palmér et al (Eds.), *Sjätte konferensen i svenska med didaktisk inriktning. Muntlighetens möjligheter - retorik, berättande, samtal.* Uppsala, Sweden: Uppsala universitet.

Silver, D., & Massanari, A. (Eds.). (2006). *Critical cyberculture studies.* New York: New York University Press.

Silverstone, R. (2005). Mediation and communication. In Calhoun, C., Rojek, C., & Turner, B. (Eds.), *International Handbook of Sociology.* London: Sage.

Simons, P. R. J. (1999). Transfer of learning: paradoxes for learners. *International Journal of Educational Research, 31*(7), 577–589. Retrieved November 31, 2009. .doi:10.1016/S0883-0355(99)00025-7

Sjöberg, U. (2002). *Screen Rites: A Study of Swedish Young People's Use and Meaning-making of Screen-based Media in Everyday Life.* Lund, Sweden: Lunds universitet.

Smahel, D., Blinka, L., & Ledabyl, O. (2008). Playing MMORPGs: Connections between addiction and identifying with a character. *Cyberpsychology & Behavior, 11*(6), 715–718. doi:10.1089/cpb.2007.0210

Smaldino, S. E., Lowther, D. L., & Russell, J. D. (2008). *Instructional technology and media for learning* (9th ed.). Upper Saddle River, NJ: Pearson Education.

Snickars, P., & Vonderau, P. (Eds.). (2009). *The YouTube Reader.* Stockholm: National Library of Sweden.

Son, J.-B., & O'Neill, S. (2006). *Enhancing Learning and Teaching: Pedagogy, Technology and Language.* Queensland, Australia: eContent Management.

Sørensen, B. H., Audon, L., & Levinsen, K. (2010). *Skole 2.0.* Aarhus: Klim.

Sørensen, B. H., Hubert, B., Risgaard, J., & Kirkeby, G. (2004). *Virtuel skole. ITMF Forskningsrapport.* København: Danmarks Pædagogiske Universitet.

Sørensen, B. H., Jessen, C., & Olesen, B. R. (Eds.). (2002). *Børn på nettet. Kommunikation og læring.* København: Gads Forlag.

Sørensen, B. H., Danielsen, O. & Nielsen, J. (2007). Children's informal learning in the context of school of knowledge society. *Education and Information Technologies.* Official Journal of the IFIP technical committee on Education, 12, 1

Squire, K. (2002). Cultural framing of computer/video games. *The International Journal of Computer Game Research, 2*(1).

Squire, K., & Jenkins, H. (2003). Harnessing the power of games in education. *Insight (American Society of Ophthalmic Registered Nurses), 3*(1), 5–33.

Squire, K. (2008). Open-ended video games: A model for developing learning for the interactive age. In K. Salen (Ed.), The ecology of games: Connecting youth, games and learning *(The John D. and Catherine T. MacArthur Foundation Series on Digital Media and Learning)* (pp. 167–198). Cambridge, MA: MIT Press.

Squire, K. (2008b). Video game literacy: A literacy of expertise. In J. Coiro, M. Knobel, C. Lankshear, & D. Leu (Eds.), *Handbook of research on new literacies* (pp. 635–669). Mahwah, NJ: Lawerence Erlbaum Associates.

Stald, G. (2009). *Globale medier – lokal unge. Institut for Medier, erkendelse, formidling.* København: Københavns Universitet.

Stehr, N. (1994). *Knowledge Societies.* London: Sage.

Sternberg, R. J. (2000). *Handbook of Intelligence.* New York: Cambridge University Press.

Stewart, K. L., & Felicetti, L. A. (1992). Learning styles of marketing majors. *Educational Research Quarterly, 15*(2), 15–23.

Strathern, M. (2000). Introduction: new accountabilities. In Strathern, M. (Ed.), *Audit cultures: Anthropological studies in accountability, ethics and the academy* (pp. 1–18). London: Routledge.

Strauss, W., & Howe, N. (2000). *Millennials rising: The next great generation.* New York: Vintage.

Street, B. V. (2001). *Literacy and Development: ethnographic perspectives.* London: Routledge. doi:10.4324/9780203468418

Sunstein, C. R. (2007). *Republic.com 2.0*. Princeton, N.J.: Princeton University Press.

Tally, B., & Burns, M. (2000). History: Mining for gold in a mountain of resources. In Gordon, D. T. (Ed.), *The digital classroom: How technology is changing the way we teach and learn* (pp. 111–116). Cambridge, MA: Harvard Education Letter.

Tan, D. (1999). *Theories of Learning Styles*. Jiangsu: Jiangsu Education Press.

Tan, K.-S. (1989). *The uses of television in primary schools. Case studies in Malaysia and England*. Unpublished PhD thesis, School of Education, University of East Anglia. Norwich, U.K.

Tapscott, D. (1998). *Growing Up Digital: The Rise of the Net Generation*. New York: McGraw-Hill.

Tapscott, D. (1996). *The Digital Economy: Promise and Peril in the Age of Networked Intelligence*. London: McGraw-Hill.

Thomas, A. (2007). *Youth online: Identity and literacy in the digital age*. New York: Peter Lang.

Thomas, A. (2006). Blurring and Breaking through the Boundaries of Narrative, Literacy and Identity in Adolescent Fan Fiction. In M. Knobel & C. Lankshear (Eds.), *A New Literacies Sampler*. Peter Lang. Retrieved December 3, 2009, from http://www.soe.jcu.edu.au/sampler/.

Thomas, A. Litzinger., et al. (2005). *A Study of the Reliability and Validity of the Felder-Soloman Index of Learning Styles*. Presented at the Proceedings of the 2005 American Society for Engineering Education Annual Conference & Exposition. Portland, Oregon, June 12-15.

Tingstad, V. (2003). *Children's chat on the net: A study of social encounters in two Norwegian chat rooms*. Norsk Center for barneforskning.

Tolmie, A. (2001). Examining learning in relation to the contexts of use of ICT. *Journal of Computer Assisted Learning*, *17*(3), 235–241. doi:10.1046/j.0266-4909.2001.00178.x

Torkzadeh, G., & Van Dyke, T. P. (2002). Effects of training on Internet self-efficacy and computer user attitudes. *Computers in Human Behavior*, *18*(5), 479–494. doi:10.1016/S0747-5632(02)00010-9

Transfer of Learning: Planning Workplace Education Programs. (2010). Retrieved November 31, 2009. from http://www.nald.ca/nls/inpub/transfer/English/page01.htm.

Trippi, J. (2004). *The Revolution Will Not Be Televised: Democracy, the Internet, and the Overthrow of Everything*. New York: Regan.

Tuman, M. (1992). *Word Perfect: Literacy in the Computer Age*. London: The Falmer Press.

Turkles, S. (1995). *Life on the screen: Identity in the age of internet*. New York: Simon & Schuster.

Turner, S. V. (2003). *Learning in a digital world: The role of technology as a catalyst for change*. Retrieved December 31, 2009, from www.neiu.edu/~ncaftori/sandy.doc

Twenge, J. M. (2006). *Generation Me: Why today's young Americans are more confident, assertive, entitled—and more miserable than ever before*. New York: Free Press.

Tyack, D., & Cuban, L. (1995). *Tinkering toward utopia: A century of public school reform*. Cambridge, MA: Harvard University Press.

Tyner, K. (1998). *Literacy in a Digital World*. Mahwah, NJ: Lawrence Erlbaum Associates.

Uimonen, P. (2004). *Information and communication technology (ICT) strategy for Bagamoyo College of Arts*. Bagamoyo College of Arts/Embassy of Sweden in Tanzania.

Uimonen, P. (2009). Internet, arts and translocality in Tanzania. *Social Anthropology*, *17*(3), 276–290. doi:10.1111/j.1469-8676.2009.00073.x

Uimonen, P. (2008). Lärande i en digitaliserad värld. In Selander, S., & Svärdemo-Åberg, E. (Eds.), *Didaktisk design i digital miljö-nya möjligheter för lärande* (pp. 54–69). Stockholm: Liber.

Uimonen, P. (2006). *ICT user study at Bagamoyo College of Arts*. Bagamoyo College of Arts and Sida/Embassy of Sweden Dar es Salaam.

Uimonen, P. (2011). *Digital drama. Art, multimedia, and transcultural liminality in Tanzania*. New York: Routledge (in process)

Undervisningsministeriet (2005). *Det nationale kompetenceregnskab – hovedrapport.* Retrieved from http://pub.uvm.dk/2005/NKRrapport/

UNESCO. (1990). Final *Report on the World Conference on Education For All: Meeting basic learning needs.* Jomtien, Thailand. Paris: UNESCO. P.43

UNESCO. (1996), *Learning: the Treasure Within.* Report to UNESCO of the International Commission on Education for the twenty-first Century.Paris, France. Retrieved October 28, 2003. from http://unesdoc.unesco.org/images/0010/001095/109590ab.pdf

UNESCO. (2003), *The Prague Declaration – 'Toward an Information Literate Society'.* Prague, Czech Republic Sept 2003. Retrieved November 28, 2009. from http://portal.unesco.org/ci/en/

Uricchio, W. (2004). Television's Next Generation: Technology/Interface Culture/Flow. In Spigel, L., & Olsson, J. (Eds.), *Television After TV. Essays on a Medium in Transition* (pp. 232–261). Durham, London: Duke University Press.

US Census Bureau. (2000). *School enrollment--Social and economic characteristics of students: October 2000* [Data file]. Available from http://www.census.gov/population/www/socdemo/school/ppl-148.html US Census Bureau. (2005). *School enrollment--social and economic characteristics of students: October 2005* [Data file]. Available from http://www.census.gov/population/www/socdemo/school/cps2005.html

US Census Bureau. (2008). *School enrollment--Social and economic characteristics of students: October 2008* [Data file]. Available from http://www.census.gov/population/www/socdemo/school/cps2008.html

US Department of Education. (2008). *Digest of education statistics.* Retrieved March 27, 2010, from http://nces.ed.gov/programs/digest/d08/tables/dt08_012.asp

van 't Hooft, M. (2007). Schools, Children and Digital Technology: Building Better Relationships for a Better Tomorrow. *Journal of Online Education 3,* (4). 20070410: http://www.innovateonline.info

van Deursen, A. J. A. M., & van Dijk, J. A. G. M. (2009). Improving Digital Skills for the Use of Online Public Information and Services. *Government Information Quarterly, 26*(2), 333–340. doi:10.1016/j.giq.2008.11.002

Van Dijk, J., & Hacker, K. (2003). The Digital Divide as a Complex and Dynamic Phenomenon. *The Information Society, 19*(4), 315–326. doi:10.1080/01972240309487

Van Eck, R. (2006). Digital game-based learning: It's not just the digital natives who are restless. *EDUCAUSE Review, 2*(14), 16–30.

Vasseur, J.-P., & Dunkels, A. (2010). *Interconnecting Smart Objects with IP - The Next Internet.* Reading, MA: Morgan Kaufmann.

Veen, V., & Vrakking, B. (2006). *Homo zappiens: growing up in a digital age.* London: Network Continuum Education.

Vogel, E. (1979). *Japan as number one: Lesson for America.* Cambridge, MA: Harvard University Press.

Von der Emde, S., Schneider, J., & Kotter, M. (2000). Technically speaking: Transforming language learning through virtual learning environments (MOOs). *Modern Language Journal, 85*(2).

Vygotsky, L. (1978). *Minds in society: The development of higher psychological processes.* Cambridge, MA: Harvard University Press.

Wallis, C. (2006, March 19). The Multitasking generation. *Time.* Retrieved from December 23, 2009, from http://www.time.com/time/magazine/article/0,9171,1174696,00.html

Ward Schofield, J. (2006). Internet Use in Schools. In Sawyer, R. K. (Ed.), *The Cambridge Handbook of the Learning Sciences* (pp. 521–534). Cambridge, UK: Cambridge University Press.

Wartella, E., O'Keefe, B., & Scantlin, R. (2000). *Children and Interactive Media: A Compendium of Current Research and Directions for the Future.* New York: MarkleFoundation. http://www.markle.org/downloadable_assets/cimcompendium.pdf

Watson, D. (2001). IT and pedagogy - teachers - change - information – knowledge. Pedagogy before Technology: Re-thinking the Relationship between IT and Teaching. *Education and Information Technologies, 6*(4), 251–266. doi:10.1023/A:1012976702296

Weigel, V. (2005). From course management to curricular capabilities: A capabilities approach for the next-generation course management system. In McGee, P., Jafari, A., & Carmean, C. (Eds.), *Course management systems for learning: Beyond accidental pedagogy* (pp. 190–205). Hershey, PA: Information Science Publishing.

Weinert, F. E. (2001) Concept of competence: a conceptual clarification. In D. S. Rychen & L. H.Salganik (Eds).*Defining and Selecting key Competencies*, 45-66 Gooettingen: Hogrefe, Germany.

Weinstein, C. E., Goetz, E. T., & Alexander, P. A. (1998). *Learning and study strategies: Issues in assessment, instruction, and evaluation.* New York: Academic Press.

Weinstein, C. E. (1987). *LASSI user's manual.* Clearwater, FL: H & H Publishing LASSI User's Manual [DB/OL] http://www.hhpublishing.com/_onlinecourses/study_strategies/BSL/admin/usersmanual.html

Weinstein, C. E., & Mayer, R. E. (1986).The teaching of learning strategies. In M.Wittrock (Ed.). *Handbook of research on teaching* (pp.3 15-327). New York: Macmillan Publishers.

Weinstein, C.E., & Richard E.M. (1983) The teaching of learning strategies. *Innovation Abstracts,*5 (32).

Weiss, B. (2002). Thug realism: Inhabiting fantasy in urban Tanzania. *Cultural Anthropology, 17*(1), 93–124. doi:10.1525/can.2002.17.1.93

Wenden, A., & Rubin, J. (1987). *Learner Strategies in Language Learning.* Upper Saddle River, NJ: Prentice Hall.

Wenger, E. (1999). *Communities of Practice: Learning; Meaning and Identity.* Cambridge, UK: Cambridge University Press.

Wheatley, M. (1999). *Leadership and the new science: Discovering order in a chaotic world* (2nd ed.). San Francisco: Berrett-Koehler.

Wheatley, M., & Kellner-Rogers, M. (1996). *A simpler way.* San Francisco: Berrett-Koehler.

Whitehead, A. (1971). *The Concept of Nature.* Cambridge, MA: Cambridge University Press. (Original work published 1920)

Wilhelm, A. G. (2004). *Digital nation: Toward an inclusive information society.* Cambridge, MA: MIT Press.

Wilhelm, A. (1999). Virtual Sounding Boards: How Deliberative Is Online Political Discussion? In Barry, N. (Ed.), *Hague & Brian D. Loader Digital Democracy: Discourse and Decision Making in the Information Age.* London: Routledge.

Williams, J. B., & Jacobs, J. (2004). Exploring the use of blogs as learning spaces in the higher education sector. *Australasian Journal of Educational Technology, 20*(2), 232-247. http://www.ascilite.org.au/ajet/ajet20/williams.html

Wilson, M., & Gerber, L. E. (2008). How generational theory can improve teaching: strategies for working with the "Millennials". *Currents in Teaching and Learning, 1*(1).

Wingrand, P., Scoff, G., & Paris, A. (1989). A Cognitive and Motivational Agenda for Reading Instruction. *Educational Leadership, 46*(4), 30–36.

Wiske, S. (2000). A new culture of teaching for the 21st century. In Gordon, D. T. (Ed.), *The digital classroom: How technology is changing the way we teach and learn* (pp. 69–77). Cambridge, MA: Harvard Education Letter.

Withrow, F. B. (2004). *Literacy in the digital age: Reading, writing, viewing, and computing.* Lanham, MD: Scarecrow Education.

Wong, W. (2007, May/June). Gaming In Education. *Ed Tech Magazine.* Retrieved April 10, 2008, from http://www.edtechmag.com/higher/may-june-2007/gaming-in-education.html

Wood, R. T. A. (2008). Problems with the concept of video game "addiction": Some case study examples. *International Journal of Mental Health and Addiction, 6*(2).

Woolard, K. (1998). Introduction: Language Ideology as a field of inquiry. In Schieffelin, B., Woolard, K., & Kroskrity, P. (Eds.), *Language ideologies: Practice and theory* (pp. 3–50). New York: Oxford University Press.

Wragg, E. C. (1993). Multi-media in education: Bane or boon? *Journal of Educational Television, 19*(2), 73–79.

Wright, S., & Rabo, A. (2010). Introduction: Anthropologies of university reform. *Social Anthropology, 18*(1), 1–14. doi:10.1111/j.1469-8676.2009.00096.x

Xenos, M. A., & Bennett, W. L. (2007). Young Voters and the Web of Politics: The Promise and Problems of Youth-oriented Political Content on the Web. In Loader, B. D. (Ed.), *Young Citizens in the Digital Age: Political Engagement, Young People, and New Media*. New York: Routledge.

Young, J. R. (2002). "Hybrid" teaching seeks to end the divide between traditional and online instruction. *The Chronicle of Higher Education, 48*(28), A33–A34.

Young, K. S. (1996). Internet addiction: The emergency of a new clinical disorder. *Cyberpsychology & Behavior, 1*(3), 237–244. doi:10.1089/cpb.1998.1.237

Young, K. S. (2004). Internet addiction. *The American Behavioral Scientist, 48*(4), 214–246. doi:10.1177/0002764204270278

Young, M., Schrader, P. G., & Zheng, D. P. (2006). MMOGs as learning environments: An ecological journey into Quest Atlantis and The Sims Online. *Innovate: Journal of Online Education, 2*(4).

Zhong, Zh. X. (2001). Information literacy: build up eight competencies for you. *China education (Newspaper)*. 02.March.2001

Ziehe, T. (2000) *Modernisierungsprozesse und Jugendkultur*. In Plebuch-Tiefenbacher, L. u.a. (Hg.), Geschlechterfrage in der Schule, Weinheim.

Zimic, S. (2009). Not so 'techno-savvy': Challenging the stereotypical images of the 'Net generation'. *Digital Culture & Education, 1*(2), 129–144.

Zolli, A. (2007, December 19). *Demographics: The Population Hourglass*. Retrieved December 15, 2009, from http://www.fastcompany.com/magazine/103/open_essay-demographics.html

Zorrilla Abascal, M. L. (2008). *Educational Television Beyond the TV Set: Educational Media Convergence in UK and a Proposal for the Mexican Model*. Unpublished PhD Thesis, School of Education and Lifelong Learning, University of East Anglia, Norwich, U.K.

About the Contributors

Elza Dunkels is a senior lecturer at the Department of Applied Educational Science at Umeå University, Sweden. Her PhD from 2007 deals with young people's own perceptions of online dangers. She is currently involved projects concerning online risk, adult's perceptions of online dangers and sexual exploitation of young people online.

Gun-Marie Frånberg is Professor in Educational Work at the Department of Applied Educational Science, Umeå University, Sweden. Her research interests include social and cultural perspectives on contemporary educational work. There is a particular focus on social values and net cultures at the intersection of age, class, gender and ethnicity.

Camilla Hällgren works as a senior lecturer at the department of Applied Educational Science at Umeå University in Sweden. She has a PhD in Educational Work, from the same university. Her research interest deals with the complexity of identity, young people, social values and online interactions.

* * *

Neriko Doerr received Ph.D. in cultural anthropology from Cornell University in New York, U.S.A. Doerr works on language and power, politics of schooling, heritage language education, regimes of difference, nationalism, and globalization in Aotearoa/New Zealand, Japan, the United States, and online space. Her publications include *Meaningful Inconsistencies: Bicultural Nationhood, the Free Market, and Schooling in Aotearoa/New Zealand* (Berghahn Books), *The Native Speaker Concept: Ethnographic Investigations of Native Speaker Effects* (Mouton de Gruyter; as the editor), *Bunka, Kotoba, and Kyoiku* (Akasho shoten; as the co-editor; in Japanese), and articles in *Anthropology and Education Quarterly*, *Critical Asian Studies, Critical Studies in Education, Identities: Global Studies in Culture and Power*, and *Journal of Language, Identity, and Education*. She currently teaches at Ramapo College, New Jersey, U.S.A.

Birgitte Holm Sørensen is professor in ICT and learning at the Danish School of Education, Aarhus University. She is a director of the Research Programme on Media and ICT in a Learning Perspective. Her research field is ICT and learning, children, young people, media and ICT. During several years she has done research with focus on ICT and learning in primary school and lower secondary school. Currently she is leader of the Danish Council for Strategic Research supported project "Serious Games in a Global Market Place" (2007-2011). Of special interest is ICT-based design for learning and teaching.

Regina Kaplan-Rakowski is a doctoral candidate in the Department of Curriculum and Instruction at the Southern Illinois University, Carbondale, USA. She has developed a deep interest in her students through years of teaching foreign languages, both in Europe and the USA, and in both the real and virtual worlds. Her current research focus is on the affordances of serious games and virtual environments for education, especially for foreign language instruction. She currently holds a B.Ed. in Teaching English as a Second Language (TESL); a M.Ed. in European Studies (both degrees from Pedagogical University, Krakow, Poland), and an M.A. in Foreign Languages and Literatures from Southern Illinois University. Kaplan-Rakowski is an author and a co-author of several peer-reviewed publications in the field of education.

Simon Lindgren is a Professor of Sociology at Umeå University in Sweden. He works in the field of cultural sociology with issues relating to media, youth and popular culture. His current research deals with people's use of digital media, network cultures, and new emerging forms of online community. He has a broad interest in social and cultural theory, and uses a wide range of research methods; discourse analysis, ethnography, network analysis etc. At present, Lindgren heads a research project on online piracy, and another on youth culture and participation. Among other things, he also takes part in a project about YouTube as a performative arena, at HUMlab, Umeå University.

Wu Liwei M.A, graduated from School of Educational Information and Technology, South China Normal University, now works in School of Continuing Education, Xiamen University, Xiamen, Fujian, P.R. China as an assisatant researcher of distance education and instructional designer of online course, and focus on learning support for Chinese distance learners and online course development. Wu is interested in providing individualized learning support for e-learning learners considering learners' learning styles. Current research focuses on the relationship between lifelong learning and self-study examination and redesign of online course aiming at improving online course quality and distance learners' learning outcome.

Liz Merkel is a Masters student in Curriculum and Instruction at the University of Victoria. She currently teaches a seminar course for students in the University of Victoria teacher education program and supervises pre-service teachers in practicum experiences. Her passion for teaching at the primary school age led her to undertake her Masters research wherein she studies how the practice of auto-ethnography research in teacher education programs critically impacts pre-service teacher practice. She is the project manager of a SSHRC (Social Sciences and Humanities Research Council of Canada) funded project entitled Literacy Learning through Video Games: Adolescent Boys' Perspectives led by Dr. Kathy Sanford.

Henry Milner is Visiting Professor of Political Science at Umeå University in Sweden, and Research Fellow at the Chair in Electoral Studies, Department of Political Science, Université de Montréal. In 2004-2005 he held the Chair in Canadian Studies at the Sorbonne, and in 2005-2006, he was Canada-US Fulbright Chair, at the State University of New York at Plattsburgh. He has also been a visiting professor or researcher at universities in Finland, Australia and New Zealand. Recent Books include *Civic Literacy: How Informed Citizens Make Democracy Work* (2002), *Social Democracy and Rational Choice (1994)*, and *Sweden: Social Democracy in Practice* (1989). He is co-publisher of *Inroads*, the Canadian journal of opinion and policy. His book: *The Internet Generation: Engaged Citizens or Political Dropouts* has recently been published.

Christina Olin-Scheller is a researcher and teacher at Karlstad University. Her main interest is young people's reading and writing in a new media landscape in general and has a special interest in how this landscape challenges traditional ways of regarding literacy. Her thesis, Mellan Dante och Big Brother. En studie om gymnasielevers textvärldar (2006), has been followed by other books and articles which turn to researchers, as well as teacher educators and teachers. Presently she is working with studies on fans, fan culture and fan fiction with focus on the relation between informal and formal learning settings. Also, she is often engaged as a lecturer for various groups of audiences.

David Rakowski is an Associate Professor of Finance at Southern Illinois University, Carbondale, USA. His Ph.D. is from Georgia State University and his B.B.A. is from Stetson University. Dr. Rakowski's interests include interdisciplinary research methodologies, pedagogy of finance, market liquidity, investor behavior, and corporate governance. His teaching interests include research methodology and corporate finance.

Kathy Sanford, Ed.D, is an Associate Professor in the Faculty of Education at University of Victoria. She currently holds the position of Associate Dean of Teacher Education. Her literacy research and teaching interests include issues of gender, assessment, and popular culture/new media. Additionally, she has been actively involved in issues related to teacher education programs, and her current writing and research involves school-based teacher education and program-wide electronic portfolios. Currently underway is a SSHRC (Social Sciences and Humanities Research Council of Canada)-funded project entitled Literacy Learning through Video Games: Adolescent Boys' Perspectives, examining a rapidly growing phenomenon, videogames, and the learning that takes place through videogame play. Additionally, working with Dr Tim Hopper she has another SSHRC funded project entitled E-Portfolios in teacher education for individual and programmatic development: Building on tradition through technological innovation. This project is exploring the development of open-source technology that encourages pre-service teachers to think more deeply about teaching and content, to be more conscious of theories and assumptions that guide their practice, and to engage in collaborative dialogues about their teaching.

Shinji Sato received his PhD degree in Anthropology and Education from Teachers College, Columbia University. His specializations are educational and linguistic anthropology, focusing language education. His works critically examine self-evident notions in language education including learning, culture, communication, competence, and creativity. Sato co-edited a book, Bunka, kotoba, kyoiku [Culture, Language, and Education], published by Akashi Shoten, Tokyo, Japan. He is currently editing books on Japanese language education for the world citizens, alternative assessment of Japanese language education, and reexamination of intercultural communication in language education. Currently he is a Japanese Lecturer at Columbia University.

Yang Sujuan, PhD, Institute of Vocational Education and Training, the University of Potsdam, Potsdam, Brandenburg, Germany; Associate professor of educational technology, member of the Research Institute of Distance Education, School of Educational Information and Technology, South China Normal University, Guangzhou, Guangdong, P.R. China. Current research focuses on competence profiles needed for online teachers and learners and its development, and on social, cognitive and teaching presence of the online teaching and learning communities with the aim to explore the nature and process of teaching and learning in Chinese online education practice, especially in the field of online vocational education and training.

Karin Tweddell Levinsen is an associate professor in online education at university level at the Danish School of Education, Aarhus University. She is a member of the internationally acknowledged Research Programme on Media and ICT in a Learning Perspective. Currently her research is focused on both university pedagogy and ICT and ICT and learning in the primary school. Of special interest is the implementation of ICT support for children with reading and writing difficulties. Karin Tweddell Levinsen has many years of experience as a professional user centred design developer of digital educational solutions. Simultaneous with her professional carrier she has kept the contact with the research community and taught at several Danish Universities, including the Danish IT-University.

Paula Uimonen, PhD, is a researcher at the Department of Social Anthropology, Stockholm University, Sweden. She is one of the founding scholars of digital anthropology, an emerging sub-discipline in anthropology that is concerned with the development and use of digital media and communication technologies in different social and cultural contexts. Her published PhD dissertation (2001) was the first comparative ethnography of Internet development in developing countries, based on multi-sited fieldwork among Internet pioneers in Southeast Asia. Her current research project focuses on digital media and intercultural interaction at a national arts and culture institute in Tanzania. In addition to her scholarly work on Internet, modernization and globalization, Dr Uimonen has advised international organizations, bilateral development agencies and government agencies on ICT for Development (ICT4D), most recently in the culture and education sectors in Tanzania. Dr Uimonen teaches courses in visual culture and digital anthropology.

Natalie Wakefield graduated from the University of British Columbia in Vancouver with a Bachelor of Arts and a Bachelor of Education in French Immersion. After several years of teaching, she returned to university to complete a Master of Arts degree at McGill University in Montreal. The focus of her graduate work was on media literacy and educational leadership. She recently returned to the classroom where plans to incorporate her research. In addition to this, she continues to work on projects dealing with issues such as cyber bullying, media literacy and student leadership.

Patrik Wikström is research fellow and research manager at the Media Management and Transformation Centre at Jönköping International Business School. His primary research area is the innovative and adaptive behaviour of media organizations. Within this area he has done research on business models in the music industry; magazine publishers' use of social media; collaborative production of online fiction; and on the competitive behaviour of small and mid-sized TV producers.

Fan Yihong, Ed D, School of Education, University of Massachusetts, Amherst, USA; guest professor of Department of Interactive Media Studies, Umeå University, Sweden (August-October, 2008); guest professor of Department of Teacher Education, Norwegian University of Science and Technology;

professor of higher education, director of Section for European Higher Education Studies, and Section for Comparative Higher Education Studies, Institute of Education, Xiamen University, Xiamen, Fujian, P.R. China. Current research project is on Comparative Research of Staff Development between Chinese and European Universities, and Information Technology Enhanced Learning. Being invited as the Educational and Cross-Cultural advisor of China-Holland Educational Competence and Knowledge Center on IT (CHECK-IT), Fan is actively engaged in this international collaborative internship project that brings 20-25 Dutch students to come to CHECK-IT each semester, working together with Chinese students on R & D of IT and Software Engineering.

Sheila Zimic is a Ph. D. Student in Informatics at Mid Sweden University. Sheila is using the national representative study conducted by World Internet Institute (a partner of World Internet Project) in her research on young people's Internet use with focus on digital competence and digital participation. The overall aim of her research is questioning the deterministic images of young people in the digital society. Sheila is also a member of the multi disciplinary research group *CITIZYS* at Mid Sweden University.

María Luisa Zorrilla Abascal is Mexican, with Bachelor and Master Degrees in Communications and PhD in Education, this last one as the result of a three year project about Educational Media Convergence at the University of East Anglia (Norwich, UK). Her career as academic is recent, but she has a long trajectory as communications professional both in Mexican government and non-profit organizations. At present she is teacher and researcher at the Autonomous University of the State of Morelos (UAEM) and is the project leader of e-UAEM, the Multimodal Educational Space at the same university, an ambitious initiative to transform traditional educational practices into an innovative b-learning concept.

Index